WRITING SPACES: READINGS ON WRITING VOLUME 5

Writing Spaces: Readings on Writing

Editors

Trace Daniels-Lerberg, University of Utah
Dana Lynn Driscoll, Indiana University of Pennsylvania
Mary K. Stewart, California State University San Marcos
Matthew Vetter, Indiana University of Pennsylvania

Associate Editors

Colin Charlton, University of Texas Rio Grande Valley
Rachel Buck, American University of Sharjah
Xiao (Katy) Tan, Duke University

Copyeditors

Isaac Adubofour, Indiana University of Pennsylvania
Sean Chadwick, University of Arizona
Analeigh Horton, University of Arizona
Melanie Gagich, Cleveland State University
Jennifer K. Johnson, University of California, Santa Barbara
Heather A. McDonald, American University
Megan Mikovits, Moravian College Melody Pugh, U.S. Air Force Academy
Thir Bahadur Budhathoki, University of Arizona

Volumes in *Writing Spaces: Readings on Writing* offer multiple perspectives on a wide range of topics about writing. In each chapter, authors present their unique views, insights, and strategies for writing by addressing the undergraduate reader directly. Drawing on their own experiences, these teachers-as-writers invite students to join in the larger conversation about the craft of writing. Consequently, each essay functions as a standalone text that can easily complement other selected readings in writing or writing-intensive courses across the disciplines at any level.

All volumes in the series are published under a Creative Commons license and available for download at the Writing Spaces website (http://www.writingspaces.org), Parlor Press (https://parlorpress.com/pages/writing-spaces), and the WAC Clearinghouse (http://wac.colostate.edu/).

WRITING SPACES

Readings on Writing
Volume 5

Edited by
Trace Daniels-Lerberg, Dana Driscoll,
Mary K. Stewart, and Matthew Vetter

Parlor Press
Anderson, South Carolina
www.parlorpress.com

Parlor Press LLC, Anderson, South Carolina, USA

© 2023 by Parlor Press. Individual essays © 2023 by the respective authors. Unless otherwise stated, these works are licensed under the Creative Commons Attribution-NonCommercial-NoDerivatives 4.0 International License (CC BY-NC-ND 4.0) and are subject to the Writing Spaces Terms of Use. To view a copy of this license, visit http://creativecommons.org/licenses/by-nc-nd/4.0/, email info@creativecommons.org, or send a letter to Creative Commons, PO Box 1866, Mountain View, CA 94042, USA. To view the Writing Spaces Terms of Use, visit http://writingspaces.org/terms-of-use.

All rights reserved.
Printed in the United States of America

S A N: 2 5 4 - 8 8 7 9

Library of Congress Cataloging-in-Publication Data

Writing spaces : readings on writing. Volume 1 / edited by Charles Lowe and Pavel Zemliansky.
   p. cm.
Includes bibliographical references and index.
   ISBN 978-1-60235-184-4 (pbk. : alk. paper) -- ISBN 978-1-60235-185-1 (adobe ebook)
  1. College readers. 2. English language--Rhetoric. I. Lowe, Charles, 1965- II. Zemliansky, Pavel.
PE1417.W735 2010
808'.0427--dc22

2010019487

1 2 3 4 5

978-1-64317-411-2 (paperback)
978-1-64317-412-9 (pdf)
978-1-64317-413-6 (epub)

Cover design by Colin Charlton.
Printed on acid-free paper.

Parlor Press, LLC is an independent publisher of scholarly and trade titles in print and multimedia formats. This book is available in paper, and eBook formats from Parlor Press on the World Wide Web at http://www.parlorpress.com or through online and brick-and-mortar bookstores. It is also available in eBook formats at http://writingspaces.org and http://wac.colostate.edu/. For submission information or to find out about Parlor Press publications, write to Parlor Press, 3015 Brackenberry Drive, Anderson, South Carolina, 29621, or email editor@parlorpress.com.

Contents

Acknowledgments   *vii*

1 We Write Because We Care: Developing Your Writerly Identity   *1*
  Glenn Lester, Taylor Lucas, Sydney Doyle, and Alison Overcash

2 Dispositions Toward Learning   *17*
  Jennifer Wells

3 "Is This for a Grade?" Understanding Assessment, Evaluation, and Low-Stakes Writing Assignments   *28*
  Jason McIntosh

4 How Writing Happens   *43*
  Zack DePiero and Ryan Dippre

5 What Color Is My Voice? Academic Writing and the Myth of Standard English   *63*
  Kristin DeMint Bailey, An Ha, and AJ Outlar

6 What Can I Add to Discourse Communities? How Writers Use Code-Meshing and Translanguaging to Negotiate Discourse   *87*
  Lisa Tremain

7 Environmental Justice: Writing Urban Spaces   *102*
  Mattius Rischard

8 Enabling the Reader   *121*
  Kefaya Diab

9 Everything's Biased: A Guide to Determining When Bias Matters   *140*
  Danielle DeRise

10 Reading in Conversation: A Writing Student's Guide to Social Annotation   *152*
  Michelle Sprouse

11 "I Passed First-Year Writing—What Now?": Adapting Strategies from First-Year Writing to Writing in the Disciplines   *168*
  Amy Cicchino

12 Strategies for Analyzing and Composing Data Stories   *189*
   Angela M. Laflen

13 "Doing Research Is Fun; Citing Sources Is Not":
   Understanding the Fuzzy Definition of Plagiarism   *217*
   Rachel Hall Buck and Silvia Vaccino-Salvadore

14 Elaborate Rhetorics   *228*
   David Blakesley

15 What Is Rhetoric? A "Choose Your Own
   Adventure" Primer   *247*
   William Duffy

16 Thinking across Modes and Media (and Baking Cake):
   Two Techniques for Writing with Video,
   Audio, and Images   *266*
   Crystal VanKooten

17 You Are Good for Wikipedia   *281*
   Matthew A. Vetter and Oksana Moroz

18 The Good, the Bad, and the Ugly of Peer Review   *299*
   Erin E. Kelly

19 Changing Your Mindset About Revision   *318*
   L. Lennie Irvin

20 What's the Diff? Version History and
   Revision Reflections   *334*
   Benjamin Miller

21 Navigating Your Collaborative Project   *352*
   Ellen Cecil-Lemkin and Tamara Gluck

22 Writing Science in the First Year of College:
   Why It Matters to STEM Students and How
   STEM Students Benefit from It   *372*
   Chris Thaiss and Stephanie Wade

Contributors   *392*

Acknowledgments

Three years ago, in the spring of 2020, Writing Spaces put out a call for proposals for Volume 4 of the *Readings on Writing* series. In many ways, that CFP marked a turning point for the Writing Spaces project since it was the first completely new volume crafted by the new editorial team of Dana Driscoll, Mary Stewart, and Matt Vetter. While we had just recently published Volume 3 of the Readings on Writing series, that particular volume included manuscripts from years previous – when Charlie Lowe and Pavel Zemliansky led the project. Our CFP for Volume 4 accepted open-topic submissions, but it also allowed us to call for essays that tackled more specific interests that emerged from our survey of readers, editorial board interests, and our review of previous issues. In other words, we wanted to both update the Writing Spaces curriculum, since the last CFP resulted in a 2011 publication, but also fill in the gaps by soliciting essays on issues such as global Englishes, translingualism, social justice, community-engaged writing, and emerging technologies, among others.

When we published the CFP for Volume 4, we never imagined the enormous response we would get, which amounted to over 150 proposals from the Writing Spaces community. The immensity of this response led to a couple of important decisions that defined the work we did in the next few years.

First, we had plenty of really great material to put out not one, but two volumes. Volume 4, consisting of nineteem unique essays on a variety of topics and issues, was published in August, 2021. And Volume 5, this volume, with twenty-two new essays, came together in August, 2023. The other significant development stemming from the overwhelming response to the 2020 CFP was the creation of the Activities and Assignments Archive or AAA (writingspaces.org/aaa). Published entirely online (at least for now), this section of Writing Spaces hosts pedagogical resources grounded in current practice and scholarship. Each document presents a pedagogical activity or assignment, curated by teacher-scholars for writing students, and reviewed by the Writing Spaces editorial team. Since initiating this project, the archive has grown to include over twenty pedagogical contributions. Originally the brainchild of Volume 4 co-editor Megan Heise, the archive is currently edited by Xiao Tan and Matt Vetter.

With the publication of Volume 4, we also did a lot of behind-the-scenes work to migrate our web presence from the Drupal content management system to Wordpress. Much of this work happened in the summer of 2021, as we sought to transfer previous volumes, create new pages for Volume 4, and begin exploring new ways to present Writing Spaces content on the web. One of these latter developments has been the development of two new features on the WS website: Essay Sequences and Essay Clusters. Both invite teachers to think about how they can use Writing Spaces essays to aid in their pedagogical and curricular decision-making. Essay Sequences provide pedagogical arrangements of Writing Spaces content that reflect common units or assignments in first year composition. This feature is meant to help instructors when designing their course units and selecting Writing Spaces content. Essay Clusters, on the other hand, are groupings of Writing Spaces content arranged by topic. We've received positive feedback about both features, but the Clusters section seems to be especially appreciated.

We have accomplished a lot these last three years. Volumes 4 and 5 provide exceptional readings for the teaching of writing. The Activities & Assignments Archive extends our curricular offerings into more practical pedagogical guidance, and the new website furthers our reach and helps to accomplish our mission to provide high-quality open educational resources for an international audience. And for these accomplishments, there are many, many people to thank. Writing Spaces is a book series, a website, and a curriculum. But more than that—Writing Spaces is a community of people dedicated to open access resources and practices for writing education.

First of all, thank you to our many authors who contributed their work to Volumes 4 and 5, and the Activities and Assignments Archive. Your dedication to the teaching of writing, and the creation of accessible teacher-to-student directed essays, is what makes Writing Spaces such a valuable resource.

To Dave Blakesley and Parlor Press, thank you for your continued guidance and for working with us on the last three volumes of Writing Spaces.

To the fifty-four blind peer reviewers who read and provided feedback on the first full drafts of the manuscripts—thank you for your thoughtful reviews and constructive recommendations!

To our copyeditors team for Volume 4 and 5, Isaac Adubofour, Thir Bahadur Budhathoki, Sean Chadwick, Melanie Gagich, Megan Heise, Analeigh Horton, Jennifer Johnson, Heather McDonald, Meg Mikovits, Melody Pugh, and John Whicker, for your patience and painstaking attention to detail.

To the editorial board team: Chris Anson, Stephen Bernhardt, Terra Williams Bradley, Colin Charlton, Robert Cummings, Douglas Eyman, Karin Evans, Alexis Hart, Craig Hulst, Carrie Leverenz, Christina McDonald, Dan Melzer, Nancy Myers, Mike Palmquist, James Purdy, Kirk St. Amant, Kyle Stedman, Christopher Thaiss, Pavel Zemliansky, your continued guidance, advice and feedback helps us imagine the project in new ways, and learn from our shared past.

To our readers and adopters—thank you for choosing to teach with Writing Spaces!

Finally, Writing Spaces has also undergone some changes in staff over the last few years. First, it is with much regret that we accept Dana Driscoll's resignation from Writing Spaces. It was Dana's energy and motivation to restart the project, so we are particularly grateful for her early guidance and determination, and will feel her absence deeply. We wish her best of luck with future endeavors.

We have also welcomed some new staff to our editorial ranks.

Welcome Trace Daniels-Lerberg to the role of Managing Co-editor.

Welcome Colin Charlton to the role of Associate Editor of Strategic Planning and Digital Initiatives.

Welcome Rachel Buck to the role of Associate Editor of International Education.

Welcome Xiao (Katy) Tan to the role of Associate Editor of Activities & Assignments Archive.

And to our first-time readers, welcome to the Writing Spaces community. We hope you find Volume 5 to be a useful pedagogical resource in your current and future classes!

On behalf of the editorial team,

Matthew Vetter

24 May 2023

1 WE WRITE BECAUSE WE CARE: DEVELOPING YOUR WRITERLY IDENTITY

Glenn Lester, Taylor Lucas, Sydney Doyle, and Alison Overcash

OVERVIEW

Many college students write for one reason and one reason only: to complete a class assignment.[1] But students who subscribe to this view of writing—writing as merely a means to an end, a tool to achieve a grade—are seriously limiting themselves. In this chapter, a writing teacher and three recently graduated writers argue that writing can be used as a tool to build personal agency, develop resilience, and achieve social goals. In doing so, we introduce you to a variety of concepts that you can use to construct your writerly identity. Ultimately, we ask you to reconsider the role of writing in your life, and invite you to take that first, radical step of calling yourself a "real" writer.

INTRODUCTION: WHAT *IS* WRITING, REALLY? (BY GLENN LESTER)

A few semesters back, I was working with a student in a writing class. The student, who I'll call Ana, was searching for a topic for an upcoming research project. The topic had to be related in some way to writing, and Ana was struggling. Ana claimed they had *no* experience with writing. Literally none.

---

1. This work is licensed under the Creative Commons Attribution-NonCommercial-NoDerivatives 4.0 International License (CC BY-NC-ND 4.0) and is subject to the Writing Spaces Terms of Use. To view a copy of this license, visit http://creativecommons.org/licenses/by-nc-nd/4.0/, email info@creativecommons.org, or send a letter to Creative Commons, PO Box 1866, Mountain View, CA 94042, USA. To view the Writing Spaces Terms of Use, visit http://writingspaces.org/terms-of-use.

A few minutes into our conversation, however, Ana told me about an art therapy program they had participated in. They had written some things there. Ana had found it helpful to write down what they were thinking and feeling.

"But that's not *really* writing," Ana told me.

"What do you mean?" I asked.

"That's what I do for me," Ana said. "That's not real writing."

"And you aren't real?"

"But this is different," Ana said. "You're talking about *real* writing. Writing for school."

Does Ana's experience sound familiar to you?

It sure sounded familiar to me. For years, I've observed that many of my students write for one reason and one reason only: to complete a class assignment. Like many other student writers, Ana found it difficult to connect the writing they did for a grade with the writing they did for individual satisfaction. And because of this, it seemed that Ana's definition of "writer" did not include Ana.

But once Ana made the connection between personal writing and school-sponsored writing, their research project suddenly opened up. They could research and document the value of writing for therapeutic and healing purposes—a value they had personally experienced. Ana ultimately realized that they had *already* developed a writerly identity—and they could further define who they were as a writer *through* school-sponsored writing.

In this chapter, we want to help you make the same conceptual leap as Ana: from thinking that writing is merely a tool to achieve a grade to understanding how you can use writing to achieve personal and community goals. Ultimately, we want you to be able to articulate your own identity as a writer.

This chapter is divided into three sections, each written by a recently graduated writer— someone who very recently sat in your shoes. Each author will share their expertise and experience with an aspect of writing that is not school-sponsored. We explore three types of writerly identity:

1. Writing for *agency* (writing is a cognitive process you can adjust and control)

2. Writing for *resilience* (writing is an expressive tool you can use for self-discovery)

3. Writing for *social engagement* (writing is a way you can get things done in a particular time and place)

Throughout the chapter, each author will explore one of these writerly identities in more detail. As you'll see, each of these critical concepts of writing aligns with the ideas and findings of writing researchers and scholars from the 1980s to today. We introduce some of these concepts and theories, not to bog you down with jargon, but to help you begin to understand and define who you are as a writer. In doing so, we want to suggest that *who you are as a writer* depends much more on *your own reasons for writing* than on any outside definition or standard.

If you are a student who has already recognized the power of writing for building personal agency, resilience, and social engagement, then great! Come along as we explore ways to use writing for these purposes. But if you are skeptical of the value of writing outside of school—or if you just plain don't like to write—then please trust us, and keep reading.

PERSONAL AGENCY AND SELF-EXPRESSION (BY TAYLOR LUCAS)

It wasn't until my first college writing course that the concept of a writer's identity came into play. Like Ana, I wasn't sure it was possible to think like a real writer and do "real" writing. In fact, the biggest lesson that introduced the concept of a writer's identity—and why writing mattered—was when my English teacher required students to get approval of their thesis statements before they could begin working on writing analytical essays. After careful consideration of the essay prompts and drafting and redrafting a thesis statement, I would finally, hesitantly, approach her with my thesis statement. She'd read it, hand my paper back to me, and ask me a question that sticks with me to this day: "*So what?*"

What she meant by that, of course, was that I needed to consider and clarify the implications of my argument, but I found the question *So what?* to be intimidating. *So what?* suggested that I had to center my focus solely around what the audience should do with my topic. I'd spent class periods carefully considering what angle and argument my teacher would want to read, hoping to write something that would please her, as she was my sole audience. Of course, the audience is important, but it is easy to forget that one of the most beneficial things that writing does is allow the writer to gain personal agency. It was easier to see the obvious answers to *So what?* I was writing for a grade, responding to predetermined prompts. As a beginning writer, it was difficult for me to accept that what I said held value beyond percentage points and grades. I knew how to strategically meet my teachers' expectations, and I knew how to tailor my message to an audience. But *So what?* encouraged me to think about how writing could benefit me, personally, in addition to my audience. Through practice, I learned that part of writing is considering what I wanted to accomplish from my work and what I wanted the words on the page to mean to me; asking these questions allows you to start developing personal agency through the act of writing.

Even if you don't feel like a writer, it is imperative to understand that, like me, you will benefit from writing, firstly by developing personal agency. Educational psychologists Barry Zimmerman and Timothy Cleary define personal agency as your "capability to originate and direct actions for given purposes" (45). To me, "originating" and "directing actions" for a purpose sounds a lot like answering the question *So what?* So, because writing helps writers develop knowledge about themselves, their interests, their goals, and how they fit into the world around them, writing contributes to personal agency. In fact, you might not even know that the writing you're doing, whether you think it's *"real* writing" or not, contributes to your identity as a person, student, and writer. According to writing scholar Peter Elbow, writing can help students discover hidden meanings, explore their feelings, and communicate (2), all of which build personal agency. The development of personal agency can be broken down into several sections, including feelings/self-expression, thoughts, and actions/goals. What you'll notice is that all of these topics can be found in all sorts of writing that you do, whether for class or for personal purposes.

Part of developing personal agency means to discover and understand your own feelings. Writing theorist James Berlin suggests that the world around us "provides sensory images that can be used in order to explore the self… Authentic self-expression can thus lead to authentic self-experience for both the writer and the reader" (485). And when the writer *is* the reader, in a sense, then the writer can gain more perspective on their own, well, perspective. In other words, using language to describe your experience helps you understand your opinions and emotions regarding your experiences. Writers do this in several ways, including journaling, blogging, and even posting on social media, in addition to the more "predictable" types of school-sponsored writing like articles and essays. While you've probably been assigned a personal narrative at some point during your education, other forms of writing that you likely do frequently and by choice have helped you learn to express yourself too.

Sometimes the thought of consistent, assigned writing can sound difficult or overwhelming. Students might think that consistent writing means that they need to sit down for hours to write an eloquent piece of work that accurately describes and portrays exactly what they want it to. This may seem intimidating, but it is not necessarily true. Even writing a few paragraphs in your journal every day can help you process your emotions and retrace your thoughts. Berlin suggests that "discovering the true self in writing will simultaneously enable the individual to discover the truth of the situation which evoked the writing" (485). In other words, change occurs on the individual level when you discover your own voice.

Writing also teaches you how to express your thoughts and feelings to others, including family members, friends, classmates, and even potential employers or professional colleagues. Writers face the challenge of explaining their opinions and ideas by blending passion and research. I call this a challenge because producing eloquently written work with the goal to inform/entertain/persuade the reader is not an easy task. First, writers have to learn to do research, which in turn teaches you how to evaluate sources and select critical information. Then, you have to relay that information, as well as expand upon it in a way that your readers can understand. This process of selecting pertinent ideas and communicating them efficiently is helpful in classroom, casual, and professional settings.

In addition to learning about self-expression and strong communication, writing teaches you to go out of your comfort zone and reach tangible goals and offers proof of self-growth. As I mentioned earlier, journal entries or casual social media posts can provide you with a physical trail of thoughts, feelings, and experiences. In fact, any writing can provide this trail of evidence of your thinking as long as you keep track of it. Writing teaches you to challenge yourself to meet goals; completing a 5-7 page essay by the deadline shows you that you were able to achieve a goal. Continuing to meet goals, both in and out of the classroom, builds your confidence. You can take this one step further by submitting your work to literary magazines and conferences. Actions like this force you to brave the next step and share your hard work with others in your field. This provides you with tangible proof that you've written work worth being shared, and in doing so, sharing your thoughts and feelings with others.

So what? You've tried your hand at writing. You're starting to recognize that any form of writing counts as "*real* writing." And now you understand that any attempt at writing, whether it be an article or a journal or a personal narrative, or creative writing story, can help you develop your personal agency. Now it's time to begin considering your identity as a writer.

You might be thinking, "There's no way I'll ever be as good of a writer as my peers," but it's important to realize that everyone's writerly identity will look different. Comparison is a normal part of many fields, writing among them; when you catch yourself comparing your work to the work of your peers, remember to ask yourself, "*So what?*" What are you learning about yourself and the communities you engage through your work? What you're likely to learn is that there's no one way to be a good writer, and there's no such thing as a perfect writer, either. Simply putting your best foot forward will be the best way to start your journey towards calling yourself a writer and developing your own personal agency. As you take this first step to calling yourself a writer, you'll see personal growth not only in your writing style but also in your personal life. Perhaps your passions might flourish as you write about them, or maybe your ability to express yourself emotionally, creatively, and critically will expand as you learn to write consistently. As you build your personal agency and start to see your voice grow through all of the writing you do, you'll learn that writing also teaches you resilience, both academically and personally. In our view, "*real* writers" ask themselves, "So what, for me?"

Building and Maintaining Resilience (by Sydney Doyle)

Personal agency acts as a stepping stone towards understanding resilience and its role in personal and academic writing. What sparked my understanding of resilience in writing was a metaphor from one of my first college writing classes: *writing is a lot like training to run a marathon.* My professor went on: "Runners have to build stamina slowly to multiply their miles while minimizing their minutes—writing, and learning to write, involves the same kind of stamina." Sounds simple enough, right? It did to me. All it would take to have me acing essays and finessing fiction would be to write as much and as I possibly could—easy! But I quickly realized that, much like training for a marathon, developing my writing skills didn't mean simple repetition. Instead, I needed to develop resilience. After all, you're not a prepared marathon runner if you spend all your time training on the treadmill at a single speed.

Don't believe my metaphor? That's okay! Instead, take wisdom from writers David Bayles and Ted Orland, who remark that what is needed to write well is "a broad sense of what you are looking for, some strategy for how to find it, and an overriding willingness to embrace mistakes and surprises along the way" (21).

So, there are in fact concrete steps you can take as a writer yourself to build the resilience I'm dwelling on, and experts agree. Stephen Koch, an experienced scholar and writing teacher, suggests these steps:

1. *Begin.* In my experience, this is the most important yet hardest part of developing writerly resilience. Whether you're brainstorming for a school assignment, tinkering around with a flashy social media post, or even journaling for yourself, no writing happens unless you start writing. This is something that requires a bit of planning. One suggestion is to set a timer. Commit to writing for 10 minutes—*all* 10 minutes. No matter why you're writing, your timer will give you 10 minutes worth of writing that you didn't have before. And it's likely that, with repetition, you'll keep going beyond those 10 minutes. Looking back at our marathon metaphor, this is a lot like planning to set your morning alarm an hour earlier than usual so you can get out the door for a training run.

2. *Work and Rework.* While I'm sure you'll be taught lots of technical advice on what makes revision work well, from a resilience perspective, I like what Elbow presents when he advises us to "[eat] like an owl: take in everything and trust your innards to digest what's useful and discard what's not" (Elbow 264). Make sure to give yourself time to avert your eyes and mind from your first draft for at least a day before you come back to revise. Having some time away allows you to make some of the tougher choices you need to make during revision. For example, discovering the need to delete filler words or add supporting evidence doesn't usually come unless you've taken this necessary break. Think of it like resting your writerly muscles so you can get up and train again tomorrow. Revision is your "innards," and it takes a lot of resilience to learn to trust yourself enough to decide not only what your writerly innards are but also what this means for your sense of self.

3. *Finish.* Finishing what you start helps you end on a note of confidence. In your final draft, Koch advises to "keep up the momentum, but festina lente [make haste slowly]" (190). Make your hard, final choices here. Do your best not to let your masterpiece become over-manicured, and keep the finish line in sight.

If you take anything from this crash course on writing resilience, take the idea that resilience is not something specific to your writerly abilities. Practicing resilience in one aspect of your life tends to flow outwards, making this something useful to you regardless of how you feel about writing. In fact, the experts agree again here. Recently, a group of scholars at the University of Michigan conducted a six-year study of how students wrote in college, ultimately concluding that "writing led students to various forms of personal and social development," especially when students took an active role in navigating their own writerly identities (Gere 320). Writing breeds resilience, and resilience breeds writing.

But, this leaves us to wonder: isn't personal resilience a very different thing from resilience in the classroom or a social setting? What does developing writerly resilience have to do with your identity as a person outside of writing, or in your community? We see some possible answers to these questions in our next section, which discusses writing for social engagement.

Writing for Social Engagement (by Alison Overcash)

My co-authors have shown how writing can build personal agency and resilience, which are two valuable intrinsic benefits that I have experienced as well. When I was in high school, I started writing in my journal every day to help me cope with my mental illness. Journaling allowed me to explore my emotions and personal goals while developing my skills as a writer. I also enjoyed writing for school, but ultimately, I found myself wishing that my words could actually make a difference in the world. I couldn't help but compare myself to my favorite authors, who seemed to have been born with a destiny to change the world, while I was simply writing into a void. While the personal benefits alone make writing a worthwhile endeavor, I didn't fully embrace my identity as a writer until I started writing for audiences besides myself and my teachers.

Once I started studying English in college, I learned that writers have the power to educate, persuade, and empower their readers by practicing the art of rhetoric. As you study composition, you will learn, just as I did, how to harness the power of language to engage with the world around you. To be a "real" writer, one must understand the rhetorical situation at hand, which encompasses the speaker, audience, and purpose. Even when the speaker and audience are the same, the act of writing that text is still powerful. Even when your audience only includes your teacher, that's still "real" writing. However, expanding this audience beyond yourself and your teachers can help you understand your own writerly identity and decide how you want to wield this unique power.

You may feel distinctly aware of your position as a student, meaning that you might feel more like a "writing student" than a "real writer." However, the writing that you do in your everyday life is just as valid as writing a novel or essay, and as Taylor points out, personal or self-sponsored writing has just as many personal benefits—and, I would argue, additional social benefits—as any piece of school-sponsored writing. You probably already practice various forms of digital writing, which involves applying the skills you learned in class to create creative arrangements of multimedia and text. Social media posts on Twitter, Facebook, Reddit, etc. frequently use the same rhetorical strategies as an argumentative essay, even if this isn't done intentionally. In the *Writing Spaces* essay, "Four Things Social Media Can Teach You about College Writing—and One Thing It Can't," Ann N. Amicucci argues that the rhetorical strategies that students use on social media can also be effective in an academic setting. As with any essay, a social media post requires the writer to understand and appeal to the rhetorical situation at hand.

During my first semester as an English major, I wrote a personal narrative about my experiences with depression. After receiving some great feedback during a peer review activity, I revised the essay extensively and eventually got to a point where I was truly proud of what I had created. My peers encouraged me to share the essay with the people close to me that were mentioned in the essay. Every time I shared my writing with someone new, I was showered with compliments and deep conversations, and it felt like I was exposing a little piece of my soul every time, but it gave me a rush of excitement to show people what I was capable of doing.

"You should post this on Facebook," my mom had suggested.

I had laughed at the idea initially, and responded, "Nobody wants to read my homework assignments except for you, mom!"

However, I was so proud of my work that I eventually decided to rewrite it as a blog post, which I published on Medium and shared to my Facebook and Twitter accounts. Several friends and family members reached out to me to thank me for putting their own complex thoughts and confusing feelings about mental illness into words. Multiple people reassured me that my voice was important, and my words were valuable. By repurposing my personal narrative as a blog post, I was able to connect with people in ways that I never would have been able to if I hadn't stepped out of my comfort zone. Anyone can become a strong writer by simply considering their own position, their audience's expectations, and the specific purpose for composing the text, but actually entering the rhetorical situation requires you to share your work with the audience you are writing for.

In studying rhetoric, I discovered that the writers I idolized were held in such high esteem because of their ability to say the right thing, the right way, at the right time. The next time you write something for a school assignment, a journal entry, or a social media post, I encourage you to reflect on the rhetorical situation as well as your own motivations for addressing that situation. These motivations may be a culmination of those we have discussed thus far, or you may have your own reasons entirely. Some writers choose to harness the transformative power of writing for personal growth, while others, like myself, use writing as a tool to promote social change. Now, it's up to you to figure out what motivates *you* to write.

Conclusion (by Glenn Lester)

I'm a writing teacher. And at this point in my career, I've worked with several hundred writers—all of them "real writers" in my book. But it's not my book that counts—it's theirs.

And yours.

Taylor, Sydney, and Alison are just three of my former students (who are now friends and colleagues). In this essay, each has discussed their own reasons for writing, and the moments, experiences, and readings that led them to construct their own writerly identities. Specifically, these concepts about writing that helped Taylor, Sydney, and Alison develop their identities as *real* writers. We hope that reading our stories will inspire you to discover your reasons for writing, and that you might try out elements of their processes and concepts as you construct your own identity.

For instance, in our "Personal Agency and Self-Expression" section, Taylor points out that she had plenty of practice writing in high school, but it wasn't until she began to consider the purpose of writing *besides* to earn a grade that she began to understand what writing meant to her. Having been challenged to go beyond her initial assumptions, Taylor began to see writing as a cognitive process that she could adjust and control. Soon, writing became a tool for Taylor to build her own personal agency. You might compare Taylor's experiences with your own as you move ahead in writing.

Likewise, Sydney's section on writing and resilience raises a series of interesting questions that you might attempt to build on in your reflections and discussions about writing in your college classes: Does writing, as Sydney suggests, provide an occasion to develop resilience in other areas of your life? If so, *how* does writing help us become more personally resilient? What does that resilience-building ability have to do with treating writing as a "series of concrete steps," as Sydney describes? Does the personal resilience built through writing act as a bridge to engaging in social action and solving the problems you want to solve?

Alison, in our "Writing for Social Engagement" section, offers a different perspective. Alison describes an early experience using writing to build resilience through journaling. But they did not *truly* construct their own identity as a writer until they discovered the power they had to affect readers through their words. The act of sharing their writing with others changed Alison's relationship to their own writing and its purpose. You might take note of how sharing your writing with peers, classmates, and friends—whether through an in-class peer review exercise, a campus literary journal, or some other informal publication—changes your thoughts about who you are as a writer.

Or take my former student Ana, who I discussed in the introduction. Ana didn't see themselves as a writer—even though they had a good deal of experience with writing—because they didn't see the writing they did "for Ana" as "*real* writing." But by conceptually reframing their experiences, Ana took the first step in the journey of understanding who they were as a writer.

So, constructing your identity as a writer is not as simple as selecting from a list of three, or five, or ten possible reasons for writing. You certainly can't learn your writerly identity from an online quiz or the Hogwarts sorting hat. What you *can* do, however, is experiment. Embrace the new. Try out a variety of purposes, genres, audiences, and processes. See if you can't alter your approach for each assignment, in order to discover what works for you—and to learn what helps you feel that both the writing you do and the writer you are are *real*.

Beyond experimentation, you might also find value in what other writers have to say about how they see themselves. For instance, in another *Writing Spaces* essay, Sarah Allen explodes the myth of inspiration by examining "The Inspired Writer vs. The Real Writer." Allen's essay resonates with me because it helps me understand that I can be a "real writer" even when I'm not feeling inspired. And in fact, as Allen argues, part of being a "real writer" might be writing even when—*especially* when—you aren't feeling inspired!

Another *Writing Spaces* essay, "Workin' Languages: Who We Are Matters In Our Writing," Sara P. Alvarez, Amy J. Wan, and Eunjeong Lee offer a striking metaphor for writerly identity: "language architects." For Alvarez, Wan, and Lee, a language architect "works" language in order to help build up their community. What an original way to think about who you are as a writer! Or take this quotation from Wendy Bishop and David Starkey's "Keywords in Creative Writing," which describes the therapeutic power of writing: "Not only does writing help authors process the events of their younger years, it also helps them grapple with the continuing . . . challenges of their lives" (180).

These three conceptions of writing can help me figure out what kind of writer I can and want to be. Like Allen, I want to be a writer who will persevere through adversity without waiting for so-called inspiration to get the writing done. Like Alvarez, Wan, and Lee, I see myself as building something—an architect of language who writes for and with my community. And, as I write, I will take heart from Bishop and Starkey's point that writing is a way of processing both past and present, and that its positive effects on me extend beyond finishing any particular piece of writing.

But just because these three perspectives resonate with *me* doesn't mean they will or even should resonate with *you*. Instead, my point is that you can start to build your writerly identity by taking note of what other writers say about *their* reasons for writing. So, as you explore writing in your college writing courses, take note of the writing advice that resonates with you—especially the writing advice that goes beyond "how to get a good grade" or "how to give your teacher what they want." Try writing it down! And take note of the new concepts you're introduced to—perhaps you'll spend time learning about *literacy sponsorship* or *discourse communities* or *social advocacy*. As you do, challenge yourself to not just learn the concepts, but also to identify which of those concepts can help you discover *your* reasons for writing, your own writerly identity.

As we composed this chapter together, one theme came up over and over: the idea that anyone can be a writer—and that everyone *should* think of themselves as a writer. There is not one "right way" to be a writer, and no one "right" reason for writing. Writing for yourself can be incredibly valuable. And writing for others can be equally valid and meaningful. But recognizing what makes *you* the *real* writer you are means recognizing your purposes and reasons for writing.

And so, we offer this new definition of a writer:

You.

You are a writer.

Works Cited

Allen, Sarah. "The Inspired Writer vs. The Real Writer." *Writing Spaces: Readings on Writing, Volume 1*, edited by Charles Lowe and Pavel Zemlinsky, Parlor Press, 2010, pp. 34-44.

Alvarez, Sara P., Amy J. Wan, and Eunjeong Lee. "Workin' Languages: Who We Are Matters." In *Writing Spaces: Readings on Writing, Volume 4*, edited by

Dana Lynn Driscoll, Megan Heise, Mary K. Stewart, and Matthew Vetter, Parlor Press, 2022, pp. 1-17.

Bayles, David, and Ted Orland. *Art & Fear: Observations On The Perils (and Rewards) of Artmaking*. The Image Continuum, 1993.

Berlin, James. "Rhetoric and Ideology in the Writing Class." *College English*, vol. 50, no. 5, 1988, pp. 497-494. *JSTOR*, https://www.jstor.org/stable/377477.

Bishop, Wendy, and David Starkey. "Therapy (and Therapeutic)." *Keywords in Creative Writing*. Utah State University Press, 2006, pp. 178-186. *JSTOR*, https://www.jstor.org/stable/j.ctt4cgr61.40.

Elbow, Peter. "Being a Writer vs. Being an Academic: A Conflict in Goals." *College Composition and Communication*, vol. 46, no. 1, 1995, pp. 72-83. *JSTOR*, https://www.jstor.org/stable/358871.

Flower, Linda. "What is Community Literacy?" *Community Literacy and the Rhetoric of Public Engagement*. Southern Illinois University Press, 2008, pp. 9-43.

Gere, Anne Ruggles, ed. *Developing Writers in Higher Education: A Longitudinal Study*. University of Michigan Press, 2019. *JSTOR*, http://www.jstor.org/stable/j.ctvdjrpt3.4.

Koch, Stephen. *Modern Library Writer's Workshop: A Guide to the Craft of Fiction*. Random House, Inc., 2003.

Zimmerman, Barry, and Tim Cleary. "Adolescents' Development of Personal Agency: The Role of Self-Efficacy Beliefs and Self-Regulatory Skill." In *Self-Efficacy Beliefs of Adolescents*, Information Age Publishing, 2006, pp. 45-69.

Teacher Resources for "We Write Because We Care: Developing Your Writerly Identity"

Overview and Teaching Strategies

"We Write Because We Care: Developing Your Writerly Identity" is best used in an introductory lesson to first year college writing students, or in conjunction with a reflective writing task, such as a portfolio introduction.

The chapter explores what it means to be a writer, both in and out of the classroom, and looks at the benefits of writing, ultimately inviting students to think of themselves as writers by constructing what we call a "writerly identity." We proposed this chapter when we realized that most writing textbooks and resources—*Writing Spaces* among them—lack much consideration of the writing that we do outside of the classroom, and often fail to invite students to take that first, radical step of calling themselves "real" writers.

With that in mind, this chapter could be paired with a class activity in which students reflect on their prior experience with and knowledge of writing. We find that students, especially first year students, often benefit from a great deal of encouragement to find the confidence to challenge themselves to even *think* of themselves as writers. In fact, as Taylor reminded us during our collaboration, one thing that Glenn said in a class has stuck with her: anyone can be a writer. To achieve that goal of helping students consider who they are as writers, we suggest pairing this chapter with other *Writing Spaces* chapters that encourage students to think about purpose, identity, and community, especially Sarah Allen's "The Inspired Writer Vs. The Real Writer," E. Shelley Reid's "Ten Ways To Think About Writing: Metaphoric Musings For College Students," Quentin Vieregge's "Exigency: What Makes My Message Indispensable to My Reader," or Sarah P. Alvarez, Amy J. Wan, and Eunjeong Lee's "Workin' Languages: Who We Are Matters in Our Writing."

Our chapter begins with an introduction that addresses a widely shared concern: what does it mean to truly write? The answer we propose is both simple (just write!) and complex (writing is connected to personal identity and community). But we argue that students can count *all* of the composing they do as "real" writing. Diaristic journaling, creative writing, therapeutic writing, researched academic essays—all of it counts as "real writing" in our book. So, a natural place for students to enter into this conversation is with the question: are we correct? Does any and all composing count as "real" writing? Even texting? What about TikTok? If so, what does this mean for the work students do in their first-year composition courses?

Our next section discusses the personal benefits of writing. Taylor grapples with the question "So what?" and concludes that every student gains knowledge, skills, and a better understanding of the self when writing. This leads into one of the most important traits that we believe writing can teach: resilience. Students face challenges in the classroom and in their personal lives that require perseverance, and the acts of writing and revision are tangible activities that help instill this practice. Sydney takes up this theme in the second section of our chapter. This section could be paired with instructional activities related to growth mindset and resilience. Or, students might be invited to speak back to us by identifying times in which writing did *not* teach resilience.

We conclude with Alison's discussion of socially engaged, community-situated writing. This section of the chapter might assist with introducing a community-oriented or service-learning writing unit, or it might open a conversation in which students discuss how they could apply class concepts to the writing and communication they already do in the communities they belong to. Glenn has seen great success in student engagement when asking his own students to identify and describe complex, ongoing problems or issues that their communities face and using those problems and issues to generate writing and research projects. Responding to these concepts could motivate students to use their writerly identity to engage with their own communities, too.

Finally, all three sections of our chapter tie back to the notion of writerly identity. The most productive use of this chapter that we can imagine is one in which students think hard about who they currently are as writers while identifying possibilities for the writers they want to become.

Discussion Questions

1. Which of the three sections of this chapter resonated with you the most, and why? Which section was most confusing or surprising? What does your response tell you about who you are as a writer?

2. What role has writing played in your personal development so far as a student? How about outside of the classroom? What ideas in this chapter do you anticipate using in this course or semester?

3. One way to develop your writerly identity is to compare various writers' reasons for writing and ideas about writing. To that end, read Sarah Allen's "The Inspired Writer Vs. The Real Writer," also found in *Writing Spaces*. Identify the common themes between that chapter and this chapter, as well as any differences in perspective.

4. Create a two-column chart. Label one column "writing for school" and the other "personal writing." Then, use the chart to describe how your experience differs when you're writing for school versus engaging in personal writing. (Remember that personal writing isn't always poetry, diaries, or short stories!)

Recommended Activities

1. To test our assertions about writing as a tool for building your agency and resilience, try this journaling exercise: use a convenient device, like a notebook or a mobile notes app, to document *one notable event each day for one week*. Write about what happened, why it was notable, and how you felt about it. At the end of the week, read through what you wrote about the week you've had and how you've felt. Then, discuss with your classmates how your attitudes about writing may have shifted as a result of using writing to document your observations and experiences. How does having a tangible record of your experiences affect your mindset and sense of your own personal agency, defined as your "capability to originate and direct actions for given purposes"?

2. Think back to the social engagement section of this chapter. Identify one community that you are a part of that is or could be impacted by writing. (Recall Linda Flower's definition of a rhetorical community, which considers how people unite for a variety of purposes around "affinities rather than visible borders.") Identify an issue, question, challenge, problem, or shared goal that the community faces. How could writing be used to approach this issue, solve this problem, or achieve the community's goal? What types of writing would most impact the community, and why? What stands in the way of addressing the issue or solving the problem—both from inside and outside the community?

2 Dispositions Toward Learning

Jennifer Wells

Overview

Many of us have something we want to learn to do that is beyond what we are currently able to do.[1] While there are a number of key factors that can influence our success (or contribute to our failure), one of the most important is our own orientation toward learning. In this chapter, you will explore the role that an individual's dispositions towards learning can play, and will discover some ways individuals can work to change dispositions that aren't serving them well.

Introduction

Recently, as in the past 36 hours, I've decided to quit my job and become a famous YouTuber. Based on my research, I will only need 2 million views a month to sustain my aspirational lifestyle.

Do I know anything about filming, video editing, sound engineering, and graphic design? No. Do I own any professional recording equipment, other than the camera and mic built into my aging cell phone that can't hold a battery charge for more than 3 hours? Also no.

Seems totally doable, right?

I start with this story because most of us have, or will have, ideas for things we want to learn to do that are beyond what we are currently able to do. Sometimes those things are hobbies, like learning to crochet adorable sweaters for penguins recovering from oil spills in Australia. Other times those might be goals related to health and wellness, like learning to run a half marathon or to cook healthy food using only a mug and a microwave.

---

1. This work is licensed under the Creative Commons Attribution-NonCommercial-NoDerivatives 4.0 International License (CC BY-NC-ND 4.0) and is subject to the Writing Spaces Terms of Use. To view a copy of this license, visit http://creativecommons.org/licenses/by-nc-nd/4.0/, email info@creativecommons.org, or send a letter to Creative Commons, PO Box 1866, Mountain View, CA 94042, USA. To view the Writing Spaces Terms of Use, visit http://writingspaces.org/terms-of-use.

And, since y'all are reading this (sorry- we say y'all in the South), my guess is you are in school, presumably to learn new things. Ok, yes, and get a degree, a job that pays as much money as being a famous YouTuber, etc. etc. All those things.

There are numerous, complex factors that can either facilitate learning, or can get in the way of learning (Roozen and Erickson). The physical environment someone is trying to learn in, for example, can make learning easier or more challenging. At some point, you probably have tried to learn in a less than ideal environment: a noisy house, or a classroom in Florida when the AC is broken. If you are learning from some sort of instructor or coach, then the way that person teaches can impact learning; similarly, if you are doing some sort of practice to learn, like baseball batting drills, then the way those practice sessions are designed can also help or hinder. Having the resources needed to learn is another important factor because, in my example above, if you are learning to play baseball but do not have a baseball bat, it is going to be more difficult than if you did have a bat.

Then, of course, there is the role of the learner themselves. Again, the factors that can impact a learner's ability to learn are numerous, and the scope of this chapter doesn't allow me to get into all of them. *How People Learn* and *How People Learn II* are great starting points for those interested in reading more. But, what I would like to talk about, and what chapter space permits, is the ways in which a learner's *beliefs about learning and about themselves as learners* can orient them towards learning, or can inhibit their learning. Recent research from the fields of education, educational psychology, and writing studies have named these beliefs "dispositions" (Costa and Kallick; Driscoll and Wells; Ennis; Nelsen). You probably are already thinking, well duh! Of course dispositions toward learning impacts learning! And that's great, because my goal is for you to be able to name and identify your own dispositions toward learning, generally, and in your writing classes, specifically, so that you can reflect on whether or not those dispositions are serving you in that particular context, and if not, you can work to change them.

DISPOSITIONS, DEFINED

But I am getting ahead of myself. First, let's get a handle on what dispositions are. Merriam-Webster's dictionary defines dispositions as, "**a:** prevailing tendency, mood, or inclination; **b:** temperamental makeup; **c:** the tendency of something to act in a certain manner under given circumstances." Using this definition, dispositions towards learning would be the tendency, mood, or inclination of the learner to learn; the temperamental makeup of the learner towards learning; and the tendency of the learner to act in a certain manner under given circumstances; i.e., in a learning situation, the learner has a tendency to act in a way that supports their learning. Baird and Dilger describe dispositions as, "individual attitudes that influence the motivation of intellectual traits." Claxton and Kallick note that, "The word itself indicates that it's not only a person's ability that counts, but also the person's perception and inclination to make good use of that ability in appropriate situations" (63).

Writing studies scholars Driscoll and Wells offer an expanded definition of dispositions by breaking down some of their features. They: Are a critical part of a larger system that includes the person, the context, the process through which learning happens, and time.

1. Are not intellectual traits like knowledge, skills, or aptitude, but rather determine how those intellectual traits are used or applied.

2. Determine students' sensitivity toward and willingness to engage in transfer.

3. Can positively or negatively impact the learning environment; they can be generative or disruptive.

4. Are dynamic and may be context-specific or broadly generalized.

Let's unpack this: as I described at the beginning of this chapter, there are a host of factors that influence learning, and dispositions are one of them. Yet, dispositions aren't the same as that knowledge. While you almost always arrive at new learning situations with previous knowledge, including "declarative knowledge" (also called content knowledge) which is knowing *that* (e.g., knowing that a topic sentence is the first one in a paragraph); "procedural knowledge," which is knowing *how* (e.g., knowing how to revise a topic sentence to fit the paragraph), when faced with a new learning challenge, your dispositions will impact the extent to which you draw from what you already know and are able to use it in that new setting (this is called *knowledge transfer*, and it is super important. You can read *Writing Spaces*, Vol. 4, "The Importance of Transfer in Your First Year Writing Course" by Kara Taczak, for more on transfer. Just as not all beliefs are positive, not all dispositions are positive, either, and some can really get in the way of your learning. Lastly, your dispositions are not static—they will change, sometimes from moment to moment, but certainly from one situation to another. For example, the way your dispositions impact your learning in a writing class may be different from how your dispositions impact your learning in a different subject.

You may have noticed I've been using the term dispositions, plural, so now let's go even deeper into some of the specific dispositions researchers have identified. From educational psychology, we have *expectancy-value, self-efficacy, self-regulation,* and *attribution.* From writing studies, we have *problem-exploring* and *answer-getting.* I have chosen to focus on these as they are the dispositions I regularly see impacting me in my own learning (including my aspirations to become a YouTube vlogger), but also in the learning that my students are doing in the writing courses I teach.

Types of Dispositions

Expectancy-Value

Expectancy-value theory (Eccles; Eccles and Wigfield; Wigfield and Eccles) explains that learners will perform better, persist longer, and make better choices when they feel that what they are working on, or learning, is valuable to them. I am sure each of you can easily think of a time when you were really interested in learning a new skill, hobby, or subject, because learning it was valuable to you. In contrast, you can also probably think of times when you didn't see the point of learning what you were being asked to learn, and therefore were probably less motivated to learn it. I am extremely motivated to watch YouTube videos in order to learn how to effectively film for my vlog. While I am not serious about getting YouTube famous and quitting my job, I do think it has the potential to be a side hustle (a time-consuming side hustle), so I am motivated to start learning what I need to learn. When it comes to my writing classes, if a student doesn't place much value on writing, if they don't think the course or skill will be useful to them in the future, they may find little about my course to be intrinsically motivating. Me shrieking, "WRITING IS IMPORTANT" is not going to convince anyone, so the best I can do is design assignments that allow them to explore the role of writing in whatever they want to study in college, or in the job they want to do after college. Like my students, if you connect developing as a writer to goals that are personally meaningful to you—if you expect the knowledge you are learning now will be valuable to you in the future—you are more likely to be motivated to learn. If you are unsure of the role writing may play for you in the future, I recommend you investigate possible career choices and explore how writing is used in those areas. More often than not, you will find that writing plays a larger role in your possible future than you may have anticipated.

SELF-EFFICACY

Self-efficacy is defined as "people's beliefs about their capabilities to produce performances that influence events affecting their lives" (Bandura 434). Several years ago, I decided to sign up for a Star-Wars themed half-marathon. Though I was not a runner, and in fact do not like running, I knew that I was capable of training to complete a half-marathon. I had self-efficacy toward Star Wars half-marathon success. Since I believed I was capable of running the half-marathon, I was more likely to do the things required to complete the race (like maintaining a training schedule), than if I believed that no matter what I did I wouldn't be able to cross the finish line.

With regards to learners, self-efficacy can be defined as learners' beliefs about their capabilities to do the things or produce the things needed to influence events affecting their lives. A student with self-efficacy will believe they can take the steps needed to succeed in a class, like visiting their professor's office hours to talk through an upcoming assignment. Side note: students, please go to your professor's office hours! We are sad and lonely when no one comes.

SELF-REGULATION

Self-regulation, according to Zimmerman, is not an inherent trait that learners either have or don't have, but rather it is a process learners go through when they choose how they will adapt to new learning situations. The ability to set reasonable goals, to choose to utilize strategies to achieve those goals, to self-evaluate progress, to manage the physical and social settings so that they serve to support and not distract from those goals, to practice effective time management, to reflect on the success of choices made or strategies used, to understand how performance leads to results, and to be able to make changes to any of these preceding actions to improve future performance—all of this falls under the umbrella of self-regulation. If it sounds like a lot, it is, and it makes sense when Zimmerman comments, "It is hardly surprising that many students have not learned to self-regulate their academic studying very well" (64). I would argue it isn't only students who haven't mastered self-regulation because there are plenty of times when the goals I set for myself are unreasonable and, as someone with ADHD, I certainly struggle with time management.

Self-regulation is linked to self-efficacy. Bandura found students with high self-efficacy were more likely than students with low-self efficacy to self-regulate their own learning. Self-regulation is the ability to make a choice for yourself and act on it, so students with strong self-regulation will decide they should visit their professor's office hours, and then actually follow through and do it. Students without strong self-regulation might have the idea of visiting office hours but then not act on it. Zimmerman found that students with self-efficacy were more persistent when faced with obstacles, and felt less anxious about the work they need to do. They also set more challenging goals for themselves, since they had the confidence in their own abilities to meet their goals. Pajares observed that students with low self-efficacy may perceive work to be harder than it actually is, which can cause negative emotions like stress and depression. Many of my students struggle with self-efficacy and I encourage them to begin by setting small, reasonable goals, like staying after class to ask the professor about an upcoming assignment instead of committing to an office hour. As they gain confidence doing the small things, they can then take on bigger challenges and build self-efficacy along the way. I encourage you to do the same: start small to build your confidence.

ATTRIBUTION

Attribution theory (Weiner and Craighead), is a theory about to who(m) or to what people attribute the causes of events that affect them. Basically, if something goes well, who gets the praise? If it doesn't, who is blamed? These attributions are sometimes referred to in terms of a person's locus of control. When a learner believes that their ability or efforts are the cause of their success or failure, they are considered to have a high internal locus of control. On the other hand, when a learner believes that the cause of their success or failure lies outside of their control, they are considered to have a high external locus of control. It is important to note that a person's locus of control is not fixed and can change from situation to situation. Learners' locus of control lies on a spectrum and is also highly dependent on the context of the event. Someone who might have a higher internal locus of control in one context may have a higher external locus of control in another. You might have a high locus of control in your computer programming class but not so much in your sculpture course. Or, like me, you might generally have an internal locus of control when things are going well but as soon as they fall apart have the instinct to blame someone else, which in some cases is warranted. While it might seem like an internal locus of control is always a good thing, having an extremely high internal locus of control can be a problem, especially when the outcome of an event is perceived as a failure. Those who believe outcomes are completely in their control may suffer from a loss of self-esteem (Abramson, Garber, and Seligman). I see this occasionally with students who enroll in college right out of high school. The students at my particular college struggle with perfectionism. So, when a student who has done very well in high school and attributes their own success to being smart and working hard gets a non-passing grade on an assignment that can sometimes send them into an emotional tailspin and lead to doubts about whether or not they are "good enough" for college. I often try to affirm these students' intelligence and work ethic while also pointing out it is totally normal for students to struggle in a new environment or in a subject or academic field they haven't studied before. A rigid internal locus of control in this context is not helpful.

Problem-Exploring and Answer-Getting

Writing studies researcher Elizabeth Wardle argues that there are two dispositions that help explain how learners manage "well-structured and ill-structured" problems they encounter during the course of their learning. A well-structured problem is one that is pretty straightforward: there is a clear answer, and that answer is not hard to find. An ill-structured problem is much messier because there is not only one answer, and the answers that do exist are not immediately obvious. Simple math is often well structured: I have two dogs and if I get three more dogs, how many dogs will I have? Too many, according to my neighbor. But the real answer is 5. An ill-structured problem might be something like how can I teach my dog to pick up a tiny basketball and drop it into a tiny hoop? There is not one obvious solution to this problem as dog training requires different approaches and techniques depending on the dog, and there would be both creative thinking and trial and error involved in figuring it out. A well-structured problem in a writing class might look like a quiz on MLA citations whereas an ill-structured problem could be like the one that Wardle describes in her article where students in a Medical Writing class identified a local health problem and then created a campaign to help solve it.

Wardle found that her students often exhibited two kinds of dispositions when faced with these types of problems: problem-exploring and answer-getting. "Problem-exploring dispositions incline a person toward curiosity, reflection, consideration of multiple possibilities, a willingness to engage in a recursive process of trial and error, and toward a recognition that more than one solution can "work." Answer-getting dispositions seek right answers quickly and are averse to open consideration of multiple possibilities." When faced with well-structured problems, students with either disposition were able to identify an answer. However, when looking at an ill-structured problem, students with answer-getting dispositions were more easily frustrated and less likely to think outside the box and approach the problem from multiple angles. Think about problems you have encountered in your own life, both in and out of school, and make a guesstimate. What percentage of those problems are well structured and what percentage are ill structured? How have you worked to solve the ill-structured ones? Can you see how your disposition towards solving that problem impacted the approach you took?

WHAT CAN YOU DO WITH KNOWLEDGE OF DISPOSITIONS?

Currently, scholars from many different fields and academic disciplines are exploring the impact of dispositions on learning within those fields. A quick search of your library's database (or, don't yell at me library friends, Google Scholar) using the key words dispositions + learning + the name of the field (e.g., computer science) will reveal the range of interesting work being done. For those interested in studying learning, dispositions offer one avenue for exploration.

For me, being able to step outside of myself and look at a learning situation to identify my own dispositions in that moment has helped me reflect on the extent to which they are working for me. In one of the writing classes I teach, we spend the first half of the semester talking about the beliefs students have about writing and about themselves as writers and reflect on the root sources of many of those beliefs. We also explore the ways in which some of those beliefs are impacting their learning-related behaviors. Then, in the second half of the course, students choose a belief or behavior that they feel is not serving them well, and design a study in which they test out three different methods or tools for making small changes to that belief or behavior. Many students choose to study one of their own dispositions, with self-regulation being the most popular.

Even though this is a book chapter and not a class, I would encourage you to do the same. As you read about dispositions, did you feel seen? In what ways are your own dispositions towards learning working for you? In what ways might they be more limiting than you previously realized? Whenever you identify one, and you think it is not working for you, reflect on concrete actions you might take to try to revise that belief.

Wherever you are on your learning journey, please remember to pack your new knowledge of dispositions. And, if I do become a wildly successful YouTuber, remember to like and subscribe.

Works Cited

Abramson, Lyn Y., Judy Garber, and Martin EP Seligman. "Learned Helplessness in Humans: An Attributional Analysis." *Human Helplessness: Theory and Applications*, vol. 3, 1980, p. 34.

Baird, Neil, and Bradley Dilger. "Dispositions in Natural Science Laboratories: The Roles of Individuals and Contexts in Writing Transfer." *Across the Disciplines*, vol. 15, no. 4, 2018, pp. 21-40.

Bandura, Albert. "Self-efficacy: Toward a Unifying Theory of Behavioral Change." *Psychological Review*, vol. 84, no. 2, 1977, p. 191.

Claxton, Guy, A. Costa, and Bena Kallick. "Hard Thinking about Soft Skills." *Educational Leadership*, vol. 73, no. 6, 2016, pp. 60-64.

Costa, Arthur L., and Bena Kallick. *Dispositions: Reframing Teaching and Learning*. Corwin Press, 2013.

Driscoll, Dana Lynn, and Jennifer Wells. "Beyond Knowledge and Skills: Writing Transfer and the Role of Student Dispositions." *Composition Forum*, vol. 26, Fall 2012. www.compositionforum.com/issue/26/beyond-knowledge-skills.php

Eccles, Jacquelynne. "Expectancies, Values and Academic Behaviors." *Achievement and Achievement Motives*, edited by Janet T. Spence, W. H. Freeman, 1983, pp. 75-146.

Eccles, Jacquelynne S. "Subjective Task Value and the Eccles et al. Model of Achievement-Related Choices." *Handbook of Competence and Motivation*, edited by Andrew J. Elliot and Carol S. Dweck, The Guilford Press, 2005, pp. 105-21.

Eccles, Jacquelynne S., and Allan Wigfield. "Motivational Beliefs, Values, and Goals." *Annual Review of Psychology*, vol. 53, no.1, 2002, pp. 109-32.

Ennis, Robert H. "Critical Thinking Dispositions: Their Nature and Assessability." *Informal Logic*, vol.18, no. 2-3, 1996, pp. 165-82.

Nelsen, Peter J. "Intelligent Dispositions: Dewey, Habits and Inquiry in Teacher Education." *Journal of Teacher Education*, vol. 66, no.1, 2015, pp. 86-97

Roozen, Kevin, and Joe Erickson. *Expanding Literate Landscapes: Persons, Practices, and Sociohistoric Perspectives of Disciplinary Development*. Utah State UP, 2017. www.ccdigitalpress.org/expanding.

Taczak, Kara. "The Importance of Transfer in Your First year Writing Course." *Writing Spaces: Readings on Writing*, vol. 4, pp. 301-15. www.writingspaces.org/past-volumes/the-importance-of-transfer-in-your-first-year-writing-course/

Wardle, Elizabeth. "Creative Repurposing for Expansive Learning: Considering 'Problem-Exploring' and 'Answer-Getting' Dispositions in Individuals and

Fields." *Composition Forum*, vol. 26, no. 1, 2012. www.compositionforum.com/issue/26/creative-repurposing.php.

Weiner, Irving B., and W. Edward Craighead, eds. *The Corsini Encyclopedia of Psychology, Volume 4*. Vol. 4. John Wiley and Sons, 2010.

Wigfield, Allan, and Jacquelynne S. Eccles. "The Development of Competence Beliefs, Expectancies for Success, and Achievement Values from Childhood through Adolescence." *Development of Achievement Motivation*, edited by Allan Wigfield and Jacquelynne S. Eccles, Academic Press, 2002, pp. 91-120. https://doi.org/10.1016/B978-012750053-9/50006-1.

Zimmerman, Barry J. "Becoming a Self-Regulated Learner: An Overview." *Theory into Practice* vol. 41, no. 2, 2002, pp. 64-70.

Teacher Resources for "Dispositions Towards Learning"

Overview and Teaching Strategies

This is a chapter that introduces students to dispositions, or the beliefs about learning and themselves as learners, and discusses the ways in which dispositions can impact learning behaviors. Specific dispositions taken up in this chapter include *expectancy-value, self-efficacy, self-regulation,* and *attribution, problem-exploring* and *answer-getting.* This chapter would be well-paired with Kara Taczak's chapter on knowledge transfer from *Writing Spaces*, Volume 4, as writing studies researchers have argued that dispositions play a crucial role in students' transfer of knowledge.

Discussion Questions

1. Before reading this chapter: think of a time that you learned something that was really challenging. What was the thing you learned and what made it so difficult? How did you eventually overcome those challenges and learn what you wanted?

2. After reading this chapter: go back to the pre-reading question #1, and ask yourself if dispositions played any role in your eventual learning success. Which ones? In what ways?

3. Thinking about the dispositions you have towards learning in general, can you think of how you developed those dispositions? What events or experiences from the past helped you form those dispositions?

4. What is something you are learning to do in school right now that is challenging? What dispositions are at play in that context? Are those dispositions serving you well? Which, if any, do you want to change?

5. If you are going to reflect on a disposition you might want to change, what steps might you take to do so?

3 "Is This for a Grade?" Understanding Assessment, Evaluation, and Low-Stakes Writing Assignments

Jason McIntosh

Overview

Grades are an important part of school.[1] Among other things, they tell students how well they met assignment outcomes, whether they are on track to pass their courses and graduate, and if they qualify for certain scholarships and extracurricular activities. However, grades are also the cause of a great deal of stress and anxiety, especially when the stakes are high. This essay examines low-stakes writing, a broad category of assignments and activities that are designed to shift students' focus away from grades and towards their writing and learning. The goal of this essay is to encourage discussion between teachers and students about the role of grades in the context of low and high-stakes writing assignments. It does so by discussing the differences between low-stake and high-stakes writing, why low-stakes writing is minimally graded or not graded at all, and how low-stakes and high-stakes writing relate to assessment and evaluation. The essay concludes with four recommendations for how students can change their mindset toward low-stakes writing.

---

1. This work is licensed under the Creative Commons Attribution-NonCommercial-NoDerivatives 4.0 International License (CC BY-NC-ND 4.0) and is subject to the Writing Spaces Terms of Use. To view a copy of this license, visit http://creativecommons.org/licenses/by-nc-nd/4.0/, email info@creativecommons.org, or send a letter to Creative Commons, PO Box 1866, Mountain View, CA 94042, USA. To view the Writing Spaces Terms of Use, visit http://writingspaces.org/terms-of-use.

Introduction

I often waited until the last minute to complete writing assignments when I was a college student. I usually started the day before the assignment was due and wrote late into the night. I didn't reread or revise. I worried that revising would slow me down, that I would realize how bad my writing was, get discouraged, and lose momentum. On the rare occasions that I got an early start, I still completed writing assignments without rereading, revising, or even proofreading typos. Completing writing assignments at the last minute and trying to "get it right" the first time meant that my *final* drafts, the ones that were graded, were really *first* drafts.

During my junior year, I took an English class with a professor who required students to write rough drafts of literary analysis essays before completing final drafts. Our rough drafts weren't graded, and the professor didn't look at them. Instead, students workshopped drafts in small groups during class. I don't remember the feedback that I received from my peers, but I do remember how helpful it was just to read my writing out loud. Not only did I find mistakes, like missing commas, but I also found places where my meaning wasn't as clear as I thought that it was. Workshopping drafts didn't suddenly transform me as a writer, but it did slowly lay the groundwork for new habits that helped me with more difficult assignments during my senior year.

Like me, you will probably turn in first drafts as final drafts at some point, maybe because you procrastinated, or you had to prioritize assignments in other classes, or life outside of school took precedence. But you will also have teachers who, like my English professor, teach you how to use *low stakes* writing practices like rough drafts and peer workshops to produce better final drafts. These teachers know that first drafts don't reflect what you are learning in the class or your writing skills. They also know that writers need feedback and that making it a habit to just write first drafts won't help you grow as a writer or prepare you to meet the challenges of *high stakes* writing in school and your everyday life.

Low-Stakes Writing Before the High-stakes Final Draft

Writing is *high stakes* when someone evaluates it and the outcome of that evaluation is important to you. The essay you write in a history class is high stakes if the essay grade impacts your standing in the course. A job application is high stakes when you really want to work for a particular employer. Even a text message to a friend can be high stakes if you are worried about what to say and how best to say it. With each of these examples, you can use low-stakes writing to help you generate, revise, and edit before turning in the final draft, uploading the completed application, or pressing send on the text.

Despite the name, *low-stakes* writing isn't the opposite of *high-stakes* writing. It's more like a constant companion, always there to provide help and support when you need it. Experienced writers make low-stakes writing a central part of their writing processes, and you can too. Consider the three examples above. If you aren't happy with your thesis statement for the history essay, you might write several new ones and pick the best. For the job application, you might write a list of the skills you acquired and job duties performed during your summer internship. You could write a rough draft of the text message and ask a trusted family member to read it and offer suggestions. Noted writing scholar and teacher Peter Elbow says that the payoff for writing like this is that "we get to throw away the low-stakes writing itself but keep the neural changes it produced in [our] heads" (5). In other words, you can use low-stakes writing strategies like brainstorming, listing, and rough drafts to assess, reflect on, and think about your writing as you work towards the final draft. It turns out that these neural changes are so transformative that educators across disciplines and subject areas have expanded the concept of low-stakes writing beyond producing better final drafts.

THE BROADER BENEFITS OF LOW-STAKES WRITING

Other kinds of low-stakes writing assignments you might encounter in school include reading responses in economics classes (Beam), letter writing in a calculus class (Jaafar), reflective journals in clinical nursing programs (Sasa), and online discussion boards in science classes (Shumskaya et al.). You might complete low-stakes writing assignments that help you study for high-stakes exams (Stevenson), prepare for class discussion (Drabick et al.), and conduct library research (Stewart-Mailhiot). Assignments like these improve your chances of earning better grades on high stakes final drafts, quizzes, exams, and major projects, but you also gain many other benefits.

In her article "Breaking Free: The Benefits of Non-expository, Low-stakes Writing Assignments in Psychology Courses," professor Dr. Rebecca D. Foushée surveys more than twenty years of empirical research about low-stakes writing assignments. Her research suggests that low-stakes writing assignments such as "in-class freewriting, letters, poems, online discussion boards, reflection exercises, journaling, short papers, group writing activities, reaction papers, and problem-solving exercises" benefit students far beyond high-stakes essay writing (40). Her research suggests that low-stakes writing assignments help you:

1. **Build your confidence as a writer.** Activities like brainstorming, rough drafts, and peer response improve your sense of ownership and agency with writing because you are the one making decisions about the quality and direction of your learning and writing, not the teacher.

2. **Improve your mental and emotional health.** While writing isn't usually assigned as a form of therapy in school, "incorporating assignments which provide opportunities to blog, journal, discuss, or share personal perspectives may promote [your] social and emotional development" in addition to helping you learn new genres (Foushée 42).

3. **Be more creative.** Because the requirements for low-stakes writing assignments are often more loosely defined, they provide you more opportunities to be creative with your thinking and writing. This kind of creative freedom gives you "psychological 'space'" to make mistakes, process course materials at a deeper level, produce personal insight, and learn from experience" (Foushée 43).

4. **Better understanding of course content and improve learning.** Foushée's research suggests that assignments like journaling and discussion boards encourage reflection and self-assessment, both of which "facilitate learning" (43). This is why you might encounter low-stakes reflective writing in a math class or personal narratives in psychology and biology, courses that traditionally focus on technical or scientific writing.

5. **Develop awareness of self and others.** Foushée's research also suggests that because of its expressive and reflective nature, low-stakes writing helps you better understand yourself and others and builds "interpersonal communication" skills that you will use throughout school and life. Small group activities are a great ex-

ample of Foushée's point because they provide a space in which to practice listening, talking, and collaborating.

Most of the low-stakes writing assignments Foushée researched were either ungraded or minimally graded, usually with a completion grade. When you are assigned a low-stakes writing assignment, you might feel like the work is less meaningful than the high stakes assignments that account for much more of your course grade. However, Foushée's research demonstrates that you will not only improve as a writer and learner, but you will gain the benefits described above. Let's look at an example of low-stakes writing and consider how grades might negatively affect the goals of that writing.

Zero Drafts: An Example of Ungraded Low-Stakes Writing

In her *Writing Spaces* essay "From Topic to Presentation: Making Choices to Develop Your Writing," Beth L. Hewett describes how she writes "zero drafts" early on in her writing process. Her zero drafts aren't "neat and tidy or super correct sentence-wise," and they aren't intended to be workshopped or shared with others, not like the more organized "first drafts" that she writes later (63). The goal of her zero draft is to "[get] the writing started" and "[begin] to organize ideas" (63). It's a way of using writing to discover what she has to say about her topic. Her zero draft can be full of unfinished thoughts and sentences, notes, sketches, lists, anything.

When you were asked to write a zero draft for class, it could be counterproductive for the teacher to grade it the same way that a final draft is graded. If your zero draft were graded, it would almost certainly affect how you wrote it. Instead of focusing on developing your ideas, you might get distracted by things like organization, word choice, and punctuation that aren't as important early on in your writing process. Ungraded low-stakes writing, as Foushée's research suggests, gives you more freedom to take risks and be creative, both of which are key to developing a sense of ownership and control over your writing.

The problem is that most of us, students and teachers, are so accustomed to everything being graded in school that it can be difficult to trust the process of writing without grades. When I introduce students to "quick writes," which are similar to zero drafts, at the beginning of the semester, someone inevitably asks, "Is this for a grade?" I would have asked the same question when I was a student. Teachers who are new to assigning low-stakes writing also have concerns about not assigning grades. I initially worried that I wasn't doing my job if I didn't grade quick writes and that students wouldn't take the assignment seriously. These are important questions and concerns, and one of the steps that students and teachers can take to find answers and reach a common understanding is to have conversations about the problems that grades create.

The Problems with Grades

Researchers and educators have long criticized grades. For example, Dr. Stephen Tchudi notes that "Grades are extremely limited in their degrees of freedom, for they take a vast array of data and condense it into a single symbol that, in itself, doesn't communicate very much" (xv). One reason they are condensed into a "single symbol" (e.g., A, B, C, D, F) is that grades need to communicate information about student performance to a wide range of audiences who each have different needs and expectations (Cizeck 17). You want to know where you stand in a class. The registrar needs to know if you have satisfied course prerequisites and are making progress towards your degree. The financial aid office might need to know your academic standing as it relates to scholarship requirements. Advisors use course grades to answer all sorts of questions, as they help you and other students decide which classes to take. Athletic departments, fraternities and sororities, student activities associations, and honors societies all use grades to determine students' standing within those programs and organizations. Dr. Gregory J. Cizek, a professor at UNC-Chapel Hill who studies grading practices, critiques this system, arguing that grades "are primitive tools for accomplishing the diverse communication demanded of them" (18). Cizek says that the depth of the information communicated by grades ends up sounding "more like two tin cans and a length of string than [cell] phones and fiber optic lines" (Cizek 18).

Prominent "ungrading" advocate and researcher, Susan D. Blum, notes that students often see grades as "arbitrary and inconsistent" with wildly ranging criteria that don't always make sense and vary greatly from class to class and teacher to teacher, even within the same subject area (56). For example, one teacher places a lot of grade weight on class attendance where another doesn't grade attendance at all. One famous study from my field of Writing Studies asked fifty-three experienced readers in six different academic and professional fields to grade 300 student essays. The study found that from the pool of 300 graded essays, "101 received every grade from 1–9; 94 percent received either seven, eight, or nine different grades;

and no essay received less than five different grades" (Diederich 6). These results illustrate how difficult it is to find consensus about writing quality, even amongst professionals. You may have noticed the differences between the grades you get on writing assignments with different teachers, even when the assignments are similar. This might be because those teachers put different weight on different aspects of writing; one teacher values originality and creativity while another values conciseness and clarity.

Educator Jesse Stommel believes that grades aren't good indicators of learning because "they too often communicate only a student's ability to follow instructions, not how much she has learned. A 4.0 or higher GPA might indicate excellence, but it might also indicate a student having to compromise their integrity for the sake of a grade" (28). Stommel's observations are echoed by Raisa Chowdhury, an Industrial Engineering and Economics major at Northwestern University. Chowdhury writes:

> If I got an A in a class, it must mean I learned everything that class had to offer. Right? Not quite. It means that I performed according to the class's requirements: turning in all homework consistently, attending classes, doing just well enough on exams, and meeting all guidelines on grading rubrics. Which means if I got an A, I performed well.

As Stommel and Chowdhury attest, grades can reflect students' abilities to meet course requirements, but meeting those requirements doesn't necessarily translate into meaningful learning.

Another problem with grades is how much time and mental energy we spend thinking about them. Sometimes it feels like accumulating grades is the whole point of school. That's understandable considering the quantity of assignments that receive grades and how much time and energy you spend thinking and talking about grades. In a typical college class, you'll receive grades for a wide range of assignments and activities related to your achievements and performance—individual assignments, group assignments, class participation, attendance, tests, quizzes, final exams, and/or online assignments. These grades determine if you pass a course, make progress towards your degree, and graduate. They also produce a two-digit Grade Point Average (GPA) that you probably won't remember a year after you graduate and that most employers won't ask for. Your teachers also spend a lot of time and energy thinking about grades, especially when we write and revise syllabi and assignments every semester, are constantly cautioned against giving too many high grades, and are limited to a single letter to communicate the richness of what students learn and achieve in a class.

Finally, there are some who argue that the excessive attention some students give to grades is unhealthy and potentially harmful to their mental and emotional well-being. Dr. Michael H. Romanowski, whose research includes the sociology of education, believes that some students' obsession with grades can lead to fears of failure (e.g., failing to meet their own and others' expectations) and that grades can become tied to their sense of self-worth. He also believes that focusing too much on grades can negatively affect learning. "Students elect not to think for themselves," Romanowski writes, "because they are more concerned with pleasing the teacher and securing a high grade than learning or developing independent, critical, and creative thinking skills" (149). Prioritizing learning over grades will help you focus on the things that matter most, such as critical thinking and engaging deeply with course material.

All of these problems with grades, their inability to convey complex information about student learning and performance, the lack of consensus about writing quality, success based on following instructions, and the distractions and stress grades cause undermine the benefits of low-stakes writing that Foushée found in her research, including building your confidence as a writer, nurturing creativity, and improving learning. This is why your teachers don't grade low-stakes writing assignments the same way that they do high-stakes writing assignments. They want you to shift your focus away from grades and toward the learning that low-stakes writing facilitates. One thing that can help you make that shift is understanding that grades are only one part of much broader systems of assessment that help teachers understand and make decisions about teaching and learning.

THE ROLE OF GRADES IN BROADER SYSTEMS OF ASSESSMENT AND EVALUATION

When I began researching grades several years ago, it became apparent to me that there is a complex web of terminology, philosophies, and definitions that often change depending on the audience (e.g. students, teachers, administrators, government entities, and others involved in education). Cizek argues for clarity in discussions about grades and provides a useful roadmap for the bigger picture of what he and others call *assessment*. According to Cizek, grades are one small part of much larger assessment processes that happen all the time in school. Assessment, he says, is "the planned process of gathering and synthesizing information relevant to the purposes of a) discovering and documenting students' strengths and weaknesses, b) planning and enhancing instruction, or c) evaluating and making decisions about students" (Cizek 16). Let's examine Cizek's definition more closely.

Cizek explains that assessment is "the planned process of gathering and synthesizing information" (16). The information gathered and synthesized can be virtually anything, from quantitative data, like how many freshmen are first-generation college students, to qualitative data, like responses to questionnaires about dining services. Teachers, academic departments, administrators, and state education boards all gather and synthesize information for *three purposes* says Cizek. To help explain those purposes, I'll use examples from first-year composition (classes like Freshman Composition or Composition I & II). Many students take a first-year composition (FYC) class, and that's where you are likely to first encounter low-stakes writing assignments in college. They are also classes that I regularly teach.

The first purpose of assessment, according to Cizek, is for "discovering and documenting students' strengths and weaknesses" (16). Despite class sizes that average from 20–25 students or more, FYC teachers try to individualize instruction as much as possible. In other words, we try to adapt our teaching to meet the learning needs of each student. It's helpful to know something about your past experiences with writing, your goals for the class, and what you see as your strengths and weaknesses with writing. FYC teachers often assign short, ungraded writing at the beginning of the semester to help us quickly assess and document these things for reference when we work with students during conferences, office hours, and/ or workshops.

The second purpose of assessment is "planning and enhancing instruction" (Cizek 16). Teachers put a lot of time and effort into planning and enhancing our classes. We consult with other teachers, share resources, attend workshops, and research "best practices" for instruction. Once the semester begins, we can gather information directly from students by observing how they interact with course material and each other during class. This is where low-stakes writing assignments fit it and provide assessment information. I read quick writes and drafts in my FYC classes to give students feedback, but I also read them to get a better idea of how students understand an assignment, where they are struggling, and where they are succeeding. I use this information to plan the next class meeting (e.g. "Let's work on our narrative essays today because we're still having trouble with scene writing.") and provide better one-on-one instruction during student conferences.

The third purpose of assessment is "evaluating and making decisions about students" (Cizek 16). Cizek is careful to point out that there is a difference between "evaluation" and the two other forms of assessment. *Evaluation* is an assessment process that involves "making judgments about student performance or ascribing value to the results of [teachers'] observations" (Cizek 17). While the other two forms of assessment are for collecting information about students' performance in order to modify our teaching, evaluation is about measuring students' performance against a set of "standards regarding what is acceptable, superior, or good enough" (Cizek 17). Those levels of performance are typically expressed in the form of a grade (Cizek 17).

Sometimes it is difficult to know what standards will be used to measure your writing performance. If you have ever had your writing graded with a rubric, then you have seen one example of how teachers attempt to make those standards transparent. If your teacher doesn't use rubrics, look for evaluation criteria on the course syllabus or assignment prompt. Jeremey Levine's essay "What Are We Being Grade On?" in *Writing Spaces Volume 4* provides helpful advice on how to read a teacher's evaluation criteria—even if those criteria aren't clear.

To summarize, teachers collect and communicate assessment information all the time. Some of this information, such as observations of small-group work, helps us adapt our teaching to improve student learning. At key points during the semester (e.g. final versions of assignments, midterm and final grades), we evaluate students' performance and learning by measuring student achievement against a set of standards. That evaluation is communicated in the form of a grade. The important takeaway here is that low-stakes writing assignments aren't just about improving your writing, creativity, understanding of course material, etc. They also improve instruction by giving teachers a more complete picture of your learning than high-stakes writing alone.

How to Change Your Mindset toward Assessment and Low-stakes Writing Assignments

It can be difficult to write without grades at first. That's why it is important for teachers and students to have conversations about grades and the expectations for both high-stakes and low-stakes writing assignments. Those conversations will help you shift from a mindset that is grade-focused to one that is learning-focused. There are also things that you can do on your own to get the most out of low-stakes writing assignments. Here are four suggestions.

1. *Attend class.* A 2010 quantitative analysis of eighty years of research about class attendance in college found a significant correlation between attending class and higher grades and GPAs. "Indeed," the researchers said, "the relationship is so strong as to suggest that dramatic improvements in average grades (and failure rates) could be achieved by efforts to increase class attendance rates among college students" (Credé 289). This is especially true when low-stakes writing assignments involve group work during class meetings. If you aren't in class, you don't get the benefits of that ungraded learning, writing, and collaboration. Even if you complete the assignment at home, you might miss out on additional instructions and examples.

2. *Faithfully participate in low-stakes writing assignments.* Not every low-stakes writing assignment or activity will work for you, but you won't know if you don't give it an honest try. You might even find a way to adapt the activity to better meet your needs. When I took FYC many years ago, the professor taught us how to write full-sentence outlines for every major essay. The process was tedious and boring; however, I kept at it and eventually found that I like writing outlines because they help me develop ideas and sentences for longer drafts.

3. *Pick one or two low-stakes practices that work for you and use them in other classes.* Pay attention to the low-stakes writing assignments that you like the most, especially the ones that help you produce better final drafts, improve your critical thinking, and/or help you understand the content of the class you are taking. These might include activities like journaling, brainstorming activities, writing outlines, reflective writing, annotating assigned readings, and peer response. Chances are that if these assignments help you in one class, they will help you in others. They will probably also help you with writing outside of school.

4. *Communicate with your teacher about grades, but understand if they are reluctant to evaluate your writing at that moment.* Remember that assessment produces feedback, while evaluation produces judgments (e.g., grades). "Is this good enough for an A?" "Am I doing this right?" "Is this what you want?" are all evaluation ques-

tions. Not only do these questions invite simple answers, but they also ask readers to judge the quality of your writing. Your teacher may not *want* to judge the quality of your writing while you are still engaging in low-stakes writing. Remember that the goals of low-stakes writing assignments include encouraging creative thought, making deeper connections with course content, and building your confidence as a writer. You can't focus on those goals if you are also focused on a grade.

One of the best ways to get better assessment feedback is to write author's notes. The next time you share a draft with someone, include a brief note that tells readers: (1) one thing that you like about your draft; (2) one thing that you don't like; (3) two or three specific questions that you want them to answer about your draft ("Revision Practices"). Writing an author's note helps you quickly assess your draft and helps readers provide better feedback by drawing their attention to the parts of the draft that you want to talk about.

More than anything, I encourage you to take full advantage of every low-stakes writing assignment. Grades are obviously important, but they don't tell you very much about your writing and learning. Low-stakes writing assignments are an opportunity to move beyond just writing for a grade. Without the constant pressure of grades, you are free to take risks, try something new, and challenge yourself.

Works Cited

Beam, Emily A. "Leveraging Outside Readings and Low-stakes Writing Assignments to Promote Student Engagement in an Economic Development Course." *The Journal of Economic Education*, vol. 52, no. 4, 2021, pp. 274–285. Taylor and Francis Online, https://doi.org/10.1080/00220485.2021.1963369.

Chowdhury, Raisa. "Don't Fall into the Grade-obsession Trap." *AmericanCampus*, 29 Jan. 2020, https://www.americancampusmag.com/blog/dont-fall-into-the-grade-obsession-trap.

Cizek, Gregory J. "Pockets of Resistance in the Assessment Revolution." *Educational Measures: Issues and Practice*, vol. 19, no. 2, pp. 16–23.

Credé, Marcus, Sylvia G. Roch, and Urszula M. Kieszczynka. "Class Attendance in College: A Meta-Analytic Review of the Relationship of Class Attendance with Grades and Student Characteristics." *Review of Educational Research*, vol. 80, no. 2, pp. 272–295. Sage Journals, https://doi.org/10.3102%2F0034654310362998.

Diederich, Paul B. *Measuring Growth in English*. National Council of Teachers of English, 1974. *ERIC*, https://eric.ed.gov/?id=ED097702.

Drabick, Deborah A. G. "Keeping It Short and Sweet: Brief, Ungraded Writing Assignments Facilitate Learning." *Teaching of Psychology*, vol. 34, no. 3, pp. 172–176. *PubMed*, http://dx.doi.org/10.1080/00986280701498558.

Elbow, Peter. "High Stakes and Low Stakes in Assigning and Responding to Writing." *New Directions for Teaching and Learning*, no. 69, 1997, pp. 5–13. *Wiley Online Library*, https://doi.org/10.1002/tl.6901.

Foushée, Rebecca D. "Breaking Free: The Benefits of Non-expository, Low-stakes Writing Assignments in Psychology Courses." *Integrating Writing into the Psychology Course: Strategies for Promoting Student Success*, edited by Tara L. Kuther, E-book, Society for the Teaching of Psychology, 2018, pp. 38–50.

Hewett, Beth L. "From Topic to Presentation: Making Choices to Develop Your Writing." *Writing Spaces Volume 1*, 2010, https://writingspaces.org/?page_id=228.

Jaafar, Reem. "Writing-to-Learn Activities to Provoke Deeper Learning in Calculus." *Primus*, vol. 26, no. 1, 2016, pp. 67–82. *Taylor and Francis Online*, https://doi.org/10.1080/10511970.2015.1053642.

Levine, Jeremy. "What Are We Being Graded on?" *Writing Spaces Volume 4*, 2022, https://writingspaces.org/?page_id=796.

"Revision Practices." *University of Nebraska-Lincoln Writing Center*. https://www.unl.edu/writing/revision-practices. Accessed 25 March 2022.

Romanowski, Michael H. "Student Obsession with Grades and Achievement." *Kappa Delta Pi Record*, vol. 40, no. 4, 2004, pp. 149–151. *Taylor & Francis Online*, https://doi.org/10.1080/00228958.2004.10516425.

Sasa, Randelle I. "Nursing Care Paper as a Writing Intensive Requirement in Clinical Nursing Courses." *Teaching and Learning in Nursing*, vol. 15, no. 2, 2020, pp. 137–144, *ScienceDirect*, https://doi.org/10.1016/j.teln.2020.01.008.

Shumskaya, Maria, et al. "Online Low-stakes Assignments to Support Scientific Lab Report Writing in Introductory Science Courses." *Journal of Microbiology and Biology Education*, vol. 21, no. 3, 2020. *ASM Journals*, https://doi.org/10.1128/jmbe.v21i3.2183.

Stevenson, Colleen M. "Benefits of a Low Stakes Write-to-Learn Assignment on Exam Performance." *Teaching of Psychology*, vol. 47, no. 1, 2020, pp. 45–49. *SagePub*, https://doi.org/10.1177%2F0098628319888088.

Stewart-Mailhiot, Amy E. "Same Song, Different Verse: Developing Research Skills with Low Stakes Assignments." *Communications in Information Literacy*, vol. 8, no. 1, 2014, pp. 32–42, 10.15760/comminfolit.2014.8.1.163.

Stommel, Jesse. "How to Ungrade." *Ungrading: Why Rating Students Undermines Learning (and What to Do Instead)*, edited by Susan D. Blum, West Virginia UP, 2020, pp. 25–41.

Tchudi, Stephen. "Introduction: Degrees of Freedom in Assessment, Evaluation, and Grading." *Alternatives to Grading Student Writing*, edited by Stephen Tchudi, National Council of Teachers of English, 1997. *WAC Clearinghouse*, https://wac.colostate.edu/books/ncte/tchudi/.

Teacher Resources for "'Is This for a Grade?'": Understanding Assessment, Evaluation, and Low-stakes Writing Assignments

Overview and Teaching Strategies

The inspiration for this article came from the many times students asked questions along the lines of, "Is this for a grade?" and "Do we have to turn this in?" These are reasonable questions. Students want to know the relative weight of individual assignments in the broader scope of coursework. This is often because they are making decisions about how best to manage their time with so many school, work, and home obligations. I was also inspired by questions like, "Is my writing good enough?" and "Is this what you want?" These are also reasonable questions. Students want to ease their fears about success in courses they see as particularly difficult or with which they've struggled in the past. However, evaluation questions like these tend to reinforce a grade mindset that can be counterproductive for low-stakes writing.

My goal with this essay is to kickstart conversations about grades—what they do and don't represent—and why there are often fewer evaluation moments in college compared to high school. I recommend that students read this chapter when low-stakes writing is first introduced in a class. You can engage students' prior knowledge about grades before they read the chapter by having them discuss the first question below. Note that students may have a difficult time understanding the difference between low-stakes and high-stakes writing. Ask them to identify and discuss examples of each that they previously encountered in school. This will give them a personal point of reference while reading this essay.

Questions and Prompts

1. Think back to the last time you completed a high-stakes writing assignment under pressure. Maybe it was a timed writing exam or a project that you waited until the last minute to complete. What was that experience like? How did you feel about what you wrote? How might those feelings and experiences have changed how you think about and approach writing now?

2. This essay is about high-stakes and low-stakes *writing*. How can *reading* be high-stakes and low-stakes? What are some examples? How might your experiences with high-stakes and low-stakes reading prepare you for reading in school and your everyday life?

3. Teachers, school administrators, and employers have argued for decades about "grade inflation." Discuss what you think "grade inflation" is and why some might see it as a problem while others don't.

4. Pick a low-stakes writing activity from the class in which you are reading this essay and try it out in your other classes. Share what you learned after a week or two. As a class, discuss how the skills you learned from the activity might transfer to other contexts, including outside of school.

4 How Writing Happens

Zack DePiero and Ryan Dippre

Overview

The writing process is often oversimplified as a series of linear steps: brainstorming, drafting, revising, editing, and publishing.[1] While this notion enables students, like you, to conceptualize writing as something that improves over time, it also conceals the chaos of writing and its social, emotional, and material messiness. To capture some of that messiness, this intentionally unconventional chapter unfolds in three parts. Part 1 offers Zack's still-in-process draft alongside his "self-talk"—an inner monologue that reveals a range of indecisive and conflicted thoughts passing through his mind as he works through his essay. The essay, itself, explores how writing is shaped by the rhetorical situation, first-order and second-order thinking, a writer's identity, genre conventions, and source usage. At the end of Part 1, Zack offers a "Top 10" list of revision and editing strategies that can help you work through the writing process. Part 2 illustrates how writers give feedback to other writers: Ryan provides constructive feedback for Zack's revision. Finally, in Part 3, Zack reacts to Ryan's feedback, then formulates a revision plan for how he plans to approach his next draft.

Introduction

Lean in close, we have a secret: we're both writing professors and we struggle with writing. It's true—even after we each went to grad school to study writing education—we still struggle. You might think that we would've graduated with a skeleton key that could unlock any obstacle that a writer would ever encounter. Nope! If anything, our

---

1. This work is licensed under the Creative Commons Attribution-NonCommercial-NoDerivatives 4.0 International License (CC BY-NC-ND 4.0) and is subject to the Writing Spaces Terms of Use. To view a copy of this license, visit http://creativecommons.org/licenses/by-nc-nd/4.0/, email info@creativecommons.org, or send a letter to Creative Commons, PO Box 1866, Mountain View, CA 94042, USA. To view the Writing Spaces Terms of Use, visit http://writingspaces.org/terms-of-use.

experience helped us realize that writing is even *more complicated* than we ever imagined. (Fun fact: we met in a fall 2012 course, ED 202C: The Development of Writing Abilities, led by Dr. Charles Bazerman, who we mention later in the chapter.)

Like many of you, we wrestle with half-baked ideas in stolen snatches of our days—jotting something down in our journal during the commute to campus, cranking out a quick paragraph between classes—and we struggle to transform those ideas into language with pen, paper, keyboards, and cell phones. If you're like us, as you're writing, you occasionally pause, re-read your words, and wonder how badly you've confused your audience with your word choice (*"Will they know what I meant by that term?"*), organization (*"Should I rearrange these paragraphs?"*), or countless other writerly decisions you've made (*"Is this quote too long?"*). And tell us if this rings a bell: when you finally think you're done, you send along your work with a mix of confidence (*"Not bad!"*), uncertainty (*"But probably not that good!"*), and manufactured apathy (*"Lol, whatever—I'm so over this!"*). All writers have those thoughts—that "self-talk," you might say—so if you think about it, it's embedded in the writing process. It's a part of how writing happens.

That self-talk appears throughout the piece you're about to read. You'll notice that some paragraphs—for instance, the very first one—are written in all italics. Those italicized areas represent the writer's (Zack's) self-talk about his piece *while* he's writing it. Why'd we decide to include that? We wanted to preserve some of those behind-the-scenes aspects of how writing happens while it was (still) happening.

We also wanted to keep another aspect about how writing (actually) happens—or at least, how we believe it can happen more effectively: by using feedback. That's why we've organized our chapter into three parts:

- Part 1: Zack's 4th Draft
- Part 2: Ryan's Feedback to Zack
- Part 3: Zack's Revision Plan for Draft #5

It's a weird piece, we know. But based on everything we know about writing—and that we've experienced as writers—writing happens in weird ways.

Part 1: Zack's 4th Draft

Damn, those first few introductions didn't pan out so well, did they? Sigh. Let's try this again. What kind of opener might make sense for me here? Hmm . . . what if I shoot for something that frames what I'll be saying in the piece—a lead-in to my argument? How about that part in Elbow's essay on freewriting where he has that borderline meltdown?! Nothing captures the spirit of how writing happens better than that!

Halfway through an essay about freewriting—a method that writers can use to get their writing to *start happening*—one of the Writing Studies field's most influential scholars, Peter Elbow, shares some of his own freewriting. Tell me if you can relate.

> Whats happening. Whats happening. Whats happening. Whats happening. Whats happening. What's happening. I don't know what's happening to me. I don't want to write. I don't know what I want to write. I don't know what I want to write. I don't know what I want to write. (47)

There's a lot to glean from that little excerpt: confusion, apathy, self-doubt, and—OK, I'll just say it: The dude was freaking out. Admit it: you've been there too. We all have. Writing is such a complicated experience; it's caught up in our emotions, our past experiences, and our future goals. It's a nightmare, really. (Only worse: you can wake up from nightmares!)

You might be wondering: didn't Zack just say that this Elbow guy was an expert on writing? And if so, shouldn't it come easy to him?

Here's the bad news: whenever you're in the process of writing something, you're probably going to get stuck in an awkward and uncomfortable space. The good news? Everyone else goes through the same thing. Writing is messy, and writing happens in different ways for different folks. To show you just what I mean, in this piece, I'll be leading you through how writing happens, from point A to point Z.

Hold on: that "A to Z" stuff is going to undermine my argument, isn't it? I'm trying to say that the act of writing *isn't* neat or tidy—that it's a marathon-like hike with disorienting turns and dead-end trails. And now I need to convey that message in a polished essay that unfolds in a linear fashion? Wouldn't that defeat my whole purpose?

Uh oh. That Peter Elbow feeling is creeping in. What's happening? What's happening? I don't know what I want to write. What's happening? OK, just keep calm and #TrustTheProcess. Write your way through this. Try recasting that previous paragraph.

Here's the truth of the matter: writing is *really* messy because it happens in different ways for different folks for different reasons. Most likely, you've learned that there's a process to writing, from brainstorming to drafting to revising to editing. And there totally is. Sort of. In reality, writing isn't a clean, linear, step-by-step process. The act of writing is a never-ending negotiation of social dilemmas, a rollercoaster of emotional hurdles, and a carousel of scattered technological tools.

Boom! There it is! That last sentence will work great as my thesis statement. It's got grammatical parallelism. The "Rule of 3" gives it that feeling of completion. It slips right off the t—actually, wait a second. It doesn't cover the more practical putting-words-on-the-page part of how writing happens. OK, no problem: I'll treat it as my "working thesis statement" and tweak it as needed. For now, I'll just keep getting ideas out and see where they take me.

Chances are, you're not aware of *just how messy* writing is, and there's a good reason why: as Writing Studies researchers Linda Adler-Kassner and Elizabeth Wardle remind us in *Naming What We Know*, "people tend to experience writing as a finished product that represents ideas in seemingly rigid forms" (15). As consumers of information—whether we're reading a scholarly journal article or watching the nightly news—we usually don't get a glimpse of how writing *actually* happens behind the scenes. (Remember: news anchors are usually reading a *written* script off of a teleprompter. And yep, that 100% counts as "writing.") By teaching you about how writing happens—in all of its weird, messy, nightmarish glory—I hope to heighten your awareness of the choices at your disposal.

The Rhetorical Situation

Believe it or not, before you even put a word on a page, writing has already *started happening.* As ideas start popping into your head, you're already thinking about how you might use language based on what's called the rhetorical situation. Every piece of writing is always *written by* someone, *written for* an audience, and *written with* a goal or purpose in mind. And it all starts with a concept called exigence: why a writer is writing a particular text in the first place. Throughout college, exigence is frequently provided by your instructors in the form of an assignment prompt. You've been *prompt*ed to write something—a rhetorical analysis, a literature review, an op-ed, an annotated bibliography, an "IMRaD" report, or some other genre—and you, in turn, respond.

How much further in depth should I go on exigence? I've got to be mindful of my 5,000-word limit here. Let's see where I'm at. Wait, what?! 1,000+ already?! Alright, well since I just offered some college-y examples of exigence, maybe I can briefly touch on how exigence functions outside of college, then keep this piece moving.

Beyond college, people experience countless new exigences every day that spark their need to write. Suppose you're seeking employment and, while scrolling through job openings on LinkedIn, you find a sweet gig to apply for. Well, stumbling upon *that* particular job description becomes the exigence for writing the application materials necessary for that position—most likely, a resume and cover letter.

*That should do the trick. Alright, now what's my next section? Time to pivot to genre? After all, there's never **not** genre. Or should I talk about brainstorming? Well, to a large degree, all that ultimately stems from our identities and lived experiences—who we are, what we've done, what we care about. But of course, that's related to stance. And stance brings us back to genre conventions and disciplinarity—which comes back to identity. Geez, this is more interconnected than I realized. Help! I'm trapped in an M.C. Escher drawing!*

I need to take a step back and get a bird's eye view. OK, so whatever I'm doing right now—literally, right now—needs to be the focus of the next section: as I'm trying to collect my immediate thoughts, I'm simultaneously planning out my long-term goals for the piece. What I'm doing is dancing in between first- and second-order thinking.

FIRST-ORDER THINKING AND SECOND-ORDER THINKING

True or false: You know *exactly* what you're going to write before you've written it.

False! Unfortunately, as a writer, you can't sit around expecting all the random information that's floating around your brain to suddenly morph into a perfect essay, *then* rush to your laptop, and *then* transcribe all that seamless language onto the page. That's just not how writing happens. Instead, *the act of writing* helps writers figure out what they actually want to say.

That's why brainstorming is such a crucial "step" in how writing happens. Contrary to popular belief, brainstorming—or related techniques like mind maps, concept clouds, or stream-of-consciousness freewriting—is more than the first "step" in the writing process; it's something that writers keep coming back to.

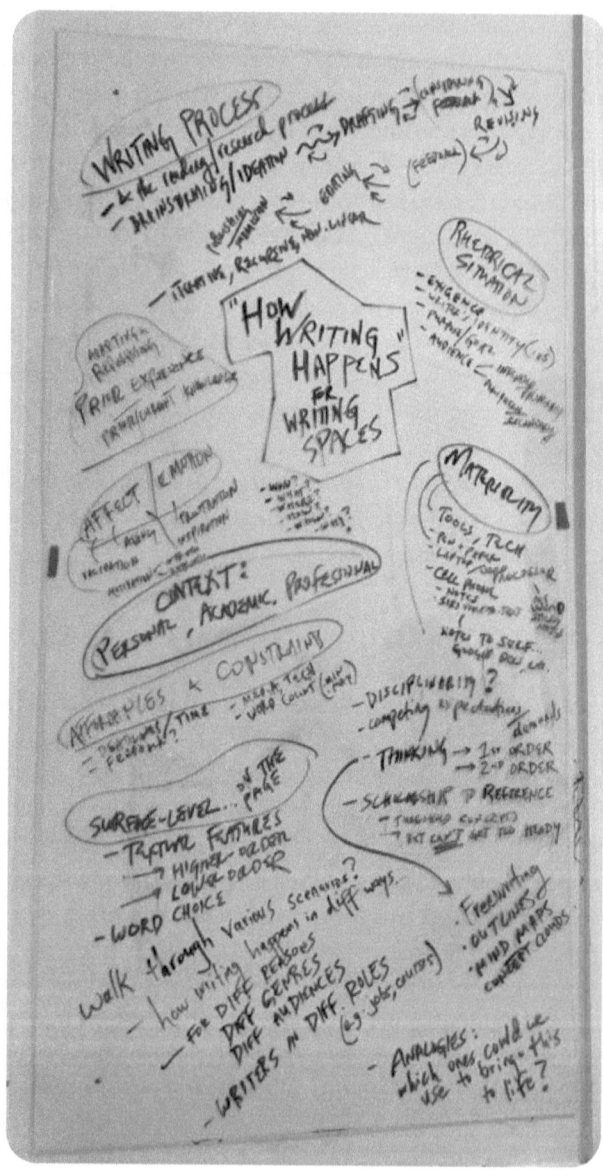

Figure 1: Zack's "How Writing Happens" Brainstorm on a Dry Erase Board. Arranged as an informal mind map with clustered bubbles and bullet points, the center of the board contains the phrase "How Writing Happens for Writing Spaces." Various ideas splinter off of the center idea such as "Writing Process," "Rhetorical Situation," "Materiality," and "Affect and Emotion," each of which include some brief language for how the concept could be explained in the chapter. Photograph by the author (DePiero).

There's this fascinating concept called first-order thinking that we engage in by capturing whatever crosses our mind: quick impressions, fleeting feelings, or random-but-maybe-relevant thoughts. As writers, we can use first-order thinking to generate interesting ideas worth writing about—and letting those ideas build off of each other—so that, later, we can shape them into something more polished. In fact, some writers (I'm not going to name names!) embrace the spirit of first-order thinking to the degree of bypassing any honest effort for correct spelling or proper punctuation.

How riding happens ideas

At the very very beginning, before I jump into the "hey I'm starting this all over again "/ elbow stuff, Ryan and I need to set up the whole piece so students understand what we're doing from the start. And really, what we're doing is modeling how the writing process actually plays out. In real time, it's draft stage. So I think we need to say something like: Here we are, we are both writing researchers, we are both writing professors, but we still struggle through drafting out our work. And we actively seek out feedback from one another because that's how we can get the most out of what we're riding.

Figure 2: Zack's "How riding happens ideas" voice-to-text memo created on the "Notes" app of his iPhone. The note contains misspelled language and very little punctuation. The exact language follows: "How riding happens ideas. At the very very beginning, before I jump into the "hey I'm starting this all over again"/ elbow stuff, Ryan and I need to set up the whole piece so students understand what we're doing from the start. And really, what we're doing is modeling how the writing process actually plays out. In real time, it's draft stage. So I think we need to say something like: Here we are, we are both writing researchers, we are both writing professors, but we still struggle through drafting our work. And we actively seek out feedback from one another because that's how we can get the most out of what we're doing." Phone screenshot by the author (DePiero).

Now would be a perfect place to reference Lamott's "Shitty First Drafts." That title, alone, is a crowd-pleaser. Gets at the whole messiness theme too. If my memory serves me correctly, though, it's a short piece. Is referencing the title enough? Maybe it's worth finding a juicy line from the piece to quote. Wouldn't hurt to go back and give it another quick look.

Anne Lamott, a narrative nonfiction author, discusses her own writing process in a piece titled "Shitty First Drafts." She says, "the only way I can get anything written at all is to write really, really shitty first drafts [...] All good writers write them. This is how they end up with good second drafts and terrific third drafts" (93). Lamott's advice is this: get your writing to *start* happening by using first-order thinking for your first draft.

Of course, if there's a first-order thinking, there must be a second-order thinking, right? Bingo! Second-order thinking is more analytical, organized, and logical. It emerges when we're in the throes of drafting and we stop to wonder, "Does this sentence build off of the previous sentence?" or "How could I support this claim with more persuasive evidence?"

But part of the reason that writing is so messy—and so resistant to a clean, step-by-step process—is because we constantly move in and out of first-order thinking and second-order thinking. Sure, during the early stages of the writing process (e.g. brainstorming, drafting), we tend to engage in much more first-order thinking because, naturally, we're ultimately interested in finding the best ideas that are worth writing about. And the flip side of that coin is true, too; during the latter stages of the writing process (e.g. revising, editing), second-order thinking is useful for polishing those ideas. But we rarely ever set either entirely aside.

Let's revisit that dry erase board and take stock of where I'm at. I've tackled a couple of the major areas—the rhetorical situation, first/second-order—and I've alluded to the range of emotions that writers experience. Check, check, check. So what's left? Oh, pretty much everything? Awesome.

Probably need to hit more on the material and social aspects of writing. Ryan will be helpful in helping me think through that—definitely looking forward to his feedback on that front. Can't breeze over genre, obviously. I've got to tackle how/when/why writers use sources: summarizing, paraphrasing, quoting. I've got some good stuff lined up for that: Bazerman's "Conversational Model," Stedman's "Annoying Ways People Use Sources." Those two texts have been influential to what I do in my writing classroom. You know, what I'm doing right now is, really, bringing my identity as a writing researcher/teacher forward within the piece. That should be a section in its own right.

Writers' Identities and Stances

Brace yourself for an incoming message from Captain Obvious: writing doesn't happen without *you* because, after all, *you're* the one writing. Simple enough!

Or is it?

Consider this: every piece of writing is unique because every writer inhabits certain identities. This impacts *what* you write about and *how* you write about it. In the Writing Studies field, this concept is sometimes referred to as *stance*. Mary Soliday, author of *Everyday Genres*, describes stance this way: "No [written] content is free floating but must be governed by [the writer's] angle of vision, or stance [...] writers do more than present information: *they perceive and judge it* in some way" (37, italics added).

Let's use social scientists as an example. Researchers from fields such as communication, education, or political science have been trained to investigate what people think, feel, or do, and why. And since we human beings are so complex, social scientists are skeptical of making sweeping, definitive claims about entire populations, especially when they're working with data that they've collected from surveys or interviews. Social scientists bring a "confident uncertainty" to their research: they're confident in the limitations of their knowledge—and this stance usually carries over in how they write. To convey their uncertainty, social scientists tend to use hedged language and qualified claims. (In fact, I did this in the last two sentences with the words "usually" and "tend.")

I'm running up against the word count wall. Got two major sections I absolutely need to include: "Using Sources" and "Genre." Let's think this through. Is there any logical relationship between these sections? That'd help me decide what might come first—what builds off of what. Seems to me that "Genre" should come before "Using Sources" because different genres necessitate using different kinds of sources—while other genres don't require/integrate sources at all.

Genre Conventions

Let's recap. You're writing something. And you're moving in and out of first- and second-order thinking—jotting down some ideas, doing a little drafting—and you've felt some mixture of confusion and curiosity, anxiety and excitement, and most likely, countless hours of self-loathing. You've got a purpose(s) for writing, and you're writing with some kind of audience(s) in mind.

Now if you turn your attention to the page itself, you might notice that you're not just writing *anything*—you're writing a text of a particular *kind*. It fulfills a distinct social action, and it's even got a certain look to it. What I'm getting at here is the elusive concept known as *genre*. Whatever you're writing—whatever anybody has ever written—can be considered some kind of genre, and this concept is absolutely crucial for your writing development, especially beyond this writing course.

To help my students grasp genre, I pose what I call the "genre question": what makes this thing *this thing*? This question encourages students to identify the *conventions* of a genre—its essential characteristics, features, ingredients, or traits. For instance, let's say you had to request a letter of recommendation from a professor. Before you begin writing, it would probably help to consider the question: what makes a letter of recommendation request *a letter of recommendation request*? And if you looked at a handful of samples, you'd likely find some patterns:

- an opening salutation ("Dear")
- a friendly beginning ("I hope your semester is going well.")
- a reminder of your relationship with the professor ("You might remember me from your ENGL 101 course.")
- your purpose for writing this email ("Would you be able to provide a letter of recommendation?")
- background info on your specific purpose ("I found a job that sounds exciting.")
- your rationale for why this particular instructor would be a good fit
- details about your accomplishments in the course
- a deadline ("The deadline for this application is May 1.")
- a closing salutation ("Sincerely,")

Each pattern is a convention of the genre. They're not rules, though, because rules are rigid. Conventions are flexible: different writers might decide to bend or defy a particular convention for good reason, and that's yet another reason why writing is so messy.

Using Sources

Behold, we're at the heart of how writing happens in academic contexts: the never-ending tango between reading and writing. Charles Bazerman, a leader in writing research for over four decades, refers to this tango as the "conversational model," and I'll let him describe what that means in his own words: "The conversational model points to the fact that writing occurs within the context of previous writing and advances the total sum of the discourse" (658). The texts that we *read* inform the texts that we *write*. As the thinking goes: the more you've read about a topic, the more you'll know about that topic, and the more you'll have to say about that topic. And depending on how precise you want to get—whether you need to record the *exact language* that somebody used or whether you're better off capturing the overall gist of a piece—you can paraphrase, summarize, or quote other writers.

In another *Writing Spaces* piece titled "Annoying Ways People Use Sources," Kyle Stedman draws an analogy between writing and driving. Similar to the way that "drivers rely on their turn signals to communicate their intentions to other drivers," Stedman suggests that, as a writer, you need to send "signals to your readers about your intentions" (255). So suppose you want to use a direct word-for-word quote from another source in your paper: you can keep readers in your rearview mirror by "prepar[ing] them] for the quotation, quot[ing], and then analy[ing] it" (246). Call it a "Quote Sandwich": the bread-meat-bread combo is your setup, then the quote, then your analysis.

Conclusion: "Top 10" Strategies for Revising and Editing Your Work

And, well, that's how writing happens! Sort of. A little bit. Until I revise this draft.

Speaking of, I've got this nagging idea in the back of my mind that I just can't shake—writing isn't just messy because it's an iterative process. Writing is *especially* messy because **throughout** that entire iterative process, there's a constant balancing act between competing forces that are simultaneously in play: first-order thinking vs. second-order thinking, summary vs. analysis, description vs. evaluation, nuance vs. gist, confidence vs. uncertainty, passion vs. reason, risk vs. predictability, affordances vs. constraints, higher-order issues vs. lower-order concerns, and of course, the mother of all Writing Studies *dualities, process vs. product. Hmmm… have I found my new working thesis statement?*

But before I wrap up, I'd like to pass along my "Top 10" list of practical strategies that might help you minimize all this messiness.

Strategy #1: Hit Pause on the Intro

When you start working on a paper, you don't *have to* start with the introduction. Really, I swear. Introductions are tricky, and it might help to hold off until you've gotten a clearer sense of what you're writing about. *Then* you can go back and hook your reader with a compelling introduction.

Strategy #2: Make a Plan, Then Set Your Priorities

Whether you're a go-getter who begins writing immediately or you're a procrastinator who keeps putting it off, you're bound to feel anxiety until your work is done. That's why managing your time is essential, and to do that, successful writers plan out their work. Step #1: Create a "To Do" list of what you want to accomplish. Step #2: Determine the appropriate order of operations that will help you prioritize what needs to get done. Step #3: Repeat steps #1 and 2 as needed.

Strategy #3: Embrace Social Interactions

The last time you wrote a research-based assignment, did you interact with anybody while you were working on it? Your teacher? Classmates? Friends, family members, or roommates? Believe it or not, by simply talking about your ideas, you'll access stored-away language associations floating around your brain and, in the process, open up new possibilities for whatever you're working on. In fact, this is precisely what your campus Writing Center tutors are trained to help you do.

Strategy #4: Find Your Habits

How do you get started? With pen and paper? Google Docs? In the morning? Or closer to dinner time? Do you write in intense 20-minute bursts, or slow and steady? We each have our habits and superstitions: as long as writing *is happening* for you, it's all good. Pro athletes try to put themselves "in the zone" before a game, and many writers do the same when they're getting ready to write. Whether you prefer up-tempo music, Mozart, or total silence, put yourself in your ideal environment to maximize your success.

Strategy #5: Understand How (and When) Outlines Might Work for You

Outlines are useful tools for bringing "second-order" thinking to your work. Tread lightly, though: for some folks, outlines can feel restrictive, particularly if you're not quite sure what you want to say just yet. If that's the case for you, you could still try making an outline *while* you're writing something. Once you've gotten going and drafted out some paragraphs, you'll be better positioned to determine what you're trying to say, so you can decide which organizational approach makes the most sense for your piece.

Strategy #6: Try a Reverse Outline

Reverse outlines: say *what*?! The next time you've written something that feels "all over the place," turn what you've already written *into* an outline. That'll help you determine how (or if) your paragraphs are connected to one another. This strategy could reveal new possibilities for re-arranging your work.

Strategy #7: Experiment with Different Styles

Writing doesn't happen without you putting your unique mark on it. Like our wardrobes, we dress our writing in our own stylistic quirks. Left to my own devices, I adorn my documents with backslashes, dashes, and exclamation points. I'll bust out a backslash when there are a couple of similar-but-not-exactly-the-same words/phrases that could get my message across. I use dashes—the most under-appreciated punctuation mark—so that readers can follow the foundation of my sentence structure a bit more easily than, say, if I buried my sentences with, oh, I don't know, too many commas. And I use exclamation points because my writing voice closely mirrors my real-life voice; I'm an excitable dude!

Experimenting with different styles can help you find out which "clothes" you feel most comfortable in. Whenever you encounter a piece of writing that you admire, pause and think: what do I like about this, exactly? Step into the "reading like a writer" shoes that another *Writing Spaces* author, Mike Bunn, suggests in "How to Read Like a Writer" so that you can consider how you might make similar decisions in your own work.

Strategy #8: Copy-and-Paste a Sentence 3x, Then Play "Syntax Tetris"

Sometimes I get stuck on a sentence. I know I'm presenting the right information. My word choice is solid. The sentence just doesn't feel smooth: the structure or *syntax* of the sentence might be an issue.

When that happens, I summon my inner video-gamer and remember an old-school classic: Tetris. Tetris is, more or less, a game of moving shapes around until they fit in neatly with one another. The core parts of a sentence—the independent clause(s), the dependent clause(s), and/or the introductory clause—function in the same way.

So here's what I do: I copy and paste a not-quite-right sentence three times, then for each version, I move the parts around and adjust the punctuation as needed. I might even break it up into two separate sentences. Once I have three different versions, I'll pick whichever one sounds the best. Here's an example:

- Version 1. When everything feels fine except for the structure or *syntax* of the sentence, I start playing a spinoff one of my favorite games from growing up: "Syntax Tetris."
- Version 2. I start playing a spinoff of one of my favorite games from growing up, "Syntax Tetris," when everything feels fine except for the structure or *syntax* of the sentence.
- Version 3. I start playing "Syntax Tetris"—a spinoff from one of my favorite games from growing up—when everything feels fine except for the structure or *syntax* of the sentence.

Strategy #9: Don't Sweat the Small Stuff

Have you ever wondered: what writing errors do college students commonly make? If so, you're in luck: two Writing Studies researchers, Andrea Lunsford and Karen Lunsford, pursued this question in their study "Mistakes Are a Fact of Life" and identified the top five most common errors:

- wrong word
- missing comma after an introductory element
- incomplete or missing documentation
- vague pronoun reference
- spelling error

What's the take-away here? Errors will also be a fact of *your* life as a writer. If you spend most of your time behind the keyboard nervously trying to avoid "errors" at all costs, you're probably *still* going to make some, and it'll also slow down your writing. So do yourself a favor: keep your eyes on the prize and stay focused on higher-order issues like your argument, claims, evidence, and organization.

STRATEGY #10: STEP AWAY FROM THE KEYBOARD

The next time you're feeling stumped or strung out, take a break. After all, writing doesn't just "happen" on the page. Ideas can seemingly spring out of nowhere when our minds are focused on other tasks. In the case of famous horror novelist, Stephen King, the big ideas underlying his best-selling books came to him "[w]hile showering, while driving, [and] while taking [his] daily walk" (169). Day in and day out, King's four-mile walk brought idea after idea until, well—until he got hit by a car.

I told you: writing is a nightmare.

(Stephen King survived! He's OK! He used his recovery to reflect on his career in *On Writing*, a memoir about his craft. So I suppose writing isn't *just* a nightmare; it can be therapeutic too.)

PART 2: RYAN'S FEEDBACK TO ZACK

Yo buddy,

This piece is shaping up! Got a few thoughts for you to consider as you take up the final revisions. I tried to (1) avoid the classic "add these 17 things and also cut 2,000 words" feedback that I seem to keep getting from reviewers and (2) balance out my praise and criticism so that you're relatively even-keeled when you finish reading it. Let me know what you think!

I wonder if, space permitting, it might be wise to say a little bit more about Peter Elbow's work at the very beginning—before you offer that example of him freaking out. I don't think undergrad readers would be familiar with him, and his work is just so pervasive in secondary and post-secondary training on writing instruction that it might be worth it to emphasize just how *accomplished* this guy is, and just how wild it is that someone so accomplished can still struggle like that. In other words, building him up could get you a bigger payoff. But otherwise, I love the intro.

In the "Using Sources" section, I think there's more connections between Bazerman, Stedman, and the quote sandwich than you have written so far. And how does that connect with the student audience that the *Writing Spaces Author Guide* asks you to consider? (And see my final comment about embracing the complexity of this conversational model of writing.) Also, perhaps you could condense this section a bit further. After you've... added in what I've asked you to add in...oh my, I've become what I hate! I'm like Anakin Skywalker hanging out in the desert! Building sandcastles! Noooooooo!

Strategy 2: Outlines don't work for everyone?! How dare you, sir?! No, I'm kidding. You're making great points here and it might help to ask not just *whether* outlines work, but *when*. In fact, I was working on two different pieces a few weeks ago, and I used an outline for one but not the other. There were good reasons for both. So a bit more about the "when" might help.

Strategy 4: I really like what you've done on this—you really tie writing style to particular choices on the page. What counts as "style" can sometimes (or even frequently) drift in conversations about it, and that explanation will help the readers using this essay to keep their attention grounded in particular writing choices. Nicely done!

I thought I'd end this feedback by annoying you a bit. You do a good job throughout emphasizing that writing is messy, and that it really isn't something that can become un-messy. But as you try to make this a useable document for undergraduates, you may—without intention—end up simplifying some aspects of writing that you're trying to leave robust. How can you give your readers useful approaches for tackling the messiness of writing without problematically simplifying the act of writing in your proposed solutions? The Roozen and Erickson digital text, *Expanding Literate Landscapes*, might be a good place to start as you're trying to double-check this. They have a lot of video interviews with writers that capture the richness of writing, so you can help first year students think through their composing choices against that backdrop.

—Ryan

Part 3: Zack's Revision Plan for Draft #5

Woooo! I get the sense that he legitimately digs it!

So I'm with him on Elbow, 100%. Great point. If I can make the case that even the King of Freewriting struggled with—you guessed it, freewriting!—I think it'll help students understand just how tough writing can be. Beyond that, too, Peter Elbow has been super-influential in how I think about teaching writing, so I might consider adding something about that. Overall, that should be a quick fix.

And yeah, I agree: slowing down on the "Using Sources" section would probably help. Sigh. There I was, talking about using your turn signals, making sure that people can follow along with you—guess I sped through that one. Maybe I can find some examples of what all that looks like in practice: paraphrasing, summarizing, quoting, etc. In fact, one area where I may have fallen short here—and the Writing Spaces *editors will be the final judge on this—is whether my piece would benefit from integrating students' work: their writing, their voices, etc. That "Using Sources" section could be an opportunity to do that.*

When to use outlines, huh? Damn, that's a tough one. I'll have to mull that over.

Roozen! How could I have guessed Ry would reference him?! And isn't that yet another element of how writing happens? We reference the people whose work has meant the most to us—at least in academia. Roozen is right up there on Ryan's Mount Rushmore of Writing Studies scholars with Bazerman and Prior.

Overall, Ryan's feedback sounds reasonable: I want this essay to be practical and usable, yes, but I also want to present—to the extent that it's possible in a published piece—an authentic account of just how messy writing really is. So I'll check out this Expanding Literate Landscapes *piece to see if that sparks any new ideas. I'll comb through this piece a couple more times for any moments when I'm sort of giving off the impression that writing is "cleaner" than it actually is.*

Finally, I can't forget: in the week since I sent this out to Ryan, some new ideas came to mind. I've been wondering: what's the writing process like for writers who are writing in a second/non-native language? And how does co-writing impact each person's approach? The mere fact that I hadn't considered these questions until my 4th draft is a useful reminder that time is the ultimate X-factor in how writing happens. As writers, we all need time to let our writing simmer.

Revision Plan

Quick Fixes
- Elbow: boost him up even further
- trim up any excess language

Medium Fixes
- "Using Sources": how can I slow down?
- "Using Sources": integrate students' voices?
- revisit the *Writing Spaces* "Author Guidelines"
- brush up on the new MLA guidelines (*Ugh!*)

Time-Intensive Revisions
- revisit Ryan's "when to use outlines?" comment
- find/read/annotate some pieces on outlining in FYC courses
- check out Roozen and Erickson's *Shaping Literate Landscapes*
- include new areas? L2? Collaborative writing? Digital texts?

Works Cited

Adler-Kassner, Linda, and Elizabeth Wardle. *Naming What We Know: Threshold Concepts of Writing Studies*. University Press of Colorado, 2015.

Bazerman, Charles. "A Relationship Between Reading and Writing: The Conversational Model." *College English*, vol. 41, no. 6, 1980, pp. 656–661.

Bunn, Mike. "How to Read Like a Writer." *Writing Spaces: Readings on Writing*, vol. 2, 2011, pp. 71-86.

Elbow, Peter. "Teaching Thinking by Teaching Writing." *Change: The Magazine of Higher Learning*, vol. 15, no. 6, 1983, pp. 37–40.

Elbow, Peter. "Toward a Phenomenology of Freewriting." *Journal of Basic Writing*, vol. 8, no. 2, 1989, pp. 42–71.

King, Stephen. *On Writing: A Memoir of the Craft*. Simon and Schuster, 2000.

Lamott, Anne. "Shitty First Drafts." *Language Awareness: Readings for College Writers*, 2005, pp. 93–96.

Lunsford, Andrea A., and Karen J. Lunsford. ""Mistakes Are a Fact of Life": A National Comparative Study." *College Composition and Communication*, 2008, pp. 781–806.

Roozen, Kevin, and Joe Erickson. *Expanding Literate Landscapes: Persons, Practices, and Sociohistoric Perspectives of Disciplinary Development*. Logan, UT: Computers and Composition Digital P/Utah State UP, 2017.

Stedman, Kyle D. "Annoying Ways People Use Sources." *Writing Spaces: Readings on Writing*, vol. 2, 2011, pp. 242–256.

Teacher Resources for "How Writing Happens"

Overview and Teaching Strategies

This essay addresses the messy realities of writing that students (and all writers) face. Contrary to the experiences that students may have had when preparing to write for standardized tests, writing—inside and outside the academy—takes on different forms, purposes, and audiences. It is also nonlinear: as writers, our ideas take shape and transform over time. Furthermore, writers must negotiate various social interactions and emotional states, all while juggling their work across a range of technological tools. By understanding a wider range of approaches, students will have more awareness, agency, and ownership of their writing processes.

In first-year writing courses, this essay could be paired with reflective assignments that focus on the writing process, revision, and metacognition. In *writing about writing*-focused courses, specifically, the various ideas surveyed in this essay (e.g. free-writing, stance, revision) could provide a springboard for a literature review about composition scholarship. Instructors might consider pairing this essay with other *Writing Spaces* pieces such as "The Inspired Writer vs. the Real Writer" by Sarah Allen, "Looking for Trouble: Finding Your Way into a Writing Assignment" by Catherine Savini, and "Find the Best Tools for the Job: Experimenting with Writing Workflows" by Derek Van Ittersum and Tim Lockridge.

Discussion Questions

1. How does writing "happen" for you? Set the scene. What **talk** (conversations with friends, classmates, tutors), **tools** (word processing programs, writing devices), and **texts** (books, articles, and websites) are around as you write?

2. Writing can be an **emotional rollercoaster**. What have been some of your highest highs? What have been some of your lowest lows? Which emotions tend to play the most significant role in your writing process, and why?

3. We've suggested a handful of **practical strategies**, from freewriting, to reverse outlining, to playing "Syntax Tetris." Which ones have you found useful, and why? Which ones are you unfamil-

iar with, and how could you use those for an upcoming writing assignment?

4. Consider how you might use this article as a springboard for an **extended research project** (e.g. a literature review). Out of the many ideas that we've introduced in this piece—for example, managing emotions, and talking with Writing Center tutors—which ones strike you as the most interesting, and why? Formulate a research question(s) that could help you dive deeper into the Writing Studies field.

5. Find someone whose writing process you'd like to learn more about. Collect some writing-related artifacts connected to their **personal life** (e.g. journal entries, "to do" lists, social media posts), **professional life** (e.g., community outreach advertisements for a public relations representative, a housing description for a real estate agent, or lesson plans for a teacher), or if they're a student, their **academic life** (e.g. an in-process draft or final submission, feedback to a classmate's draft, an email to members of a club/organization). Use that data to ask questions that pique your curiosity as it relates to how writing happens for them. That data could become the basis for what Writing Studies researchers call a text-based interview, and you could ask them to walk you through the various decisions they made while writing each of those various documents.

5 What Color Is My Voice? Academic Writing and the Myth of Standard English

Kristin DeMint Bailey, An Ha, and AJ Outlar

Overview

In this chapter, a community college writing professor and two of her first-year writing students collaboratively address the issue of Whiteness in academic writing.[1] Specifically, we challenge the notion that academic language is neutral as well as the expectation that all academic writers should strive for uniformity. We question notions of correctness and clarity, adopting Jacqueline Jones Royster's definition of voice as "the power and authority to speak and make meaning" (31), and we challenge students to ask hard questions about language, identity, and power. We explain the inextricable bonds between language and community, examine the connections between language and racial identity, and explore the political nature of language, all of which affect a person's voice as Royster has defined it. Then, the two of us who are students share our experiences with writing for school, reflecting on what we've learned both in and out of school about our language and our voice. Together, we invite students to reflect on their own voice in academic writing, asking themselves, "Whose voice do I hear in my writing, and why? What does this voice reveal about my identity as a writer, and how do I feel about what I uncover? What might I want to do more or differently?"

> . . . *survival is not an academic skill. It is learning how to stand alone, unpopular and sometimes reviled, and how to make common cause with those others identified as outside the*

---

[1]. This work is licensed under the Creative Commons Attribution-NonCommercial-NoDerivatives 4.0 International License (CC BY-NC-ND 4.0) and is subject to the Writing Spaces Terms of Use. To view a copy of this license, visit http://creativecommons.org/licenses/by-nc-nd/4.0/, email info@creativecommons.org, or send a letter to Creative Commons, PO Box 1866, Mountain View, CA 94042, USA. To view the Writing Spaces Terms of Use, visit http://writingspaces.org/terms-of-use.

> structures in order to define and seek a world in which we can all flourish. It is learning how to take our differences and make them strengths. For the master's tools will never dismantle the master's house. They may allow us temporarily to beat him at his own game, but they will never enable us to bring about genuine change."
>
> —Audre Lorde, *The Master's Tools Will Never Dismantle the Master's House*

Introduction

In school, we're often asked to write using strict formats and formal language. Writing isn't about personal expression or style; it's about mastering "standard English," "edited American English," "formal English"—whatever you call it. It's about communicating ideas and showing others (usually teachers, sometimes classmates, sometimes ourselves) what we know and understand about whatever it is we're studying. And for many of us (if we're being honest), it's about sounding smart—writing the right things in the right ways to show that we belong, that we're capable of doing the work. Because ultimately, we *need* people to know we're capable so we can pass our classes and get that diploma.

Our success, as we all know, is usually determined by how well we meet the standards that have been indoctrinated into us through feedback and grades for most of our lives. We accept those standards as the ideal because we see them played out in the texts we're assigned to read. We believe that good academic writing is complicated and abstract, that it uses words we don't know or hear very often, that it is objective and neutral and essentially personality-less. We believe that academic writing doesn't have a voice.

Oh, but it *does*.

Many people don't notice a voice in academic writing because the voice that *is* there has been normalized and disembodied. In other words, when people talk about "academic" writing, they don't talk about the *people* who are doing that writing, who set those standards. Those standards, we think, simply reflect "correct" language usage, which we think is just how things are. Consider this: How often do you think about what the speaking voice of the person writing the academic texts you're reading *sounds like*? How often do you think about what that person *looks like*?

Regardless of whether you *notice* a voice in academic writing, however, that voice is still there. And because this is college, where you'll learn to ask questions and dig deep for understanding, we're asking you in this chapter to look closely at that normalized academic voice, to ask hard questions about what that voice reflects—and what it covers up.

These kinds of questions are what many researchers in the field of rhetoric and composition, especially Black, Indigenous, and People of Color (BIPOC), have been asking for decades. One leading scholar in the field, Jacqueline Jones Royster, argues that a voice is a "central manifestation of subjectivity" (30). In other words, our relationship to power, as well as the opportunities it affords and the constraints it places on us, is revealed through our voice. Royster defines a voice as something "that is constructed and expressed visually and orally, *and* [...] a *thing* heard, perceived, and reconstructed" (31). Why does this distinction matter for Royster? Because it points our attention not only to who is *doing* the speaking, but also who is being *heard*. To have a voice, Royster argues, is to have "the power and authority to speak and make meaning" (31). This is the definition of voice we're thinking of as we write this chapter.

In a sense, Royster is bringing us back to that old saying, "If a tree falls in the forest, and there's no one there to hear it, does it make a sound?" To have a voice means someone has to hear you. But what does it really mean to be heard? What kinds of sounds are meaningful, and to whom? What assumptions do we make about the listener (or reader) when we think about sounds that are meaningful?

As you'll learn in college if you haven't already, sometimes the best answer to a question is another question. In this chapter, our goal isn't to tell you what to think or how to write. Instead, we share with you what we know and leave you with challenging questions—questions about language, identity, and power that we ourselves don't have good answers for. But we join many scholars who believe that those who write and teach writing in school *need* to be asking them. You might feel uncomfortable at times, and that's okay—because discomfort can be productive. We hope that you'll leave this chapter inspired to explore those questions and to work through any discomfort that comes up along the way.

How We Acquire Language: It's All About Community

It's hard to talk about voice without talking about language, because language is one of the primary ways most people communicate. So in order to think critically about voice in academic writing, we first need to think critically about language. Luckily for us, there's an entire academic discipline called Linguistics where people study language. Linguistics scholars study how sounds and words form patterns, how humans develop language, what features all languages have in common, how language varieties differ, and more.

One of the most fundamental things linguists have found that's relevant to our discussion is this: language really isn't something we *learn* through conscious effort; it's something we *acquire*. In other words, language is sort of something that happens as we interact with other human beings. Research has shown that one of the best ways to acquire language is simply by using it with others, out of necessity to communicate. Language acquisition is one reason why language immersion programs and dual-language programs have become so popular, and it's one benefit of study-abroad programs as well.

Because language is acquired by interacting with others, it's as diverse as the communities we're part of: communities organized by where we live, our religious traditions, our interest groups, and so on. In each of our communities, the language we use is specific to those groups; for example, we use certain words or expressions, we focus on particular things, and we share certain beliefs that form the basis for our interactions. The language we use is also what creates a sense of community; it separates people who are in that community from those who are outside it. For example, writer and cultural theorist Gloria Anzaldúa says that Chicano Spanish "sprang out of the Chicanos' need to identify ourselves as a distinct people" (33). This language is one "they can connect their identity to, one capable of communicating the realities and values true to themselves—a language with terms that are neither *espanol ni ingles,* but both" (33).

Language is also connected to racial identity but not for the reasons most people think. "[R]ace does not determine what language a child will speak, there is no such thing as a 'racial language,' and no race or ethnic group is born with a particular language," explains Geneva Smitherman, a groundbreaking and important Black linguist who has spent the last 50 years researching Black Language, also known as Black English, African American Language (AAL), and African American Vernacular English (AAVE), and formerly known as Ebonics. She continues:

> Children acquire their language from the community of speakers they play, live, grow up, and socialize with. [... S]ince communities in the U.S. have been separated and continue to exist along distinct racial lines, language follows suit. An African American child will more than likely play, live, grow up, and socialize in any one of the numerous African American communities of the U.S. and thus will acquire the African American Language of her com-

munity. [...] Even though race does not determine what language a child will speak, race does determine what community a child grows up in, and it is that community which provides the child with language. (5)

In short, what Smitherman is arguing is that language tends to differ among differently raced people, but that isn't because language and race are inextricable from one another. That is, being Black doesn't determine which language and dialect you'll know and use most any more than being Mexican American means you'll know and use Chicano/a Spanish or being white means you'll speak middle-class English.

Why Language Is Political: The Silencing Power of Stigma

The discussion of communities and language gets tricky when we start to talk about *value*, specifically how different communities and languages are valued differently. At its most basic, value is attached to resources: land, money, time, materials, people, and other assets that we need in order to live. The more resources we have access to or possess, the more value we possess. The more value we possess, the more power we have, because we live in a world where resources are finite. More power means more authority, including authority to set standards and make the rules that govern society.

Authority is inextricably connected to language because people are inextricably connected to language. In other words, language is political because politics is all about how humans living in groups make decisions. They make those decisions by *using* language, and in many settings, they make decisions *about* language: what is and isn't valued, appropriate, correct, and so on. The issue, of course, is *who* is making those decisions—or historically has made those decisions—and whose values are accounted for in the decisions that they make, in the standards that they set.

One of the most difficult concepts for non-linguists to grasp about language is that there really is no such thing as an objective "standard" version of a language. The idea that there *is* one is a myth. To the contrary, language doesn't exist on its own; it's created through interaction and changes over time, two truths that linguists have discovered through careful observation and deduction. In other words, there simply is no "pure" form of a language, no standard. The belief that standard English exists is called *standard language ideology*.

Nevertheless, people try to *standardize* language—to create and uphold some notion of the "pure" form of a language—out of perceived necessity. Sociolinguist Rosina Lippi-Green explains that because we write to remember things and help others to remember them, and to preserve ideas we find valuable, we place a lot of demands on written language: "we want it to span time and space, and we want it to do that in a social vacuum, without the aid of paralinguistic features and often without shared context of any kind" (18). As a result, she says, people think that "written language needs to be free of variation: it must be consistent in every way, from spelling to sentence structure" (18).

The problem, though, is that language *doesn't* happen in a vacuum; it happens among people of diverse cultures, nationalities, religious traditions, and socioeconomic classes who have different orientations toward gender, sexuality, physical ability, neurotypicality, and so on. The demand for language consistency necessarily results in standards that reflect a particular worldview: the worldview of the people in positions of power. In the United States, these were the people who historically had access to education (until roughly the 1970s, most were wealthy white men). Smitherman raises a good point: "If Black people were in power in this country," she says, "Black English would be the prestige idiom" (63).

Language diversity in educational and professional spaces isn't itself a *problem,* however. People in countries outside the U.S. have found ways to value such diversity; the American system of education is unique in its insistence on standardizing one language variety, says late writer and teacher June Jordan:

> In contrast to India, where at least fourteen languages co-exist as legitimate Indian languages, in contrast to Nicaragua, where all citizens are legally entitled to formal school instruction in their regional or tribal languages, compulsory education in America compels accommodation to exclusively White forms of "English." White English, in America, is "Standard English." (364)

In other words, kids in the U.S. from ages 5-ish to 18-ish are required to learn and demonstrate proficiency in what Jordan calls "White English," the language variety that has been standardized by people in power. In effect, the notion that written language must adhere to these standardized rules is a power play that inevitably reproduces white supremacist systems. It is the *systems* that are problematic, not the language differences within them.

These systems are even more problematic because of how they influence our thoughts about one another. In judging language, we judge the *people* who use that language. Judgements[1] are made through comparison, usually to some standard or ideal. So when someone who accepts standard language ideology judges our language, assessing it in terms of "correctness" and/or "appropriateness," they're effectively judging our own proximity to that ideal. In effect, they "devalue the intelligence and character of students, employees, and colleagues, who [...] don't speak or write ['standard' English] by labeling their language improper, inappropriate, or incorrect," explains writing scholar Anjali Pattanayak (84).

Over time, humans internalize beliefs about ourselves and others based on judgements of language. Elaine Richardson, an influential Black professor of Literacy Studies at The Ohio State University, writes about these judgements in her memoir, entitled *PHD (Po H# on Dope) to Ph.D.: How Education Saved My Life*: "I had entered this class, this university and been told in so many words that I was illiterate because the words I used were *awkward*, not recognized as college format, because I didn't know how to punctuate sentences" (202). She later recaps feedback from a writing professor:

> Miss Richardson, when your prose breaks down it's because your logic has broken down ... syntax problems come up not just when someone doesn't have a command of the language or grammar, but because he or she hasn't thought the argument through carefully enough. The language from your home and neighborhood is fine in that context, but it doesn't work for the kind of careful analysis and expression expected in academic writing. (207)

In other words, according to this professor, Black English doesn't make possible the logical and analytical thinking expected of college students. Her white mentor's suggestion? "Write more like I talk," which meant code-switching like she did when "trying to project a positive self-image, especially when speaking to White folks" (207).

Never mind that White linguist William Labov's analyses of Black speech, published in 1970, clearly "dispel the racist myth that African American Language is illogical or ungrammatical [...] reveal[ing] the language to be rule-governed and systematic, not a collection of haphazard errors" (Smitherman 11). Never mind that they correct "false impressions about language, race and intelligence" (11). Never mind that Black English "comes out of the experience of U.S. slave descendants" and was developed through communal resistance to slavery, that it "meld[ed] diverse African ethnic groups into one community [and] was created as a communication system unintelligible to speakers of the dominant master class" (3). Standard language ideology is a powerful thing. "Black English don't make it own-self oppressed," argues Vershawn Ashanti Young, a prominent Black scholar of African American Studies. "It be negative views about other people usin they own language [...] that make it so" (110).

This stigmatization can have serious consequences for people who speak and/or write anything other than what sociolinguists H. Samy Alim and Geneva Smitherman call White Mainstream English, a term literacy scholar April Baker-Bell uses "to emphasize how white ways of speaking become the invisible—or better, inaudible—norm" (3). Consider, for example, George Zimmerman's 2013 trial for the murder of Trayvon Martin. The star witness for the prosecution on whose testimony Zimmerman's verdict hinged was a 19-year-old Black woman named Rachel Jeantel, a speaker of Black Language. An extensive (and dense) analysis of the trial by Stanford linguists John R. Rickford and Sharese King reveals that Jeantel's "AAVE, though systematic, was misheard and maligned. Her testimony, which provided crucial evidence, was disregarded because of its unfamiliarity to most jurors and social biases against AAVE speakers" (980).

Prejudices about language inferiority and intellectual ability are so deeply engrained through standard language ideology that peoples' bodies themselves are stigmatized even when they haven't uttered a word. This, of course, is an inevitable consequence of what writing and rhetoric scholar Asao Inoue calls "white language supremacy" and what Baker-Bell calls "anti-Black linguistic racism." "When we read the words that come from [others'] bodies [...], we read those bodies as well," argues Inoue, "and by reading those bodies we also read the words they present to us; some may bear/bare stigmas, some may not" ("Friday Plenary Address" 144).

It is because of this shared concern that we urge you to ask, "What color is my voice?"

As you'll see in the narratives that follow, which were written by the two of us coauthors who were community college students in Kristin's first-year writing courses, we believe this reflective work is an important first step in resisting white language supremacy. It's especially important to do this work in educational settings, because education influences society, and because a collective voice (such as many voices of students in a class or a school) are more powerful than a single voice. We have three hopes for sharing our stories. We hope that those who've been forced to surrender their voice to an impossible standard will find solidarity. We hope that all readers will begin or continue to ask hard questions about voice and power.

And we hope that all readers will do something in response, writing our way into finding our voice even in academic writing.

WRITING PRIVILEGES FROM THE "GOOD WRITER": AN'S STORY

I was lucky enough to grow up in a house that loved reading. My mom was a bookworm who read to me while I was still in the womb. Childhood was full of fairy tales and endless books using all kinds of language. The thee's and the thou's and the damsels in distress, I gobbled those stories up like Cheerios. Often, I would get busted for reading under the covers with my Hello Kitty flashlight. I'd say I was sorry, but it wasn't my fault that stories got so much better after dark. Over the years my books and personal libraries were replaced by an iPhone, late-night reads became late-night texts, and "fancy language" went from being words of kings and queens to MLA format. As far away as childhood was, I can still say that my background affects the verbiage I use today.

Speaking of background, let's take it back, way back to 1991, the year my parents arrived.

My parents are Vietnamese immigrants who came to this country riding on the promise of a better future for their not-yet-born kids (me and my sister). America was their ticket to success, and they made sure not to squander a second of it. Both of my parents graduated with Bachelor's degrees in New York and made it a point to value education above all else. My mom was a Special Ed teacher before she had me, and my dad was a math substitute all throughout my adolescence. As for me, I started preschool ASAP and although I only remember how fun it was to play with giant bins of sand, I'm sure that going there benefitted me linguistically. Going on to elementary school, I recall reading absolutely anything and everything from cereal boxes to captions on the TV. In middle school the reading tests we did were my best tests (sorry, math teachers). I loved the thrill of reading faster and faster, zooming through the paragraphs and climbing the ladder of success. Sooner rather than later, it was clear to me that I was equipped with an arsenal of vocabulary. Reading felt like a train steadily chugging along with no reason to stop. But this was not the case for everyone. While I counted down the minutes left in class so I could race to the library, others around me avoided reading like the plague. Some simply had better things to do, like talk to their crushes at their lockers or gossip in the bathrooms. However, for some of my peers, the thought of picking up a book for leisure caused more stress than comfort. They only read books assigned for class, and even then those stories felt boring or overwhelming—the farthest thing from enjoyable. While reading for me felt like my greatest escape, my friends saw it as the greatest chore. I did not fully understand why this may have been until entering college. This was when I started learning more about how reading and writing experiences in childhood can affect people for the rest of their lives.

As an Early Childhood Education major, I am taking courses about childhood development, and some of the things I've learned have been truly eye opening. For example, one of my classes focuses on how to use Art Integration in all subjects in order to give students creative outlets. Something we recently discussed was the concept of "art scars." Art scars refer to past traumas that students have around art. Often, in childhood, students will experience shame or harsh criticism of their creativity from their peers or their teachers. This trauma can cause people to lose their sense of creativity entirely and can affect them well into adulthood. An example we spoke about in class was a story of a student applying to college. He flew through his application with full confidence, but when he was asked to draw an image of what represented him as a person, he broke down in tears, and ended up throwing his application away.

In the same way, I believe that people have "writing scars." Throughout school, I had various friends tell me that they were bad at writing. I took that statement as a call to action and stepped in as human Grammarly—reading through numerous essays, tweaking them here and there so that they sounded "more academic." What I ended up noticing is that the essays that they gave me ended up sounding nothing like the final product that I produced. In making their writing "better," what I actually did was censor their voices, stripping their colorful essays of what made them profound and thought provoking. Without knowing it, I was reinforcing what their past writing scars had told them, that they were no good at writing and that their language was not deemed academic. Perhaps, and I hate to admit this, *I* was the one giving them the writing scars and making them feel inadequate about their writing ability. This realization especially sucks because at the time, I genuinely felt that I was being a good friend by helping. I now understand how critical it is to believe that everyone's stories are important, not just those who use "suburban" vocab or have perfected their citations. Looking back, I wish that I had just encouraged them to use more of the language that made them feel comfortable and heard. Instead, I took their narratives and shoved them into a box when I should have been the friend to set them free.

To me, writing is freedom.

I am a woman who feels with ferocity, and I love to express those feelings and be loud and pissed off and powerful. Writing should be used to empower people, not make them doubt their abilities. Often, writing can be cathartic or an emotional release. I know that that is what it feels like to me. The problem is that the academic writing standards that we currently have in place are way too rigid and, quite frankly, boring. Which is not how it's supposed to be. When it comes to my own assignments, I find that in order to do well, my deep connection to my writing is something that I have to erase completely. But that SUCKS! I want to write the way I speak and to be able to share my story. I want to use expressions and italics and exclamation points. I want my bold points to be **bold** and for my essays to make people laugh or cry. Ultimately, I want my writing to sound like *me*. I recognize that it is much easier for me to excel in writing than it is for others who do not share my background. All my life I have had every chance to do well in English class, and this in itself is a blessing. My language doesn't get nearly as much scrutiny as others do, and that's not fair. I am not "better" at writing, I am not smarter or superior or even the best at writing this. The only thing that separates me from someone who is deemed a "bad writer" is access to opportunities. *Everyone* is a good writer. Because everyone who writes tells a story.

I have so much love for writing, and I wish that everyone else had the opportunity to feel the same. But truly, all it comes down to is the fact that I was lucky enough to grow up in a house that loved reading.

WRITING WHILE BLACK: AJ'S STORY

Growing up as a young Black man in the white suburbs of Chicago, I have experienced so much judgement and backlash when writing and how I'm viewed as uneducated due to my writing. **Even after completing my associate's degree.** I still feel stuck in writer's block every time I am tasked with a writing project or assignment. Recently I was involved in a motorcycle accident that temporarily made me unable to type. Both writer's block and this accident have made it really hard to write this chapter. So what I decided to do is get creative and try from a different angle. Kristin and I decided to have a conversation, transcribe it, and share pieces of our conversation with you.[2] Sometimes, life circumstances limit what we can do, so we gotta be flexible, and this is one of those situations.

> Kristin: Can you talk to me about some experiences you've had that stand out to you about your writing for school?

AJ: So you know how when you're a kid, you're taught—what is it called, the—the correct ***"English,"*** or the correct way how you should write or say things. But then once you're—as you grow up, especially when—growing up Black [...] it's like learning two languages because you go to school and they teach you, "Oh, this word, you know, means this. And this is how you should use this word, this is how you should use it in a sentence, and you use this many words in a sentence and you use a comma, and this is how you properly do something." And then you go home and then you pick up on vocabulary words, you pick up on how your [...] culture speaks and you're [...] going in two different worlds because you tryna learn about your culture and how *they* speak, and then you grasp onto *that*. But then you going back to school and you tryna grasp onto *that*. But then let's say a teacher writes you an assignment about "what do you think?" Oh, like a perfect question I just had recently asked: "What do you think, why is police recruiting down nationwide?" And then "what do you see as the problem, and do you see a remedy?" Now, you could choose two different options on how you can respond. [...] You can respond to the white version and use what you think that the audience would like, which is the white audience, or you could respond [...] how you truly feel about it, but when you try to respond how you truly feel about it, [...] you have to worry about who's gonna be reading it and [...] what the type of audience is going to be reading it and how people will judge you on writing that. Does that make sense?

Kristin: Yeah. So are you talking about the *response* that you give, or are you talking about the way that you—your voice in your writing?

AJ: Yeah—it's kind of both [...], because if you give the response that you believe in [...] I might get graded poorly on it, and I can't voice how I really feel or speak how I really feel about the [thing I'm supposed to be writing about]. [...] In your mind you thinkin, am I writing for a white audience? When I get the assignment, I gotta think, "OK, who's gonna be reading it?" If you know your teacher is white, then you'd be like, "OK, my teacher is white. So let me sound *this* way because I think this'll impress my teacher, but I really don't *like* how I'm putting this." I'm not gonna really add *flavor* to it, or add how I really *feel* about it. But I wanna respond how I think that the teacher would like. Does that make sense?

Kristin: Yeah. So would you say that race is the first, or one of the first, considerations that you think about when you're writing for someone else?

AJ: Oh absolutely. That's the *first* thing that comes to my mind.

Kristin: So what about a topic that's not about police, like anything having to do with law enforcement, for example? Like for your meteorology class, or—

AJ: Doesn't matter. Because the first thing comes to my mind is that—I'm writing something, right? I'm gonna get judged automatically about what I'm writing about. Regardless. And there's always gonna be somebody that don't like what I say, but [...] I'm gonna to try to sound *proper* [...] regardless of if I don't know if the teacher is white or black, whatever. I'm gonna try to sound proper because if I try to speak [...] using African-American Ebonics language, if I speak with slang and talk using slang words, then I'm gonna be viewed as *uneducated* or poor—poor choice of words, you know. People are not gonna try to validate my argument because the type of words that I'm using. Now, if I were to sound very *proper,* I'm still gonna get judged, but I may have a slim chance than if I were to use slang words to explain where I'm coming from.

Kristin: Have you ever felt like you could write in ways that felt really authentic to you?

AJ: No, I don't think so. Not at all. I feel like it's all sugar-coated and watered down. It's like you're beating around the bush. You're at the *top* of the surface, but you're not going *underneath* the surface. Because why even try if [...] Black people incapable of, aren't capable of writing in a efficient and proper way.

Kristin: Where do you get that message from?

AJ: I just think it's the *experiences* like, you know—I think it has to probably tie back to going to middle school and high school, being shamed in front of the whole class. I just feel like those experiences shape our way of thinking—when you go through an experience like that, it makes you think, like, damn, maybe I *am* not good enough to do this.

Kristin: Would you be comfortable telling me about those experiences?

AJ: Yeah. I had to write this essay for high school; it was called the Pettus Bridge Essay. Of course, it was about violence against Black people, and I fucking hated it. It was traumatizing learning about that in a white setting when you're one of the only Black people in the class. And this teacher—it's not the shit that he would *say* that would be racist, it was the *antagonizing* shit that he would *do* that made me believe he was racist. We would turn in our essays on Friday, and during class on Monday, he would call groups of people up, have them stand in a line, give them back their essays, and talk to each person for 30 to 45 seconds on what they can do to improve. And he got to the last three people—and what a coincidence that we're all Black—and everybody was up and down in their seats, and no problems. And then like, the three Black people, it was like—I feel like I was standing in the courtroom in front of a fuckin judge, because we're *all* standing in front of him, he's all telling us how, "Oh, this isn't good. Look how all the Black students didn't do well on their assignments." We all got like Cs and Ds, and we still talk about it to this day, [the teacher said,] "Oh, if you want a good grade, you'll have to rewrite it over again in a different way—if you do it this way, improve here and there. And that shapes the way of you writing in the future, because now you thinking like, "Damn, I can't really explain how I feel or what I think about this situation, because now I'm second-guessing every goddamn thing, thinking like, 'I don't know where to start. Does this sound good?'" And you know, *that's* what makes writing so difficult. That shit right there. Experiences like that. Where you have someone that kinda shames you growing up, or someone shames you for your writing like that, it shapes you into a way of thinking that you're not capable of being a good writer or not being a good, efficient, and proper writer, because everything you do, you feel like it's not good enough.

Kristin: Are there situations in school where you've been having to write and you felt like you *were* able to move past that writer's block?

AJ: It's not something that you could just move past. I'm *still* not past it, cuz it's like even with different teachers, I still have that in the back of my mind when it comes to writing. That's not the first experience of me dealing with something like that one teacher, but just that one experience could impact you writing in your whole life because it's just like—that was just too much for me, you know? That was *sophomore year in high school*. And to this day, I *still* have that same problem of second-guessing everything, and that's [...] why I hate writing assignments so much. I mean,

I'll rather do a essay than do math. But it's just like it takes so much longer to write because you're second guessing everything. You write two pages? "Oh, that don't sound— that don't—I don't think that's right." You know? You're thinking you're not good enough to write. [. . .] All it takes is one experience, is a white person to say—or, put you, like, make you feel like you're *beneath* them, and then it just impacts your writing, and then it'll fuck you up writing moving forward.

Kristin: And you can't—

AJ: And you can't get past it because that one experience is in your mind.

Where We Go from Here

The goal of empowering writers by preparing them to write in contexts where they *will* be judged for deviations from the "standard" might seem like a good one—people trying to help others to succeed in life. But with code-switching, the fact that the "standard" was set by the people who have historically had the most resources remains unchallenged—and that, we believe, is a huge oversight. "For the master's tools will never dismantle the master's house," wrote Audre Lorde in a book titled for that quote. "They may allow us to temporarily beat him at his own game, but they will never enable us to bring about genuine change." In other words, if we continue to follow the status quo with our academic writing and the teaching of it, we'll never change white language supremacy. Black women like Rachel Jeantel still won't be believed or taken seriously because she talks (or writes) in a stigmatized dialect (or language, depending on how you categorize AAVE). So even though students in higher education have become more diverse, the standards and expectations have not changed to reflect that diversity—and white supremacy lives on.

Looking back on all the reading we've done for college, the books and articles that have stayed with us most are written by Black, Indigenous, and People of Color who've written about brilliant, complex ideas—*with a voice*. The language they use reflects the *person* behind those words and ideas. Their radical academic writing pushes us to ask hard questions about language and power, questions that unsettle the paralyzing fear of failure that so many students *always* carry because they've been socialized to believe their language and thus their intelligence is inferior, as AJ's story exemplifies. It is for these students and *all* students who believe their voice doesn't belong in higher education or professional workplaces—a belief rooted in white supremacy—that we urge us all to ponder how our own voices show up in our academic writing—or how they're silenced, and what we want to do with that knowledge.

Notes

1. Throughout this chapter, we've adopted Asao Inoue's (2021) intentional spelling of "judgement" with an "e" to emphasize that there is always a *person* doing the judging, acting as judge.

2. Whenever you see [...] (an ellipsis), we've cut out a word or words to keep focused on the parts we feel are most important to share.

Works Cited

Alim, H. Samy, and Geneva Smitherman. *Articulate While Black: Barack Obama, Language, and Race in the U.S.* Oxford University Press, 2012.

Alvarez, Sara P., et al. "Workin' Languages: Who We Are Matters in Our Writing." *Writing Spaces: Readings on Writing, Volume 4*, edited by Dana Lynn Driscoll, Megan Heise, Mary K. Stewart, and Matthew Vetter. Parlor Press, 2021, pp. 1-17.

Anzaldua, Gloria. "How to Tame a Wild Tongue." *Language Diversity and Academic Writing*, edited by Samantha Looker-Koenigs, Bedford/St. Martin's, 2018, pp. 31-42.

Baker-Bell, April. *Linguistic Justice: Black Language, Literacy, Identity, and Pedagogy*. Routledge, 2020.

Boroditsky, Lera. "How Language Shapes the Way We Think." *TED: Ideas Worth Spreading*, May 2018, www.ted.com/talks/lera_boroditsky_how_language_shapes_the_way_we_think. Accessed 29 July 2022.

—. "Lost in Translation." *Language Awareness: Readings for College Writers*, 12th ed., edited by Paul Eschholz, Alfred Rosa, and Virginia Clark, Bedford / St. Martin's, 2016, pp. 141-46.

DiAngelo, Robin. *White Fragility: Why It's So Hard for White People to Talk About Racism*. Beacon Press, 2018.

Frye, Marilyn. "White Woman Feminist." *Willful Virgin: Essays in Feminism*, The Crossing Press, 1992, feminist-reprise.org/library/race-and-class/white-woman-feminist/. Accessed 29 July 2022.

Grayson, Mara Lee. "Writing toward Racial Literacy." *Writing Spaces: Readings on Writing, Volume 4*, edited by Dana Lynn Driscoll, Megan Heise, Mary K. Stewart, and Matthew Vetter. Parlor Press, 2021, pp. 166-183.

Inoue, Asao B. *Above The Well: An Antiracist Literacy Argument From A Boy of Color*. The WAC Clearinghouse; Utah State University Press, 2021, doi: 10.37514/PER-B.2021.1244.

—. *Antiracist Writing Assessment Ecologies: Teaching and Assessing Writing for a Socially Just Future*. Parlor Press, 2015.

—. "Friday Plenary Address: Racism in Writing Programs and the CWPA." *WPA: Writing Program Administration*, vol. 40, no. 1, 2016, pp. 134–54.

—. "How Do We Language So People Stop Killing Each Other, or What Do We Do about White Language Supremacy?" *College Composition and Communication*, vol. 71, no. 2, Dec. 2019, pp. 352–69.

Jordan, June. "Nobody Mean More to Me Than You and the Future Life of Willie Jordan." *Harvard Educational Review*, vol. 58, no. 3, Aug. 1988, pp. 363–74.

Kim, Dae-Joong, and Bobbi Olson. "Deconstructing Whiteliness in the Globalized Classroom." *Performing Antiracist Pedagogy in Rhetoric, Writing, and Communication*, edited by Frankie Condon and Vershawn Ashanti Young, WAC Clearinghouse, 2017, pp. 123–58.

Lippi-Green, Rosina. *English with an Accent: Language, Ideology, and Discrimination in the United States*, 2nd ed. Routledge, 2012.

Lorde, Audre. *The Master's Tools Will Never Dismantle the Master's House*. Penguin Classics, 2018.

Morrison, Toni. "Nobel Lecture." *The Nobel Prize in Literature*, Dec. 7 1993, www.nobelprize.org/prizes/literature/1993/morrison/lecture/. Accessed 29 July 2022.

Pattanayak, Anjali. "There Is One Correct Way of Writing and Speaking." *Bad Ideas about Writing*, edited by Cheryl E. Ball and Drew M. Loewe, West Virginia University, 2017, pp. 82-87.

Richardson, Elaine. *PHD to Ph.D.: How Education Saved My Life*. Parlor Press, 2013.

Rickford, John R., and Sharese King. "Language and Linguistics on Trial: Hearing Rachel Jeantel (and Other Vernacular Speakers) in the Courtroom and Beyond." *Language*, vol. 92, no. 4, 2016, pp. 948–88. doi: 10.1353/lan.2016.0078.

Royster, Jacqueline Jones. "When the First Voice You Hear Is Not Your Own." *College Composition and Communication*, vol. 47, no. 1, 1996, pp. 29–40.

Sánchez-Martín, Cristina. "Beyond Language Difference in Writing: Investigating Complex and Equitable Language Practices." *Writing Spaces: Readings on Writing, Volume 4*, edited by Dana Lynn Driscoll, Megan Heise, Mary K. Stewart, and Matthew Vetter. Parlor Press, 2021, pp. 269-280.

Smitherman, Geneva. *Word from the Mother: Language and African Americans*. Routledge, 2006.

Young, Vershawn Ashanti. "Should Writers Use They Own English?" *Iowa Journal of Cultural Studies*, vol. 12, no. 1, 2010, pp. 110–17.

Young, Vershawn Ashanti, Aja Y. Martinez, and Julie Naviaux. Introduction. *Code-Meshing as World English: Pedagogy, Policy, Performance*, edited by Vershawn Ashanti Young and Aja Y. Martinez, NCTE, 2011, pp. xix-xxxi.

Teacher Resources for "What Color Is My Voice? Academic Writing and the Myth of Standard English"

Overview and Teaching Strategies

One thing I (Kristin) have learned through experience with doing antiracist work in writing classes—such as engaging students in discussions about white language supremacy—is the importance of working through the material and hard questions that come up before I ever introduce the concepts to students. I've also learned the importance of developing my own racial literacy beyond a basic understanding of white privilege and structural racism as a precursor to doing this work, because antiracism is personal and powerful, white fragility (DiAngelo) is real, and whiteliness (Frye) doesn't depend on a person's racial identity (though of course white people are more likely to be whitely). And I've learned both firsthand and through collaborating with colleagues how difficult this internal work is and how easy to is to unconsciously slip into Habits of White Language (HOWL; Inoue, *Above the Well*) even while we're consciously trying to confront them.

For these reasons, our teaching strategies begin with the recommendation that teachers do some difficult introspective work first. Write out your responses to the questions for writing and discussion below. Think about your own voice in academic writing, what you like about your voice and what you dislike about it, what your thoughts are on language diversity in academic writing, what unresolved questions linger for you and how you're working through those questions, who some of your favorite academic writers and/or texts are, and so on. Reflect on the identities you bring to the classroom, how those identities impact your stance on language diversity and antiracism, and in what ways you will need to pay careful attention to those identities (i.e., worldviews and habits) as you engage students in these conversations. Also think about how your grading policy and assessment practices function in your class alongside these discussions about voice. We strongly urge you to read Asao Inoue's *Antiracist Writing Assessment Ecologies*, ensuring that your policies and other elements of the assessment ecology that is your writing class will support the critical work this chapter invites students to do. Once you've laid that groundwork you can think about how this chapter will fit into your overall plans for the course.

We envision this chapter as being most useful early in a course, because it introduces students to concepts that we hope will impact their writing throughout that course. The longer students have to engage with these ideas and think critically about their own voice and the value of language diversity in academic writing, and the more practice students get writing with these ideas in mind, the better equipped they will be to continue and defend this revolutionary work in future classes. In turn, the antiracist work you begin here will be more likely to extend beyond your class.

Because race and voice are deeply connected, and because the nature of race as a social and political construct (and not a biological one) is often unfamiliar and/or controversial, you will likely need to teach students about racial literacy. You will also need to make explicit connections between racial literacy and writing classes, especially when those classes are gen-ed requirements meant to teach writing for academic purposes. We intend for this chapter to help make that connection, drawing students' attention to normalized values and perspectives that inform the standards we're taught are objective and innocuous. We recommend that you and students read this chapter alongside a few other open-access texts that we describe below. These texts will help contextualize and deepen readers' understanding of the inescapably political nature of writing. They will also stimulate critical thought about how students might use their writing for social change.

Three chapters in *Writing Spaces,* Vol. 4 complement this chapter. Mary Lee Grayson's "Writing toward Racial Literacy" explains the relevance of race and racism to writing classes and guides readers in thinking through how race and racism impact their lives no matter their racial identity. We recommend that students read Grayson's chapter before ours to develop a foundational understanding of the systemic issues underlying voice as we discuss it here. Students might also find Cristina Sánchez-Martín's chapter, "Beyond Language Difference in Writing: Investigating Complex and Equitable Language Practices," helpful for thinking about how multilingual writers commonly engage in "'translingual' practices by which writers move across traditional understandings of separate languages" (270). Sánchez-Martín shares multiple examples of translingualism in both popular *and* academic texts, arguing that translingual approaches to writing can address issues of diversity, equity, and inclusion. Translingualism and its contributions to academic writing are also core concepts in "Workin' Languages: Who We Are Matters in Our Writing," by Sara P. Alvarez, Amy J. Wan, and Eunjeong Lee. In this chapter, Alvarez, Wan, and Lee offer strategies for and approaches to integrating diverse language practices in academic writing that they have gleaned through personal experience.

This chapter might be especially useful as a follow-up to our discussion of voice because it provides a theoretical lens that students can adopt as they write: that of the "language architect." Significantly, these authors account for the constraints a writer's subjectivity places on her rhetorical situation, clarifying that "many of us whose languages are racialized in various ways may have to work their academic writing contexts more so, or differently" (6). This point alone yields opportunities for discussing how voice and subjectivity function in tandem, which we discuss in our chapter, and how that reality impacts the choices available to individual writers.

In addition to these *Writing Spaces* chapters, we recommend that teachers (and possibly students) familiarize themselves with the concept of *whiteliness*, which Marilyn Frye distinguishes from whiteness and defines as "a deeply ingrained way of being in the world" (qtd. in Kim and Olson 87) and Dae-Joong Kim and Bobbi Olson add is an "epistemological worldview, a lens of judgment" (124). This distinction might help to mitigate eruptions of students' (and teachers') white fragility by conveying that just as race isn't a biological reality, so too the whitely worldview that sustains white language supremacy (Inoue, *Antiracist Writing*) isn't intrinsic or limited to white people. In other words, some Black, Indigenous, and People of Color adopt whitely perspectives about language, and some white people actively challenge those perspectives. This clarification can help to abate tension that might otherwise stall important and productive conversations about linguistic racism.

Following are some questions to stimulate critical thought and activity suggestions to help students identify standard language ideology in their everyday worlds and reflect on its impact on their own and others' lives.

Questions for Writing and Discussion

The following questions would work well for writing in class or out of class and then discussing. They could also be seeds for projects investigating language difference and ideology, perhaps resulting in presentations or a gallery of multimodal or written texts about students' findings.

1. Often, we don't notice something's existence until we feel its absence, so you might not realize how important language is to your identity or your communities. It might help to think of a time when you felt you couldn't write or speak in ways that felt natural to you, authentic. Or a time when you felt like you had to translate a concept from one of your communities (for example, a religious community, a scientific community, or a cultural/heritage com-

munity) to someone outside that community. It could be a minor moment or a more involved conversation about a concept. What was that experience like? How did you feel during it? What made you realize that you were a part of that community to begin with?

2. Make a list or draw a mind map of four or five communities you're part of, like a church community, a neighborhood, an online interest group, etc. Then, for each community listed, answer the following questions: What does it mean to be part of this community? In other words, what values do you share? What interests do you share? What specific beliefs about people, things, reality, etc. do you share? What are some common terms or phrases that you use—terms or phrases that someone outside your community might not understand but that anyone in your community would most likely understand? What do those terms or phrases mean to you, and why are they significant to your community? How do they reflect what is important to you?

3. In a speech addressing college writing teachers, Asao Inoue asked, "Which bodies historically have had the privilege to speak and write the most in civic life and in the academy? Whose words have been validated as history, truth, knowledge, story, the most throughout history? Who sits in the teacher's chair [...]?" ("How Do We Language" 136). Based on your experiences in K-12 and even college so far, how would you answer Inoue's questions? How might sharing identity characteristics (like race, gender, socioeconomic class, etc.) with these teachers, writers, speakers, politicians, and so on affect students who share them both in school and outside school? Think broadly about potential effects on students' thoughts and/or emotions as well as situations they might (or might not) encounter. Make your ideas here as specific as you can. Then consider the alternative. What is at stake for the people who do *not* share these identity characteristics? How might their experiences in school be impacted? How might their thoughts and emotions be impacted, and how might those impacts affect their experiences?

4. "The idea that there is one correct way of writing devalues the writing, thoughts, intelligence, and identities of people from lower-class backgrounds," argues Anjali Pattanayak (85). What are some examples of interactions you've either experienced or observed where a strongly held belief in standard English led someone's intelligence

or identity to be stigmatized? Have *you* had these thoughts yourself? What do you make of them given what you've read in this chapter?

5. Spend a few minutes reflecting, in writing, on these questions: Whose voice do I hear in my writing, and why? What does this voice reveal about my identity as a writer, and how do I feel about what I uncover? What might I want to do more of, or differently? What might happen if I make these changes, and how do I feel about those potential outcomes? What kinds of support do I need for finding my voice in academic writing, and where can I find that support at this school?

6. In their introduction to *Code-Meshing as World English*, Vershawn Ashanti Young, Aja Y. Martinez, and Julie Naviaux pose an incisive question: "What if, during formal language instruction, native English speakers and English language learners were exposed to a variety of Englishes, both from regions of their countries and from around the globe? [...] What if all English users were not only encouraged to understand varieties of English but also allowed to fluidly use them in both formal and informal contexts?" (*xx*). What do you think of this proposal to resist standard language ideology in classes where writing is taught? How might this change affect teachers? How might it affect students? Do you think it might affect life outside of school? If so, what possibilities do you imagine?

Sample Activities

Following are a couple of activities or activity ideas that I (Kristin) have used to raise students' awareness of standard language ideology and its implications for diversity, equity, and inclusion and of the central role of language to being human.

Standard Language Ideology in Memes and TikToks

Have students find memes or short videos (like TikToks) about language that demonstrate standard language ideology. One I often bring to class is a meme with a white man in a three-piece suit holding a top hat and saying, "When you say 'I seen,' I assume you won't finish that sentence with 'the inside of a book.' I see. I saw. I have seen." We discuss whose languaging the meme critiques (speakers of Black English) and what it communicates about the people associated with that languaging (Black Americans). We also discuss the significance of the image and what it communicates, and we discuss the sociocultural significance of memes in general, connecting back to the roles that educational institutions play in reproducing and/or resisting harmful stereotypes.

After students find their own memes or short videos, ask students to write about each one, describing it and answering the following questions: 1) What does this meme/video communicate or imply about "correctness" in language use?, 2) How does this meme/video affect, reinforce, or challenge your own perceptions of people?, 3) What assumptions is the creator of this text making about communication, and how do those assumptions connect to your own?, 4) How might these assumptions and perceptions reinforce inequality? You can also have students analyze the rhetorical situation of the text and where they found it and reflect on the significance of various parts of this rhetorical situation (like when and where it's published and how it circulates).

Languaging as "The Measure of Our Lives"

Assign students to watch, listen to, and/or read Toni Morrison's Nobel Lecture for the Nobel Prize in Literature in 1993, available as an audio file and transcript at NobelPrize.org. In this lecture, Toni Morrison speaks of language as a living being—a bird—held in the hands of some young people who visit a wise, old, blind Black woman to mock her for her blindness. The old woman considers this bird they bring—language—to be "partly [. . .] a system, partly [. . .] a living thing over which one has control, but mostly [. . .] agency—as an act with consequences." In the story Morrison tells, the woman draws the young people's attention away from the hands holding the bird, those with power over it, and to the bird itself—language—"the instrument through which that power is exercised." Near the end of the lecture, Morrison says, "We die. That may be the meaning of life. But we do language. That may be the measure of our lives." That agency, the verb-y-ness of language, and the extent to which we use it is our legacy.

Morrison's lecture is especially relevant to this chapter because in it, she identifies several threats to language-as-agency, or voice as we have used it in this chapter. For example, she directly critiques "the proud but calcified language of the academy" and "the commodity driven language of science" as "oppressive language," which she says "does more than represent violence; it is violence; does more than represent the limits of knowledge; it limits knowledge." And she explicitly connects "the policing languages of mastery" to discrimination, to "sexist language, racist language, theistic language." Just as the story Morrison tells ends by calling attention to the young people's agency—"[W]hat I do know is that [the bird] is in your hands. It is in your hands," says the old blind woman—so Morrison concludes the lecture by imagining the woman's response as a reflection on the agentive power of languaging together. Having read Morrison's text and this chapter side-by-side, students could then develop a written or multimodal project where they create their own metaphor for their own voice and explain that metaphor along with its significance to them, especially in light of this chapter. I (Kristin) am purposefully leaving assignment possibilities vague here to encourage creative teacher responses that 1) make use of the wide-ranging analog and digital technologies available to students and 2) honor individual teachers' knowledge of/comfort with assigning and responding to multimodal projects.

Language Structure and Style in Students' Own Communities

If you're using this chapter with advanced undergraduates and beyond, you might want to invite students to think even more deeply and critically about the relationships between language and identity (specifically, worldview). You could, for example, ask students to find texts in their communities and analyze the language in those texts, looking carefully at sentence structure, style, and so on. Two texts that work well to set up such more advanced assignments are Lera Boroditsky's 2018 TED Talk, "How Language Shapes the Way We Think," and June Jordan's "Nobody Mean More to Me than You and the Future Life of Willie Jordan."

Language isn't just something we create, Boroditsky, a cognitive scientist, argues; it creates *us*, how we think and view the world: "research shows us that the languages we speak not only reflect or express our thoughts, but also shape the very thoughts we wish to express. The structures that exist in our languages profoundly shape how we construct reality" ("Lost" 145). For example, languages shape how we think about space and time as well as cause-and-effect relationships. They also reflect and shape our value system. Black English, for example, reveals a person-first value system, "a distinctive Black value system" embodied through "the presence of life, voice, and clarity" in words and sentence structures, explained the late writer and professor June Jordan (367). "You cannot 'translate' instances of Standard English preoccupied with abstraction or with nothing/nobody evidently alive, into Black English," she continued. "That would warp the language into uses antithetical to the guiding perspective of its community of users. Rather you must first change those Standard English sentences, themselves, into ideas consistent with the person-centered assumptions of Black English" (368).

6 What Can I Add to Discourse Communities? How Writers Use Code-Meshing and Translanguaging to Negotiate Discourse

Lisa Tremain

Overview

This essay explores how discourse communities change over time and through participation, and it shows how we can negotiate the expectations for discourse through translanguaging and code-meshing.[1] As discourse community members learn and practice the language rules of a community, they also act as agents to develop, change, or resist these rules. The essay traces iterations of a popular internet meme to show how creative approaches to language, changing memberships, and modes of communication help negotiate and revise discourse community expectations. Translanguaging and code-meshing are two frameworks writers and speakers can use to understand, interrogate, and negotiate discourse community expectations as they establish agency as members in them.

Introduction

Let's say you're having a meal with your closest family members or friends. And let's say the conversation at the table is about a recent topic in the news, something everyone has been talking about and about which folks have a wide range of opinions. Pause to imagine how language might be used in this conversation. Who is there? Would some

---

1. This work is licensed under the Creative Commons Attribution-NonCommercial-NoDerivatives 4.0 International License (CC BY-NC-ND 4.0) and is subject to the Writing Spaces Terms of Use. To view a copy of this license, visit http://creativecommons.org/licenses/by-nc-nd/4.0/, email info@creativecommons.org, or send a letter to Creative Commons, PO Box 1866, Mountain View, CA 94042, USA. To view the Writing Spaces Terms of Use, visit http://writingspaces.org/terms-of-use.

folks at the table use specific words or phrases, hand gestures or voices in ways that only the group might understand? Are there inside jokes that only this group knows? Would there be more than one language spoken or a blend across languages in the conversation? Which individuals would likely lead the conversation and how?

Now imagine you're having a conversation about the same topic, but you're in a classroom where you are a student; maybe it's your first-year writing course. To what extent does your sense of how you'd use language, voice, or gesture about the topic change in this community? How do the people in the classroom make choices about how to add to this conversation—and what would make them feel invited to add to it—or not? How many languages are spoken or blended during the classroom conversation? What kinds of language styles would be valued there, and how are these language styles different from or similar to the conversation at the dinner table?

In this chapter, we'll look at how we use language in different ways across different discourse communities—and we'll consider the degree of agency we have to negotiate the expectations for language in these spaces. In his essay "Understanding Discourse Communities" (*Writing Spaces* Vol. 3), Dan Melzer explains that we can apply the concept of *discourse community* to "describe a community of people who share the same goals, the same methods of communicating, the same genres, and the same lexis (specialized language)" (102). Melzer's definition of discourse community anchors this chapter's exploration of why dinner table and classroom conversations can feel different. This chapter also explores how specialized language (the lexis) works in discourse communities, and how a lexis can change over time and through negotiated participation. Because we all belong to and move into and out of various discourse communities, we'll take up (and slightly modify) Melzer's closing question in his chapter: *What can I add to discourse communities?*

As members of different discourse communities, we *can* and *do* change discourses through the choices we make with language, but the types of language we use (or feel we are able to use) often depend upon power structures, our positionalities, and our type of membership in them. Perhaps, you are a leader in one discourse community and more of a listener in another. Maybe you're louder and more opinionated with your family or friends (aren't we all?) and more quiet or formal in the classroom. At some time, you have probably felt like a novice in one community and an expert in another. No matter what identities we take on across the communities we belong to, we help to shape and change the discourses in them—sometimes to a great extent and sometimes in ways that are hardly noticeable, but that are more powerful than we might think.

Discourse Communities Change Across Time and Through Participation

Melzer's chapter helps us consider the many features that make up a discourse community through an example that analyzes his guitar jam group. Melzer examines this group through John Swales' six characteristics for discourse communities, which include a set of commonly understood community goals, mechanisms of intercommunication, and a specific lexis. Language sits at the center of Swales' characteristics—and language helps us to understand how discourse communities work. But language isn't just speaking; it's also gesture and body language, images, and written text. The ways that we use our language resources in any given discourse community—as speakers and writers—changes depending on the values, common practices, and the lexis, dialect, or vernacular "rules" that we learn and use in them.

Discourse communities are also fluid; they are always changing across time and as participants move in and out of them, though some discourse communities are more fluid than others (we'll discuss this a bit later in this chapter). This means that language expectations are negotiated across time and participation. When I was a high school teacher in the early 2000s, for example, students often appreciated something or someone in their peer group by saying it was *tight*, as in "That movie was *tight*." A few years later, the appreciative term changed to *sick*, as in "Our beach trip was *sick*." But neither of these terms was used in the same ways a decade or so earlier when I was in high school. Back then, pants were *tight* or the dog was *sick*, maybe, but we weren't appreciating either. And because I was the teacher (and not part of the student peer group), it would have been humorous if I told my students "This play we're about to read is *sick*." As you're reading this, there are likely new terms of appreciation you might be using in peer settings—terms that you wouldn't use in other settings or that someone with a different identity could only use ironically or badly. This is just one example that exhibits the ways that languages are always shifting and evolving, and they do so through use, location, and time.

It might seem obvious to say that languages change over time and are used differently across different groups. But take a second to think about how many different groups (or discourse communities) you already belong to. How have you—consciously or not—learned and practiced the expectations of language in each of them? Teams, clubs, campus groups, workplaces, online groups, gaming communities, and undergraduate major programs are all examples of discourse communities you are or likely have been a member of at one time or another. The discourse that is used in and across these groups changes through members' negotiation of language over time. In the following section, we'll test this claim by examining a popular internet meme.

Tracing a Discourse: The LOL Cats and Internet Meme Aesthetic

The term *meme* is derived from the Greek word *memeia* - that which is imitated. A meme is a *genre*, and different memes become dominant in a discourse through retention and repetition. Memes, like language, are a genre we learn and practice through imitation. I'm sure you can think of more than one popular meme, and you might have even designed a few memes yourself. As a textual genre, a meme shows us not only what we were thinking about a particular topic at a moment in time, but also how we applied, negotiated, or resisted language rules in this textual form. As a genre, memes use language and image to become an expression of culture shared by particular groups of people. Any one meme is like a signpost on a giant map of how language is used on the internet. By tracing memes across time and communities, we can explore how rules for language change through participation.

Consider the (now pretty ancient) LOLcat meme (fig. 1).

Figure 1. An image of a small, gray and white kitten standing on its hind legs and looking up at the photographer, with the words "CAN I HAZ" placed at the top of the photo, and "CHEEZBURGER PLZ" at the bottom of the photo.

So, why the cat? Why does the cat ask to *haz* as opposed to *have* a *cheezburger*? What does this meme *mean*? Though we know that cats don't really eat cheeseburgers (or *cheez*burgers), there are literally thousands of cat memes with "haz" in place of "have" in them, including memes of cats asking, "I can haz cat memes?" This genre is culturally known as the LOLcats meme (https://en.wikipedia.org/wiki/Lolcat), and this particular image was made with a meme generator for a burger restaurant (https://tinyurl.com/274akjmh). LOLcats memes are cousins of (or intertextual with) other genres, such as viral cat videos and cute kitten images and gifs—and they are one of the earliest examples of the internet meme.

A function of the LOLcats is that they present us with an archive of early internet aesthetic, a genre where writers designed and posted digitized blasts of communication through images and words, usually for comic effect. LOLcats memes capture and interpret cultural practices at one point in time, and they present us with the expectations for language in this meme-specific genre and discourse. We immediately know this is an LOLcats meme not only because it shows a cat, but because it uses the internet language forms of *plz* and *haz*. The LOLcats memes are an example of how a discourse community uses language, including visual and linguistic patterns to reveal, develop, contribute, or change a cultural practice or to establish a user's membership in the community.

Other discourse communities have taken up the genre of the LOLcat meme to speak internally to their members. In fact, while the first LOLcats memes appeared long before there were meme generator sites, now we can play Minecraft in LOLcat language (https://www.youtube.com/watch?v=Nbgjaoww4Rs). We can also see how specific discourse communities with specialized languages (the lexis) meshed their discourses with the language of the LOLcats, like this example (fig. 2):

Figure 2. A brown cat who has apparently crawled inside of a computer tower pokes its head out, with the words "REDUNDANT VARIABLE CAT IZ IN UR DATASET" placed at the top of the photo, and "BOOSTIN UR R^2" at the bottom of the photo (https://tinyurl.com/mr3fxudy).

Whether you understand the specialized language in this LOLcat meme or not (which uses the lexis of statistics), you can see the LOLcat language conventions of *iz* and *ur*. This meme is also highly representative of the statistics discourse community. It uses the disciplinary terms *redundant variable, dataset,* and *r^2*, and the joke in it makes little sense to those of us outside of its membership.

You might pause here to take a few minutes to do an image search of meme + one of your favorite hobbies, activities, or areas of study to see what comes up. What kinds of community or cultural practices are revealed through the memes you find? How do these memes reveal the language expectations of the community? This same approach can occur by examining the genres and language expectations of college majors, workplaces, groups, or clubs.

So far, I've attempted to show how, across our lifetimes and even in a single day, we move across complex linguistic landscapes. Still, we don't simply close a drawer in our brain when we're done using one discourse and then open another as we move across communities. Regardless of the group we're in at any given moment, our brain wants us to use all of our linguistic resources to communicate and connect with one another, to develop ideas, to create and design and live. As we navigate the expectations of a discourse community, we draw from and creatively adapt our language resources to communicate. The ways that we have learned and experienced language, especially the language(s) or dialects we first learned as children, are *always* present, *always* part of our tool box, no matter what discourse community we are navigating.

At the same time, language is inseparable from power. Sometimes we are asked to perform certain kinds of language to show the worthiness of our membership in a discourse community. Sometimes the way we are asked to perform language is connected to a paycheck or a promotion or a grade. And sometimes we are asked to deny a way that we speak or write. Language is not neutral. While practicing and using a specialized lexis *does* help us to establish membership and identity in the discourse communities we belong to (or want to belong to), it can sometimes feel like we need to hide languages or discourses we know and value. When we make and share a meme on the socials, the stakes aren't as high as they are as when we write for a college course assignment or draft an email to request a raise at our job. As Melzer points out, you may "find yourself struggling a bit with trying to learn the writing conventions of the discourse community of your workplace" (110) or your major or any other specialized group. How, then, do we use (and show the value of) the language resources we already have and, at the same time, how can we practice and learn the language expectations of a specific discourse community?

There Is No Single Story for Writing and Speaking

Consider, once again, the differences between the conversations at the dinner table and the first-year writing classroom. It's unlikely that the conversational rules and language expectations are exactly the same across these two situations. We are consciously (and often unconsciously) aware that there are certain ways to use language (and certain languages) in certain spaces. These ways of knowing highlight the very deep relationships between language, identity, and power.

Through our experiences as readers and writers, especially in school settings where we are required to learn communication and language skills in what is known as "standard English," we tend to internalize beliefs about how language (and English) works. Sometimes this looks like a single story of speaking or developing a belief about how writing "should be done." It also means we have been trained to evaluate others based on their ability or willingness to "do it the way it should be done."

But a focus on standard English (also known as Edited American English in the U.S.) as the achievable and desirable mode of "correct writing" is far too simplified to help us deal with the writing and communication we do in the world every day. The teaching of standard English rarely includes a transparent acknowledgement that requiring it upholds White Western norms and values about "correct" speaking and writing. Mara Lee Grayson speaks to the ways pervasive requirements to use standard English across discourse communities uphold Whiteness and White supremacy in her essay "Writing Toward Racial Literacy": "These so-called rules have been passed down through systems and people, like schooling and teachers, for so long that we might think they're the only way to write" (168). But in fact, "correct" writing and language use—including certain kinds of English—are *constructions* or beliefs; they have become standards because people (often people in power) have made them so. When you take a close look at how language rules function differently across communities, you can see that "correctness" is contingent and flexible.

As Meltzer tells us at the end of his essay, "Discourse community norms can silence and marginalize people, but discourse communities can also be transformed by new members who challenge the goals and assumptions and research methods and genre conventions of the community" (110). How we make certain choices about language is shaped by each discourse community we are part of, by the communicative situations in them and by their norms or "rules" for language—rules that we learn, break, and participate in changing. While language often functions as a gatekeeper, letting some folks into a community while keeping others out, language rules are also always in negotiation—between speaker and listener, and between writer and audience.

Language That Negotiates Discourse Community Expectations: Translanguaging and Code-meshing

Translanguaging and *code-meshing* are two frameworks that can help us see language in negotiation. These frameworks can help us understand our various linguistic resources as we navigate—and potentially challenge or change—the expectations of discourse communities. Translanguaging and code-meshing are especially useful in helping us see the ways that language, identity, and power intersect—and how much linguistic agency we have in the discourse communities that we are (or hope to be) part of.

Translanguaging can be understood in part by looking at the Latin root *trans* (to cross); when we cross or blend languages in order communicate, we are translanguaging. Hybridized cultural languages, such as Spanglish, are examples of how translanguaging works. Examples like *"Actualmente, I will join you,"* or *"Wacha le"* show translanguaging in action. We also commonly see translanguaging in internet speak, like "I *googled* it" or "It was *gr8* to see you." People don't use translanguaging without purpose; rather, we translanguage to help us communicate creatively and accurately with others. When we translanguage, we create and co-construct new meanings for and values about how language works in discourse communities.

While translanguaging blends languages, *code-meshing* occurs when we mesh dialects (or codes) of one language as we speak or write. In English, for example, we might consider *y'all* as a regional term associated with Southern United States dialects. Code-meshing is similar to translanguaging in that when we use it, we are performing a type of membership. If I write in this essay that I hope *y'all* are able to observe or use translanguaging and code-meshing in college, I've meshed the sentence to include a regional southern English dialectical term with the more academic English language I've primarily used to shape it. Yet I am almost sure you've had a teacher that would correct you if you used *y'all* or *gr8* or *actualmente* in an essay or research paper for school; you also probably wouldn't use *sick* or *tight* as an appreciative term in an academic text. In other words, we often consider and do our best to apply the rules of "acceptable" discourse in each situation, and what's "acceptable" is generally the discourse that we recognize as dominant in the community. This is because we understand that many discourse communities, including academic or college-level disciplinary communities, require highly specific forms of language of their members. Meeting these requirements means knowing the right terms (or *lexis*) to use, but also the right kind of English.

But cultivating a sense of how (and how often), as a writer or speaker, you and others can use translanguaging or code-meshing can reveal the negotiated nature of communication in discourse communities. For example, translanguaging and code-meshing in certain communities can be beneficial: these practices can help writers share or create new meanings and knowledge, and they reveal the degree of linguistic flexibility we might have in a discourse community. However, translanguaging and code-meshing can also be risky: by using them, a writer or speaker might fail to meet a discourse community's standards, which could mean losing a job, lower grades, marginalization, or exclusion.

In her well-known essay "How to Tame a Wild Tongue," Gloria Anzaldua reflects on these tensions, including which languages to speak—and when—in relationship to her Chicana identity:

> [B]ecause we internalize how our language has been used against us by the dominant culture, we use our language differences against each other...Even among Chicanas we tend to speak English at parties or conferences. Yet, at the same time, we're afraid the other will think we're *agingadas* because we don't speak Chicano Spanish...There is no one Chicano language just as there is no one Chicano experience. (58)

Like English, as Anzaldua notices, there is no one Chicano language. She notices the ways that the English language has been used to assert dominance, to gatekeep, and to exclude. If Chicano Spanish or *y'all* or *gr8* are all part of a writer's or speaker's linguistic knowledge, what happens when that knowledge is not valued inside a discourse community?

In requiring each member of the discourse community to use (and be fluent in) its discourse (for example, standard English), it stands to reason that *some* members of the discourse community advance more quickly when they perform language the "right" way, while others do not. And because language gatekeeping continues to occur, some folks might believe that having fluency in the dominant discourse is necessary for success. But it's useful to interrogate these claims. How does language gatekeeping work in relationship to membership and power in a discourse community? Whose language is allowed to thrive in the discourse community and whose is not? In one of his many scholarly essays in support of code-meshing, Vershawn Ashanti Young argues against the idea that "prescriptive standard English is all that students need for academic and financial success" (140). Instead, Young argues that

> When we operate as if it's a fact that standard English is what all professionals and academics use, we ignore that real fact that not all successful professionals and academics write in standard English. We ignore the many examples of effective formal writing composed in accents, in varieties of English other than what's considered standard. Further, we ignore that standard English has been and continues to be a contested concept. (144)

When we take a step back and see the various ways we use language in our lives—and how our individual approaches to language are constantly being negotiated across discourse communities, we can see that standard English is a contested concept. A broadly constructed understanding of English asks us to understand and acknowledge that, in the same ways that there are multiple languages and discourses, there are multiple English*es*.

WHAT CAN I ADD TO THE DISCOURSE COMMUNITY?

When it comes to written communication, we can acknowledge translanguaging, code-meshing, and Englishes as *flexible* ways to communicate rather than *right* or *wrong* ways to communicate. Aimee Krall-Lanoue suggests, "If we believe that language is not fixed or static and that it is shifting according to the needs, desires, and interests of users, we must also ask ourselves [...] to critically and intensely read what *is* on the page rather than what *ought* to be on the page" (233-4). This doesn't mean that we shouldn't pay attention to (and probably learn and practice) the codes and expectations of a discourse; rather, it means that we can have a critical awareness of these codes and expectations.

As you attempt different kinds of writing and communication across the discourse communities you'll join (or want to join), you can assess language expectations through a critical lens. In the essay "Beyond Language Difference in Writing: Investigating Complex and Equitable Language Practices," author Cristina Sánchez-Martín suggests that we ask: "[H]ow much space is there for language difference is there in this type of writing? Are the audiences receptive to it? [...] What would happen if I decide to ignore the audience's preferences?" Sánchez-Martín encourages us to "look at the larger situations, ideologies, histories, and conditions that put us, writers, in a position to really be strategically 'linguistically diverse' in our writing on our own terms" (276–77).

While a specific lexis helps establish the boundaries of what makes a discourse community, the specialized language in it can be negotiated and transformed through a type of a balancing act. On one side, members develop and progress in a discourse community as they learn to enact its values and beliefs by writing and speaking in its specialized language and genres. On the other side, members can and do participate in shifting a discourse community's communication practices and values by purposefully making language choices that reflect our hybridized identities, multiple literacies, linguistic backgrounds, and cultural heritages.

Another way to think about the balancing act of negotiating discourse: as the expectations of a discourse community acts upon us, we also act upon it. We change discourse communities by bringing our prior knowledges, especially our social, cultural, linguistic and discoursal knowledges to them. Because we work, live, and write across a range of cultures and communities, we must engage in conscious efforts to think about how attitudes about and practices of writing and communication are negotiated in them. We also might seek to understand, as writers, how, why, and when we alter our writing (or the genres we use) to address the needs of various cultures and communities.

Works Cited

Anzaldúa, Gloria. *Borderlands = La Frontera: The New Mestiza*. Aunt Lute Books, 2007.

Grayson, Mara Lee. "Writing toward Racial Literacy." *Writing Spaces: Readings on Writing, Volume 4*, edited by Dana Lynn Driscoll, Megan Heise, Mary K. Stewart, and Matthew Vetter. Parlor Press, 2021, pp. 166-183.

"Can I Haz Cheezburger Plz?" *The Salted Cracker Sandwich Shop Facebook Page* https://tinyurl.com/274akjmh. Accessed 4 June, 2022.

"I Played Minecraft in the LOLCAT Language." *YouTube*. https://www.youtube.com/watch?v=Nbgjaoww4Rs. Accessed 1 June, 2022.

Krall-Lanoue, Aimee. "'And Yea I'm Venting, but Hey I'm Writing Isn't I': A Translingual Approach to Error in a Multilingual Context." *Literacy as Translingual Practice: Between Communities and Classrooms*, edited by A. Suresh Canagarajah, Routledge, 2013, pp. 228-234.

"Lolcats." *Wikipedia, The Free Encyclopedia*. https://en.wikipedia.org/wiki/Lolcat. Accessed 1 June, 2022.

Melzer, Dan. "Understanding Discourse Communities." *Writing Spaces: Readings on Writing, Volume 3*, edited by Dana Lynn Driscoll, Mary K. Stewart, and Matthew Vetter, Parlor Press, 2020, pp. 100-115.

"Redundant Variable Cat Iz In Ur Data Set." *Keynesian Cat Facebook Page*. https://tinyurl.com/mr3fxudy. Accessed 4 June, 2022.

Sánchez-Martín, Cristina. "Beyond Language Difference in Writing: Investigating Complex and Equitable Language Practices." *Writing Spaces: Readings on Writing, Volume 4*, edited by Dana Lynn Driscoll, Megan Heise, Mary K. Stewart, and Matthew Vetter. Parlor Press, 2021, pp. 269-280.

Young, Vershawn Ashanti. "Keep Code-Meshing." *Literacy as Translingual Practice*, edited by A. Suresh Canagarajah, Routledge, 2013, pp. 139-146.

Teacher Resources for "What Can I Add to Discourse Communities? How Writers Use Code-Meshing and Translanguaging to Negotiate Discourse"

Overview and Teaching Strategies

This essay can be used when teaching students about the concept of discourse community and is appropriate when discussing the ways that discourse communities communicate their goals and values through language expectations, especially via written genres. It might be read alongside Cristina Sánchez-Martín's essay "Beyond Language Difference in Writing: Investigating Complex and Equitable Language Practices" or Mara Lee Grayson's "Writing toward Racial Literacy," both in *Writing Spaces 4* (2022). This essay may also be read as a follow up to Kerry Dirk's text "Navigating Genres" in *Writing Spaces 1* and/or Dan Melzer's essay "Understanding Discourse Communities" in *Writing Spaces 3*.

The claims in this text regarding the characteristics of translanguaging, code-meshing and language as negotiation are presented as companion *and* counterpoint to the discourse community characteristic of *lexis* or specialized language. As students explore discourse communities, including academic disciplines or majors, and as they notice how language expectations establish or uphold goals, values, and beliefs, they can turn to investigating how translanguaging or code-meshing appears or might be part of negotiating discourse community expectations. Students might analyze: 1) the extent to which a specific discourse community values monolingual and/or multilingual language practices; 2) the potentialities of translingualism and/or code-meshing as tools to challenge the dominant language practices of the discourse communities in which they are (or want to be) members; 3) the possible risks and benefits of using these practices in relationship to their membership in a given discourse community. In addition to the questions for discussion for students shared below, instructors might consider specific questions in the context of this essay for their own teaching, such as:

- How can writing instructors consider concepts like monolingualism, Whiteness and/or White language supremacy, in our teaching of writing, or of discourse community as a concept?

- How can instructors explore or allow translingual and/or code-meshing practices in students' language work (talk or text) as a viable and visible way to promote linguistic justice?

Questions, Activities and Prompts for Discussion

1. Find and evaluate a meme as representative of a discourse community.
   - Justify the extent to which the meme is or is not representative of a particular discourse community and explain your rationale.
   - Analyze language expectations of the discourse community by comparing the meme to another genre from the discourse community.
   - Evaluate the meme use (if present) of translanguaging or code-meshing. If no translanguaging or code-meshing is present, evaluate how well the meme adheres to its discourse community's language expectations.
2. Design a meme for a particular discourse community using its lexis *and* integrating translanguaging or code-meshing practices as appropriate to your linguistic resources. Be respectful and do not appropriate another cultural language practice or dialect that is not your own.
3. Consider your language background and history. To what extent has your language use and literacy changed through your participation in a specific discourse community? If you are/are not a monolingual English speaker, for example, how does this interact with your membership in and access to the discourse communities where standard English is expected?
4. Why do we use the English*es* that we do in particular discourse communities? How is audience a key factor for our communication choices?
5. How are English*es* different across the communities where you am a member and when does it really matter what language choices you make in the discourse community?

6. Choose a discourse community that you are a member of—or that you want to join. Analyze the language expectations of this discourse community by considering the following questions:
    o What would it look like for you or others to utilize linguistic resources, such as the dialects or language styles a person feels most comfortable with, in this community? What are the risks and benefits of doing so?
    o What do you notice about language expectations and which languages or dialects are and are not valued in this discourse communities?
    o What are the benefits or challenges of using translanguaging and/or code-meshing in this community? When are the stakes high and where are they low?
7. How can we better understand the choices people make as writers and speakers and learn to value diverse and interesting language practices?

7 Environmental Justice: Writing Urban Spaces

Mattius Rischard

Overview

Our sense of place not only affects our perspective, but also the way in which we represent our home to others.[1] It is vital that students learn to write about spaces that civically engage them on a personal level. The structural elements of the built environment that contribute to pollution, dilapidated housing, food and housing insecurity, and natural catastrophe are often ignored in favor of focusing on the violent results of these problems; yet, from downtown arboretums to rooftop hydroponics, undergraduates have sought to argue for compelling solutions through an urban ecology lens for environmental justice. Urban ecology promotes resilient and sustainable urban spaces where humans and nature coexist. When argued in the right way, it can help decrease air and water pollution while enabling new methods of food production, more efficient transportation, and improved housing. This chapter offers students a method of activist writing for building urban environmental justice arguments in genres of papers often expected of college writing courses, such as the personal narrative and the rhetorical analysis. It also gives examples of what environmental rhetoric can look like in the city by highlighting thematic patterns in student essays.

Part I: Introduction

You wake up one morning, and your sink suddenly vomits up a corrosive sludge as you turn it on, while the power simultaneously goes out. What is your plan? Do you tell the landlord? Call a plumber

---

1. This work is licensed under the Creative Commons Attribution-NonCommercial-NoDerivatives 4.0 International License (CC BY-NC-ND 4.0) and is subject to the Writing Spaces Terms of Use. To view a copy of this license, visit http://creativecommons.org/licenses/by-nc-nd/4.0/, email info@creativecommons.org, or send a letter to Creative Commons, PO Box 1866, Mountain View, CA 94042, USA. To view the Writing Spaces Terms of Use, visit http://writingspaces.org/terms-of-use.

or electrician? Do you need first responders? A lawyer? How much money or tools or parts will you need? Do you have insurance? Who or what is causing this crisis, and how do you make it stop?

Many readers could probably dismiss this question as being outside the realm of possibilities in their lives: maybe you have a brand new home, maybe your loved ones would handle it, or maybe you don't have a sink to begin with. Regardless, there are real living and working environments in cities where the idea of being "urban" might not seem compatible with "environmentalist" rhetoric for constructing arguments or narratives about urban spaces and crises, being that cities are rarely thought of as belonging to "the environment." Donna Haraway, Greg Gerrard, Cronon, McKibben, and other post-human and ecocritical scholars have decried the way in which human civilizations are historically conceptualized as relying upon the unbuilt environment or "wilderness," and yet they are also imagined as separate from that wilderness, given that the wilderness is defined by the lack human settlements. The problem with framing environmentalism as only concerned with wilderness is that it conceals the structural elements of the *built* environment that contribute to pollution, dilapidated housing, food insecurity, and natural catastrophe, in favor of focusing on their violent results, like inner-city crime or poor educational outcomes. We tend to conceptually separate wilderness from manufactured spaces, but it is not necessary to do so; even worse, it harms both the inhabitants of wilderness and built communities. Just as the natural environment must sustain life, human dwellings must also support their inhabitants within the constraints of the natural environment. But the only way to ensure that our dwellings and other places of human life continue to sustain it is if you can get others to care about them too.

However, in a place as diverse as the American city, the invisibility of environmental concerns in select spaces limits the impact of community advocacy. These spaces, from the individual alleys and kitchens to the systems of ghettos and subways, are selectively avoided by the media and the public, creating the perception of them as underwhelming and dangerous spaces that are unworthy of public attention, except in moments of crisis.

In responding to urban issues with new forms of human-environmental interaction that promote community agency and equity, students use the rhetoric of space to lay out the geography of a communicative event, such as the reporting around a chemical spill or the leveling of a slum. Like all landscapes, a rhetoric of spaces may detail both the cultural and material arrangement of people and objects, both synthetic and organic, to lay out the significance of a location. Developing a rhetoric of space in your work as a critical-thinking college student and citizen of our democracy helps you learn to inscribe a sense of meaning and identity into the places in which you live and work. Being capable of representing your community in new ways also helps you to advocate for those places and critique its competing representations, such as those in the media that you find to be flawed in some way. In writing and reading each other's experiences of the streets in which we live, we can understand the broader forces shaping differences and similarities in experience and formulate even larger networks in resolving the issues presented to the community.

Part II: The SHOWED Method

Communicating effectively is a crucial skill for solving wide-scale problems in something as complex as an urban environment. General techniques for this kind of writing have been previously addressed in "Public Writing for Social Change," from *Writing Spaces, Vol. 4*. Yet regardless of whether you are tasked with writing in an analytic or narrative mode, you will need to articulate your specific ecological problem and its relevance to the reader in order to mobilize them in some way towards a solution.

Urban ecologists and public health officials around the world have used the SHOWED method to conceptualize their writing topics through providing opportunities to people "who seldom have access to those who make decisions over their lives" (Wang et al. 1391) to visually document their environment. It is a practice of sending advocates into their own communities of interest to photograph, draw, describe, or collect other depictions of the realities they perceive. SHOWED itself is an acronym rooted in the teaching philosophy of critical theorist Paolo Freire's *Pedagogy of the Oppressed* (1970) and stands for a set of research questions that one poses in response to the problematic imagery collected from an environment. From these questions, a logical sequence to the sections or paragraphs of the analysis or narrative becomes possible in framing an urban problem and highlighting the environmental solution. I invite you to draw upon common themes from Section III to "fill in" the components of the SHOWED schema below:

- S: What do you SEE here?
- H: HOW is it problematic?
- O: How does the problem relate to OUR lives?
- W: WHY does this issue exist?
- E: How do people become EMPOWERED in response to the issue?
- D: What do we DO about it?

There are obviously more questions that one could ask about the problem. For example, let's say your issue is income inequality in your neighborhood leading to evictions during the COVID pandemic. Obviously, access to safe shelter is a key tenet of environmental justice. One aspect of this issue is the way that poor and rich people talk about each other in the neighborhoods to decide who should live where. Does your community think that the government should raise taxes on the rich to pay for eviction deferrals? Should universal basic income pay for rent? You use the SHOWED method to narrow down an issue to a specific topic and begin to generate explanations. The way in which one responds and the evidence they choose to use is dependent upon genre: i.e., narrative or analysis.

Using SHOWED for Analysis

A student of mine was concerned about the condition of public schools and institutions in his North Philly neighborhood. He began with an image from Google Streetview, which the *Philly Voice* published to depict the rowhouse displays outside of North Philadelphia's Urban Crisis Response Center, and Streetview images of an entry point to the Northeastern suburbs used in the same local news source. Juxtaposing the conditions of streets, schools, and housing in a part of North Philly (also popularly known as "the Badlands") with the relatively affluent parts of nearby Northeast Philadelphia, he was able to use the SHOWED method to make his problem clearer in analysis (see reprinted images below). Essentially, he wanted to highlight that the selective visibility of marginal spaces such as "the Badlands" is part of defining them as ghettos that are selectively avoided by the media and constituted as unworthy of public attention, except in moments of crisis. Through its own environmental neglect, the city is able to "blame the victims" for creating the Badlands, while also neglecting to improve their public services, from school quality to sanitation.

Figure 1: Rowhouse displays outside of North Philadelphia's Urban Crisis Response Center (Source: Dominic McNeal)

Figure 2: Northeastern Philadelphia Rowhouses (Source: Dominic McNeal)

This student's analysis had to back up his position with evidence. If you were to apply the SHOWED questions to his imagery, how would you answer them, and what kind of evidence would the analysis need? In Fig. 1, we see that there is a crowded set of partially inhabited, ivy-covered rowhouses graffitied with the statement "I WANT TO LIVE" next to a coffin, which is also labelled with a sign claiming "All Lives Matter." In Fig. 2, we see newer rowhouses further back from the street, with lawns and walkways to the backyards, and ample parking. We cannot problematize these pictures without understanding how they are connected: while merely a few blocks apart, these spaces have very different socioeconomic, racial, and cultural groups, who either directly profit or suffer from the segregation of their communities and the way in which their local taxes fund local services. Since property taxes are used to fund a good portion of school budgets, for instance, one community has a much higher-performing school than the other because a poorer community will inevitably have lower-value properties on which to pay taxes, and because a good deal of rentiers whom make up low-income groups will not be paying property taxes, such that the schools in their region will have less resources to work with.

To explain why the issue exists, you must then posit a theory. In this student example, he argued that these regions are not just physical places that become sites of struggle over human rights in urban areas. In highlighting urban "pathologies" to address an issue rather than its effects on a community, the media appeals to an audience to imagine the impoverished culture of the ghettoized urban folk as non-deserving of political rights. This mass media-dominated narrative appeals to the suburban ideology of what urban "decay" should "look like" to justify the continuation of its existence.

How do you wrap up analysis in a satisfying way? The student wanted to begin his conclusion by explaining the first steps towards empowerment that a community can take, before ending with a call to action (i.e., the "E" and "D" in SHOWED). He pointed out that hyper-invisibility of ghettoized communities is dependent on outside evaluations that try to limit the community's power to define itself and leverage action to improve its environmental conditions. By redefining the community's limitations as assets and training individuals to highlight the inequities created by the urban environment, he showed that it was possible to empower community advocates to voice their public concerns. For instance, he was able to use his research into the school district achievement scores for the largest North and Northeast Philadelphia public schools, producing a graph that he was able to include in his paper showing the differences in math and English proficiency and AP enrollment (see below). This kind of evidence helps to support community activists in presentations to stakeholders, such as school district officials or politicians, where the problem needs to be succinctly conceptualized.

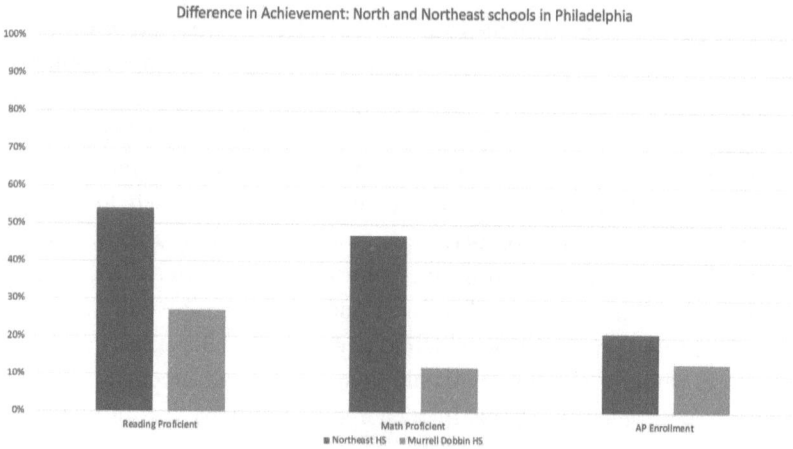

Figure 3: A Student Example of a Graph for Problematizing the School Environments in Philadelphia (Source: Dominic McNeal)

But more literate eyes on the street and more education in the community only serve the causes of ecological sustainability if they are informed by environmental initiatives in cities. For instance, one student has recommended that campus arboretums, already a hallmark feature of many flagship universities, be extended via public-private partnerships to increase their urban foot traffic as well as their visibility as a site of biological research. She even proved, using local press, that people were commenting and calling in since the 1980s to use the local campus arboretum to entertain tourists and visiting relatives, as a way to promote its expansion. Another student started a coalition of rock climbing enthusiasts with the local Forest Service to create cleanup sites at nearby bouldering and rock climbing sites that were hard to reach without training, and had become defaced by heavy traffic in recent years. Through their careful study of the problem, students have produced a variety of creative responses to environmental issues facing their cities that are not only effective, but also fairly viable with relatively few resources.

Using SHOWED for Narrative

The narrative style of writing is distinct from genres of analytic prose for many reasons, but these formal differences are due to the fact that they address a unique rhetorical purpose: analysis takes information apart in order to highlight new insights from the topic, while narrative synthesizes information into a story-like format with a beginning, middle, and end. How do you make your story meaningful in relation to the details of the environment that shapes your needs and wants? If one is, for instance, a female member of an immigrant community that only has access to rudimentary medical care in her area, her narrative of experiencing this disparity is evidence enough for the SHOWED method to help articulate the problem in an alternative mode. A student stated in her personal narrative that "[i]f you ever ask a woman if she's felt dismissed and discriminated against at the doctor's, it is more likely she'll say yes than no." (Casarez 2). Why not ask her what happened, then? We can learn to identify the problem just as easily through her story as we can through rhetorical analysis of evidence from other sources.

The introduction sentence still involves giving an overview of the community issue—in the student's instance, discrimination and low-quality healthcare spaces resulting in limited access to services for vulnerable communities of people. However, from this point the narrative essay can include paragraphs addressing the SHOWED components in any particular order that serves the plot and keep the reader interested in the issue through your anecdote. The student richly describes what she sees when commuting with her mother to see her grandmother at home and in the hospital, due to diabetes and dementia-related complications. Traversing her hometown to the outskirts near the Mexican border, she comments that it feels like moving from the "second to the third world," and that an insurmountable set of socioeconomic conditions make it difficult to bring quality care into the border town environment. Despite the beauty of the sunsets and the "cool air drying her face" on the long drives, the periods of "empty" and "abandoned" lots and buildings remind her that "[t]here are millions of lives that are lost due to health complications that could have easily been treated, but the lack of medical care [...] has caused unnecessary disparities and deaths." (Casarez 3).

She then explains that this problem relates to our lives because many patients suffer not so much from their disease as from an environment plagued by a lack of adequate medical attention and supplies. Despite the pain and suffering she witnesses and vividly describes, she realizes that "the longevity of [her] great-grandmother's life was most likely cut short due to the fact that medical attention was not nearly as comparable as that of the attention in first world countries." (Casarez 4). A border had separated the community across generational lines, and it taught the author that certain groups were left vulnerable as a result. However, it also taught her that these issues affected urban environments more broadly.

Just as in the analytic genre, your narratives still require a unifying theory that answers the question as to "why" this issue exists. In continuing with the same student, she theorized early on that "In many underdeveloped countries, education is not nearly as good as the education here in the States, and I would love to spread my knowledge and support." (Casarez 4). This awareness becomes a motivating factor in studying medicine herself. More specifically, she also implies that her grandmother's lack of adequate dementia care is a larger problem because "in most countries neurological disorders are often treated last, for many people are ignorant to them." (Casarez 4). Thus, she is able to move into the final sections of her reflection upon the experience by explaining the consequences of ignoring the problem of a lack of access to care for chronic and debilitating disease. She proposes that these medically disenfranchised communities can become empowered by the organization of larger numbers of minority doctors and funding for their education, especially if it is earmarked for doctors intending to return to serve in their communities post-graduation.

Her call to action involves leading by example, because the narrative itself is oriented towards reflecting upon what her experience can teach her (and, by extension, the reader). While she wants to study neuroscience specifically, she refers to the narrative as the reason why she hopes "to aid in research focused on neurological disorders. Alongside that, [she] really wants to help families like mine down in Mexico. [She] wanted to help people receive treatment to prevent stories like my grandmothers." (Casarez 5). While she welcomes more doctors willing to do this work with "disadvantaged people here in Arizona, I believe that my help would prove significantly more beneficial in Mexico" (Casarez 5) where inequities in healthcare are even more exaggerated. The conclusion returns to the issue and again emphasizes the need to address the problem or mystery, but it is also her place to leave the audience with a strong impression of the need for her solution and how it can ease the problem. Narratives are not merely justifications for solving a problem by describing the environment at hand; they can be a form of knowledge in themselves, or a lesson on how we can protect and improve upon that environment. Students have written about their experiences, such as personal health crises, attending rallies, or road cleanups, where subjective experience can yield valuable information.

Part III: Urban Environmental Themes for Approaching Your Essay

Common themes of the urban ecology framework that students can frequently address include 1) confronting benign neglect of urban environments, 2) desegregation of urban environments, 3) highlighting and responding to pollutants or natural catastrophes/climate change, 4) reframing gentrification as urban recolonization, and 5) enhancing accessibility to urban environments. Each theme is merely a conceptual grouping of the most common patterns identified in student writing, but they nevertheless have a significant history and impact on public policy and our cultural practices. In each section, readers can learn about the significance, applications, and popular examples of the theme before moving on to learn about ways other students have employed them in their assignments.

Urban Segregation: Where it all Started

Segregation, be it religious, ethnic, racial, or otherwise, has not only a cultural impact, but also an environmental one as well. It can produce material damage to the living conditions of the more vulnerable groups in a society, as well as require forms of policing to separate people that can damage the environment itself. However, individual student advocates and popular environmental movements have worked to highlight the injustices of systems that rely upon segregation. Common student topics have included school district funding inequalities, policing/ICE practices, political gerrymandering, the construction of gated communities, housing deficits, the neglect of public projects, and the history of mortgage redlining in their area. These are only some of the possible issues you might address, but beginning from one of these topics can serve as a lens into the significant cultural differences in signage, language, architecture, and types of institutions that form the human ecology of segregated areas.

In *Barrio Anita,* an historic Mexican neighborhood near our university in Tucson, for instance, it was the ethnographic research from the students' historical analysis and resulting artworks that contributed to the continuing success of the *Barrio Stories* project and fundraiser, which is aimed at preserving historic neighborhoods from being bulldozed. Indeed, you can consult the *Barrio Stories* Project online (http://www.barriostories.org/barrio-anita/), where it has been hosted as a contemporary digital archive since 2018, to learn more about the specific ways in which communities are collaborating to promote the equitable inclusion of their neighborhood in the city environment. Working with Anita residents looking to reestablish an official neighborhood association, project artists designed the culminating event as a way to organize collaboration for addressing growing environmental issues, such as poor drainage in the face of flooding, the dereliction of historic housing and schools, and lack of serviceable public roads.

Why is segregation so important to study in the context of urban ecology? Because urban authorities attempt to exert individual control through division and classification (who, where, and what someone is), there will inevitably emerge a hierarchy of spaces in which some communities are more or less environmentally disposable for the sake of industry and economy. Through division and representation, often inequitably, States turn portions of cities into thriving cultural centers and commercial zones, while relegating dangerous industries, violent crime, and public housing to other areas.

Differential Exposure to Pollutants or Catastrophes: A Bayou Tale

Hurricane Katrina famously demolished large swaths of New Orleans, leading to starvation, dehydration, and death among those trapped in their attics and on their roofs, turning the majority-Black 9th Ward into a swamp and the majority-White Chalmette into an oil spill. The streets had not even been drained before the Whites in Chalmette, fearing the takeover of their enclave by outside investors and non-White tenants, attempted to legislate a 2006 city ordinance requiring that owners rent their property to blood relatives. This legal move sought to protect the racial makeup of the community, but it did nothing to rebuild the city or the broken levees (Wise 12). Just a bit further upriver, in another majority-Black and working-class area of the bayou, the petroleum refineries financing the Louisiana state and city budgets were simultaneously poisoning the communities now popularly known as "Cancer Alley" (Baurick et al.). Media and research over the last few decades revealed the extent to which the petrochemical corridor between Baton Rouge and New Orleans have adversely exposed working class minorities to pollutants, in addition to catastrophes like Katrina. Surveying the petroleum plants, researchers found that they only hired "between 4.9% and 19.4% African Americans" (Berry 3), which is very low relative to the surrounding population. Thus, the manufacturing plants in Cancer Alley poisoned African American people while simultaneously excluding their communities from job opportunities.

Segregation on the Lower Mississippi from St. John's Parish to St. Bernard's Parish has left minority groups vulnerable to pollution and environmental disaster, but it is not a phenomenon unique to the South. Students can apply the notion of environmental racism and injustice to a variety of topics that help highlight the multiple mechanisms whereby legal and social practices subordinate the needs of environmentally vulnerable communities to global economic interests. Questions you might ask to identify topics related to your own community might include: where are carcinogens concentrated? Where are they spreading? Where are nuclear waste facilities, heavy metal processing sites and toxic chemicals, such as those in Cancer Alley? What might we suggest for the target audience to respond to climate change, natural disasters, and manmade pollution in their city spaces? Shall they coordinate harbor cleanup proposals, carbon tax proposals? A letter-writing campaign to improve public housing and homeless shelters around your university in response to intensifying climate conditions?

BENIGN NEGLECT AND THE DENIAL OF SERVICES

How does a community become vulnerable to catastrophes like the Katrina in the first place? What makes a community transform into the ghetto as it is recognized on TV? It is not a self-imposed process of destroying one's own home; rather, some spaces are targeted for benign neglect and the denial of public and private services by the larger political economy of the city. This "benign neglect" (69) is a term used in a 1970 government memo by Daniel P. Moynihan, LBJ's Secretary of Labor who would later become Nixon's Advisor on Urban Affairs, to describe his strategy for hollowing out the culture of an area through the defunding of public services, and a simultaneous crackdown on crime. This policy shift resulted in the planned shrinkage, intentional dereliction, and the knowing deprivation of basic services in American inner cities since the end of the Civil Rights Era.

So, how have students reimagine and redefine ghettoes, such that their narratives and analyses capture the problems confronting their communities without giving policymakers rhetorical opportunities to blame the vulnerable, and leave them in "benign neglect?" With topics such as food deserts, water and electric outages, the lack of transit, and police brutality, students have been able to compare the ways in which certain communities are systemically exposed to both more violent policing and crime, a relative lack of healthy food, a relatively slow reaction time for first responders or city workers, and more blackouts, sewage spills, and plumbing issues, than the surrounding regions. Using this information, you can make a significant case for reframing these problems as opportunities for empowerment. From attending and recording a narrative of the goings-on at school district budget meetings to analyzing urban rezoning proposals, you can produce creative solutions to benign neglect that demanded accountability from their municipality while also highlighting opportunities for collective agency.

Gentrification as Urban Recolonization

Urban reinvestment through gentrification is often seen in urban ecology as a kind of "colonizing" the city through opportunistic outsiders. The central concern of both scholars and activists is that gentrification is defined not by enhancing or refining the community inhabiting an area, but by wealthier people moving in, improving housing, and attracting new businesses, typically displacing current inhabitants in the process. In my own walks in downtown Tucson, I have followed the Tucson streetcar development quite closely. While it started as a gaping ditch in the middle of downtown's historic streets, it slowly grew into a bustling cornerstone of pedestrian commerce. New, flashy buildings went up on street corners where dilapidated lofts or brick warehouses had stood. Gone were so many of the homeless, the graffiti and the murals. But so too went businesses that had served those neighborhoods and Barrios for generations. Cafes and community centers were bought out by fancy restaurateurs and high-end art galleries. Microbreweries and gastropubs replaced corner stores and local bars, and many historic homes started to disappear behind the imposing concrete-and-glass of the new condos and apartments.

But in order to interrogate this "colonizing" aspect of gentrification in your work, you must ask the questions: why do people need to leave their neighborhood as it is improved? If a city is looking to improve an area, why not empower those who already have a stake in occupying it, rather than prioritizing those who already have the resources to move where they please? And how might a city do so? A good example of a place to start might be the Gary, IN "Art Archive + Guide" (https://www.destination-gary.com/gary-art-archive-guide), which presently contains over 194 documented installations and community initiatives aimed at neighborhood renovation that address structural decay and environmental degradation without displacing its inhabitants. it is a living archive representing a diverse range of creative contributions seen in one of the nation's most prosperous 20th Century Steel Towns, which has in more recent years become emblematic of white flight, crime, and pollution. It also recognizes the many ways of art-making and place-making. Mapping and documenting new, old, and lost temporary, semi-permanent, and permanent artworks that enhance the buildings, storefronts, and historic sites of Gary will be an ongoing archival project that can serve as a model for other cities to revitalize their environmental image without sacrificing their culture.

ACCESSIBILITY TO URBAN ENVIRONMENTS

Your sensory experience is your first set of ecological instruments. Trust your senses in the environment, and your topic can arise from a variety of subjective experiences that allow you to identify the material and immaterial borders that make spaces harder or easier—even painful or pleasant—to pass through and access. Of course, there are examples of spaces that are segregated according to handicap access for the deaf and blind or physically disabled, but also the way in which buildings and transit are structured around gendered norms in bathroom design. An older building on campus, for instance, only had one bathroom at each floor in the stairwell. Was this because they had gender-neutral bathrooms in Tucson before the World Wars, or more likely because there were primarily white males at the universities at the beginning of the 20th Century? Other students also highlighted certain spatial practices that are permitted or forbidden according to patriarchal norms of conduct, such as the proper places to breastfeed, or dress cis-gendered. By contrast, it is interesting to think of places where women or children in general are excluded in the design of campus and workplace environments.

In order to help you understand how to approach this theme, you might study the architecture of an older campus building: what kind of experience does it encourage, and what does it restrict or ignore? You might notice that there is a concentration of flowers and trees right at the entrance as a way to invite the walker in. You might notice that there is not brail on the signs, or that the hallways or bathroom stalls might be too narrow to accommodate a wheelchair. I once had a student who commented on the pleasant fragrance upon entering a courtyard garden. She was interrupted by another, who claimed upon entering the garden that "it smelled like shit" because he had to take the wheelchair ramp, which was only accessible behind a putrid dumpster. This experience taught all of us that, through the five senses, there are limitless ways to positively and negatively experience a space or how to access it. Who did or did not have power over designing it thus sets the norm of the environment, determining who will be able to access it, and how they should do so.

Part IV: Conclusion

Lots of first year writing assignments fall into narrative and analytical genres of essay-writing. Whether you are assigned a genre research project, a rhetorical analysis, or a personal literacy reflection, they fall into two general categories of approach: one is either telling a story, or breaking down an object of study. It should therefore be noted that writing in the narrative as opposed to the analytic genre typically requires a different set of skills. One typically reads a novel and a dishwasher self-help-manual with different intentions in mind, and thus the texts have differing arrangements.

But let us think of these genres in terms of their tactical relationship to representing an urban environment: obviously, narrative tells a story with a plot, sensory detail, dialogue, and concrete imagery that allows the reader to experience a space. Rhetorical analysis uses a claim, topics or themes of approach, and components that are classifiable in their character or relation to each other in order to support the thesis about the space. They enable you to do different, but no less important, actions for your community. On the one hand, narratives should "grip" the reader with what it "feels" like to be in such a space, or to understand how it is to live in that space through its representation. On the other, analysis allows you to "look back" at the representations of your community, or at those of others, and reflect upon how they are emphasized in their portrayals. The former allows you to move a readership to action based upon a story, the latter protects the community from the biases of a depiction by explaining the biases for the reader.

From automated cleanup vehicles to carbon taxes, you can join other students in advocating for a better world in which you can actually see a future for on this planet. We do not have to do away with cities altogether in order to make our environments livable again—nor should we. While they are imperfect, cities still represent the greatest attempt at human collectivity in our social history. We just need to reimagine the ultimate function of our collectivizing, and our methods of sustaining it.

Works Cited

Berry, Gregory. "Organizing against Multinational Corporate Power in Cancer Alley: The Activist Community as Primary Stakeholder." *Organization and Environment*, vol. 16, no. 1, 2003, pp. 3-33. https://doi.org/10.1177/108602660225

Baurick, Tristan, et al. "Welcome to 'Cancer Alley,' Where Toxic Air Is About to Get Worse." *ProPublica,* 30 Oct. 2019. https://www.propublica.org/article/welcome-to-cancer-alley-where-toxic-air-is-about-to-get-worse

Casarez, Selina. "Medicine without Borders: Personal Narrative." 4 Sept. 2019. English 109, University of Arizona, student paper.
Freire, Paolo. *Pedagogy of the Oppressed*. New York: Continuum Press, 1996.
McNeal, Dominic. "School Inequality in North/East Philly." 3 Jul. 2017. English 101, University of Arizona, student paper.
Moynihan, Daniel Patrick. *The Negro Family: The Case for National Action*. US Government Printing Office, 1965.
—. "Text of the Moynihan Memorandum on the Status of the Negroes." *New York Times*, 1 March 1970, p. 69.
Wang, Caroline, Mary Ann Burris, and Xiang Yue Ping. "Chinese Village Women as Visual Anthropologists: A Participatory Approach to Reaching Policymakers." *Social Science & Medicine*, vol. 42, no. 10, 1996, pp. 1391-1400. https://doi.org/10.1016/0277-9536(95)00287-1
Wise, Tim. "The Pathology of Privilege: Racism, White Denial & the Costs of Inequality." *Media Education Foundation*, 2008. https://www.mediaed.org/transcripts/Tim-Wise-On-White-Privilege-Transcript.pdf

Teacher Resources for "Understanding Environmental Justice: Writing Urban Spaces"

Overview and Teaching Strategies

Maintaining a healthy democracy requires a literate citizenry capable of articulating the significance of their sociopolitical environment based upon a rhetorically compelling explanation of the issues confronting their local context. Therefore, it is vital that students learn to write about spaces that civically engage them on a personal level; over the past three semesters of gathering feedback on my teaching social justice and urban studies in first-year writing courses, students have voiced this civic interest towards writing about environmentalist themes related to their local spaces that can be tied to social justice discourses more broadly. Their lived spaces are overwhelmingly urban, necessitating a rhetorical framework that addresses common environmental themes observed in built environments (i.e., cities) to fit student interests while also developing a method for scaffolding their ability to research and write on their selected issue using critical awareness of the sociopolitical context that gives rise to that issue.

This chapter can be taught as part of a social justice, environmentalist, or urban studies theme, within units that accord with most first year writing curricula, such as personal reflection narratives and rhetorical analyses. Part I highlights why it is important to study rhetorical themes in urban environmental justice, while Part II describes the SHOWED method you can use in class to prompt students to collect spatial data for analysis through the lens of the given topics as a starting point. The essay concludes with a description of the five most common environmental themes under which we can suggest topics for student writing. They are also free to generate new themes grounded in the data, using a deductive approach to answer the questions and formulate a topic.

Students may have to develop different sets of skills to collect and analyze data; however, these can be major-specific and benefit students in their discipline-specific literacy. For analysis of photography and video, graphical representations, and particularly dense or jargon-laden sources on a topic, getting instructor feedback on their questions and the scope of their research is important. Teaching students how to narrate their experience and use it as data for representing environmental injustice is another necessary skill set. Therefore, I have included several activities and reading questions to help teachers map their unit and for students to effectively comprehend and apply the chapter.

DISCUSSION QUESTIONS

1. What are some examples of environmental issues in your own neighborhood that might fit under one of the five themes in the chapter?

2. Typical environmental issues in the city involve a certain region being compared to others in order to establish an exploitative or neglectful relationship between them. Can you think of any other themes besides the five listed that might fit this criteria?

3. Select a picture of your community from the internet that you feel most positively represents it. Now select one that you feel most negatively represents it. Explain the difference between the two and why you selected them, and then answer the SHOWED questions to express a problem that relates the two.

4. Do you think it is more useful to write about an urban environmental issue through the narrative or analytic mode, based on the examples you read about in the chapter? Why?

ACTIVITIES FOR ANALYTICAL OR NARRATIVE WRITING ASSIGNMENTS

1. In a first year writing unit on urban ecology or environmental justice that requires an analytical piece of writing, the first session before engaging in the photovoice methods of the chapter would focus on creating and sharing urban maps around communities of interest. Then, groups or individuals could generate some word clouds about those spaces regarding concepts they connote with it. After that, students can think about how others have represented these places, by doing a quick media or image search for a point of reference. This experience will allow them to triangulate their experience among others who co-construct the meaning of that space. Hopefully, as they begin to gather data (perhaps through the third discussion question attached with the chapter), this ini-

tial discovery will shape their final essay towards synthesizing their own feelings about place with the formal research of others. These opinions might include those of cultural geographers, sociologists, folklorists, autobiographers, urban planners, real estate specialists, politicians, or others who speak on a particular issue affecting the area.

2. For a narrative product, it is more important that students learn the elements of craft, such as plot, rich description, sensory detail, and figurative language, than it for them to spend time developing the kinds of critical data literacy needed for rhetorical analysis. However, it must still relate an urban injustice in such a rhetorically compelling way as to advocate for change. An assignment that could address these two needs would use urban narratives, even canonical literature if the instructor is so inclined, to connect their experiences of environmental injustice with an understanding of various techniques for expressing them. For instance, in the urban novel *Bleak House*, Dickens satirized Mrs. Jellyby for her "telescopic philanthropy" (see Chapter 4, which is titled with this term). She dedicates her life to charity in Africa while her children, neighbors, and local Londoners went unclothed and ill-fed. She could not see that the East Londoners lived in dark and airless tenements that "Africans," whom she so monolithically patronized, would decline flat out. Have the students read the sections on Mrs. Jellyby and then really challenge them by asking how they may see any local analogies in their own experience. At the same time, have students highlight the basics of craft within the passage: instances of dialogue, creative use of punctuation, rich description, sensory details, figurative language, etc.

8 Enabling the Reader

Kefaya Diab

Overview

Students in writing courses often circulate inaccessible and hard-to-read digital documents to their teachers and peers, thus disabling the readers.[1] This essay is inspired by my experience with my students and the activities I design to help them notice the importance of composing readable and accessible digital texts. The essay draws on feminist and critical disability studies that perceive environments and social norms as disabling rather than the body as disabled from within. Therefore, the essay holds the author accountable for designing texts that enable the reader. The essay focuses on the context of student authors and their readers within the class community. The focus serves as a starting point to taking what students learn in class to their targeted audiences in the world. The essay brings examples of digital texts that disable the reader and works some out to show examples that enable the readers. The essay also includes exercises for individual homework and in-class group activities.

Introduction

In many rhetorical histories and traditions, rhetoric and composition serve as tools to enact active citizenship and civic engagement. That means a rhetor, speaker, or writer can utilize rhetoric and composition to act as a good citizen and contribute to positive change in the world. As educated citizens and students of rhetoric and writing, you have the responsibility and capacity to contribute to making the world around you a better place to live. However, I wish to warn you that writing and rhetoric

---

1. This work is licensed under the Creative Commons Attribution-NonCommercial-NoDerivatives 4.0 International License (CC BY-NC-ND 4.0) and is subject to the Writing Spaces Terms of Use. To view a copy of this license, visit http://creativecommons.org/licenses/by-nc-nd/4.0/, email info@creativecommons.org, or send a letter to Creative Commons, PO Box 1866, Mountain View, CA 94042, USA. To view the Writing Spaces Terms of Use, visit http://writingspaces.org/terms-of-use.

could also be tools to contribute to an adverse change in the world. For instance, intentionally or unintentionally writing to a targeted audience can disable them.

Have you ever thought that when you write for targeted readers, you might be disabling them? Perhaps the question makes you uncomfortable as it implies violence committed against the readers. But what does it mean to disable the reader?

Unlike what some might think, I am not implying breaking the reader's arm or leg and leaving them[1] with a disability. Rather, I am talking about writing practices that might disable the reader's access to the author's texts. By access, I mean what the accessibility and usability scholar, Janice Redish, describes as enabling the reader to: "Find what they need," "Understand what they find," and "Use what they understand appropriately" (163). According to Redish then, accessibility includes three levels of:

1. reading the text,
2. comprehending it, and
3. using it to serve the reader's purposes.

Any author can enable or disable the reader's access to their text on these three levels.

To better explain what it means to disable the reader, let me back up a little bit and start with a theory about disability. According to Rosemarie Garland-Thomson who is a feminist disability studies scholar: "disability . . . is not a natural state or corporeal inferiority, inadequacy, excess, or a stroke of misfortune... The ability/disability system produces subjects by differentiating and marking bodies" (5). I understand from Rosemarie Garland-Thomson that disability is not something that happens in the body from within but rather something that is done to it. Disability does not reside in any given human body but is created by the surrounding cultural environment of that body. The theory that Garland-Thomson offers flips the equation. Someone doesn't have a less than ordinary capability in their bodies. Instead, the cultural environments discriminate against someone by limiting their access to and mobility within their environments. The result is privileging particular bodies by marking them as adequate and normal while marking other bodies as inadequate and abnormal.

Of course, environments do not act on their own. Humans contribute to constructing and impacting these environments. Take, for instance, engineers who alter environments following intentional plans. Imagine that engineers in your school designed high steps and long stairs at the entrances of the school buildings. When they do so, engineers decide that only particular bodies would enter the building. The engineers' architecture design excludes a student with a broken leg, a staff member with arthritis in their knees, a toddler visitor with their parent, and a faculty member in a wheelchair. The student, staff member, toddler, and faculty member might be able to make it and enter the building but with much struggle or with the help of others around them. If instead, engineers included a ramp option for entering the school buildings, all the listed above would be able to enter the buildings more easily.

Looking at the situation that way makes disability not something natural within any given body of the student, staff member, toddler, or faculty member but a result of engineers' design decisions. When designing steps rather than a ramp to enter the buildings, engineers exclude particular bodies from entering the buildings and restrain particular bodies' mobility. That exclusion is unjust and discriminative because it privileges certain bodies over others and overlooks the needs of the buildings' visitors. Thus, it disables them.

If you agree with Garland-Thomson on what she forwards as a feminist disability theory, perhaps you still wonder, "how does that theory relate to writing and the writer and disabling the reader?" The answer that I have for you is that, like the engineers who design and construct buildings, writers, including you and I, design and construct digital texts that can disable or enable the readers. Whether through the design or content, we as writers can make our texts difficult to access, read, comprehend, and use appropriately. Such a case compromises our mission as educated citizens and students of rhetoric and composition to make the world a better place for living.

In her article, "What Does It Mean to Move," Christina V. Cedillo, a disability studies scholar, calls for teachers to "contest conditions that create exclusion" by teaching students in ways "that recognize and foreground bodily diversity so that students learn to compose for accessibility and inclusivity" (par. 2). This essay responds to Cedillo's call by inviting you to internalize inclusive practices in your document design and composition. In this essay, I provide several examples of how writers might enable or disable the reader by designing and constructing their digital texts. You might relate to at least some of the situations I present here. However, these examples don't account for all possibilities of disabling/enabling the readers. As ethical writers and designers, we always need to facilitate access to and readability of our texts. Thus, we always need to think of our diverse readers and targeted audiences' needs and not assume that everyone is just like us, able to access what is accessible to us.

Centering the Reader

In any case, educated digital authors need to account for the rhetorical situation within which they compose their texts. A rhetorical situation includes the message, targeted audience, and medium of the message. The medium always imposes particular capabilities and constraints.

Perhaps you have been advised before to organize and format your text well so that you'd appear credible in the eyes of the reader. A principle that seems valid, we all should care about the image that we project about ourselves through our texts' content and design. For instance, you are likely to want a resume to look professional and respond to the job advertisement requirements that you're applying for. Also, you probably want your research paper to be supported by credible resources and evidence beyond your own opinion and formatted consistently according to a particular formatting or citation style. But you need to remember that how the reader perceives the author's image is highly related to how accessible the author's text is. If the text is not accessible to the reader, it doesn't matter how professional it looks or how it is supported by credible evidence. That's simply because the reader can't access it, to begin with. What's the point of a document that the targeted audience cannot read!

To think of examples of how documents might disable the reader, let's look at readability and accessibility from the reader's point of view on the three levels of reading the text, understanding it, and using it appropriately for the reader's purposes. These three levels of readability and accessibility overlap; the following examples will show you how. In what follows, I provide examples of textual content and design that could disable or enable the readers on the readability and accessibility three levels. These examples are inspired by my experience reading hundreds of texts from students each semester.

Enabling the Reader to Read the Text

As Redish indicates, for the text to be accessible, readers should be able to read the text, which is the first level that an author needs to grant to their readers. What follows are two examples that show how the author could enable or disable the readability of their texts.

Enabling the Reader by Font Type and Size

It might be obvious that some font types and sizes could hinder readability and accessibility to the reader. A font that is too small or too decorative will likely make readability harder for the targeted audience. Take, for example, the following textual examples (table 1, which contains figures 1-6). Which text in each row is easier to read?

Table 1

Examples that Demonstrate how Font Type and Size Contribute to Enhancing or Hindering the Readability and Accessibility of Texts from my own Perspective as a Reader. The first column shows the number of each example. The second column shows font types and sizes that make it difficult for me to read and understand the text. The third column shows font types and sizes that enhance the readability of texts to me.

Ex. #	Textual Option #1	Textual Option # 2
1	*What do you think?* Figure 1: The question "What do you think?" written in font type Brush Script Std size 14	What do you think? Figure 2: The question "What do you think?" written in font type Times New Roman size 14
2	What do you think? Figure 3: The question "What do you think?" written in font type Times New Roman size 10	What do you think? Figure 4: The question "What do you think?" written in font type Times New Roman size 14
3	What do you think? Figure 5: The question "What do you think?" written in font type Baguet Script size 12	What do you think? Figure 6: The question "What do you think?" written in font type Comic Sans MS size 12

Notice that the examples in table 1 are given from my own perspective as a reader with particular capabilities. The font type and size might enable or disable me, but I don't represent all variations of readers. For instance, readers with Dyslexia find it hard to distinguish letters and words from each other in written texts, which impacts the time required for reading and comprehending written words (Rello and Baeza-Yates). According to Rello and Baeza-Yates, font types in written texts are critical for readers with Dyslexia. See figure 7 for reading comprehension time required by readers with Dyslexia for 12 font types.

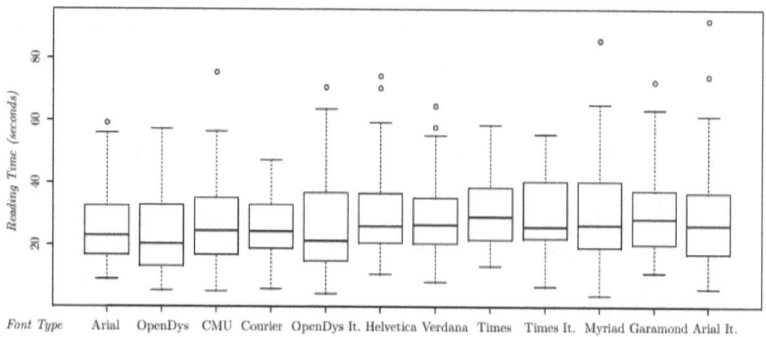

Figure 7. A figure created by Rello and Baeza-Yates shows how 12 font types impact the time required for reading and comprehending texts by readers with Dyslexia. The X axis shows the font types of Arial, OpenDys, CMU, Courier, OpenDys It., Helvetica, Verdana, Times, Times It., Myriad, Garamond, and Arial It, arranged by the readability time, where Arial has the shortest readability time and Arial It. Has the longest readability time. The Y axis shows the time in seconds required to read each font including the median, mean, and standard deviation of the readability time. Thus, the font types with the least time needed for reading, point to better readability. See "Good Fonts for Dyslexia" for more comprehensive study results. (The figure was reproduced for this chapter with the permission of the authors.)

Figure 7 shows the time required to read 12 different fonts by readers diagnosed with Dyslexia. As Rello and Baeza-Yates' study shows, font types such as Arial, OpenDys, and CMU are more readable to readers with Dyslexia than font types of Myriad, Garamond, and Arial Italic, for instance. For us as good authors and citizens, such results mean that we need to consider readers with Dyslexia when composing any text. If we focus on what looks "professional" or "nice" to us, we risk disabling particular readers, such as ones with Dyslexia, from reading and comprehending our texts.

Exercise 1: Conduct research about font types and sizes that facilitate readability to readers with different conditions and capabilities. What would be the implications of your findings on your choice of font size and type selection as a writer?

Enabling the Reader by Email Subject Lines

Like font type and size, subject lines play a role in facilitating the process of reading the email text to grant the reader the first level of accessibility, as indicated by Redish. The purpose of a subject line for an email is to give the reader an idea about the content of the email. Considering that emails often require a response from the reader, a subject line could facilitate or hinder the author's access to a particular email when one has tenths of emails to respond to.

If you ever received an email with no subject line or with a generic subject line such as "Hi," you probably noticed how the lack of a subject line disables you from knowing what the email is about until you open and read it. Your lack of knowledge of the subject might influence whether you open the email, read it, and respond to it in a timely manner. For example, which email from your roommate are you more likely to open right away? An email with the subject line "Hey," or "Our apartment is on fire?" Although not often email subjects would be that tragic, you get the point. A meaningful subject line is essential to motivate the reader to open an email and read it, which constitutes the first level of readability and accessibility.

Let's now imagine that for some reason, in the future you needed to find a particular email in your mailbox. How would you search for it without having a meaningful subject line? You might, of course, find the email by searching for the person who sent it. However, if you forget who sent that particular email or when, or if you received many emails from the same person, what would you do? A teacher who has many students might forget who sent a particular email. Without a meaningful subject line, it might be near impossible to search for and find such an email a few days after it was received by the teacher. Consider also readers who use screen reader software. It would confuse them when the software keeps reading the phrase "no subject line, no subject line" repeatedly. Thus, using a generic subject line or not including a subject line is like not providing a suitable ramp to a building. In that case, both the author and engineer prevent their targeted users from accessing their products easily and equitably.

ENABLING THE READER TO COMPREHEND A TEXT

The second level of readability and accessibility per Redish's definition is comprehending a text, which includes getting the idea of the text and being able to remember it. In what follows, I include an example of how an author could disable or enable the reader to comprehend a text.

Disabling the Readers by Long Paragraph Blocks

Have you ever noticed that textbook texts can be organized under headers, sub-headers, short paragraphs, and lists, making it easier for you to comprehend them? Contrary to that, a text presented as a whole block of many ideas mixing together, making it hard to comprehend and remember. Take, for example, the following writing assignment that I composed for my students:

An Assignment Example

Whether in an educational, social, or work context, authors often need feedback from their peers, teachers, family members, or supervisors to enhance their texts. A genre through which the author could ask for feedback is an author's memo. When explaining the rhetorical situation of a text to the reviewers and indicating the aspects of feedback needed, an author enables the reviewers to comprehend the text and respond to it by providing helpful feedback. To help the reviewers (peers and teachers) to provide you with specific and helpful feedback for your revision, you need to compose an author's memo as follows: Provide the rhetorical situation of your essay (exigency, readers, purpose) to help the reader, understand where you're headed with your essay (5 points). Provide details of the revisions that you implemented so far on the latest draft of the essay (5 points). Provide details about the revisions you intend to do in the future. Provide a prioritized list concerning the feedback you wish to receive from your readers (5 points). Read your classmates' memos and comment and respond to 2 of them using tactful rhetoric by the end of the day of 1/23/2020 (2.5 points for each response, 5 points total). Use a template of a memo—as we learned earlier in the semester—that facilitates readability and accessibility. Use a black font color of size 14 (2 points). Use a font type that facilitates readability (2 points). Make sure to have page numbers at the top or the bottom of the page (2 points). Use headers and sub-headers as designated in MS Word (2 points). Run the accessibility checker feature of MS Word on the memo, and fix anything that's not accessible according to the accessibility checker. Save the memo as a pdf file named "First & Last Name-Personal Author's Memo" and submit it here. (2 points).

The Revised Assignment Example

Now, notice how I revised the design of the assignment text with readability and accessibility in mind. Which do you find easier to comprehend and remember? Is it the original assignment or the revised one?

Introduction

Whether in an educational, social, or work context, authors often need feedback from their peers, teachers, family members, or supervisors to enhance their texts. A genre through which the author could ask for feedback is an author's memo. When explaining the rhetorical situation of a text to the reviewers and indicating the aspects of feedback needed, and author enables the reviewers to comprehend the text and respond to it by providing helpful feedback.

Content Requirements (60-90 minutes)

To help the reviewers (peers and teachers) to provide you with specific and helpful feedback for your revision, you need to compose an author's memo as follows:

1. Provide the rhetorical situation of your essay (exigency, readers, purpose) to help the reader understand where you're headed with your essay. **(5 points)**

2. Provide details of the revisions you implemented so far on the latest draft of the essay. **(5 points)**

3. Provide details about the revisions that you intend to do in the future. Provide a prioritized list concerning the feedback you wish to receive from your readers. **(5 points)**

4. Read your classmates' memos and comment and respond to 2 of them using tactful rhetoric by the end of the day of 1/23/2020. **(2.5 points for each response, 5 points total)**

Readability and Accessibility Requirements (14 points)

Use a template of a memo—as we learned earlier in the semester—that facilitates readability and accessibility.

1. Use a black font color of size 14. **(2 points)**

2. Use a font type that facilitates readability **(2 points)**

3. Make sure to have page numbers at the top or the bottom of the page. **(2 points)**

4. Use headers and sub-headers as designated in MS Word. **(2 points)**

5. Run the accessibility checker feature of MS Word on the memo, and fix anything that's not accessible according to the accessibility checker.

6. Save the memo as a pdf file named "First & Last Name-Personal Author's Memo" and submit it here. **(2 points)**

Do you notice how I revised the text so that it is divided into sections under headers, sub headers, and lists? Do you recognize how I used bold font type to purposefully emphasize particular parts of the text? Although it is initially important that student readers read the assignment word for word, the new revision makes it easier for them to comprehend the text, remember it, and relocate a particular part that they might need at a certain moment.

Exercise 2: Go back to a past text that you composed and revise it into sections using headers, sub-headers, and lists as designated on MS Word. If you don't know how to use headers, sub-headers, and lists in MS Word, consult search engines and YouTube to find many tutorials about that.

Enabling the Reader to Use the Text Appropriately

Using a text purposefully and appropriately comprises the third level of accessibility as indicated by Redish. One of the genres that require action from the readers is what's called a memo. You're likely to use this genre extensively in the workplace. As a starting point to learn about writing accessible memos, I introduce you in the next section to the author's memo, a genre writers use extensively.

Enabling the Reader by Accessible Author's Memo

When an author writes for a particular reader, the author usually has a purpose to accomplish. Likewise, the reader will likely have their own purpose in reading a particular text. In the previous assignment example, the author is supposed to compose a memo to acquire feedback from the reviewer. If the author provided their texts to the reader/reviewer without any explanation about the rhetorical context of the text and the particular feedback needed, the reviewer might provide feedback that doesn't respond to the author's needs. Without enough guidance, when a reviewer is asked to provide feedback, they are likely to look for places in the text that need revision. Because the author and readers' purposes might contradict, it is important for the author to make themselves clear about the feedback that they wish to receive from the reviewer.

Let's see how an author, Priya Samoni[2] responded to the requirement of an author's memo that she submitted with her essay's draft.

Personal Essay Draft #2: Studying in a Foreign Land | Author's Memo

> Notice how the student author provided a full comprehensive title of the memo that included the assignment type, draft #, and title of the essay.

To: Reviewers (Nina, Tory, and Dr. Diab)

From: Priya Samoni

> The genre of a memo requires a clear designation of both the writer and readers.

Dear Nina, Tory, and Dr. Diab,

I'd appreciate your feedback on my essay draft#2. In this memo, I explain the rhetorical situation of my essay so far, the revisions I've implemented on the previous draft, and the feedback I wish to receive from you at this point.

> This tactful introduction helps the readers know what to expect in the rest of the memo and how the memo will be organized. Thus, the author helps the reviewers read and comprehend the essay, which comprises the first and second level of accessibility as indicated by Redish.

Rhetorical Situation (Exigence, Targeted Audience, and Purpose) of the Essay

> Knowing where the author is aiming with their essay helps the reviewers use the text appropriately to provide feedback that would help the reader to achieve their goal.

The issue that I attempt to respond to is the struggle I went through as an international student and non-native English speaker pursuing my bachelor's degree in psychology in the US.

As readers of this essay, I target students and teachers in undergraduate education in the US who might unintentionally contribute to the struggle of international students in the US.

I hope that after reading my essay, the targeted audience would think of their own actions or lack of action that might contribute to foreign students' struggles and amend their behaviors toward foreign students accordingly to help foreign students succeed.

> The author divided the parts of the rhetorical situation (exigency, readers, and purpose) into three separate paragraphs which helps the reader locate each easily, thus read, comprehend, and use the text appropriately.
>
> Another thing that the author could have done is including these in a bulleted point list or under subheadings.

Implemented Revisions

After I received feedback from my peers on the first draft, I cut parts from the essay that made it unfocused, such as the part about my travel from my country to the U.S., and the extended details about my high school in my own country. The cut parts happened in paragraphs 1, 2, 6, 7 in draft #1.

> The author indicates what they done specifically, which helps the reviewers locate the differences between draft #1 and draft#2.
>
> They also explain why they've done their revisions, which helps the reviewers provide feedback that takes in consideration the author's purpose.
>
> By explaining where the revisions happened, the author helps the reviewers locate the revised parts.

Responding to the feedback that I received, I elaborated on my struggle understanding basic aspects in the process of registering for my classes and communicating with my mentors. These details set the stage for the idea that even the smallest things contribute to international students' stressful education experiences. You can see these revisions highlighted in blue color in paragraphs 2, 3, 4.

On my own, I read the essay out loudly, shortened many sentences, and made revisions on word level in some places. I highlighted these in light blue.

Specific Revisions to Implement in the Future

I already spent 6 hours revising draft#1 into draft#2. However, I still feel that my story doesn't flow well as I feel I jump from one topic to another in some places without having enough transition. See, for instance, the topic that ends in paragraph 5 and the one which starts in paragraph 6. I plan to think of ways to reorganize my essay's parts to flow more cohesively.

> Often authors know what needs to be revised but because of time constraint they can't do all the desired revisions at once. By acknowledging what the author already is aware of, the reviewers can focus on giving feedback about something else that the author needs help with. In that case, the author's text enables the reviewers to use the text appropriately.

Prioritized Feedback

What I would appreciate your help with at this time are:

> The author specifically helps the reviewers understand what the author needs help with.

1. How to make better connections between the various incidents that I show in my essay so that they don't sound like a list of incidents but rather a cohesive essay.

2. I am struggling with the conclusion and am not sure what to do there. It seems to me that repeating the main points in my essay might be boring. How could I highlight the main purpose of my essay without saying, "this is the purpose of my essay"?

3. Any other suggestions you might have would be great because I am sure I couldn't capture all the weaknesses in my essay.

> The author allows the reviewers to provide feedback from their perspective and in that way the author would receive a comprehensive feedback that covers both the author and reviewers' purposes.

Thank you in advance for your help. I am looking forward to receiving and discussing your feedback next week.

Do you notice how the memo text and design help the reviewers read and comprehend the memo? Do you notice how the memo's specificity helps the readers read and understand the essay and helps them provide meaningful feedback to the author? Notice how the student in this example responded to the teacher's expectations. The student used a readable and accessible template and responded to the memo assignment requirements by sorting out the contents under subheadings and list, when necessary, for instance.

Exercise 3: If you composed any author's memos in the past, check out at least one of them. Does it comply with the readability and accessibility guidelines that are indicated in this article? If not, what could you do to enhance the readability and accessibility of your memo? If you have never submitted an author's memo with a draft before, try to do so next time you submit a draft, and ask the reviewers whether the memo helped them provide you with meaningful feedback.

Accessibility Checkers

The previous examples of enabling and disabling texts aim to give you a place to start from. Once you compose a text, it is a good idea to check it against the readability and accessibility guidelines provided in some software. For instance, Moodle, Canvas, M.S. Word, and Acrobat Reader software all have built-in accessibility checkers that give you details about what needs to be enhanced to make your texts more accessible. However, you should be careful not to fully rely on these checkers as they can miss some necessary aspects of readability and accessibility.

Exercise 4: Search the internet for tutorials about accessibility checkers in M.S. Word and Acrobat Reader. Follow the instructions in the tutorials to check the readability and accessibility of M.S. Word or PDF documents on your computer. Follow the instructions to enhance the readability and accessibility of the checked text(s). Share what you learn from the process with your teacher and classmates.

Language Transparency and Readability and Accessibility as Work in Progress

Both engineers and writers are makers who could contribute to constructing enabling and disabling environments for their targeted audiences.

While engineers could enable or disable users by the way how they design buildings and products, writers can enable or disable their targeted audiences by the way how they compose their texts. The examples I provided in this book chapter offer a few strategies to enhance the readability and accessibility of authors' texts so that you act as a writer who is aware of their capability to enable and disable the reader. However, although these strategies might help make texts clearer and easier for readers to read and comprehend, they don't guarantee that the readers would understand from the text what the author intended. That's because of two reasons. First, language is not transparent, so different readers might interpret and comprehend texts differently. The second reason is that we, as authors, can never account for all the situations that might make our texts readable and accessible for particular readers. Therefore, one strategy we can continue to pursue is to communicate with our readers as much as possible and ask for their feedback about the readability and accessibility of our texts. In a classroom context, you could always ask your peers and teachers whether it was easy for them to read your text, comprehend it, and use it for their own purposes productively. You could also ask them to tell you what they understood from your text and compare it with what you intended. Depending on the answers, you can revise your texts and document design accordingly.

The examples and activities provided in this book chapter about readability and accessibility can't exhaust all possibilities for creating accessible and readable texts. The technologies of composition change every day. Therefore, the technology examples that might be helpful to you in this chapter this year 2023 might become irrelevant in 2024 or after. What remains, however, is the principle of being aware of your capability of disabling the reader and the need for lots of thinking, research, laboring, and revision to guarantee that you won't oppress the reader or deny them the chance of accessing and comprehending your texts. As Jay Dolmage—a disability studies scholar—warns us: when we think of accessibility as checklists, we risk believing that accessibility is fully achieved "if the boxes were all checked." Instead, Dolmage argues, we need to work with any list as a place "to *start* thinking, doing, acting, and moving" (par. 2). I, therefore, invite you to work with this chapter as a starting step in an ongoing process toward maintaining readability and accessibility in texts that you produce.

Notes

1. I use the pronouns "them", "they", and "theirs" intentionally when speaking of individual humans to disrupt the gender binary and account for humans who don't abide by that binary in defining themselves.

2. I made up the example and student's name to show an example of an author's memo that facilitates the readers' access to both the memo and essay draft.

Works Cited

Cedillo, Christina V. "What Does It Mean to Move?: Race, Disability, and Critical Embodiment Pedagogy." *Composition Forum*, vol. 39, https://compositionforum.com/issue/39/to-move.php

Dolmage, Jay. "Universal Design: Places to Start." *Disability Studies Quarterly*, vol. 35, no. 2, 2015, https://dsq-sds.org/article/view/4632/3946

Garland-Thomson, Rosemarie. "Integrating Disability, Transforming Feminist Theory." *NWSA Journal*, vol. 14, no. 3, 2002, pp. 1-32.

Redish, Janice C. Ginny. "What is Information Design?" *Technical Communication*, vol. 47, no. 2, 2000, pp. 163-166.

Rello, Luz, and Ricardo Baeza-Yates. "Good Fonts for Dyslexia." *Proceedings of the 15th International ACM SIGACCESS Conference on Computers and Accessibility*, 21-23 October 2013, Bellevue, WA. doi: https://doi.org/10.1145/2513383.2513447

Teacher Resources for "Enabling the Reader"

Overview and Teaching Strategies

This chapter draws on feminist disability studies that perceive disability as a defect in the surrounding environment of disabled bodies rather than the bodies themselves. Within that framework, student authors are invited to recognize themselves as contributors to environments that could disable the readers at times. This chapter can be used as a foundation to maintain readability and accessibility in students' produced documents as social justice action throughout the semester. Thus, it might be more beneficial to introduce readability and accessibility and assign the chapter to students at the very beginning of the semester. The chapter can be assigned for reading as a whole or in parts, depending on the teacher's agenda and course scope. Exercises and discussion questions are embedded inside the text for accessibility reasons.

The chapter draws on the information design theory forwarded by Janice Redish, "What Is Information Design?", to identify three levels of readability and accessibility of texts. The three levels are:

- Reading the text
- Comprehending it
- Using it appropriately

Thus, the examples in the chapter reiterate the three levels of readability and accessibility to help students internalize Redish's definition of readability and accessibility.

Activities

Purposefully, exercises were suggested to students in-text to relate to a particular example of text that disables/enables the reader. These exercises can be assigned to students as homework that they do individually or as group work to do in class. In what follows, I provide five more activities that aim to engage students in research around readability and accessibility in and outside the classroom. You might introduce these activities as actions that respond to Jay Dolmage's invitation for an ongoing performance of action toward composing readable and accessible texts.

Interviews Concerning Emails' Readability and Accessibility

This activity starts and ends in the classroom, but the research component occurs outside the classroom.

1. Introduce the activity to students indicating that each needs to interview someone who has a profession that requires extensive email communication. Each student needs to ask their interviewee about practices they perceive in the email communication that makes it hard for them to read, understand, and/or respond to emails.

2. Ask students to compose the interview questions together, first in small groups, and after that as a whole class. Prompt students to use the examples in this book chapter to inspire their questions and make sure they bring questions about new aspects of readability and accessibility that the book chapter didn't include.

3. After students conduct their interviews, let them share their findings in class. Help students arrange their findings in categories of readability and accessibility and draw conclusions accordingly.

4. Ask students how their research findings might influence their future composition of emails.

Professional Document Analysis

This activity aims to analyze professional documents with an eye on readability and accessibility.

1. Depending on the focus of your course, provide students with professional documents (brochures, flyers, resumes, instructions, etc.) to analyze in groups in class.

2. Ask students to create two lists: one about what was done well to facilitate the document readability and accessibility, and one about what violated readability and accessibility guidelines.

3. Ask the groups to share their findings with the whole class. Help students create class guidelines for readability and accessibility that they'd commit to in their document design.

Conducting Internet Research about Accessibility Checkers

This activity introduces students to accessibility checkers that are embedded in various software such as MS Word, Acrobat Reader, and Learning Management Systems.

- Ask students to search the internet for tutorials about accessibility checkers in M.S. Word, Acrobat Reader, and the Learning Management System that they use in your school.
- Require students to follow the instructions in the tutorials to check the readability and accessibility of M.S. Word or PDF documents on their computers.
- Ask students to follow the instructions to enhance the readability and accessibility of the checked text(s).
- Ask students to share what they learn from the process with their class community.

Font Types, Colors, and Sizes as Rhetorical Choices

1. Ask students to conduct research about font types, colors, and sizes that facilitate readability to readers with different conditions and capabilities, such as Dyslexia and color-blind readers.

2. Encourage students to think of the implications of their findings on their rhetorical choices of font size, type, and color as writers.

Naming Files Meaningfully

1. Introduce file names as a pointer to file contents that function similarly to email subject lines and document titles.

2. Ask students to go back to the last three assignment files submitted to their teacher and/or peers through the learning management system they use.

3. Ask students to pay attention to how they named their files.

4. Ask students to reflect on whether they made it easy for their teacher and/or peers to know who submitted what by reading the file names.

5. Ask students to revise the file names, when necessary, to point out the author and what they submitted to the reader.

9 Everything's Biased: A Guide to Determining When Bias Matters

Danielle DeRise

Overview

The polarization of American society means almost every topic is ripe for controversy.[1] Students in first year writing classes reflect this noisy information ecosystem, commonly, by focusing on the degree of bias an author displays. In some cases, these observations result in savvy choices about source credibility, but in other instances, a focus on bias can lead students astray, even steering them away from reputable information. This chapter provides four classroom strategies—context awareness, genre awareness, classifying opinions, and evaluating counterarguments—to encourage students toward a more nuanced understanding of bias, which also can be applied to real-world situations.

In *Biased*, a 2019 book about racial bias, author and psychology professor Jennifer Eberhardt likens bias to a categorization effort by the human brain. Eberhardt also acknowledges that this trait is universal: it's our version of a short cut for processing vast amounts of information, "bringing coherence to a chaotic world" (24). However, these very same shortcuts have significant limitations, as they "impede our efforts to embrace and understand people who are deemed not like us" (24). This idea is at the heart of Eberhardt's research about implicit racial bias and its life-or-death consequences.

Tragically, in the years since Eberhardt's book was published, acts of violence have continued against Black individuals by law enforcement. Also,

---

1. This work is licensed under the Creative Commons Attribution-NonCommercial-NoDerivatives 4.0 International License (CC BY-NC-ND 4.0) and is subject to the Writing Spaces Terms of Use. To view a copy of this license, visit http://creativecommons.org/licenses/by-nc-nd/4.0/, email info@creativecommons.org, or send a letter to Creative Commons, PO Box 1866, Mountain View, CA 94042, USA. To view the Writing Spaces Terms of Use, visit http://writingspaces.org/terms-of-use.

the COVID-19 pandemic began claiming lives globally, but disproportionately affected those over 65, those with compromised immune systems, people of color, people living in poverty, and those with limited access to information or health care.

It matters to first acknowledge the dire consequences of bias—such as violence against people of color, or policies rooted in ableism that threaten those who are vulnerable—to establish how systemic injustice, fueled by implicit biases, manifests in extreme forms. Misinformation can exacerbate these problems, further polarizing individuals on consequential issues. Many college students are aware of and upset by these realities. However, there is a lot of societal confusion over bias, too. Without more clarity about what bias is, when it matters, and when it does not, these egregious examples can get lost alongside inconsequential ones, leading to further confusion and division. In this chapter, I provide four strategies to help you better understand bias in a more nuanced way as both a reader and a writer. I also explain how bias conversations that start in our classrooms are also relevant to us as citizens.

Tip #1: Determine Writer and Reader Contexts

In their textbook, *So What? The Writer's Argument,* composition instructors Kurt Schick and Laura Miller describe context as the "where and when" of a writer's circumstances (8). In other words, it's useful to consider what sparked the writer's need to communicate a particular message. Now, let's consider an example. For Devoney Looser, author of the 2017 personal narrative, "Why I Teach Online," the spark was a family health emergency, which led her to seek the flexibility of remote teaching. Previously dismissive of online classes, she came to realize their value as her own experience disproved stigmas she previously believed.

Recently, it's been common for students reading this essay to remark that Looser seems "too biased in favor of online classes" to be credible. At first, these critiques may seem puzzling to you—wouldn't a professor who teaches online have *something* worthwhile to say about the subject? However, considering many students' experiences with online learning in 2020 and 2021, with technology platforms that didn't work and classes requiring them to read entire chemistry textbooks without guidance and teachers who had seemingly disappeared off the planet, it becomes clear that *readers'* contexts matter, too. Quite simply, COVID was making it too hard for some readers to imagine online classes in a positive light.

My own positive experiences teaching online for years *before* the pandemic probably led me to Looser's essay in the first place. In Fall of 2020, hearing students bemoan another semester online, I felt...defensive. It took some reflection on my part to separate my past context from the present reality: it just wasn't the same when everyone was being forced into it while a global pandemic raged around us. Noticing where my context diverged from many reader contexts in 2020 helped me acknowledge my own bias. I also encourage you to look beyond any of yours. For example, we shouldn't assume online learning was terrible for all students in the pandemic, as some individuals with disabilities reported feeling *more* connected by the same virtual experiences that led to others feeling isolated (Belle).

In conclusion, take inventory when you read: what was going on for the writer? How were those circumstances different from what's going on for you now? How are your experiences different from other readers'? Context awareness can train you to be a bit more receptive to potentially meaningful information that you might miss by dismissing it due to bias.

Tip #2: Clear Up Misconceptions about Genre

Chances are you've heard the word genre describing a TV show or movie, with labels like sci-fi and comedy guiding your expectations. Such labels are useful for any genre of the written word, too, for which Schick and Miller provide the following definition: "a typical, commonly recognized form of communication used to achieve a recurring (that is, repeating) purpose" (21). The more we read, then, the more we discover patterns in these categories that shape our expectations for the content.

Below are three genres you'll likely encounter as a student: academic, news, and opinion. We'll determine how the presence of bias impacts credibility in each. From there, hopefully you'll start to see that the word *bias* alone is too simplistic a way of expressing a complex set of reading and writing possibilities.

Academic

For college-level reading, the academic genre often refers to a scholarly article obtained from a library database. For writing, *academic* might describe the genre in which many professors expect you to compose. You might be quick to say academic work should be completely unbiased, which is correct *to an extent*, but let's go deeper.

If you tend to read a scholarly article and see it in terms of "biased in favor of x" or "biased against y," it may help to differentiate between bias and argument. There are indeed biases that threaten the integrity of academic work. One is called confirmation bias, or when a writer ignores evidence that complicates or disproves a claim; another is failure to disclose conflicts of interest, such as receiving funding from a company that monetarily benefits from certain findings.

However, writers seeking academic publication must undergo a peer review conducted by other subject experts, a process that checks not only for accuracy, but also for these troublesome biases. A writer favorably reviewed by peers, then, gets to confidently assert a position. A claim supported by responsibly-collected evidence is no longer a bias—it's a new academic finding. Sure, that finding might be refuted later, which doesn't mean the original work was biased, either; only that an academic perspective is subject to change.

Now that we've discussed the relationship between genre and bias for *readers*, let's consider how we can apply this knowledge to *our* academic *writing*. Schick and Miller note, "genre knowledge can provide instructions for how to write effectively" (23). Another composition expert, Amy Devitt, asserts that genre is a "dynamic patterning of human experience, [one that] enable[s] us to construct our writing world" (573). Combined, these ideas emphasize how a careful choice of genre not only gives writers control over their purpose but may even help determine their purpose.

The answer to the question about bias in your own work, then, depends on two factors:

(1) **The assignment's genre and purpose expectations.** Are you sure you're being asked to write a report, or is the assignment asking for something else? After all, how could a personal narrative possibly remain unbiased? What would an unbiased analysis of a poem even look like? To motivate peers into recycling, would you want to only list facts? Or might you want to do some strategic persuading?

(2) **What, precisely, you mean by bias.** Do you mean compiling facts with no original content from you? Chances are that's not what your professor wants, even in the most traditionally academic of assignments. On the other hand, if you mean researching multiple perspectives and citing a variety of sources, then, yes, that's what academic writing involves.

NEWS VS. OPINION

Students often describe news articles as unbiased, which reflects what they *should* be, not what they always are. In some cases, bias creeps in, either through word choices that suggest a preference (or distaste) for one side, or from the glossing over or omitting of details that might have presented a more comprehensive report. News bias is actually quite problematic and is likely to go undetected, because we have to be knowledgeable about a topic to even spot instances of bias. Check out the *Writing Spaces* chapter "Effectively and Efficiently Reading the Credibility of Online Sources" by composition scholars Ellen Carillo and Alice Horning for some excellent source evaluation strategies. Among other tips, they remind us that it's a writer's job to "negotiate bias" shown in sources, remembering that we "can't somehow remove bias from these sources" (42), but that rather, it matters how we present these slants to our readers. For example, we can indicate to readers if an otherwise credible source is published in an outlet that leans to the political left, right, or center. We can also choose to disclose background information about authors we cite, especially if we think those details may be relevant to a particular viewpoint or position.

On the opposite end of the genre spectrum, an opinion article is often described by students as very biased, which isn't completely wrong, either; after all, the writer is favoring a side. However, with few exceptions (such as hateful language or deliberately false claims), readers aren't harmed by a clearly disclosed opinion, so you need not reject the content on bias alone. Although you don't want to depend solely on opinions, they can be useful because they're often short and easy to read. Hastily discarding an opinion for its bias may even prolong your information-seeking task, making you rely on dense articles intended for expert audiences.

Media literacy specialists, including *AllSides* marketing director Julie Mastrine, acknowledge that bias is everywhere and unavoidable. Like Eberhardt, Mastrine accepts that human beings are biased by nature. Specifically related to media, though, Mastrine argues that bias only becomes a problem when not disclosed, which may result in readers "being manipulated into (a biased outlet's) point of view and not able to evaluate it critically and objectively" (qtd in Sheridan). Experts like Mastrine also note that media outlets improve their credibility with the public by labeling content as news or opinion.

Tip #3: Categorize Opinions

While we're at it, the word opinion is pretty vague, so labeling alone might not be enough. In the article, "No, You're Not Entitled to Your Opinion," author Patrick Stokes notes that in everyday conversation, we toss the word around inconsistently, to describe anything from a preference, to a deeply held conviction, to an evidence-based argument (Stokes). Only in the last instance, though, does a writer's degree of bias really matter.

Let's dig into Stokes' categories, remembering from Tip #2 that it's a waste of energy to worry about author bias for a (clearly labeled) opinion or narrative. An author is writing about a preference to be vegetarian? So what? You're welcome to write an ode to carnivores in response, but unless the author hurls insults at meat eaters, author bias is mostly irrelevant to evaluating credibility here. Maybe the author expresses moral, ethical, or religious convictions against killing animals, a classic example of a bias, in this case a deeply personal belief unlikely to be changed. Without evidence to "prove" morality, bias doesn't matter much here, either. If your conscience permits you to eat meat, then you can agree to disagree.

On the other hand, if an author claims beef production should be reduced for climate reasons, a statement for which there is concrete evidence, then you can apply the following checklist, where an answer of "no" might indicate a credibility-reducing bias:

- Does the author have the appropriate credentials, experience, knowledge, or expertise to cover this issue? Be careful with credentials: does an astrophysicist necessarily know more about vegetarianism than a lifelong vegetarian?
- Does the author cite credible sources?
- Does the author mention any valid counterarguments and treat these fairly?
- Does the author use professional/respectful language?
- Does the author have any conflicts of interest? If so, are they candidly revealed?

In his essay, Stokes also discusses why this categorization matters beyond the classroom: a lack of precision about the word opinion can lead us down the dangerous road, societally, of affording the same merit to *all* opinions. Shielding bad faith ideas under the defense of supposedly "harmless opinions" can even contribute to implicit biases that erupt in racist violence, or to unsubstantiated ideas about a public health crisis that lead individuals toward risky behaviors.

Tip #4: Seek Valid Counterarguments Only

The previous paragraph may seem to contradict what you've likely been taught, which is to avoid bias by acknowledging the other side. Often, this is an advisable move. In an article about argument writing, authors Warrington et al. note, "…[representing] only one side of an argument… could make the audience believe that the author is either not knowledgeable about other possible arguments or not interested in these arguments" (191). Warrington et al. classify this one-sidedness as a type of bias, and it certainly can be. As readers, we need a balanced portrayal of a topic, particularly one new to us. As writers, one way to achieve this balance for readers is to cite high-quality sources from a variety of perspectives, a move that shows our familiarity with other viewpoints and a confidence in our own.

For a topic familiar to many students, such as pet ownership, the imbalance in a source that rambles about the joys of pets without acknowledging any challenges is probably easy to spot. But what about for a less familiar topic? How do you know what the counterarguments even are or if they're good ones to consider? First, you have to read many sources to determine if there are reasonable perspectives beyond what you plan to argue. You probably don't want to bother with a topic for which no sensible counterarguments exist. Sure, you *could* mention the flat earth theory, but what would that accomplish other than playing a not-very-meaningful game of Devil's Advocate? In fact, devoting time to bad counterarguments—much like treating all opinions as equally worthy—not only reduces your credibility as a writer, but it also perpetuates the false equivalence fallacy, mentioned earlier by Stokes, that is so pervasive in society.

When meritless positions are repeated over and over, as they often are on social media, they can *seem* more widespread than they are. Mere prevalence can convey an air of legitimacy. For example, First Draft, an organization dedicated to debunking misinformation, analyzed thousands of Twitter accounts in the summer of 2020, shortly after many countries had imposed mask mandates to control COVID spread. Casual social media users around this time might have been quick to conclude there were equal numbers of pro-maskers as anti-maskers; and therefore, that this was an issue worthy of a thoughtful two-sided debate. However, the organization's investigation revealed that while there were some opponents, a majority accepted the mandates, with only "a small minority provoking a backlash that end[ed] up amplifying their messaging."

The takeaway? Before you accuse someone of bias for not mentioning "the other side," make sure the side in question has credible evidence to back it up.

Putting It All Together

Have you ever heard anyone say they wish the media and experts would just "stick to the facts?" Sounds sensible, but here's the problem: I could read so-called "facts" 24/7 and still wind up dangerously misinformed if I'm not consulting reputable sources, or if I'm relying on a single outlet while ignoring other credible perspectives.

Let's revisit an idea from Tip #2, that opinions can offer valuable insights, and now apply it to the real world. You'd probably listen, for example, if your two closest friends warned you against a popular nutritional supplement after experiencing severe stomach pain. Sure, they're doing something other than just sticking to the facts, but because you trust your friends, their opinions might be more credible than any fact available to you on the supplement's website, which exists to sell the product.

In other words, *intent* matters too. If you're thinking, "But how can I possibly know someone's intent?" you're right. We can't know the motivations of every person or organization. But just because we can't know *every single* time doesn't mean we shouldn't make educated guesses some of the time. Here again, a checklist helps:

- Is the author being published by an organization (such as a national newspaper) that has a reputation to uphold?
- Is the publishing organization known for quality journalism or reports?
- If the claim is being made on social media, can the individual's identity be verified and deemed credible?
- Does the person stand to gain monetarily or in some other way [fame, attention, prestige] by putting out less-than-honest information?

In a blog post for Nieman Lab, Mike Caulfield, head of the Digital Polarization Initiative, writes that most COVID misinformation follows predictable patterns, meaning one way to combat it can involve our getting better at "pre-bunking" the claims instead of treating each one as worthy of serious explanation. Training ourselves to pay more attention to a source's intent may be one way to do this. If you notice that a particular Twitter user constantly posts about hoaxes just to provoke heated debates, then meticulously refuting each claim may have the unintended effect of elevating a bad-faith user's credibility.

Another way to combat misinformation is to become more attentive to our own biases, and how these might prime us to overly criticize viewpoints that go against ours, while also remaining too receptive to poor quality content *just because* we agree with it. Zeynep Tufekci, a sociologist who studies technology's effects on the information ecosystem, writes the following in a 2018 *MIT Technology Review* article:

> ...the new, algorithmic gatekeepers aren't merely (as they like to believe) neutral conduits for both truth and falsehood. They make their money by keeping people on their sites and apps; that aligns their incentives closely with those who stoke outrage, spread misinformation, and appeal to people's existing biases and preferences.

The entities mentioned by Tufekci have interests other than keeping us educated. It's a common tactic among those who deliberately spread bad information—either for monetary gain, or to sow political discord—to hide behind the veneer of plausible-sounding facts, while accusing any challenger of being biased. Here, a charge of bias even functions as a form of misinformation *in itself* by making people overly skeptical of writers or organizations who publish the truth. Unfortunately, once truth is doubted on a large enough scale, societal chaos can ensue. Some people will remain in a perpetual state of skepticism; others may even reach for conspiracy theories in an attempt to make sense of a confusing situation.

To summarize, I've book-ended this chapter with two examples of urgent importance, first where biases can lead to life-or-death consequences for people, and where the language around the word *bias* is used as a tool of manipulation. In the middle, we discussed some strategies for sharpening your own critical thinking so that you can be better equipped to determine for yourself—in the classroom and beyond—when bias matters and how much.

Works Cited

Belle, Elly. "How 2020 Created Community for Disabled People." *Teen Vogue*. 24 December 2020. https://www.teenvogue.com/story/how-2020-created-community-for-disabled-people.

Carillo, Ellen and Alice Horning. "Effectively and Efficiently Reading the Credibility of Online Sources." *Writing Spaces: Readings on Writing*, edited by Dana

Driscoll, Megan Heise, Mary Stewart, and Matthew Vetter, vol. 4, 2021, pp. 35-50. https://writingspaces.org/?page_id=758

Caulfield, Mike. "2021's Misinformation Will Look a Lot Like 2020's (and 2019's, and . . .)." *Nieman Lab.* https://www.niemanlab.org/2020/12/2021s-misinformation-will-look-a-lot-like-2020s-and-2019s-and/

"Coronavirus: How Pro-Mask Posts Boost the Anti-Mask Movement." *First Draft.* 20 August 2020. https://firstdraftnews.org/articles/coronavirus-how-pro-mask-posts-boost-the-anti-mask-movement/

Devitt, Amy J. "Generalizing about Genre: New Conceptions of an Old Concept." *College Composition and Communication,* vol. 44, no. 4, Dec. 1993, pp. 573-586. *JSTOR,* doi.org/10.2307/358391.

Eberhardt, Jennifer. *Biased: Uncovering the Hidden Prejudice That Shapes What We See, Think, and Do.* New York: Viking, 2019.

Looser, Devoney. "Why I Teach Online." *The Chronicle of Higher Education.* 20 March 2017. https://www.chronicle.com/article/why-i-teach-online/

Schick, Kurt and Laura Miller. *So What? The Writer's Argument.* 3rd Ed. New York: Oxford, 2021.

Sheridan, Jake. "Should You Trust Media Bias Charts?" *Poynter.* 18 May 2021.https://www.poynter.org/fact-checking/media-literacy/2021/should-you-trust-media-bias-charts/

Stokes, Patrick. "No, you're not entitled to your opinion." *The Conversation.* 4 October 2012. https://theconversation.com/no-youre-not-entitled-to-your-opinion-9978

Tufekci, Zeynep. "How Social Media Took us from Tahrir Square to Donald Trump." *MIT Technology Review.* 14 Aug. 2018, https://www.technologyreview.com/2018/08/14/240325/how-social-media-took-us-from-tahrir-square-to-donald-trump/

Warrington, Kate et al. "Assessing Source Credibility for a Well-Informed Argument." *Writing Spaces: Readings on Writing,* edited by Charles Lowe and Pavel Zemliansky, vol. 3, 2020, pp. 189-203. https://writingspaces.org/wp-content/uploads/2021/04/warrington-kovalyova-king-assessing-source-credibility-1.pdf

Teacher Resources for "Everything's Biased: A Guide to Determining When Bias Matters"

Overview and Teaching Strategies

Building on students' natural tendencies to recognize bias, this chapter might fit into a critical reading or research unit. I have found that if students can identify relevant instances of bias as they read, they become not only better at choosing high-quality sources for their writing projects, but also more aware of how their own biases might impact their approach to writing topics.

For claims of author bias that may more accurately describe students' own strong feelings about a topic, the discussion of context may help identify where tensions could occur between readers and writers. For students using the word bias to describe any non-neutral material, a review of genre may prompt them to differentiate among actual biases, academic arguments, and accepted features of some genres.

Discussion Questions

1. How many different **genres** do you encounter in a typical day? For which does the author's or publisher's bias affect your understanding the most? The least? Why?

2. Free-write about a past experience of significant importance to you. How does the **context** surrounding this experience contribute to your memory and retelling? How does your present context compare or contrast with your past context?

3. Which topics of controversy often simplified into two sides actually have more than two valid positions? How should writers handle topics for which a pervasive **viewpoint** has little or no credible supporting evidence?

4. Write down an **opinion** about which you feel strongly. Is it a preference, a moral belief, or an informed viewpoint? What would it take (if anything) for you to change your mind?

Activities

Inhabiting a biased reader's perspective. This activity can be done in small groups, or it can be the subject of a low-stakes exercise. First, ask students to imagine a strongly negative response to an assigned text. Next, ask students to write a summary of the text using this biased tone/style. Finally, discuss how these loaded summaries can be revised for more neutrality. (Note: I suggest asking students to embody a *hypothetical* reader rather than prompting them to use their own biases as examples. Of course, the latter is the eventual goal as they begin to transition from thinking of these concepts as readers to applying them in their own writing.)

Viewpoint Summary Project. Assign students to small groups (3-4 is ideal). As a group, students will choose a debatable issue for which there are several reputable viewpoints. Next, they will summarize various articles that express opinions on the topic. Finally, they will present their neutral summaries to a peer audience. This can be a stand-alone project to reinforce skills of source evaluation and summary, or it can serve as an early annotated bibliography if you plan to scaffold this activity to a research assignment.

10 Reading in Conversation: A Writing Student's Guide to Social Annotation

Michelle Sprouse

Overview

Students are often encouraged to annotate while reading.[1] However, annotation is often framed as an individual undertaking, a conversation between a reader and text. This chapter repositions annotation in the writing classroom as a social activity that can support students' literacy development. Beginning with opportunities for students to reflect on their experiences with annotation, the chapter argues that social annotation can help students practice reading for different purposes as members of learning communities. Using examples from writing students and public annotators, students will learn about social annotation in classroom and public contexts. Students will then consider several affordances of social annotation technologies—expanded marginal space, hashtagging, and multimedia enrichment—that they can use for more productive marginal conversations. Because navigating a core text and its annotations can be challenging, the chapter concludes with a discussion of reading workflows that integrate skimming, close reading, and extending to help students get the most from social annotation.

Easing open the cover of J.D. Salinger's *Nine Stories* that I annotated two decades ago, I can see in the rounded letters of my adolescent handwriting are notes about Salinger's life and the underlined heading "3 Themes" followed by the bulleted points "communication, innocence of children, perversion of adults." Squeezed on the bottom of a page

1. This work is licensed under the Creative Commons Attribution-NonCommercial-NoDerivatives 4.0 International License (CC BY-NC-ND 4.0) and is subject to the Writing Spaces Terms of Use. To view a copy of this license, visit http://creativecommons.org/licenses/by-nc-nd/4.0/, email info@creativecommons.org, or send a letter to Creative Commons, PO Box 1866, Mountain View, CA 94042, USA. To view the Writing Spaces Terms of Use, visit http://writingspaces.org/terms-of-use.

much later in the book was my annotation, "Ramona's glasses—child's view, scratched." Even though the term paper they helped me to write has been lost, the first steps on my journey toward becoming an English scholar remain mapped in the pages.

An annotation is a note added to text. Like many of my students, you may have had experience annotating in high school. Perhaps your teachers asked you to add notes to printed documents or in the margins of paperback books. You may have used digital annotation tools. But, if you're like many of my students, annotation might have been a reading strategy you practiced alone.

In this essay, I will introduce you to social annotation, a practice where groups of readers annotate in the shared margins of the text to engage in conversations about texts and reading. You'll learn about what social annotation may offer as a tool for engaging with the communities in which you read.

Whether you are an annotation expert or novice, I invite you to make and share your own annotations on this chapter. You might use Hypothesis (web.hypothes.is/start) or another tool suggested by your instructor. There are questions embedded throughout to help you reflect on your own reading practices and to engage in conversation with others as you read. I also hope you will feel inspired to respond to other parts of this chapter.

Let's start by reflecting on your own experiences. *What experiences have you had with annotation? How might those experiences prepare you to read in community with others?*

Learning is Social

Annotation has been practiced for thousands of years as a way to improve reading. Readers annotating texts individually to aid learning is an old practice, one recommended by Erasmus as early as the sixteenth century (Jackson 48). Social annotations can help us learn about what we're reading too. In the Jewish tradition, published Talmudic annotations help readers make sense of the Talmud (Kalir & Garcia 78). Before the invention of the printing press, it was common to share a text and annotations among groups of readers even though the technology made reproducing the text and annotations time consuming.

But new tools for digital social annotation afford readers new possibilities not only for making annotations that are shared with others, but also for annotating at the same time and across distances. Digital annotation thus creates a more expansive space for the social practice of annotation.

Let's pause again. *Whether written into the margins of texts, integrated into the print, or digitally superimposed, in what contexts have you encountered annotations written by another person? In what ways have you shared your annotations with other readers?*

When I annotated in high school, I thought all annotations focused on the literary elements of texts. But I've learned since, by annotating and reading with others, that different communities of readers annotate for different purposes. In a composition course, successful reading may differ depending on a writer's purpose. Seeing what and how you are reading is an important first step toward more effective reading. Social annotation can help you practice reading for different purposes.

Social annotation makes visible the different ways people read to accomplish their goals. You might need to "read like a writer" (Bunn 72), evaluating an author's writerly choices and deciding how similar choices might or might not work in your own writing. Seeing how others respond to those same choices might help you decide how best to address your own audience. Or, you might read a source text, analyzing the author's findings to make an argument of your own. Social annotations might help you understand how others interpret the evidence so that you can tailor your own argument to the values of your readers.

Learning is a social act; we learn from others and from helping others learn. When you share the margins of a text in social annotation, adding your thoughts and questions and considering others' interpretations, you contribute to a community in conversation about texts.

SOCIAL ANNOTATION IS CONVERSATION

In the sections below, I will share examples of how writing students use social annotation to engage in conversations through course-based and public social annotation.

COURSE-BASED SOCIAL ANNOTATION

You are an important part of your classroom community. Through social annotation, you can contribute to conversations about reading and writing to enrich learning in the course, much like when you participate in class discussions.

Many of my students that find it difficult to speak up in whole-class discussions find social annotation a meaningful way to participate. Social annotation also gives you a chance to revise your thinking before you share it with a group. You can edit your words in the margins in a way that is impossible when speaking up in class.

Reading others' annotations can help you see more in the text than you might find on your own. During a think aloud, my former student Chloe noted how reading her classmate's annotation changed her thinking about a text:

> When I was first reading this, although I guess I didn't question it as much, I see Layla's comment and how she really questioned it. It got me thinking more and now I'm reading it once again just to see what the author meant by that term.

You might help your classmates, for example, notice the significance of a term that they might otherwise overlook. Reading their annotations can also give you insight into what matters to other readers. This knowledge can help you learn about others' perspectives. As a writer, this insight might help you see how people respond differently to the same writerly choice, or how a readers' experiences shape their interpretation of an argument.

My students were reviewing research papers for our class and encountered a number of citation strategies. In their readings, Elizabeth and Tom[1] used their annotations to raise important questions about the citation strategies they were encountering (Fig. 1):

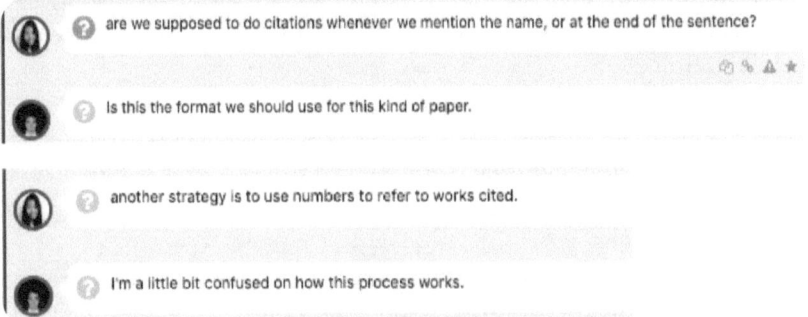

Figure 1. Screenshot of student annotations exploring citation strategies. (Permission to use this image was obtained from students.)

Your classmates might also ask questions to which you can respond. In the annotations below (Fig. 2), Elizabeth is able to answer Cole's question about an author's cultural background.

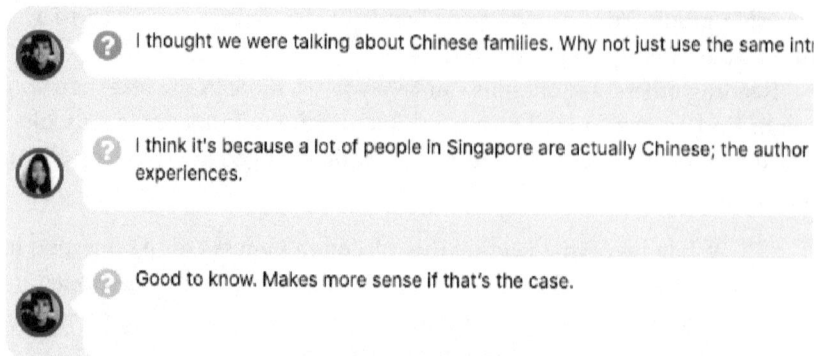

Figure 2. Screenshot of annotations with replies to student questions. (Permission to use this image was obtained from students.)

Community is an important aspect of social annotation. So that you and your peers can learn well together, it is important to establish and follow norms for respectful communication. Treat the margins of your shared text like you would a physical classroom space, as a place where different opinions and experiences can be valued and discussed safely.

Public Annotation

In addition to building community within a class, social annotation also offers opportunities for you to contribute to conversations about texts with public audiences.

Have you ever wondered about the inspiration for the lyrics to your favorite song? The popular lyrics site, Genius (genius.com) for example, allows readers to annotate song lyrics. Annotators use research and links to other sources to support interpretations and contribute to collaboratively written annotations.

As I'm drafting this chapter, Harry Style's song "As It Was" is number one on the Genius list. The first annotation (Fig. 3) combines the work of four contributors who have crafted an explanation of the introduction using quotes from interviews, links to his music video, and an analysis of how the line might fit with broader themes in Styles' music ("Harry Styles As It Was Lyrics"). Ratings for the annotation as a whole and individual contributors help other readers evaluate the annotation.

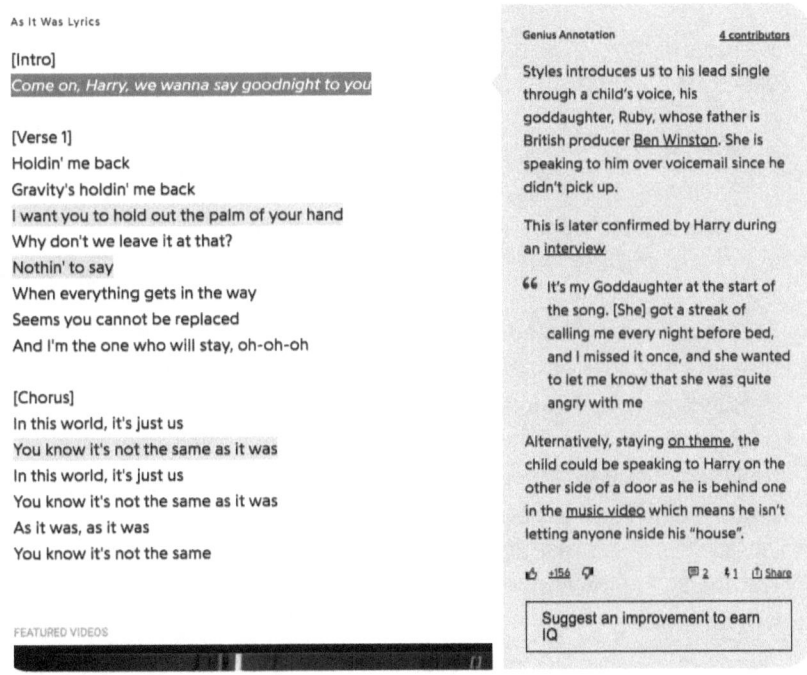

Figure 3. Screenshot of public annotation of Harry Styles' "As It Was" lyrics by four contributors. This image does not fall within the CC license for this work.

Public social annotation can help us to understand and share our interpretations of texts. Shared annotations can also help us to understand the responses readers might have to an authors' writing choices.

Figure 4 is an example of an annotation contributed to the UM Press Annotates project where readers were invited to add annotations to open access ebooks around several themes, including disability studies.

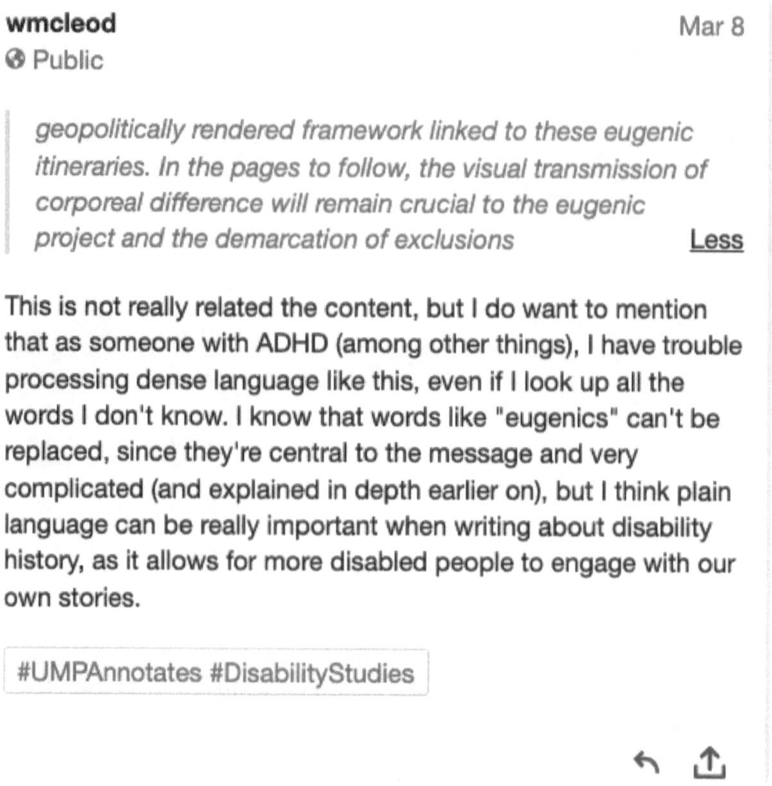

> **wmcleod** Mar 8
> 🌐 Public
>
> > geopolitically rendered framework linked to these eugenic itineraries. In the pages to follow, the visual transmission of corporeal difference will remain crucial to the eugenic project and the demarcation of exclusions **Less**
>
> This is not really related the content, but I do want to mention that as someone with ADHD (among other things), I have trouble processing dense language like this, even if I look up all the words I don't know. I know that words like "eugenics" can't be replaced, since they're central to the message and very complicated (and explained in depth earlier on), but I think plain language can be really important when writing about disability history, as it allows for more disabled people to engage with our own stories.
>
> #UMPAnnotates #DisabilityStudies

Figure 4. Screenshot of wmcleod's annotation of Susan Antebi's Embodied Archive with the hashtags #UMPAnnotates and #DisabilityStudies. This image does not fall within the CC license for this work.

Social annotator wmcleod responds to a passage in Susan Antebi's *Embodied Archive: Disability in Post-Revolutionary Mexican Cultural Production* with a critique of the author's language choices for her intended audience. As a writer, you can use this annotation to reflect on when and how you might choose to use technical vocabulary to make your own writing more accessible for a wider audience.

These are just two of many social annotation projects you might explore. You might also be interested in seeing how annotators have contributed to historical documents in Speculative Annotation hosted by the Library of Congress (https://labs.loc.gov/work/experiments/annotation) or literary texts like Frankenstein (https://www.frankenbook.org).

Affordances of Digital Spaces for Social Annotation

Now that we've had a chance to think about some of the conversations social annotation can facilitate, I want to share some of the affordances of digital tools that we can use to get the most out of social annotation.

One way to think about affordances is to imagine the possible uses of the tools. Texting, for example, affords nearly instant sharing of brief messages across wide geographic distances. Texting also allows for silent, more private communication in a shared space.

There are three important affordances of digital, social annotation that you can leverage for more productive conversations: expansive marginal space, hashtag organization, and multimedia enrichment.

Expansive Marginal Space

If you've ever annotated a paperback book, you've probably found yourself short on space to write notes. One of the major affordances of digital and social annotation is the expansive marginal space.

Whereas I could hardly squeeze three words into the margins of the inexpensive paperbacks I used to annotate for my high school English classes, the digital margins give you room to write much more. Tye, one of my students, appreciates this affordance, explaining, "I feel like it makes you do a deeper read because I can just highlight and do an analysis of a line instead of trying to squeeze [in] little words."

Use this extra space to share enough of your thinking so that others, including your future self, can converse with your ideas. Compare Evan's two annotations below (Figs. 5-6). First, he makes a brief response that would fit into the margins of a trade paperback.

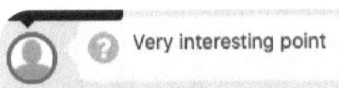

Figure 5. Screenshot of brief student annotation, "Very interesting point." (Permission to use this image was obtained from student.)

While we can read how a bit about what he's thinking, there's not much to respond to. Visually, we can see too that there's space for him to elaborate.

Now read Evan's longer annotation (Fig. 6).

> I was really able to connect to the author in this story as me too, leaving for college, have left my house behind. I wonder what will change in my house while I am gone.
>
> Sep 10 11:00 pm

Figure 6. Screenshot of longer student annotation, "I was really able to connect to the author in this story as me too, leaving for college, have left my house behind. I wonder what will change in my house while I am gone." (Permission to use this image was obtained from student.)

Notice how this longer annotation more fully explains Evan's thinking. In the expansive digital margins, more complete thoughts actually open space for a dialogue to develop. You might add to the conversation about how your home might change if you too are away for college.

Of course, just like in class, you don't need an extended monologue that leaves no room for anyone to respond. The sweet spot for my students seems to be about two or three sentences. Enough to share a complete thought, but not so much that it takes over.

If you are composing a longer annotation, you might use line breaks as in the Genius example to separate points and make your annotations easier to skim on screens.

Hashtag Organization

As you share your thinking and begin to participate in marginal conversations, you may find yourself wanting a way to sort and organize the notes. Enter hashtags.

Most social annotation technologies allow readers to create hashtags to label and organize annotations. These can be especially helpful when you're looking for themes or patterns across texts.

The hashtags which will prove most helpful will depend on your course goals and the audience. One place to start to identify important themes for your social annotations is the course syllabus. My students, for example, create a set of hashtags to represent the goals outlined in the syllabus. They also add hashtags to represent their personal learning goals for the course. The list from a recent first year writing class included #audience, #wordChoice, #ethos, #structure, and #style.

For your instructors and classmates, you might also create hashtags that signal questions or issues you want to discuss in class. Some annotation technologies, like Perusall, have built in features that allow you to mark important questions as you write or second the question asked by your peers.

Hashtagging public annotations can also make conversations searchable within an annotation tool like Hypothesis or even across social media platforms.

Multimedia Enrichment

Not only can you add hashtags to existing resources on the web, but you can also embed multimedia resources within your annotations using most modern social annotation technologies.

Images, including gifs, function in many social annotation platforms. Sometimes writers use these humorously to illustrate their reactions, especially when I ask them to annotate our syllabus and assignment sheets. Reginald, one of my students, included a gif of a man throwing a cell phone against a wall to illustrate his response to a request to keep cell phone notifications off during class.

As we saw earlier in wmcleod's public annotation (Fig. 4), we should also consider the accessibility of our annotations for diverse audiences. When you include multimedia annotations, captions and alt text descriptions can help audience members who use screen reading technology access your annotation.

You can also use multimedia hyperlinks to help clarify confusing sections of text for yourself and your classmates. You can find the correct pronunciation of an unfamiliar name or a word in a new language. Or, if you're reading a description of a process that's difficult to follow, you might consider finding and embedding a video that illustrates the process. Consider adding a brief explanatory note to make clear why you are including the multimedia.

What other affordances might social annotation tools offer?

Reading Workflows

There are many affordances of digital and social annotation that can enhance your learning. But as with most things, there are also tradeoffs. In technology terms, we might call these constraints. Constraints are the challenges and limitations associated with using any tool, including social annotation technologies.

One of the constraints social annotators may face is finding a path through an annotated text. Do you read the text all the way through and then read your peers' comments from top to bottom? Do you pause as you encounter new highlights and read and respond to the comments left by your peers? Are you the first to read and responsible for annotating for the readers yet to arrive?

There is no single path through a socially annotated text, or any text for that matter. But there are three flows readers can use to get the most from their readings: skimming, digging in, and extending.

Skimming

Skimming can give you an overview of the text and the conversation. Skim through the introduction and the conclusion and the headings of the text—what does it seem to be about?

Skim through the social annotations. Are there any spots that seem, as my student Phil says, important because lots of folks have annotated them already? And, importantly, are there places where folks haven't annotated that you might be able to add something new to the conversation?

Digging In

Social annotators often spend most of their time digging in. Many writers like to dig deep into the primary text first, reading carefully and sometimes annotating as they go. In their first full read, they might mostly ignore others' annotations. Chloe, for example, prefers using tools that allow her to temporarily hide others' annotations and highlights for a more focused first reading. When they finish the assigned text, they go back and dig into the annotations, reading carefully and crafting responses to their peers.

Other annotators choose a lateral dig that moves back and forth between the text and the social annotations. They might read a paragraph or section of the assigned text and then pause to review and respond to any annotations and leave their own before continuing to the next.

I have worked with a few writers who prefer to dig into the social annotations first. You won't have much to add to a conversation about a text you haven't read. So, even if you start with a careful reading of the annotations, plan to dig into the text before you write your responses. Otherwise, you'll miss out on the opportunity to develop your own thoughts and compare them to other writers. The direction you dig is up to you.

Extending

Social annotators also extend their reading by sharing connections to other texts. Have you or other readers asked any questions that remain unanswered? If some research will help you answer them, do the research, add your answer, and cite or link to your source in the annotation. If you still can't answer a peer's question, consider marking it if your social annotation tool allows or add a reply that says you also have this question. This signals to other readers your interest in learning more and may help you to crowd source answers.

REFLECTIONS

Whatever your social annotation workflow, I encourage you to take time to reflect on your reading purpose and summarize what you're taking away from the conversation. If you've been "reading like a writer" to identify strategies for writing in the genre (Bunn 72), record the key writerly strategies named in the social annotations you want to try out. If you've been learning about a new topic or interpreting an argument, summarize the key point in your own words. One writer, Tye, explains his process for using my pre-reading instructions to review his annotations:

> I use the notes function whenever I want to look back at your questions. I normally answer your questions in that section just because I feel like you're asking them because we're going to need them later. And it's just easier to find my thoughts.

This practice of reviewing the reading prompts and summarizing his thoughts, he explains, prepares him to revisit and categorize annotations again later in class. Spending just a few minutes preparing to move the annotation work you did with your peers to the next step—class discussion, an exam, or a writing project—will help you to get the most from your reading.

Public annotation can help you to connect with other readers and writers—sharing knowledge well beyond the classroom.

What is your typical reading workflow? How do you anticipate it changing when you socially annotate?

Taking the time to review your annotations will also teach you about yourself as a reader. Reviewing the social annotations, Tye learns about how his thinking compares to his peers, "I see things in a different way than I think most of my classmates do." You can learn about your identity and strengths as a reader—what kinds of questions and ideas do you readily notice? You can also use your peers' annotations to identify places to grow as a reader.

Most importantly, socially annotating can help you to form a community of readers. My students sometimes tell me that our class feels "like high school." Annotating with their peers helps them to feel more connected to each other, to be more ready to share and receive feedback in writing workshop, and to build friendships that sometimes extend beyond the classroom.

Discussion Questions

1. What experiences have you had with paper, digital, and social annotation?

2. When might you choose to share annotations with your class and when might you make your annotations public? How would you annotate differently for the two audiences?

3. What hashtags would you create to summarize the major themes in this chapter? How would you categorize them?

4. Describe your workflow for reading and annotating this chapter. What worked well? What might you change to be more strategic?

5. How might social annotation fit into your course? For what purposes might you begin conversations in the margins of the texts you read with your class?

Note

1. All student names are pseudonyms.

Works Cited

Bunn, Mike. "How to Read Like a Writer." *Writing Spaces: Readings on Writing*, edited by Charles Lowe & Pavel Zemliansky, Vol. 2. Parlor Press, 2011, pp. 71–86.

Jackson, H. J. *Marginalia: Readers Writing in Books*. Yale UP, 2001.

"Harry Styles As It Was Lyrics." *Genius*, https://genius.com/Harry-styles-as-it-was-lyrics. Accessed 12 April 2022.

Kalir, Remi H., & Antero Garcia. *Annotation*. MIT Press, 2021.

wmcleod. "This is not really related the content, but I do want to mention that as someone with ADHD (among other." *Hypothesis*, 8 March 2022, https://www.fulcrum.org/epubs/f1881p00r?locale=en#/6/22[Antebi-0011]!/4/2[ch02]/2[-header0201]/2/2[p68]/1:0.

Teacher Resources for "Reading in Conversation: A Writing Student's Guide to Social Annotation"

Overview and Teaching Strategies

This essay is intended to help you make reading a visible practice in your classroom, whether that is face-to-face, virtual, or hybrid. I encourage instructors to assign "Reading in Conversation" early in the semester to set the stage for an ongoing investigation into the ways writers and communities of writers use reading to improve their practice. Other essays in *Writing Spaces* might be used as companion pieces that introduce how to read for different purposes:

- Mike Bunn's "How to Read Like a Writer,"
- Ellen Carillo and Alice Horning's "Effectively and Efficiently Reading the Credibility of Online Sources,"
- Laura Bolin Carroll's "Backpacks vs. Briefcases," and
- Karen Rosenburg's "Reading Games: Strategies for Reading Scholarly Sources."

Students can practice the strategies outlined in these and other how-to-read pieces using social annotation technologies.

Before assigning this essay, I encourage you to select an annotation technology and introduce students to its basic functions so that they can practice socially annotating as they read this chapter. Instructors have many options for social annotation technologies, including at the time I am writing, Hypothesis, Perusall, and even Google Docs. Balance the available features and the demands of adopting a new technology for your students. Perusall and Hypothesis are two applications designed specifically for social annotation but may require more time for students to create accounts and familiarize themselves with available features. While Google Docs offers less in terms of grouping, hashtagging, and note-taking, many students are familiar with the tool and will need less onboarding instruction. Instructors may also wish to consider whether the social annotation tool integrates with the school Learning Management System. This can reduce the need for additional login accounts and make annotation assignments easier for students to complete.

When possible, I encourage instructors to introduce the social annotation technology in class. Begin by modeling how to access the tool, make and reply to annotations, and use basic accessibility features such as text-to-speech, adjusting text size, and keyboard navigation. Give students time to make their first social annotations when instructors and classmates are nearby in time and space to offer support. Depending on your class size, you might choose to break students into smaller groups of three or four so the number of annotations they see is not overwhelming.

Most importantly, use students' annotations in your instruction. I suggest integrating social annotations as discussion starters regularly to build on students' ideas and give them incentives for beginning thoughtful conversations. Address key questions posed in the margins, by responding yourself or reposting to the larger group. Regularly ask students to review annotations. You might ask them to identify and describe the characteristics of the most helpful social annotations or create lists or charts that summarize key ideas about course readings.

Other Activities

Below, I offer four suggestions to extend social annotation in the classroom and in the public sphere.

Annotate the Syllabus

Remi Kalir (http://remikalir.com/courses/annotate-your-syllabus-2-0/) encourages instructors to have students annotate the syllabus. Do this and avoid the blank stares when you ask if there are any questions. They'll be right there in the margins and so will your answers for students to refer back.

I ask my students:

- What questions do you have about the syllabus?
- What #RelatedExperience have you had? What will be #New for you?
- What #Excites you? What #Concerns you?
- Where do you see your #PersonalGoals reflected in the syllabus? What changes might you suggest better reflect your #PersonalGoals?

Then, repeat for the assignment sheets for each major unit.

Integrate Social Annotation into Peer Review

Social annotation practices can also be integrated into peer review. First, ask students to share their documents in your social annotation tool or a collaborative word processor like Google Docs. Then, ask students to annotate their own texts—pointing to the places and issues where they want to solicit feedback. Their peer reviewers can then continue the conversation in the margins, adding their own noticing as they write.

Give students opportunities to synthesize their reviews in peer review letters or synchronous workshop sessions. You might even ask students to annotate their own texts with their revision goals and plans in response.

Use Social Annotation to Support Student Reflection

For each unit, I ask students to write cover letters introducing their work. As part of letters, students review their annotations and reflect on how individual and social annotation supported their work as readers and writers. Not only does this support students in developing the metacognitive skills to connect their reading and writing, but their letters help me to reflect on the usefulness of the reading and annotation assignments to improve my instructional practice over time.

Converse with the Author

Social annotation also affords opportunities to engage with authors. Projects like UM Press Annotates invite authors to share their work for social annotation. Students' annotations can help to spark conversations with authors in the margins. Or, you might invite an author as a guest speaker for a course or event where they incorporate responses from readers.

11 "I Passed First-Year Writing—What Now?": Adapting Strategies from First-Year Writing to Writing in the Disciplines

Amy Cicchino

Overview

This chapter foreshadows challenges you can experience as you adapt your writing beyond your first-year writing course to become a writer in your discipline.[1] The essay contains a student scenario, defines key rhetorical concepts within discipline-specific writing situations, and gives you strategies for adapting these rhetorical concepts to new writing situations. After reading this chapter, you will better understand how the concepts introduced in first-year writing connect to the writing you will encounter in your upper-level, disciplinary courses and identify strategies that will help you intentionally adapt writing knowledge to new discipline-specific contexts.

Introduction

"C minus?!" Angel was stunned. Angel was not a C- student; they had always done well in writing courses in the past and had just earned an "A" in Composition II last semester. Yet, while looking at their grade for their first writing assignment in BIO 2030, they began to doubt their ability.

Professor Smith introduced the assignment six weeks ago, and it seemed simple enough: each student would create a scientific poster on a series of lab experiments they had completed on the culturable microbes they had found in dirt samples. The assignment sheet told students to create a poster for a scientific audience with complete sections and a polished design.

---

1. This work is licensed under the Creative Commons Attribution-NonCommercial-NoDerivatives 4.0 International License (CC BY-NC-ND 4.0) and is subject to the Writing Spaces Terms of Use. To view a copy of this license, visit http://creativecommons.org/licenses/by-nc-nd/4.0/, email info@creativecommons.org, or send a letter to Creative Commons, PO Box 1866, Mountain View, CA 94042, USA. To view the Writing Spaces Terms of Use, visit http://writingspaces.org/terms-of-use.

Sure, Angel hadn't started the assignment until a few days before it was due, but the professor hadn't asked to see drafts before the final due date.

Angel brought up the poster when they went to lunch with their friend, Akeelah, who was also in the class. "How did you do on the poster project?" Angel asked.

"Okay," Akeelah said absentmindedly.

"What is okay?" Angel pried.

"B minus," Akeelah said, putting down her phone and turning her attention more towards Angel, who was obviously concerned about the assignment, "Why?"

"I got a C minus," Angel admitted, "I'm a good writer. I don't understand what Prof. Smith wants from me."

"Have you thought about asking?" Akeelah posed, "You can go and talk to her during office hours. That's what I did. It was weird at first, but I felt a lot better afterwards."

Angel shrugged, they hated having awkward conversations with professors, "Can't I just see your poster?"

Akeelah paused, "I'll show you my poster, but only after you talk with Prof. Smith." Angel sighed and opened their email; they began an email asking Prof. Smith to come and discuss the grade during office hours. Angel needed to know what they could do better for the next assignment.

A few days later, Angel sat with Prof. Smith in office hours. Prof. Smith explained why Angel had earned the C-. She said Angel wasn't writing in a way that was effective for scientists or for the purpose of the assignment. The sentences were too wordy, the writing style was not appropriate for scientific readers, some expected poster sections were missing, and the conclusion only summarized without making specific recommendations for the scientific community. Prof. Smith did not see the conventions she expected to see in scientific posters: a presentation of findings and data using relevant graphs or images, an evaluation of methods and processes, and specific recommendations based on data. Instead, she argued, Angel had written the poster as if it were an essay. Angel was confused, "Was the writing they had done in their composition class less good than the writing they were doing now?"

"Not less good," Prof. Smith said, "but *different* in its purpose, audience, style, and form."

Prof. Smith then asked Angel what they had done to prepare for the assignment: Had they looked at example scientific posters? Had they researched scientific writing styles? Had they arranged to meet with another classmate to look over drafts? Had they taken their writing to the writing center for feedback? Prof. Smith had talked about these steps when the poster assignment was introduced. Angel struggled to remember that class day—it was a long day, and they had felt overloaded with all the information they had received. Together Prof. Smith and Angel logged into Canvas, their course learning management system, and located the course syllabus. They downloaded and opened the file—Angel was guilty that they hadn't thought to do that while completing the poster. Sure enough, there was a section of the syllabus devoted to resources on scientific writing (Kinsley's 2009 *A Student Handbook for Writing in Biology, 3rd edition* and Weaver et al.'s *Scientific Posters: A Learner's Guide*) and even links to example scientific posters by former students.

Angel had used writing strategies that had worked well for them in the past: they had participated in class activities and done every bit of the homework. When they were ready to start the poster, they had outlined their ideas into sections, written in complete and engaging sentences, and cited their sources in MLA. They had moved their written sections onto a poster and added a visual. However, they hadn't done enough to consider this new writing context, its new expectations, and the more independent responsibility they would have to take on as a writer. Being asked to write in new forms for new audiences demanded Angel adapt their writing strategies.

Before we move on, let's look at the posters created by Angel and Akleelah. What differences do you notice? Table 1 summarizes several differences as well.

Microbiomes in Soil
Angel Martinez

Introduction
According to the University of Minnesota Center for Infectious Disease Research, as we continue to overprescribe antibiotics in the medical community, we risk a greater likelihood of antibiotic resistance. However, we can respond to this problem by spending more time examining the dirt around us. Bacteria with the potential to create new antibiotics live in the ground we walk on every day, but it takes significant time and labor to discover them. Unfortunately, pharmaceutical researchers do not have any incentive to explore these potential antibiotics because they already profit from existing antibiotics and treatments. The Tiny Earth project seeks to respond to this dilemma by training students to collect, review, and analyze bacteria in their science lab courses. Through lab experiments in BIO2030 designed by Dr. Smith, I have sought to do this work in collaboration with my classmates. This poster summarizes what I found.

Conclusion
The soil sample did show positive for two kinds of isolates, AIB09 and AIB11, which are capable of producing antibiotics. However, because of insufficient data and issues in testing samples, I was unable to further explore the samples. Future studies should be conducted using further samples from the Auburn River to further explore what isolates are present in these samples.

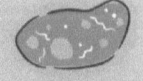

Research and Lab Work
As a sophomore, this was my first opportunity to conduct lab-based research. We began by collecting soil samples from the Auburn River. I chose to take my samples from the river bank where standing water had pooled with the hope that more bacteria would be present in the soil. Aseptic Technique protected samples from contamination. The samples were then plated, purified, and stained so that soil isolates could be examined.
After 24 hours of growth, staphylococcus epidermidis and psydomonas putida was present in the samples. While 16 PCRs were attempted, further testing did not produce significant results related to metabolic characterization.

Works Cited
Handelsman, Jo, Hernandez, Simon, Bascom-Slack, Carol, Broderick, Nichole. *Tiny Earth: A Research Guide to Studentsourcing Antibiotic Discovery.* XanEdu, 2021. Print.

University of Minnesota Center for Infectious Disease Research and Policy. "Overuse of Overprescribing of Antibiotics." CIDRAP, 2021, https://www.cidrap.umn.edu/asp/overuse-overprescribing-of-antibiotics. Accessed March 14 2022.

Acknowledgments
I want to thank my lab partners and professor, Dr. Smith

Figure 1: Angel's scientific poster, mock examples created by the author. This poster has a lengthy introduction with an attention grabber to start. The research and lab work section discusses the student's experience in the lab, not the scientific methods or lab processes. The conclusion offers a quick summary of the points already explored. Research is cited in MLA format, and the only visual is a microbe cartoon.

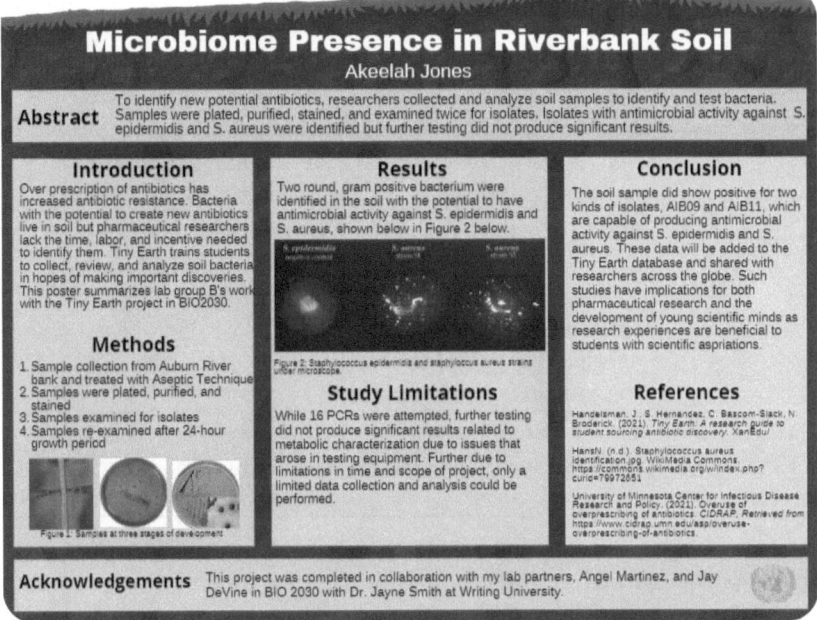

figure 2: Akeelah's scientific poster, mock examples created by the author. This poster starts with an abstract. Its introduction is short, offering brief context for the project. The methods are a simple list that focuses on scientific lab processes and includes a figure showing the three stages of development. The results also include a single takeaway with an image showing the antimicrobial activity in its microscopic form. There is a section on limitations. The conclusion offers a brief summary and calls for the Tiny Earth project to be continued to promote pharmaceutical research among young scientists. References are in APA format.

Angel's challenge isn't uncommon for students as they move into their discipline-specific courses (also called courses in the major). Angel's composition professor had taught them the importance of audience, purpose, and genre, and they had been successful applying those concepts in their composition course. However, it was more difficult for Angel to apply those concepts and manage their writing process in this new discipline-specific course. Prof. Smith expected Angel to do the work of learning about writing within the scientific community and the genre of a scientific poster more independently. Prof. Smith also didn't provide checkpoints in draft development like Angel's composition professor had, making it easy for Angel to wait to begin the project until just before it was due.

Table 1

A comparison between Angel's and Akeelah's posters

	Angel's Poster	Akeelah's Poster
Style/ Word Choice	Uses "I" language, narrative style, and lengthy transitions to elaborate on the topic. MLA format	Uses more concise scientific language with tightly focused paragraphs. APA format
Organization	Emphasizes the introduction and conclusion sections as being the most important while methods focus on what they gained from engaging in research	Mirrors the IMRAD structure with methods detailing lab procedures
Design	Mostly written text with a single cartoonish graphic	Balanced between concise writing and visuals, including labeled figures

    This chapter will help you understand how you can use the rhetorical concepts you learned in your composition course to decode new writing situations and genres that you'll likely encounter in your upper-level, discipline-specific courses in your major. You might assume that writing is just writing, but Angel's scientific poster shows that is not the case. While you might receive more support in your discipline-specific courses than Prof. Smith provided in the example, you will be expected to be more independent as you develop and revise your writing projects. You also could be expected to learn about disciplinary writing styles and genre conventions by seeking out resources on your own.

Discipline-Specific Courses and Discourse Communities

In Volume 3 of *Writing Spaces*, Dan Melzer helps readers learn about discourse communities, which are named so because they have specific communal expectations related to speaking and writing. Your majors represent discourse communities created by individuals within your discipline and future profession: biologists, nutritionists, professional writers, athletic trainers, hospitality professionals, nurses, and engineers are all different discourse communities.

When you begin taking courses in your major, your professors (who are members of those discourse communities), will develop assignments that help you to practice speaking and writing like members of those discourse communities. To do this, you will need to learn writing styles and genres that are popular in those discourse communities, although this purpose may not be formally explained in class. Professors may not unpack discourse community expectations clearly, or they might expect you to do more independent work learning about writing style and format.

Mary Soliday notes that attempting new genres can be difficult and "disorienting," even for professionals, because you are juggling a lot of newness all at once—"exploring new subject matter, trying on new roles, and meeting unknown audiences" (14). However, you can use the rhetorical concepts you have learned in your composition course to investigate writing in these new situations. And you are more likely to do this successfully when you have opportunity to engage in "bridging practices" to reflect on how your learning in composition can be framed to transfer to a new context (Rounsaville).

Take our issue at hand—the presence of microbiomes in soil. Different discourse communities would approach writing on this topic in different ways, using different formats. A biologist interested in the systematic study of these microbiomes will engage in research projects to collect and analyze soil samples, and share those analytical findings in scientific forms of communication, like a research poster, presentation, or article. A nurse, however, would focus more on educating individuals so that they avoid coming into contact with infection-causing bacteria. Because the nurse has a different purpose and audience, they would produce a genre focused on the general reader, like an informational health pamphlet or newspaper editorial. The writing styles of the biologist and nurse also differ because of their different audiences and purposes, even though they both study within the sciences.

The rest of this chapter will help you develop strategies for using rhetorical concepts (key terms like audience, purpose, rhetoric, genre, and conventions) to decode or investigate discipline-specific writing situations. The section below defines these common rhetorical concepts and explains why these concepts are relevant in your discipline-specific courses. The chapter ends with another scenario: one that shows Angel using the knowledge in the chapter to do better on their poster assignment.

Important Concepts and Definitions

Each rhetorical concept below has a general definition alongside how the concept might be applied in your discipline-specific courses. These terms give us a language to talk about our writing choices and transfer existing writing knowledge to new contexts (Rounsaville 12).

Purpose

Every communicative act has a purpose, or an impact you would like your writing to have on your audience. In Angel's case, their scientific poster was intended to communicate a research experience and its findings to other scientists. Your purpose can be affected by other situational details, like the topic, audience, and genre. Similarly, your purpose can impact your writing style and word choice (i.e., are you writing to inform, persuade, call to action?).

Applying Purpose to New Writing Situations

The purpose of writing in your discipline-specific courses might not always be clear through assignment sheets. For example, scientific posters communicate a research project—its goal, methods, data, key findings, and implications—in a highly visual and easy-to-read fashion. When creating a poster, you need to consider visual design and how your photos, graphs, and tables from the research can support concise writing. Too much writing, and you lose the visual appeal of the scientific poster genre. Too many visuals and the audience does not have enough information to know how to interpret and connect the visual elements.

Consider how Angel and Akeelah each used visuals in their poster examples: Angel included a single, cartoonish visual while Akeelah included several labeled figures from her lab research. It's appropriate for you to ask your professor to explain the single or multiple purposes of an assignment, either during class, in an email, or during office hours. You might say something like, "I know that there should be a specific purpose this writing assignment aims to achieve. Can you help me understand it?"

Audience

The people you are writing to engage, which in turns affects your writing style, format, and choices. When writing for an audience, you will want to consider their shared experiences and needs and write with those details in mind.

Applying Audience to New Writing Situations

Your audience can vary widely depending on the assignment. A good first question to ask is if your audience will be other experts in your discipline. To revisit our example, scientific posters can differ by their audience. Expert audiences will expect to see methods and terminology that show you are also an expert in their field and that your research project meets rigorous research expectations. If you are writing to other experts in your profession, you can use more technical language and assume a certain level of background knowledge. General audiences care more about the larger implications your research has on the general public, but they may need your help understanding the scientific concepts and terms. If your audience is not in your professional community, you will need to write using language and a style that is approachable to someone who does not have background knowledge in your discipline.

Rhetoric

The words, images, media, sounds, and body language you use to communicate your purpose to your audience. Choose rhetoric that will be effective and meaningful for your audience.

Applying Rhetoric to New Writing Situations

Rhetoric in your disciplinary communities includes more than written words: graphics, figures, and design (e.g., section headings, font size, color choice, layout) also hold value. You'll want to remember this as you are investigating new genres. For example, when viewing a scientific poster, you'll want to pay attention to how visuals like graphics and figures are used to communicate data as well as how design helps make the complex scientific topic being discussed more approachable to the audience. Further, when presenting your poster, your body language and oral delivery can be as influential as your word choice and poster design in helping your audience understand your research.

Genre

Most people think about genres that appear on their Netflix account: action, drama, documentary. But in writing, genres are different forms of writing. These formats have come to exist over time as individuals responded to the same rhetorical situation and needed to solve recurring communication problems. For instance, a resume is a particular genre that quickly tells an employer about your qualifications and background before the interview stage of hiring. You write a resume for a specific audience to achieve a particular purpose, persuading them to offer you an interview or job. Resumes help employers solve a problem: how can they review every applicant without expending too much time or labor?

While genres do not have concrete rules, they do contain conventions related to their structure, organization, language, and style (Miller 163). My use of in-text citations throughout this chapter is a genre convention that has come to be associated with forms of academic writing: I am expected to link my thought and ideas to existing scholars on a topic. So, as I discuss genre, I cite Carolyn Miller's foundational text on how genres perform social actions, but I paraphrase Miller's point so that her ideas are more accessible to my chapter's audience.

Applying Genre to New Writing Situations

Inevitably, you will encounter new genres in your discipline-specific courses: lab reports, presentations, memos, posters, case studies. It is important to ask questions and learn about new genres as they represent ways that professionals in your discourse community communicate with one another. The first time you complete a writing assignment in a new genre, it is common to struggle and want additional support. As you develop drafts of these assignments, seek out models of successful examples, feedback from peers and experts in your discipline (like your professor), and writing about the genre, which may exist within your professional community (for an example, see Andrea Gilpin and Patricia Patchet-Golubev's *A Guide to Writing in the Sciences* or Suzan Last's *Technical Writing Essentials: Introduction to Professional Communications in the Technical Fields*). Prof. Smith included some of these resources in her syllabus, but Angel had forgotten about them. You may want to refer to course documents, like the syllabus, or other institutional resources, like subject-librarians.

CONVENTIONS

The characteristics that an audience associates with a particular genre and thus expects to see. These conventions can relate to the writing's purpose, content, structure, organization, style, tone, language, and formatting.

APPLYING CONVENTIONS TO NEW WRITING SITUATIONS

As you encounter new genres, you should ask what conventions are associated with each genre. When attempting to write in a new genre, you want to be aware of conventions because your audience will expect to see them. These might be (but are not always) described in the assignment sheet. They should be observable in successful examples of the genre, so look for models of the genre in which you are writing. Ask questions about what writing in these genres typically looks like and does and seek out examples when you can.

Conventions can vary because of your audience, discipline, or culture. For instance, the conventions associated with a research poster can vary across disciplines: a research poster you create in a biology course may have different conventions than a research poster you create in a history course. While both will still purposefully communicate research, biologists expect concise informative writing, a straightforward design, and want to see scientific methods, while historians allow for more creative design with persuasive moments in writing and research methods drawn from the humanities. Conventions can vary across cultures and national contexts, too. Poster conventions that are typical for American professionals might differ from posters that those in the same profession in Japan or Ghana create because different cultures appreciate different aesthetic designs and have different ways to logically make meaning.

Writers do sometimes purposefully reject conventions because they want to challenge the expected to impact the audience. You should always deviate from conventions intentionally. Because conventions come to be expected by your audience, deviating from them might leave your audience confused or questioning your expertise. For instance, a biologist presenting their scientific poster to an audience of high schoolers might reduce their technical terms and play with a more colorful, creative design. Departing from conventions in this case makes the information more accessible and appealing to the biologist's audience and helps the biologist achieve their purpose: to engage high schoolers in learning about biology research.

Table 1

This table briefly summarizes these rhetorical concepts and offers some guiding questions to get you thinking about these concepts in your writing.

RHETORICAL CONCEPT	DEFINITION	GUIDING QUESTIONS
Purpose	An impact you would like your writing to have on your audience (e.g., inform, persuade, call to act)	• What do I want readers to do while and after engaging with this writing? • Where do professionals use this type of writing in the real world? • When will I use this type of writing after graduation? • How do my choices in writing style and design align with this writing's purpose?
Audience	The people you are writing to engage, which in turns affects your writing style, format, and choices. When writing for an audience, you will want to consider their shared experiences and needs.	• What does my audience know about my topic? What background information should I assume they already know, and what information will need to be introduced or explained to them? • What does my audience expect to see because of the genre I'm writing in? How can I meet those expectations or intentionally stray from them to achieve a greater rhetorical impact? • What specific needs, interests, and goals do members of my audience share?
Rhetoric	The words, images, media, sounds, and body language you use to communicate your purpose to your audience	• How can my writing be designed to achieve a visual impact? Can I **bold**, *italicize*, or otherwise format my words for rhetorical effect? Can I break my ideas down into sections, subsections, and lists for brevity? • What visual elements, like figures and graphs, can I include to support my audience's understanding? • What visual genres might be most appealing to my audience? Would they be more likely to engage with infographics, short videos, or one-page overviews rather than the traditional essay?
Genre	Different forms of writing that have come to exist because they solve communication problems. Because genres recur, audiences come to expect to see certain genre conventions.	• What problem does this genre solve? What is its purpose? • What similarities are shared by successful examples of this genre? • What writing resources exist that discuss how one can approach writing in this genre? • What does my audience expect to see because of the genre I'm writing in? How can I meet those expectations or intentionally stray from them to achieve a greater rhetorical impact?
Genre Conventions	The characteristics that an audience associates with a particular genre and thus expects to see. These conventions can relate to the writing's purpose, content, structure, organization, style, tone, language, and formatting.	• What expectations are identified in the assignment sheet and rubric? • What conventions can I observe by looking at successful examples of this genre in my discipline? • What does my audience expect to see because of the genre I'm writing in? How can I meet those expectations or intentionally stray from them to achieve a greater rhetorical impact? • Do I want to follow the genre conventions, or should I intentionally subvert or deviate from them to impact my audience in a particular way?

Strategies for Approaching New Writing Situations in Your Discipline

This section will lead you through strategies that can help you intentionally apply these rhetorical concepts in new writing situations. Before you begin writing,

- Carefully examine materials, like assignment sheets and rubrics. Pay attention to the purpose in the prompt (it can usually be identified through the verbs that are used, like "justify," "reflect," "analyze," "research"). Nelms and Dively remind us that these verbs can take on different meanings across the disciplines: "research" might imply reviewing library sources in a writing course but might refer to data collected in a lab setting in science courses (227). When unclear, you should ask professors for examples and further explanation.
- Identify each rhetorical concept for the assignment and check that what you've identified matches what the professor is requiring.
- Genre matters! Ask experts to talk to you about genre conventions. If possible, locate examples of this genre from within your discipline and analyze the rhetorical moves that the writer is making. Then, reflect on the rhetorical choices you made in your draft and why you made them. Consider how you would justify *why* you wrote the project in this way if asked.
- Locate resources related to writing in your discipline, like examples and guidebooks. Seek out feedback from your peers in the course, professor, subject-librarians, TAs, writing center tutors, among others.
- Make a plan: when will you begin the project, how will you get feedback, and what resources will you draw from when you have questions? Give yourself time to engage in a writing process. This means you'll need to start a project when it's introduced to have ample time to revise higher-order elements like organization and structure as well as lower-order elements like sentence-level clarity, consistency in language, and proofreading.

After doing this work, I would still recommend visiting your professor during office hours to confirm that what you've found aligns with their expectations for the assignment. Coming to office hours with questions that have emerged from this investigatory process will show your initiative as a student while also ensuring you meet expectations. Remember, joining a discipline takes time. Don't be discouraged if you struggle at first. Being able to use feedback to grow and learn will help you gain the disciplinary expertise that you need to feel more confident as a writer in this new space.

Applying These Strategies to a Scenario

Let's revisit Angel's story again. This time, consider what you would do if you were in their position:

In BIO 2030, Prof. Smith, introduced a new assignment, a scientific poster. The assignment prompt asks students to communicate the research they've been doing in their labs to a scientific audience. The assignment will be due in one month but will not be worked on during the class although some of the readings and lectures might be relevant to the assignment. What should Angel do next? Help them consider the important questions they should ask as well as what resources they can locate to help them begin their project.

What Might Angel Do Next?

I hope you had some sensible advice for Angel this time around. For one, they should begin by seeing if there is an extended assignment sheet or rubric that they can reference to get more information on the purpose, audience, genre, and conventions. They should also look back to the course syllabus to see if additional writing resources are listed there.

Next, they can locate resources and examples on scientific posters in biology. Once they feel they have a sense of what Prof. Smith might be expecting in this assignment, Angel could email her or visit office hours to make sure they are meeting her expectations. In this meeting, they should bring their resources and talk through them, showing Prof. Smith that they have done some initial research and found good examples to build from. This is a good point in the process for Prof. Smith to let Angel know if they are missing key assignment expectations.

After Angel is confident, they can create a first draft and get feedback. Ideally, they should find someone familiar with scientific writing, like a peer in Biology or a writing center consultant with a background in STEM writing. Angel shouldn't rely on friends without experience with scientific writing as their English major friend will likely be using different writing conventions than their professor expects. This feedback will help Angel know if what they are intending to communicate is coming across clearly to a real reader. As they revise, Angel could continue to use the resources they found, the assignment materials, and additional opportunities for feedback.

Aside from potentially doing better on the assignment, Angel will feel more confident as a writer in biology. Also, Angel will engage in important strategies that are necessary to developing writing: considering genre and context, embracing the writing process, and integrating feedback. These steps are taken by all writers—even writers who are experienced with their professional community and its expectations.

Conclusion

While you have established a solid foundation through your composition course, all students, new professionals, even experts continue to learn about writing well beyond composition. I hold multiple graduate degrees in English and participate in a discipline with others who study and teach writing. Despite our expertise in writing studies, *even we frequently commiserate that writing is a taxing and troublesome act.*

When you are adapting to discipline-specific writing, those challenges are heightened, and sometimes you might even experience failure in your initial attempts to write something new. Those feelings of confusion that might be overwhelming at first are very normal experiences! If you take the time to evaluate each new writing situation and apply the rhetorical concepts you have learned, you can transfer your writing habits and take advantage of available resources. I hope these tips prepare you to anticipate new writing challenges and give you some strategies for tackling them.

Note

Thank you to Noah Flood, a talented peer consultant in Auburn University's Miller Writing Center, for his feedback on this chapter.

Works Cited

Bunn, Mike. "How to Read Like a Writer." *Writing Spaces, Vol. 2.* Parlor Press and WAC Clearinghouse, 2011, pp. 71–86. Retrieved from https://writingspaces.org/sites/default/files/bunn--how-to-read.pdf

Gilpin, Andrea and Patricia Patchet-Golubev. *A Guide to Writing in the Sciences.* University of Toronto Press, 2000.

Kinsley, Karin. *A Student Handbook for Writing in Biology, 3rd edition.* Sinauer Associates, Inc. and W.H. Freeman and Co, 2009.

Last, Suzan. *Technical Writing Essentials: Introduction to Professional Communications in the Technical Fields*. British Columbia/Yukon Open Authoring Platform, 2021. Retrieved from https://pressbooks.bccampus.ca/technicalwriting/.

Melzer, Dan. "Understanding Discourse Communities." *Writing Spaces. Vol. 3*. Parlor Press and WAC Clearinghouse, 2020, pp.100–115. Retrieved from https://writingspaces.org/sites/default/files/melzer-understanding-discourse-communities.pdf.

Miller, Carolyn R. "Genre as Social Action." *Quarterly Journal of Speech*, vol. 70, 1984, pp.151–167.

Nelms, Gerald and Ronda Leathers Dively. "Perceived Roadblocks to Transferring Knowledge from First-Year Composition to Writing-Intensive Major Courses: A Pilot Study." *WPA: Writing Program Administration*, vol. 31, no. 1–2, Fall 2007, pp. 214–240.

Rounsaville, Angela. "Selecting Genres for Transfer: The Role of Uptake in Students' Antecedent Genre Knowledge." *Composition Forum*, vol. 26, Fall 2012, pp. 1–16.

Soliday, Mary. *Everyday Genres: Writing Assignments across the Disciplines*. Southern Illinois University Press, 2011.

Weaver, Ella, Kylienne A. Shaul, Henry Griffy, and Brian H. Lower. *Scientific Posters: A Learner's Guide*. National Science Foundation and The Ohio State University, n.d., https://ohiostate.pressbooks.pub/scientificposterguide/. Accessed 1 April 2022.

Teacher Resources for "'I Passed First-Year Writing—What Now?' Adapting Strategies from First-Year Writing in the Disciplines"

Overview and Teaching Strategies

Thank you for reading—and potentially teaching—this chapter! This chapter is meant to help students consider how they will adapt the strategies that they learned in composition when they enter discipline-specific courses in their major. As an administrator in a WAC program, I really hope that students are asked to write in meaningful ways beyond their general education writing courses. Research in writing across the curriculum, writing in the disciplines, and career success identify the ability to communicate effectively as integral for professional preparation. This chapter is meant to resist the assumption that the completion of their general education writing courses means students are done learning about writing. Moreover, it encourages students to critically think about how they can take more agency in writing transfer and anticipate that writing in their disciplinary courses will likely have less scaffolding and support than they experienced in composition courses.

This chapter opens with a scenario describing a student who experienced success in composition but could not transfer the skills they learned to a biology scientific poster assignment. Then, it explains how key rhetorical concepts can be applied in a writing in the disciplines setting. After, it gives students some tips they can use to guide their writing in these new contexts. It ends by revisiting the scenario and asking students how they might advise the student featured in this story. The conclusion reminds readers the work of learning writing never ends.

I encourage you to use this chapter alongside other WAC/WID activities, such as researching genres and writing situations common to students' professional and disciplinary communities or speaking with experts in their future fields about writing. In my own composition course, I ask students to complete a genre analysis of a genre that is used often within their future professions. Then, after analyzing the genre and researching a topic relevant to professional conversations in their discipline, they compose the genre for the first time. I would ask students to read this chapter after that final project alongside a reflective activity that asks them to imagine their future writing tasks and articulate how their writing strategies can help them complete these tasks. The discussion questions below can facilitate this reflective process.

Discussion Questions

Please use these discussion questions to guide synchronous or asynchronous discussion. They are broken into two sections: one that asks about the chapter's content and another that asks students to begin reflecting on their future disciplinary writing.

Reviewing the Chapter's Content

1. Review the key rhetorical concepts that the author uses in this chapter. Which concepts are familiar to you and which are new? How do you see these concepts at work in the writing you've done for this course?

2. In your opinion, is the scenario that opens and closes this chapter realistic to writing assignments in other courses? What challenges related to how you understand writing in your discipline are understated or missing? What do you wish the author had considered or added when creating the opening scenario?

3. The author has a list of writing strategies that she encourages you to consider. In looking over this list, which strategies complement your writing process? Which strategies do you think would be more difficult to integrate into your writing habits?

Reflecting as a Writer

1. The author mentions the role that failure and frustration plays in adapting to new writing situations. Think about a particular time you felt frustrated by a writing situation: what did you do? How did you overcome the challenges? What would you have done differently? How did this past challenge prepare you to better respond to future writing-related challenges?

2. In reflecting on your future professional community, identify some writing situations (purposes, audiences, genres, and forms of rhetoric) that are commonly used in that community. What do you know about these writing situations? If you were to engage in these

situations as a writer, what questions would you need answered to be successful?

3. Open an internet search and type in "Writing in..." completing the phrase with your future professional or disciplinary community. Take 10–15 minutes to review some resources that come up. Then, do some freewriting about what you found: what resources did you find, and do you believe they reliably represent writing in your future profession? What organization or individual created these resources, and are they good authorities of writing in your discipline? What did you learn about writing in this professional community? How is this approach to writing different than writing you have done? What excites you about writing in these new ways? What do you want the writing you do in your profession to accomplish?

Optional Activities: Read-Like-a-Writer

This activity has been developed from Mike Bunn's chapter "How to Read Like a Writer" chapter in Writing Spaces, *vol. 2.*

For Teachers

I use this brainstorming activity to open a genre analysis assignment. I model with students how to engage in answering these questions. If it's early in the semester, I model using the syllabus (which can actually be helpful in teaching students how to read syllabi), but if that is not a timely suggestion, you can use pop culture genres (like Instagram posts, memes, blogs) or other familiar genres. When I'm teaching online, this is a shared discussion board, Google doc, or Padlet thread that everyone contributes to. When I'm teaching face-to-face, we orally discuss the example while I take notes on a shared doc or visible whiteboard. After we discuss a shared example, I ask students to complete the read-like-a-writer questions for the genre they would like to focus on the for the genre analysis. Students will then build on their answers to these questions to create a first draft of their genre analysis assignment.

Disciplinary instructors could use this activity to introduce a genre that students will be creating—like a scientific poster. This will help students learn about the new genre and create a conversational space where the instructor can emphasize assignment expectations.

For Students

Find 1–3 examples of a genre used by your professional community. If you are working with a longer genre, just read one part across all examples (e.g., if you are reading academic journal articles in your future discipline, maybe just look at a single section of each article).

Take time to read through each example. Instead of worrying about the content, read these examples with the goal of learning how the writer put them together: the choices they made and the writing strategies they used. The questions below will help you by leading you to look at specific features within the text(s). By reflecting on how the writing is designed to achieve its rhetorical goals, we can learn about writing in our professional disciplinary communities and begin to consider which strategies we would like to bring into our own writing.

Rhetorical Considerations

1. What is the purpose of this writing? To answer this question, look for clues in the text, but also consider where is has been published or shared.

2. Who is the audience? The answer is not everyone. Who would be interested in reading this text and who is it meant to reach given its purpose?

3. What forms of rhetoric are used throughout this text? Is the purpose achieved through alphabetic writing, visual rhetoric, embodied rhetoric, oral rhetorical cues, etc. Where are key moments in this text where you think the rhetoric is particularly strong in achieving its purpose?

4. What is the genre of this text? How does this genre relate to the text's audience and purpose?

5. What are the conventions of this genre? Put differently, what would someone expect to see because you are writing in this genre? Where do you see the writer pushing against the conventions and where do you see them following those conventions?

Text Design

1. How is the example organized? What logic guides how the text is put together?

2. How long is the text overall? Does that overall length get evenly distributed across all sections of the text or are certain sections longer than others?

3. What are the text's main parts or components?

4. How does the writer introduce or open the text? How long is the introduction? What rhetorical moves are made to bring the audience into the text and inform them of its purpose?

5. How long are paragraphs within the text? If the text doesn't have paragraphs, how long are sentences?

6. How does the writer close or conclude the text? How long is the conclusion? What rhetorical moves are made to wrap up the text and reinforce the text's purpose?

7. Does the writer attribute or cite ideas and sources? If so, what does that referencing process look like: are there in-text citations, footnotes, end notes, hyperlinks, tags?

8. What do you notice about the writer's language and style of writing? Is it formal or informal? Does it use technical or generalized language? How does it fit the audience and purpose of the text?

Process of Creation

1. What do you think was the writer's process for creating this text? Where might they have gotten feedback? What did the revision process perhaps take into account? How might they have known when the text was "done" or done enough to publish?

2. What steps did the writer take to make this text accessible? Accessibility includes steps taken in the design process to make it readable for those using assistive technologies, like screen readers, but it can also include language and design considerations that make the text

more approachable to readers with different disciplinary, professional, educational, and cultural backgrounds.

Adding to Your Writing Toolkit

1. What about this text complements how you write? These can be rhetorical strategies or design characteristics that appeal to you, or aspects of the process that fit your own process for writing.

2. What about this text is new or different from your writing? Do you have any interest adopting any of these strategies?

3. What challenges might you experience trying to write in this genre for the first time?

4. What resources or support could help you write in this genre for this audience and purpose?

12 Strategies for Analyzing and Composing Data Stories

Angela M. Laflen

Overview

Data stories are multimodal texts that combine data with words and images to tell a story to or make an argument for a particular audience.[1] They are increasingly common in everyday life as technology has resulted in an information explosion. Data often do not make sense unless someone takes the time to explain them—to tell a story about them. Data stories help to turn raw data into information that readers can understand and use to make decisions. Data storytelling has become an essential strategy for managing data, and students need to cultivate their skills in reading and composing data stories so they can critically analyze the data stories they encounter and in order to use data ethically and effectively in their writing. This chapter offers strategies to help students read data stories critically and use data in composing their own multimodal texts. It demonstrates how to use these strategies by working through the process of analyzing and composing sample data stories.

Introduction

While scrolling through Instagram, the following post catches your attention:

---

1. This work is licensed under the Creative Commons Attribution-NonCommercial-NoDerivatives 4.0 International License (CC BY-NC-ND 4.0) and is subject to the Writing Spaces Terms of Use. To view a copy of this license, visit http://creativecommons.org/licenses/by-nc-nd/4.0/, email info@creativecommons.org, or send a letter to Creative Commons, PO Box 1866, Mountain View, CA 94042, USA. To view the Writing Spaces Terms of Use, visit http://writingspaces.org/terms-of-use.

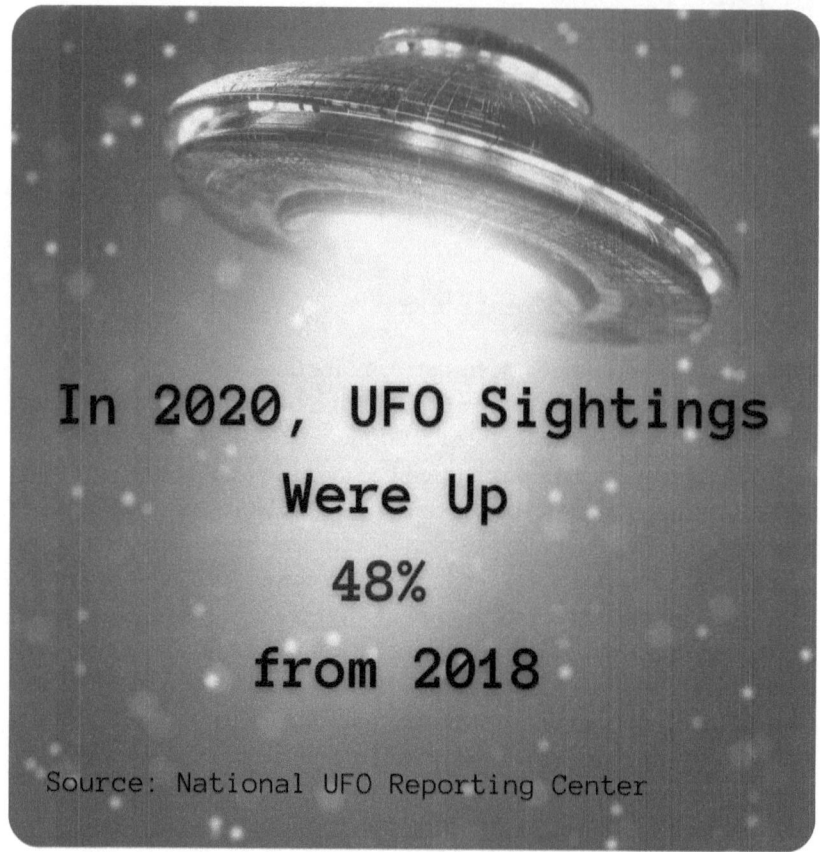

Figure 1. A sample Instagram post. Source: Angela Laflen.

You wonder if the post is true since you know there is a lot of misinformation circulating on social media. Working your way through questions you use to assess whether information is credible, you consider who posted it (your generally reliable cousin), why she posted it (because she is fascinated by UFOs), and its original source (the National UFO Reporting Center, which sounds official). So far, the post seems credible, but what to make of the statistic itself? If you are like many readers, you may tend to either dismiss it out of hand (since everyone knows statistics can be made up) or accept that it's accurate (since there's nothing obviously off about it).

These two responses to numerical information are very common. However, neither is particularly effective at helping you make good decisions about the "data stories" you encounter in daily life. In the case of Figure 1, the National UFO Reporting Center is a real organization that allows people to report sightings of UFOs, and the statistic in the post is technically true, but it is also misleading. A quick search of the National UFO Reporting Center reveals that 2018 was anomalous for the low number of reported sightings that year, so the 48% increase reported in Figure 1 is the result of cherry-picking data to create the impression that UFO sightings rose drastically over a 2-year period. Cherry picking of data means we look for particular data and statistics that help to illustrate our point of view, and it is a common way that data are misused in data storytelling. Notice that no complicated math—or really any math at all—was required to determine that this statistic is flawed; just some simple fact checking. Though not all data stories can be fact-checked so easily, it is possible to read many data stories and to write your own credible data stories using basic reasoning skills.

What Are Data Stories?

Whether or not you have heard the phrase "data stories" before, you have certainly seen data stories because they are widespread on social media, in news publications, and in advertising of all kinds. In addition to social media posts such as Figure 1, data stories often take the form of infographics (such as Figure 2) or online articles (such as Figure 3). Whatever form they take, data stories are multimodal texts that combine data with words and images to tell a story or make an argument for a particular audience. As infographic guru Alberto Cairo explains, data stories are texts that "give shape to data, so that relevant patterns become visible" (16).

You may have even used data in your own writing by including a graph or table as evidence to support an argument in a research paper. In fact, writers have always turned to data for evidence, and data stories of all kinds have long helped make data comprehensible to members of the public, decision makers, and other audiences. Today, though, data stories have become more common because there are simply more data to work with. According to writing and digital studies scholar Brenta Blevins, "the omnipresence of computers in every aspect of human life means we're recording and capturing ever-increasing amounts of data." Indeed, according to a 2021 article published in *TechJury*, "the majority of the world's data has been generated within the last two years alone" (Bulao).

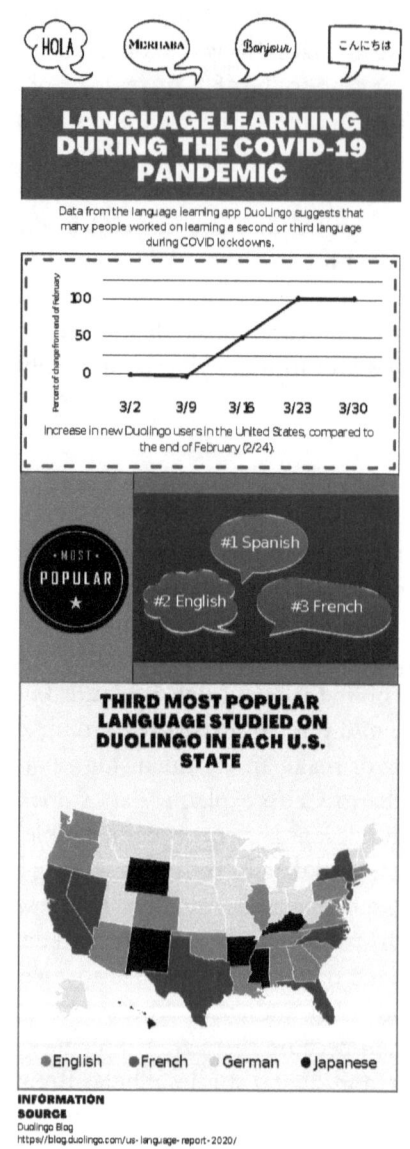

Figure 2. Infographic that charts the increase in language learning using the DuoLingo app during the COVID-19 pandemic. Source: Angela Laflen.

Which Plant Milk is the Most Sustainable?

Consumers often turn to plant milk as an alternative to cow's milk, which is far less sustainable in terms of the carbon dioxide emissions, land use, and water consumption associated with its production. But which plant milk is the most sustainable? It turns out that there is not a simple answer, as reported in a recent study published in Science and a recent New York Times interactive article.

Almond milk consumes the most water of the plant milks at 371 liters per liter of almond milk. But rice milk generates more pollution than almond milk does, with 1.2 kgs of CO_2 generated per liter of rice milk produced. Soy and oat milk are more sustainable options when it comes to water use, requiring only 28 and 48 liters of water respectively, but they both require more land to produce than do rice or almond milk. Oat and soy milk also still impose packaging and transportation costs on the environment. According to a BBC report, depending on the location of the consumer, oat or soy milk can travel a considerable distance, and it is not always easy to find out where the products used in a specific plant milk originated.

When it comes to choosing a plant milk alternative to cow's milk, consumers face a variety of choices, each of which comes with caveats and trade-offs. In contrast to cow's milk, though, each plant milk option is more sustainable.

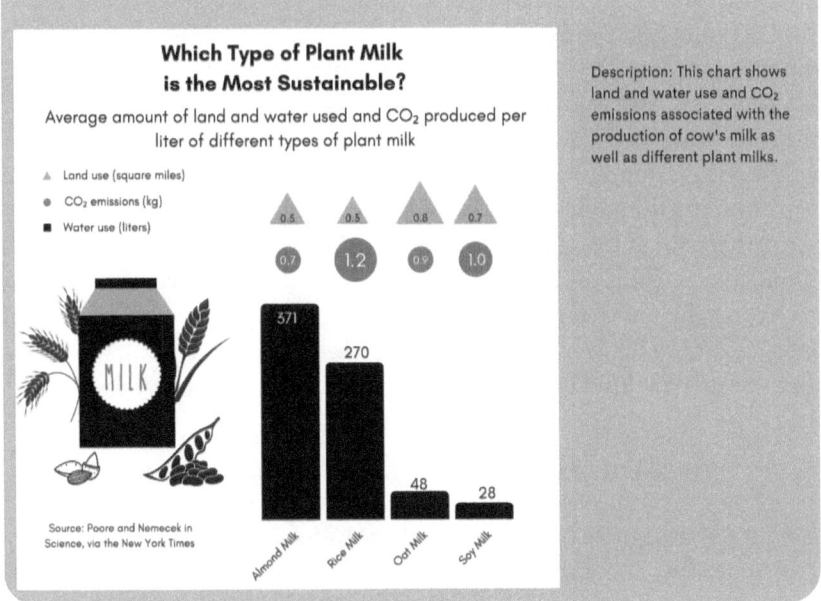

Figure 3. Online news article that compares plant milks based on their CO2 emissions, land use, and water use. Source: Angela Laflen.

Although not all of this information is numeric, a lot of it is, and most of it doesn't make sense unless someone takes the time to explain it—to tell a story about it. Data stories help to turn raw data into information that readers can understand and use to make decisions. In fact, even the way news is reported reflects the increasing importance of data. Data journalism is a type of journalism in which reporters use large databases as sources to produce stories. As they tell complex stories through the use of infographics and data visualizations, data journalists practice data storytelling.

Data storytellers rely on multiple modes of communication to make data comprehensible for readers, relying heavily on linguistic (words) and visual (images) modes of communication. The authors of *Writer/Designer: A Guide to Making Multimodal Projects* explain that the word multimodal

> "is a mash-up of *multiple* and *mode*. A mode is a way of communicating, such as the words we're using to explain our ideas in this paragraph or the images we use through this book to illustrate various concepts. Multimodal describes how we combine multiple different ways of communicating in everyday life" (Ball et al., 3).

For example, the UFO post in Figure 1 is a multimodal text. It combines an image of a UFO with a statistic about UFO sightings to create a text that uses images, words, and numbers—multiple modes—to try to convince readers that UFO sightings have increased over a short period of time.

You might also wonder whether an Instagram post like the UFO example is really a text. In an essay titled "An Introduction to and Strategies for Multimodal Composing" in volume 3 of *Writing Spaces*, Melanie Gagich explains that although the word text is "often only associated with writing (or perhaps the messages you receive or write on your phone)," in composition courses the term is often used to refer to "a piece of communication that can take many forms. For instance, a text is a movie, meme, social media post, essay, website, podcast, and the list goes on" (66). An Instagram post is the kind of multimodal text you likely encounter daily.

Why Do Data Stories Matter to Writing?

Even if you recognize how common data stories are, you may wonder why you are reading about them in a writing course; don't they belong better in a math or statistics course? Data storytelling is about more than being able to perform mathematical operations. Since technology has resulted in an information explosion, data storytelling has become an essential strategy for managing data, and as you develop your skills as a writer, it is important to cultivate data storytelling skills so that you can read data stories critically and are prepared to use data ethically and effectively in your writing. As Janae Cohn discusses in the essay "Understanding Visual Rhetoric" in volume 3 of *Writing Spaces*, "if we limit ourselves to words in our arguments, we may not successfully reach our audiences at all. Some audiences need visuals to think through an idea, and using graphs and diagrams can express some ideas *more* clearly than text can" (21).

Often, students encounter data stories when they are assigned to write—or read—multimodal texts such as infographics. Strategies for evaluating and composing multimodal texts more generally are useful with data stories, but they do not provide all the tools we need to work with data. Although often we do not need advanced mathematics or sophisticated statistical knowledge to analyze or compose data stories, we can become stronger readers and writers of data stories by being familiar with critical questions for data stories and the data story composing process.

Scholars have identified four different types of citizens according to the situations in which they use data: communicators, readers, makers, and scientists (Wolff et al., 18). Although scientists—and to some extent makers—do need advanced statistical training to be able to work with data at an appropriate level, for most people, the skills of a communicator or reader will help them "use data intelligently for solving real world problems" (Wolff et al. 18). Communicators are those who "make sense of and tell stories about data for others to digest," while readers "need skills to interpret data that is increasingly presented as part of their everyday life" (Wolff et al. 18).

This chapter focuses on how you can cultivate the skills of a reader and communicator of data stories. Though the strategies in this chapter will not be sufficient for those who need to work with data as a scientist or maker, they will help you in your writing courses to read data stories critically and use data in composing your own multimodal texts.

Strategies for Analyzing Data Stories

You can apply all of the critical reading strategies you already use to analyze other kinds of texts to data stories. For example, you can preview a data story to get a quick sense of its author, general design, and structure, or you can read a data story rhetorically to consider how the author's purpose, audience, and other elements of the text's context influence you as a reader. You can learn more about reading strategies in Mike Bunn's essay "How to Read Like a Writer" found in volume 2 of *Writing Spaces*. In addition, to analyze data stories, consider 1) the data source, 2) data alteration, 3) data analysis, and 4) data presentation. Table 1 provides a checklist of questions you can ask during analysis. In this section, I will show you how to use these questions to analyze a sample data story.

Table 1

Critical Questions for Data Stories

1	Data Source	Who conducted the study that this data story is based on and why?
2	Data Alteration	How were the data manipulated from their raw form into the visualization that we see? Are details about the data alteration provided?
3	Data Analysis	What terms are central to the writer's argument (quantitative and otherwise)? How does the writer define the terms? Who would disagree with the way the terms have been defined, and why? Would the writer's argument change if the definition of the term(s) changed; if so, how?
4	Data Presentation	Who is the audience for this data story and what are they supposed to do with this information? How do the data, images, and design elements work together to draw the audience into feeling a particular way about the topic of the data story?
5	Data Presentation	What story does this data story tell? What organizational pattern(s) did the writer use to tell that story? How would using a different organizational pattern change the argument?

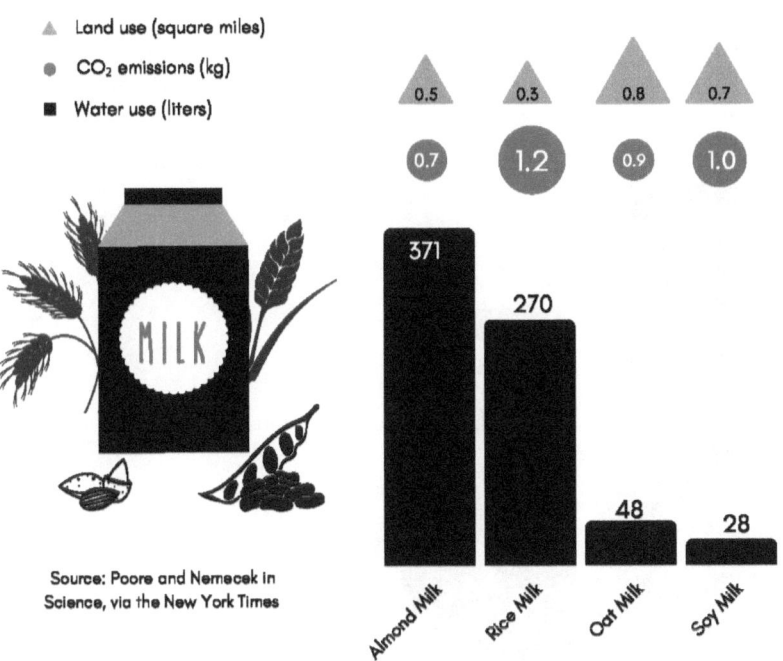

Figure 4. An example of "data journalism," which refers to short news articles designed for sharing online. This graph was written to be published alongside the news article in Figure 3, but texts like this can also circulate online via social media without their original articles.

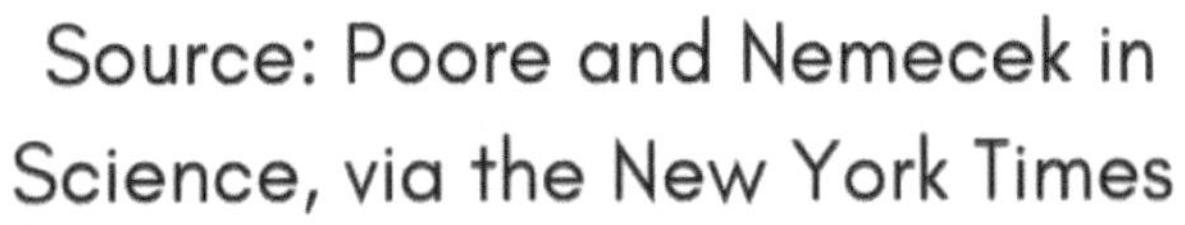

Source: Poore and Nemecek in Science, via the New York Times

Figure 5. Closeup on source information from Fig. 4. Source: Angela Laflen.

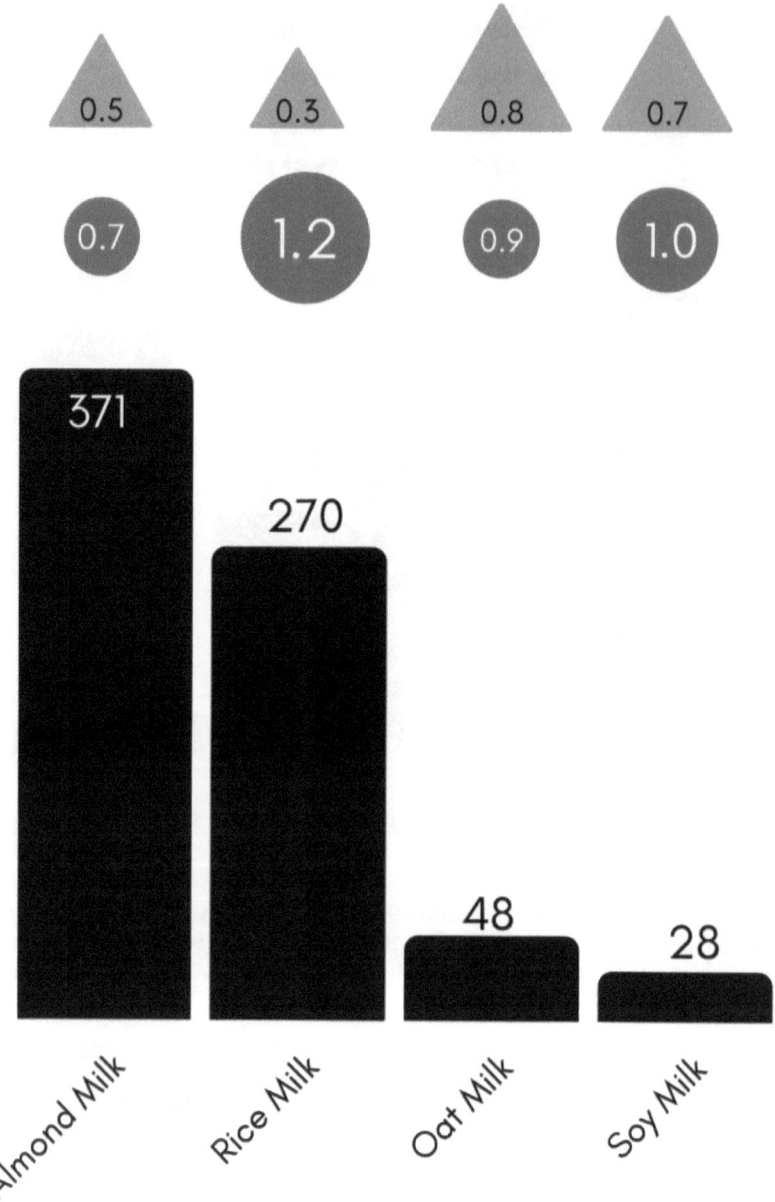

Figure 6. Closeup on bar graph in Fig. 4. that compares plant milks based on their CO_2 emissions, land use, and water use. Source: Angela Laflen.

Data Source

In order to analyze this story, our first step is to check the data source. All credible data stories should cite their source(s) of information. This citation serves the same function as citing your sources in an academic research paper: crediting the source of information and allowing readers to find that source for themselves. Do note that data stories do not always use a formal documentation style like MLA to credit sources. Sometimes data stories are so succinct that there is not space for complete citation, and data stories designed to be read online often rely on embedded links to their sources as a way to identify them. Additionally, some of the programs used to create data stories do not support formatting features we have come to expect from word processing programs such as indenting or italicizing specific words. Nevertheless, data stories should provide enough information about their source(s) that readers can find the source(s) for themselves. Also, be sure to do an Internet search for any source that is credited in a data story to make sure it really exists because some deliberately falsified data stories make up fictional sources that sound credible. It goes without saying that falsifying data for use in a data story is unethical.

In the case of Figure 4, the source is credited as Poore and Nemecek in *Science* via *New York Times*, but without any other information to help readers find the source such as article title or date (Figure 5). The online article that accompanies the data story includes a link to the *New York Times* article "Your Questions About Food and Climate Change, Answered," which includes a link to a peer-reviewed research article published in *Science* titled "Reducing Food's Environmental Impacts through Producers and Consumers." Though it takes a little work to identify the source(s) used in Figure 4, they are the kinds of credible scholarly and news sources that students like yourself are often encouraged to use in making academic arguments.

Data Alteration

Checking the data alteration means asking how the data were manipulated from their raw form into the visualization that we see. Ideally, writers will share details about how the data alteration was performed. Figure 4 is based on data from one table in the *New York Times* article (Moskin et al.), which lists data on water use in liters, land use in meters, and CO_2 emissions in kg and also includes data on cow's milk in addition to 4 types of plant milk. Figure 4 makes the comparison of different types of plant milk easier to see by moving data from a table into a bar graph to compare CO_2

emissions and by using bubbles and triangles to depict the relative sizes of water and land use (Figure 6).

By separating them out, readers can see that the milks compare differently depending on whether they are looking at CO_2 emissions, land use, or water use. Figure 4 also omits cow's milk, which helps the reader to directly compare plant milks to one another.

Data Analysis

We should also ask how data were analyzed and consider the terms the writer used in the data story. Though several terms are used in Figure 4, "sustainable" is the most significant term to examine because it can be defined in multiple ways (Figure 7). Figure 4 implicitly defines sustainability in terms of CO_2 emissions and water and land use, but no explicit definition is included. The data story could change drastically if sustainability were to be defined differently.

Which Type of Plant Milk is the Most Sustainable?

Average amount of land and water used and CO_2 produced per liter of different types of plant milk

Figure 7. Closeup on title in Fig. 4. Source: Angela Laflen.

Data Presentation

To check the data presentation, we ask how data, images, and other design elements work together to draw the audience into feeling and thinking a particular way about the topic of the data story. We also ask what the main story or argument is and how it is organized. The presentation of Figure 4 seems rather simple at first. When we look closer, though, we see that the presentation is designed to make reading easy, although the story's title could be revised for clarity. Different shades of gray, black, and white are used to help distinguish elements of the data story from each other.

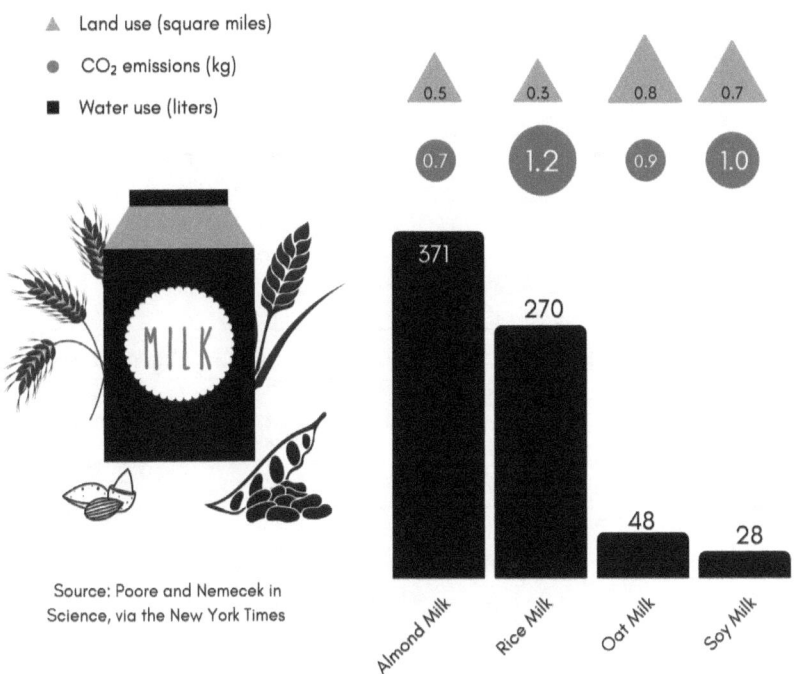

Figure 8. Closeup of milk carton image and bar graph in Fig. 4. Source: Angela Laflen.

Most obviously, Figure 4 includes a bar graph and bubbles and triangles to present data, which make the visual comparison of the plant milks easy for readers. The story also includes an image of a milk carton surrounded by the four types of plants included in the comparison of plant milks: rice, oats, soy, and almonds (Figure 8). This imagery helps the reader to visualize the types of milk being discussed in the data story. A large title at the top of the story asks "Which Type of Plant Milk is the Most Sustainable?," a question the story ultimately does not answer since the data indicate that no single plant milk is most sustainable in terms of carbon emissions, water use, and land use. The title could be revised to highlight this fact.

STRATEGIES FOR COMPOSING DATA STORIES

The process of composing data stories is similar to the process you would use to create any multimodal text; however, we have to take extra steps to ensure that we represent data in ethical and rhetorically effective ways.

Figure 9 shows how we might visualize the data storytelling composing process.

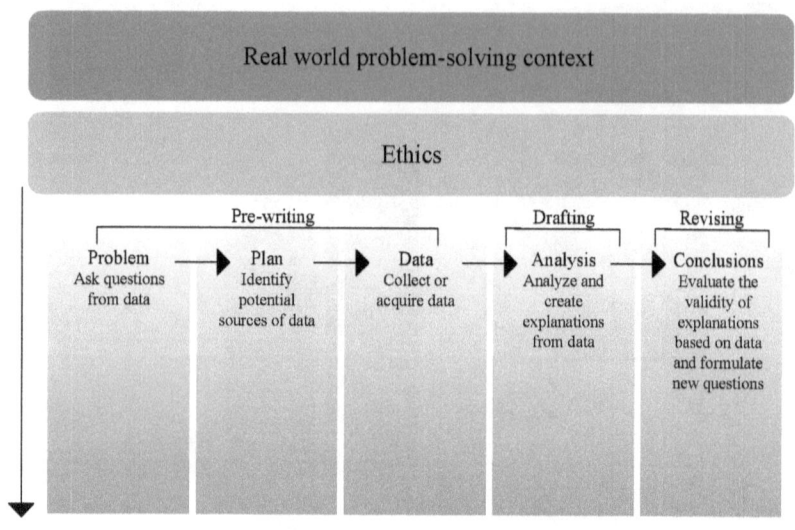

Figure 9. Data Storytelling Composing Process. Adapted from Wolff, Annika, et al. "Creating an Understanding of Data Literacy for a Data-Driven Society." *The Journal of Community Informatics*, vol. 12, no. 3, 2016, p. 15. Source: Angela Laflen.

As this map illustrates, real-world problem-solving contexts and ethics determine how a writer moves through the data storytelling composing process. We can think of them as defining the writer's rhetorical situation when composing a data story. A rhetorical situation refers to the surrounding circumstances and contexts that shape a piece of writing (usually discussed in terms of audience, purpose, exigence, genre, and rhetor). Data stories, like all texts, are shaped by their rhetorical situation. The real-world problem-solving context includes the reason a writer creates a data story, the audience they are writing to, and how they will disseminate the story.

In addition to the real-world problem-solving context, ethics also dictate the choices a writer can make when composing a data story. This means that a writer cannot choose to exaggerate or cherry-pick data just because this makes for a more interesting or persuasive story. All of a writer's decisions are bound by the need to be as accurate as possible in working with data.

In this section, I'll show you how I worked through the composing process to draft a story about Americans' preferences in pizza toppings.

The real-world problem-solving context for this story is the need to make an eye-catching Facebook post for National Pizza Day (celebrated annually in the United States on February 9). My ethical obligation as a writer is to accurately report the data I use in my story and to cite my source(s) of information so readers can fact check the story for themselves.

Prewriting Steps

It is common to spend more time on prewriting for a data story than on drafting the story. This is because writers need to work through at least three pre-writing steps:

1. Asking questions from data
2. Choosing data sources
3. Collecting data

Asking Questions from Data

Asking questions from data means thinking about possible questions data might be able to answer about a topic (this does not mean you will be able to find data to answer all of the questions you can think up). In the case of my National Pizza Day post, there are a number of questions I could ask, including: how much pizza do Americans eat each day/month/year? What kind of pizza do Americans like best/least? How do preferences for pizza (types of crust, toppings, etc.) differ by state or region? How much do Americans spend on pizza each year and how does this compare to spending on other types of food? I usually begin a data story by brainstorming lots of possible questions before I start looking to see what data is available to work with. This way, I can adjust my story depending on what I find.

Choosing Data Sources

After I identify questions I might be able to answer with data, I search for possible sources of data. I start my search by Googling "Americans' pizza preferences," which yields over a million results. However, given my rhetorical situation, I want to work with a large, national opinion poll, and I also want a source that allows me to see the raw data, which refers to the original data that was collected. There are many fewer options that meet these criteria. In fact, I quickly discovered that YouGov, a British international Internet-based market research and data analytics firm that specializes in market research through online methods, is the best source for my data story. YouGov has published data from a 2021 survey of Americans (over 6000 adults participated from different regions of the country). Since this survey only focused on pizza topping preferences, I can also narrow down the topic for my data story.

Collecting Data

The last prewriting step is collecting data. As you collect data, you have flexibility to further refine or change your topic based on the data you collect. It is important to develop a data story that supports the data you are working with rather than trying to make data fit a narrative you already have in mind, which can result in cherry-picking of data or other data distortions that undermine your credibility as a writer.

Collecting data from a source such as YouGov that makes the raw data from their surveys available online is easy and quick. I prefer to work with sources that let me see raw data because then I don't have to worry about how data were altered during analysis or for presentation. However, you will often not have access to raw data and will have to work with data from secondary sources, or data that has been reported by others. For example, the data stories in Figures 2 and 3 are based on data reported by secondary sources. Any time you work with data that have been gathered and reported by others, it is crucial to choose data from a credible source that clearly explains how they gathered and altered data and what their purpose was. In other cases, you may conduct primary research yourself and collect your own raw data for the project. In that case, data collection can be the most time-consuming part of your work. For more information about conducting primary research, check out Dana Lynn Driscoll's essay "Introduction to Primary Research: Observations, Surveys, and Interviews" in volume 2 of *Writing Spaces*.

Drafting and Revising

Analyzing Data

You begin drafting your data story by analyzing the data you have collected. Analysis involves thinking about the terms you'll use in your story and how you will represent data for readers. The terms you use can impact how well readers understand your data story and how accurate it is. For example, can you see the difference between saying that anchovies are Americans' "most disliked" topping versus that they are the "least popular" topping in America? While the difference is subtle, saying something is "most disliked" has a more strongly negative meaning than saying it is "least popular" (which implies it has some degree of popularity). To determine which phrase to use in my data story, I need to know what the original survey asked because that language influenced how survey participants responded. In the case of the YouGov survey, 61% of respondents indicated that they dislike anchovies, so it is accurate to say they are the most disliked topping in the survey.

Another of the main ways that writers analyze data is by deciding whether or not to use a graph to represent it and, if so, what type of graph to use. Sometimes, a simple table will help you present data more clearly than a graph would, and in other cases you might just present a statistic in the text of your story. In any case, your choices should be deliberate and intended to make data easy for your readers to understand.

If you think a graph is needed to communicate data clearly, you should choose the type of graph based on what you want it to show about your data. The flowchart in Figure 10 shows you how you can use the purpose of your graph and the kind of data you are working with to determine what graph might work for your data story. More information about each of these graphs and choosing the graph to use is available at the website Storytelling with Data (storytellingwithdata.com).

For the National Pizza Day post, I want to show a comparison, and specifically a comparison among items (pizza toppings in this case). The flowchart suggests I should consider a graph such as a vertical bar chart, horizontal bar chart, variable width column chart, or embedded table with graphs. Given that I only have one variable to graph—preference for pizza toppings—the vertical bar chart or horizontal bar chart are my best options.

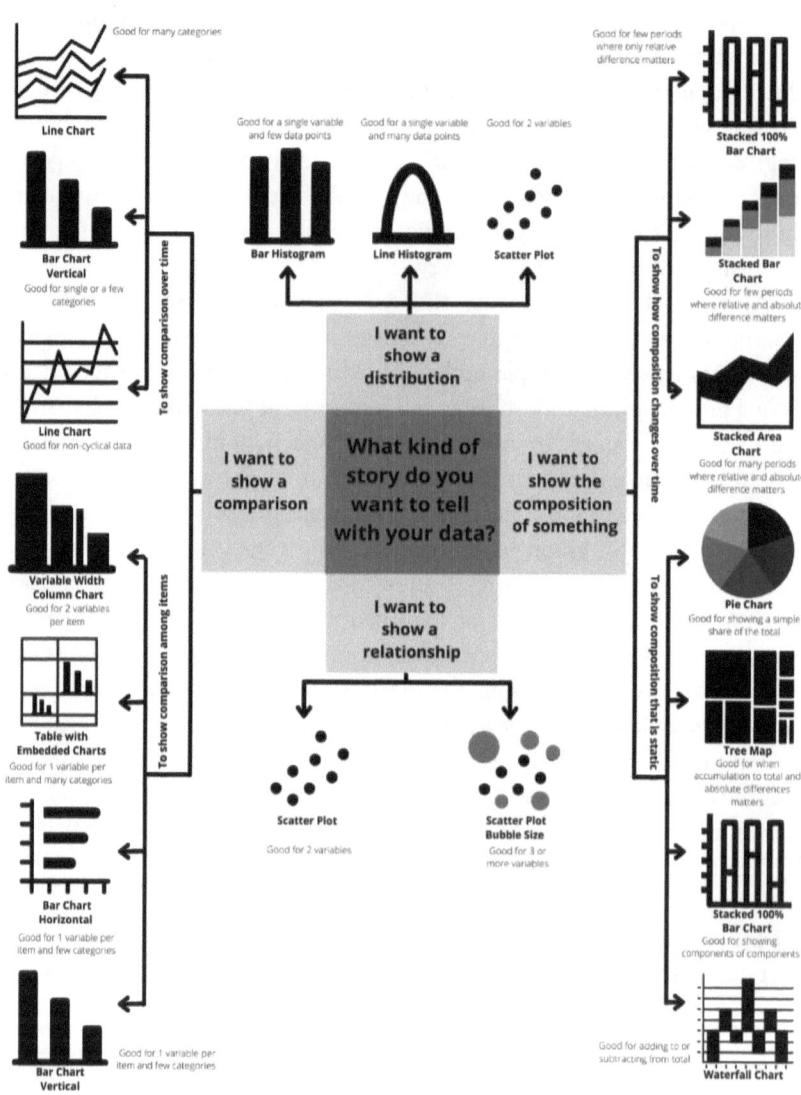

Figure 10. Flowchart to determine graph type based on data storytelling purpose. Source: Angela Laflen.

Create Explanations from Data and Test These with Readers

Though the simplest data stories may just present data in a clearly labeled graph, it is more common for data stories to make a larger argument about their topic using data as evidence to persuade readers that the argument is true. Writers create these larger arguments by combining words and images to help readers understand what is important or meaningful in the data they are working with. Since it takes time to compose multimodal texts that combine words and images effectively, we can borrow drafting strategies from the field of graphic design to help us work efficiently. Specifically, tools called thumbnails and mock-ups are useful to help writers plan the design of multimodal texts.

Graphic designers use thumbnails, which are small, quick sketches of possible designs, to rough out their initial ideas about how they might combine words and images (Figure 11). I like to create several different thumbnails to see the pros and cons of my different ideas. Often, I end up combining elements from different thumbnails together in my final design.

Figure 11. Two sample hand-drawn thumbnails for my pizza story. Source: Angela Laflen.

After you decide on an approach for your design, you create a mock-up, which is a rough layout of a screen or page. Think of your mock-up as a "visual outline of a project" (Ball, et al. 189) that includes the layout, colors, images, fonts, and headers you plan to use for your project. Mock-ups may or may not also include the actual text you plan to use. Although you can create a mock-up by hand, I prefer to create mock-ups using the software program I plan to use for my data story. Several free online programs are available to create multimodal texts including Canva, Piktochart, and Visme, along with pro tools such as Adobe Illustrator. Although these programs can make the composition process easier, document or slide programs (e.g. Word, Google Docs, Pages, PowerPoint, Google Slides, Keynote) can also work.

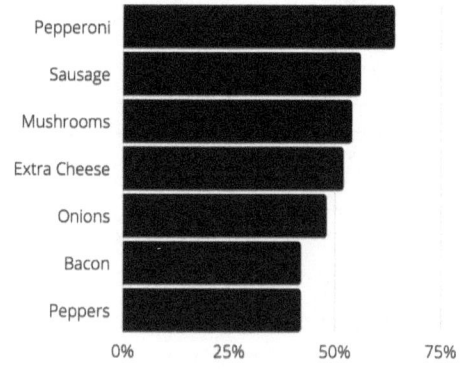

Figure 12. Mock-up of my National Pizza Day story. Source: Angela Laflen.

I used Canva to create the mock-up of my National Pizza Day post (Figure 12). I decided to focus my story on how united Americans are in their preferences for pizza toppings. The implicit argument in this story is that there are still some questions on which Americans agree strongly regardless of region, gender, age, politics, or income level. Since pepperoni is Americans' favorite topping across all these categories, I used a large image of a pepperoni pizza as the focal point for this story, and I wrote a title that communicates the argument of my story about national unity around pizza topping preferences. I drafted short text to present key results from the survey and included a bar graph to show more of the survey results. This mock-up helped me to see that the story has two distinct parts that aren't clearly linked yet, and I used it to write down a list of changes I wanted to make moving forward. Figure 13 shows how my data story evolved from the mock-up. Though some elements remained the same, including my main argument, I spent time on the images and text to make the story more cohesive. A cohesive data story is one in which the relationship between the different components of the text—the words, the images, the data, and any other elements included—is clear and logical to the audience. For example, in my mock-up it is not clear how the image of a hand reaching for a piece of pizza logically relates to the title "The United States of Pizza." Similarly, because I used different fonts for the two different parts of the story, there is no clear visual relationship between the parts. I made changes during revision to improve these elements. I included an image of a pepperoni pizza shaped like the United States to relate more clearly to the title. I also used two consistent fonts throughout the data story, one for headings and the other for the rest of the text. The consistent use of fonts creates visual unity between the two parts of the text.

Figure 13. My National Pizza Day Facebook post. Source: Angela Laflen.

The next step in my composing process is to test my story with readers. Based on this feedback, I might make additional revisions to the story. Like all texts, data stories are subject to an ongoing drafting and revision process, and I usually only finish working on a data story because I run into a deadline.

Concluding Thoughts and More Information

This chapter introduced you to data storytelling and to strategies that will help you get started as a reader and communicator of data stories. The main takeaway is that you can analyze data stories critically and use data ethically and effectively in your writing whether or not you consider yourself a "numbers person." Although these strategies are just a starting point, regular practice reading and composing data stories will help you to improve your analysis and composition skills. I also encourage you to learn more about the process of designing your data story. I touched only briefly on design in this chapter, and I recommend the following for more information:

- Michael J. Klein and Kristi L. Shackelford's *Writing Spaces* volume 2 chapter, "Beyond Black on White: Document Design and Formatting in the Writing Classroom" gives an overview of document design and how it impacts the way readers perceive a text.
- Janae Cohn's *Writing Spaces* volume 3 chapter, "Understanding Visual Rhetoric" focuses on the visual mode and would be useful as you choose visuals for your data story.
- Melanie Gagich's *Writing Spaces* volume 3 chapter, "An Introduction to and Strategies for Multimodal Composing" discusses five strategies for composing multimodal texts that should inform the drafting of your data story.

Works Cited

Ball, Cheryl E., et al. *Writer/Designer: A Guide to Making Multimodal Projects.* 2nd ed., Bedford/St. Martin's, 2018.

Blevins, Brenta. "Visualizing Data through Infographics." *Digital Rhetoric Collaborative.* 14 Nov. 2013, https://www.digitalrhetoriccollaborative.org/2013/11/14/visualizing-data-through-infographics/. Accessed 15 June 2021.

Bulao, Jacqueline. "How Much Data Is Created Every Day in 2021?" *TechJury.* 18 May 2021, https://techjury.net/blog/how-much-data-is-created-every-day/. Accessed 21 June 2021.

Bunn, Mike. "How to Read Like a Writer." *Writing Spaces: Readings on Writings*, vol. 2, 2011, pp. 71-86, https://wac.colostate.edu/docs/books/writingspaces2/bunn--how-to-read.pdf. Accessed 15 March 2022.

Cairo, Alberto. *The Functional Art: An Introduction to Information Graphics and Visualization.* New Riders, 2013.

Cohn, Janae. "Understanding Visual Rhetoric." *Writing Spaces: Readings on Writings*, vol. 3, 2020, pp. 18-39, https://wac.colostate.edu/docs/books/writingspaces3/cohn.pdf. Accessed 18 June 2021.

Driscoll, Dana Lynn. "Introduction to Primary Research: Observations, Surveys, and Interviews." *Writing Spaces: Readings on Writings*, vol. 2, 2011, pp. 153-174, https://wac.colostate.edu/docs/books/writingspaces2/driscoll--introduction-to-primary-research.pdf. Accessed 15 March 2022.

Gagich, Melanie. "An Introduction to and Strategies for Multimodal Composing." *Writing Spaces: Readings on Writings*, vol. 3, 2020, pp. 65-85, https://writingspaces.org/wp-content/uploads/2021/04/1gagich-introduction-strategies-multimodal-composing-1.pdf. Accessed 18 June 2021.

Klein, Michael J. and Kristi L. Shackelford. "Beyond Black on White: Document Design and Formatting in the Writing Classroom." *Writing Spaces: Readings on Writings*, vol. 2, 2011, pp. 333-349, https://wac.colostate.edu/docs/books/writingspaces2/klein-and-shackelford--beyond-black-on-white.pdf. Accessed 20 June 2021.

Poore, Joseph and T. Nemecek. "Reducing Food's Environmental Impacts through Producers and Consumers." *Science*, vol. 360, no. 6392, 2018, pp. 987-92.

Wolff, Annika, et al. "Creating an Understanding of Data Literacy for a Data-Driven Society." *The Journal of Community Informatics*, vol. 12, no. 3, 2016, pp. 9-26.

Moskin, Julia, et al. "Your Questions About Food and Climate Change, Answered," *New York Times*, 30 April 2019, https://www.nytimes.com/interactive/2019/04/30/dining/climate-change-food-eating-habits.html. Accessed 1 June 2021.

Pizza Toppings. YouGov. 21 Feb. 2021, https://today.yougov.com/topics/food/survey-results/daily/2021/02/04/72784/2. Accessed 3 June 2021. Dataset.

Teacher Resources for "Strategies for Analyzing and Composing Data Stories"

Overview and Teaching Strategies

This essay introduces data storytelling in the context of multimodal composing. I assign it to students when I introduce multimodality because data storytelling plays a central role in multimodal genres ranging from infographics and white papers to social media posts. That said, the chapter could also be beneficial to help students learning to write about data they have collected through their own surveys or interviews. Without explicit instruction in the use of data, students often struggle to both analyze the use of data in multimodal texts as well as to use data effectively and ethically in their own multimodal texts. Multimodal composition pedagogy prepares students to discuss multimodal texts in terms of different types of media and modes of communication. While this vocabulary helps students to analyze the data stories they encounter and to plan their own data stories, it is not fully sufficient. Students need additional vocabulary to understand the strategies available for working with data. In this essay, I share a checklist of critical questions students can use to analyze the use of data in multimodal texts and apply the checklist to the analysis of a sample data story. I also introduce students to the data storytelling composing process and model this process by demonstrating how I worked through it to produce a data story.

This chapter focuses on introducing strategies for reading and composing data stories, and it does not go into detail about design principles or modes of communication. Consequently, it is best to combine this chapter with additional readings that discuss multimodal composing more generally and the vocabulary of page design. In my own courses, I also provide more information to students about specific graph types to help them make informed choices, and I spend time in class showing them how to use free online programs for composing multimodal texts such as Canva, Piktochart, and Adobe Illustrator. Some of the questions and activities that I use with my students are included below:

Discussion Questions

1. Keep track of the data stories you see on social media over the course of a day or a week. What patterns do you notice in the kinds of stories or arguments made in these texts?

2. Use the critical analysis questions in Table 1 to analyze one of the data stories you saw on social media. Discuss why you think the data story does or does not use data effectively.

3. I suggested that the title of Figure 4 should probably be revised for accuracy. Discuss what a more accurate title for this data story might be.

4. Choose a topic you are working on or have recently worked on. Generate a list of questions about that topic you might be able to answer about it using data. Can you identify good sources of data that might help you answer any of those questions?

5. Use the flowchart in Figure 10 to determine the best options you have for showing data in the following scenarios:
   a. You want to show how house prices in your community have changed over time.
   b. You want to present data for 7 online stores, their monthly e-commerce sales, and online advertising costs for the last year.
   c. You want to show which student services on campus bring in the biggest share of total visitors.

6. Try using a different graph type to represent the data in the horizontal bar chart in Figure 13. Which graph is easiest to read and understand? Why?

7. This chapter includes several examples of data stories. Choose one of them and discuss how you could revise its genre (as one example, you might consider how you would turn the infographic in Figure 2 into a social media post). What changes would you make to the story to suit the changed rhetorical situation?

Activities

The following three activities help to scaffold the data storytelling composing process for students by helping them become familiar with data stories, giving them practice creating different types of graphs, and using free, online programs for composing multimodal texts.

Data Storytelling Scorecard

When I introduce data stories to my students, I like to give them several examples of data stories, from effective data stories to examples that have serious problems in the design or use of data. I put them in groups with a scorecard, below, and ask them to rank the stories on a scale from Great to Horrible.

Directions:

1. Examine the data story. What is it trying to communicate?

2. Discuss with your team: Is the story clear? Is it misleading? How could it be improved?

3. Rate the data story and make a short note about why you gave the rating you did.

Number	Your Rating	Comments/Notes
1	Great Good Bad Horrible	
2	Great Good Bad Horrible	
3	Great Good Bad Horrible	
4	Great Good Bad Horrible	

5	Great Good Bad Horrible	
6	Great Good Bad Horrible	

After the groups have a chance to rank the data stories, we have a whole class discussion about how we ranked each data story. This is a good way to talk about what makes a story effective and how content and design work together in these texts.

Graph Creation Practice

To help students become more comfortable creating graphs, I use a class day to give them the opportunity to practice making different kinds of graphs. They do need access to computers on this day. I project a simple spreadsheet with population data on it at the front of the class and ask them to enter the data into their own Excel or Google Sheets spreadsheet. Then I show them how to create a variety of graphs including pie charts, horizontal bar charts, vertical bar charts, line charts, and scatterplots. After we work together for a few minutes, I ask them to continue trying out different graph types and to choose the one they think makes the population data easiest to see and understand. Once they choose the graph they think is most effective, I show them how to add and change labels on their graph, how to change the color palette, and how to save and download their graph. In the last section of the class, we share the different graphs students made and talk through their strengths and weaknesses for depicting the data.

Reverse Engineer a Data Story

Having students reverse engineer a data story in class or as homework is useful in several ways. To reverse engineer the story, students have to recreate it using a software program designed for multimodal composing, such as Canva, Piktochart, or Adobe Illustrator (depending on what the students have access to and will use for their own projects). Students gain experience manipulating text and images using the program without having to worry about the content. They see how text and visuals work together in the story, and they also quickly see what the software program is capable of and what its limitations are. This helps them to plan their own projects more realistically and to appreciate the time involved in composing multimodal texts. The entire class can be asked to reverse engineer the same data story that is provided by the instructor, or students can choose to work with a data story they think is particularly effective.

13 "Doing Research Is Fun; Citing Sources Is Not": Understanding the Fuzzy Definition of Plagiarism

Rachel Hall Buck and Silvia Vaccino-Salvadore

Overview

For many students, the word "plagiarism" invokes a sense of fear: a fear of being caught for doing something wrong and facing sometimes very harsh penalties such as receiving a failing grade on an assignment or being expelled from college.[1] You might be familiar with these feelings and associating plagiarism with stealing someone else's words and ideas and claiming them as your own. But, as we hope you understand by the end of this chapter, plagiarism is much more complex, especially as some of you can probably remember a writing instructor at some point telling you to write a text "in your own words." So, when does an idea or a word become your own? When does an idea or language that you read need to be cited and when is it "common knowledge"? In this chapter, we hope to dispel some of the fear you might have about plagiarism by sharing experiences of our own students, presenting some academic definitions of plagiarism, and then discussing an activity that we completed with Rachel's students in a first year writing course at a 4-year university in the United Arab Emirates. We'll end with some ways you can better identify plagiarism in your own writing, especially when writing a research paper so you'll be able to focus on how to develop ownership of your own language and ideas rather than being concerned about the consequences of plagiarism.

---

1. This work is licensed under the Creative Commons Attribution-NonCommercial-NoDerivatives 4.0 International License (CC BY-NC-ND 4.0) and is subject to the Writing Spaces Terms of Use. To view a copy of this license, visit http://creativecommons.org/licenses/by-nc-nd/4.0/, email info@creativecommons.org, or send a letter to Creative Commons, PO Box 1866, Mountain View, CA 94042, USA. To view the Writing Spaces Terms of Use, visit http://writingspaces.org/terms-of-use.

Introduction

After spending an entire unit researching a paper about the relationship between childhood trauma and serial killers, Mueller[1], a first-year engineering student, determined that "researching about a topic is interesting, citing the sources is not. Although, citing needs to be done to avoid plagiarism." Many of you might agree with this sentiment. You get really excited when you learn about a new topic that interests you, but actually finding sources to incorporate into the paper without being accused of plagiarism can be stressful. You might even feel that you don't understand what plagiarism actually is and how you're supposed to avoid it. So what is plagiarism? Let's look at a couple of definitions.

Definitions of Plagiarism

Most of you will probably agree that buying an entire paper off a website or having someone else write your entire paper for you is a clear example of academic dishonesty. But many cases of plagiarism happen unintentionally because plagiarism is not always so easy to identify.

One often cited definition of plagiarism is when you present "words or ideas as [your] own" (Howard 799). Your college or university most likely has its own institutional policy on plagiarism. Many are found on your institution's website or in your student handbook. Take a look at this policy on plagiarism (paying attention to the language used in the policy). Does your school's policy use verbs such as "use" or harsher verbs such as "stealing" or "copying"? Do you think the policy offers clear guidelines that help when writing a paper?

Let's compare your institution's policy with the two examples from US universities below. You will notice similarities, but also that much of the language and what counts as plagiarism changes between policies.

1. At the University of Berkeley, plagiarism is defined as the "use of intellectual material produced by another person without acknowledging its source," for example:

    - Wholesale copying of passages from works of others into your homework, essay, term paper, or dissertation without acknowledgment.
    - Use of the views, opinions, or insights of another without acknowledgment.

- Paraphrasing of another person's characteristic or original phraseology, metaphor, or other literary device without acknowledgment. ("Academic Honesty")
2. In Arizona State University's (ASU) plagiarism policy, the school gives students some helpful advice about what doesn't need to be cited in research papers:
   - Your opinion
   - Common knowledge
   - Accepted factual information
   - Things you personally observe and record
   - Personal experiences ("Plagiarism").

At Berkeley, it is plagiarism to use the "views, opinions and insights without acknowledgement." At ASU, your own opinion does not need to be cited, however, your opinions and ideas are so often influenced by what we have read, especially in higher education classrooms where it's expected that your opinions are formed by reading others' works. In other words, at what point does your opinion, which has likely been influenced by another's, need to be cited? If you have read some idea or opinion that you readily agree with, do you need to cite that person if you feel like you now own the sentiment? Determining when opinions need to be cited can be problematic because we often feel that we align ourselves with certain ideas and opinions, but these still often need to be cited.

What Is Being Plagiarized?

In this section, we will present the results of an activity Rachel and Silvia designed for the first year writing course Rachel taught where students were put into groups and given examples of what might be considered plagiarism. Let's now look at some specific examples and using the definitions above about plagiarism, determine what, if anything, is being plagiarized.

As you read through the following quotes from popular social media pages from four individuals, ask yourself if these are examples of plagiarism. If so, what do you think is being plagiarized?

1. "Reading is the inhale, writing is the exhale." —Justine Musk

2. "Reading is inhaling. Writing is exhaling."
   —Armaja Bandyopadhyay.

3. "Reading is like inhaling. Writing is like exhaling."
   —Aditi Bharadwaj.

4. "Reading is like breathing in. Writing is like breathing out."—Pam Allyn.

Do you think the idea or the language is plagiarized? What else do you think you need to know to determine if this is plagiarism?

In our classroom, one group of students agreed that this is an example of plagiarism saying: "The meaning behind each picture [showing quotes about reading and writing] is the same for all four quotes. They are all structured in the same way where reading comes first then writing comes next. They all tried to use different words between the sentences however, their idea is the same" (Jade and Tea). Another group agreed saying: "we don't know who is the original source of this quote and there are many quotes that give the same idea by changing the wording. The idea is being plagiarized because they all share the same thought about reading and writing, but they paraphrased the original quote" (Mishoo and Zamir). Most of the students in the class agreed the four quotes are an example of plagiarism, but one group also disagreed: "The idea seems to be more plagiarized than the language. Since there is no stark difference in the idea and language of the given example, we believe that this is an example of plagiarism. And since the use of different words can subtly alter the meaning of the phrase, some of us believe that this is not an example of plagiarism" (Sneha, Bilbo, and Talida).

These students notice some very interesting aspects of plagiarism including ideas of originality, structure, meaning, and the language. While discussing plagiarism, Diane Pecorari, a noted scholar of plagiarism, states, "While an idea can be the object of plagiarism even if it is expressed in an entirely new way, it is often the repetition of the wording of an earlier text which enables the plagiarism to be detected or which is persuasive in convincing gatekeepers that plagiarism has in fact occurred" (538). In other words, ideas can be plagiarized even if the language is different. Coming up with original ideas or fear of being accused of plagiarizing someone else's ideas can be a very scary thought as you are still developing your opinions and ideas about new subjects. However, Edward White, a scholar in writing studies, tells students, "We get to own others' ideas by understanding and thinking about them, by *making* them our own through reflection and integration into our own thinking processes" (207). Being able to articulate and defend why you think the way you do is part of this learning process.

Can you think of an idea that you read about in a book that has influenced the way you currently think? Would you cite the source? Or do you think the idea is now your opinion and doesn't need to be cited?

Let's look at another example. Politicians often use similar words, phrases, and ideas when giving speeches. So, when does this become plagiarism? In this example, we have two sections of speeches given by Michelle Obama in 2008 ("Transcript") and Melania Trump in 2016 (Drabold, "Watch Melania Trump's"). Look through the speeches and highlight words, phrases, or ideas that you think are plagiarized in these sections of the longer speeches.

Michelle Obama (2008 speech)	Melania Trump (2016 speech)
"And Barack and I were raised with so many of the same values: that you work hard for what you want in life; that your word is your bond and you do what you say you're going to do; that you treat people with dignity and respect, even if you don't know them, and even if you don't agree with them.	"My parents impressed on me the values that you work hard for what you want in life; that your word is your bond and you do what you say and keep your promise; that you treat people with respect."
…	…
"And Barack Obama and I set out to build lives guided by these values, and pass them on to the next generations. Because we want our children, and all children in this nation, to know that the only limit to the height of your achievement is the reach of your dreams and your willingness to work for them."	"[My parents] taught me to show the values and morals in my daily life. That is the lesson that I continue to pass along to our son."
	…
	"And we need to pass those lessons on to the many generations to follow, because we want our children in this nation to know that the only limit to your achievements is the strength of your dreams and your willingness to work for them."

One group said of Trump's speech: "The wording is exactly the same, the format (the outline of the ideas) are exactly the same, the order of those ideas are exactly the same. The language and tone are similar. And so is the context. No new ideas were added" (Maya, Malar, and Ruby).

Another group discussed the concept of owning ideas by saying "The idea isn't being plagiarized as it's a common idea shared by people around the world, and the language used was different but still served the same purpose" (Mishoo and Zamir). Agatha and Maddi extended this by saying that "Both the ideas and the language are being plagiarized. At times, the language is even copied word for word."

Zamir and Ruby added to the issue of ideas and language by also taking into account the speaker's position in society saying in our class discussion:

> Ruby: Melania should have taken full of advantage of her higher position, her power and resources, yet, she didn't make use of what she had; it's annoying [what Melania did].

> Zamir: I mean if the person doesn't have that much power I can kind of understand.

> Ruby: In the classroom, everyone has some importance or value; it is not about money or status; plagiarism would be the way you word it, the language you use, the tone, idea is the same, then yes, it's plagiarism.

These ideas spurred an even lengthier conversation in our classroom about how plagiarism can be connected to language and ideas, but also positionality. Do you agree that a person's position in society should be considered when discussing issues of plagiarism? Why or why not?

Reading and Keeping Track of Your Sources

Now it's time to apply the ideas we've discussed above related to public figures and plagiarizing to the practicalities of completing your own research in your various classes. You can see that so many mistakes about plagiarism happen because of incorrect citation and not paraphrasing—not giving credit to the author who influenced the idea or language in your own writing—but also because of a misunderstanding of when an idea is common knowledge or original. There is pressure to come up with original ideas or put someone else's ideas into your own words. Peter Elbow, another writing studies scholar, tells students, "In your natural way of producing words there is a sound, a texture, a rhythm, a voice which is the main source of power in your writing…This voice is the force that will make a reader listen to you, the energy that drives the meaning" (7). Writing any paper is a complicated process involving you reading ideas of others, discussing ideas with others, discovering your own ideas, developing your own opinions, and combining these all in a way that makes you feel like you own the paper.

In the book *Bad Ideas about Writing*, Dustin Edwards and Enrique Pas dispel the myth that writers are solitary geniuses, sitting alone in the woods waiting for original ideas and inspiration to flow into their minds (64). They make the point that this is not how writing works for most writers. We are certainly included in this! We read others' work, draft our own, talk about it with others, revise again, and again. We are often inspired and get ideas from those around us.

You might feel some pressure to come up with original ideas for your papers, but hopefully you can see that "originality" involves more than just ideas. As Maddi determined after reflecting on her final research paper for the course: "As I was writing this research, I realized that for a paper to be yours not every single word in the text must be original, but the way that you guide the reader throughout the text and the way that you portray the message is owned by you."

So how do you keep track of all these concepts as you write your own research paper? Diane Pecorari, a scholar of students' source use and plagiarism, suggests that skilled writers "articulate more consciously what they have learned from which sources" (68). In order to do this, Rachel had students in her class keep a research log that helped them better see how the sources they were reading influenced their understanding of their chosen research topic, but also gave them a clearer idea of how to cite the particular source in their final paper. Before beginning the research paper, it is helpful to first write down what you know about your chosen topic. Then you can more easily see how each of your sources is adding to or changing your current understanding. You can also see ways to incorporate the source into your final paper. For example, let's look at one entry in Maddi's Research Log:

Article citation (APA)	Clark, P. A. (2006). Physician participation in executions: Care giver or executioner? *The Journal of Law, Medicine &Ethics*, *34*(1), 95–104. doi:10.1111/j.1748-720x.2006. 00012.x
How did this article change or add to your understanding of the topic?	Other than being a reliable source, this article allowed me to understand the topic in terms of known ethical principles rather than in the terms of the physician's personal ethical stance.

Article summary	The author explores the role of physicians in executions and analyzes the ethical arguments for and against physician involvement in the process. It discusses the urgency in resolving the ethical conflicts. The text analyzes the situation in accordance to certain medical ethical principles such as respect for persons, beneficence, nonmaleficence and justice. Clark argues that physicians should abide by the Code of Medical Ethics regardless of their personal beliefs. Moreover, the author emphasizes that physician participation in the death sentence is unethical.
Quote that you might use in your paper	"This would be a very cruel way to die: awake, paralyzed, unable to move or breathe, while potassium chloride burned through your veins" (Clark, 2006, p. 100).
How much time did you spend reading and summarizing this article?	Reading and summarizing: 40 min; Research: 20 min

In the course, students were introduced to APA citation style guides, and then we could discuss in class how this source might be acknowledged in the paper in order to avoid plagiarism. You can see in column 4, Maddi has cited a direct quotation that she might want to use in her final paper. But she also knows that if she is going to use information that she wrote in her summary in column 3, she will also need to cite it, although she won't use quotation marks because she is paraphrasing the author's ideas.

Using a log like this might seem time consuming but remember that writing a research paper is a process that takes some time. You won't complete it all in one sitting, so it is especially helpful to have your notes in a log like this. If you do have any questions about whether or not you need to cite something, it would be helpful if you have some specific examples you can talk about with your writing instructor, writing center tutor, or peers.

Above all, we want you to ask your instructor when you have questions! So many students are scared to ask about plagiarism because of the stigma associated with this word. We hope that you can see after reading this short chapter, that plagiarism is a really complex issue that involves concepts related to originality, language, ideas, structure, phrases, context, and of course, the particular assignment. These factors interact in ways that make you feel like you have ownership over your research process and also the final product. We hope that you will feel connected to these as you begin (and continue) to read more authors and develop your own opinions throughout your educational careers, and that even though citing sources may not be fun, as Mueller mentions in the title of this chapter, the process of doing research can still be fun.

Note

1. Mueller, and all student names mentioned in this chapter, are self-selected pseudonyms by the students in Rachel's class.

Works Cited

"Academic Honesty." *Berkeley Writing*, Berkeley University of California, 2021. https://writing.berkeley.edu/academic-honesty. Accessed 27 Jan. 2021.

Drabold, Will. "Watch Melanie Trump's Speech at the Republican Convention." *Time*, 18 Jul. 2016. https://time.com/4412008/republican-convention-melania-trump-2/. Accessed 27 Jan. 2021.

Edwards, Dustin, and Enrique Pas. "Only Geniuses can be Writers." *Bad Ideas about Writing*, edited by Cheryl E. Ball and Drew M. Loewe, West Virginia University Libraries, 2017, pp. 64-70.

Elbow, Peter. *Writing Without Teachers*. 2nd ed., Oxford University Press, 1998.

Farooqui, Mazhar. "College Essays, Thesis for Sale in the UAE." *Gulf News*, 9 March 2020. https://gulfnews.com/uae/college-essays-thesis-for-sale-in-the-uae-1.69509784. Accessed 9 Jan. 2022.

Howard, Rebecca Moore. "Plagiarisms, Authorships, and the Academic Death Penalty." *College English*, vol. 57, 1995, pp. 788-806.

Obama, Michelle. "Transcript: Michelle Obama's Convention Speech." *NPR*, 2008. https://www.npr.org/templates/story/story.php?storyId=93963863. Accessed 27 Jan. 2021.

Pecorari, Diane. *Teaching to Avoid Plagiarism: How to Promote Good Source Use*. Open University Press, 2013.

"Plagiarism." *ASU Library*, Arizona State University, 2021. https://libguides.asu.edu/citing/AcadIntegrity. Accessed 27 Jan. 2021.

White, Edward M. "Student Plagiarism as an Institutional and Social Issue." *Perspectives on Plagiarism and Intellectual Property in a Postmodern World*, edited by Lise Buranen and Alice Myers Roy, SUNY Press, 1999, pp. 205-210.

Teacher Resources for "'Doing Research Is Fun; Citing Sources Is Not'": Understanding the Fuzzy Definition of Plagiarism

Overview and Teaching Strategies

As composition teachers, we find that students are not aware of the complex nature of plagiarism, and because of the stigma associated with it, are not willing to discuss this topic or ask their teachers questions because of a fear of being "caught" plagiarizing. To remedy these situations, writing instructors can use this chapter to help students understand the complexity of what plagiarism entails, to start having open discussions of plagiarism with students in and outside the classroom, and ultimately to help students take ownership of their own research process.

The chapter describes three activities (the similar quotes activity, the two speeches activity, and the research log activity) which we believe are apt to classroom discussions and are eye-openers for many students. In terms of process, we find it interesting to start by asking what students believe plagiarism is and if they believe they own the language and ideas that they write. This can begin with asking students what it means to "write in your own words." Once we have answers to these questions, we build on their understanding by assigning the three activities mentioned above. We also like to include a newspaper article about paper-mills as a first assignment (Farooqui), as this is a clear-cut example of plagiarism, and then move on to the similar quotes activity followed by the speech activity. We then ask students to use a research log while conducting research on their writing topic and discuss some examples of student writings in class.

Discussion Questions

1. How do you define plagiarism? Do you think you own the ideas and language you write?

2. How did the activities about plagiarism challenge or change your definition of plagiarism?

3. How might your own revised definition of plagiarism influence the way you can integrate the ideas and language of your scholarly sources into your own research paper?

4. Plagiarism is often discussed in terms of ownership. One helpful activity after you've written your final research paper is to identify areas that you feel are "yours" and sections that "belong" to others. Why might this be a difficult activity?

5. In what ways do you think you "own" your final research paper?

14 Elaborate Rhetorics

David Blakesley

Overview

This essay presents a working definition of rhetoric, then explores its key terms to help you understand rhetoric's nature as both an applied art of performance and a heuristic art of invention and creation.[1] The definition also situates rhetoric in the social processes of identification and division. The definition goes as follows: "Rhetoric is the art of elaborating or exploiting ambiguity to foster identification or division." The chapter develops the meaning of rhetoric, art, elaboration, exploitation, identification, and division, modeling a process that anyone can follow with their own definitions of this or any complex concept. In the end, you should see rhetoric as more than "mere rhetoric" or "the art of persuasion." You will learn to see rhetoric's presence in all situations that involve people using words and images to teach, delight, persuade, or identify and divide. You will also learn the value of rhetorical listening for understanding the social, cultural, and plural nature of identity and, thus, our capacity for identification (or division) across contexts.

You are a writer, so I'm going to presume that you don't need to hear much about *why* you should bother learning more about rhetoric. Instead, I hope to illuminate its nature as an art so that you can put it to work to change the world or to reimagine it or even re-create it.

People use rhetoric everyday for a wide variety of purposes: to persuade, move, entertain, teach, plead, divide, portray, protest, amuse, complain, inspire, empathize, debate, inquire, charm, and to do just about anything one person can communicate to others with words and other symbols, sounds, or images. This essay presumes that, as a writer yourself, you'll

---

1. This work is licensed under the Creative Commons Attribution-NonCommercial-NoDerivatives 4.0 International License (CC BY-NC-ND 4.0) and is subject to the Writing Spaces Terms of Use. To view a copy of this license, visit http://creativecommons.org/licenses/by-nc-nd/4.0/, email info@creativecommons.org, or send a letter to Creative Commons, PO Box 1866, Mountain View, CA 94042, USA. To view the Writing Spaces Terms of Use, visit http://writingspaces.org/terms-of-use.

benefit from a better understanding of what the term *rhetoric* means—its definition—because it can help you not only decide what to write (invention) and how to write it but also make sense of (analyze) what you and others write and why it matters. Understanding rhetoric will help you become a better writer and reader. Like most complex concepts, people have widely divergent ideas about what rhetoric means. That's okay and to be expected. At the same time, and because we think *with* concepts and not just *about* them, developing your own workable definition of rhetoric—drawing from what others say about it—can make your writing and reading more purposeful, more of a habit or art than a happy accident.

Everyday Rhetorics

Before I discuss a definition of rhetoric that I have found useful and that I hope you will as well, I want to spend a few moments making the case that rhetoric is everywhere. Rhetoric has traditionally and most commonly been defined simply as "the art of persuasion." In popular usage nowadays, rhetoric refers to the use of language, symbols, or images to influence opinion or beliefs, often with the intent of moving people to change their minds or actions. Sometimes people use the term *rhetoric* to name an exaggerated emphasis on style and manipulation at the expense of substance or even truth. In that usage, rhetoric (sometimes referred to as "mere rhetoric") embellishes the truth or, even worse, hides it with lies or misinformation. In this sense, rhetoric is also the use of symbols for partisan or individual interests with a goal of gaining or maintaining an advantage or privilege, winning an argument, proving a point (with gusto!), or forming special interest groups

Let's suppose, however, that rhetoric involves more than just persuasion or lying. After all, not all occasions for writing or speaking involve changing someone's mind or misleading them. Writers also teach and inform. They entertain and tell stories. They invite us to wonder about the nature of things, lives, experience, history. Writers defend principles, expose injustice, create community, and, not surprisingly, attack others. Persuasion, in other words, is only one aim of rhetoric and usually associated with speechmaking, debates, or formal arguments in public forums. You might ask, then, "How can we define rhetoric to account for and understand the many forms and purposes of writing we now use to get along in the world?" How does rhetoric bring people together or, the opposite, divide them?

Rhetoric can help us understand the everyday situations that create or threaten community. When you tell a joke, for instance, you might want simply to make people laugh, but whether you intend them to or not, jokes also invite a bond (identity) between you and your audience. When the hearer "gets it," there has been some identification, an "I see what you did there" moment. The hearer may also recognize the form of a joke (the setup, the punchline) and swing along with its rhythm. That recognition of form also creates some identification that helps you know, for example, when it's time to laugh, the Aha! Moment, the spontaneous recognition of form. Jokes aren't always funny, of course. We may not get them right away or at all. They may be painful or embarrassing to hear, especially when the laughter comes at another's expense. Jokes may create division, in other words, marking a difference or distinction between an "us" and "them" or self and other.

Even the kind of everyday humor we find on the news satire website *The Onion* functions rhetorically to foster identification or division. Consider this headline: "Taliban Criticized for Failure to Include Diverse Array of Extremist Perspectives in Government." (To read the full story from September 9, 2021, search the headline at www.theonion.com.) Here, we see both identification and division: the Taliban would of course not share the democratic value that diverse perspectives (extremist or not) make governments better. The joke is on those who indiscriminately apply their own values (pluralism) to people who don't share them. We may criticize the Taliban for being extremist, misogynist, or racist, but criticizing them for not adopting the principles of deliberative democracy would be like blaming a duck for having feathers. If you get the joke, you understand this point. The humor in this headline, if you see any, directs attention to the media's habit of manufacturing controversies as click-bait and ridicules those who criticize others because they don't know any better or simply for the sake of critique itself. The joke divides *us* (those who know) from *them* (those who don't) and exposes the extremist nature of confirmation bias, which simply reaffirms what we already know or think we know.

A Working Definition of Rhetoric

A good definition will include terms and concepts in a formal, grammatical relationship that helps you generate knowledge, much the same way that a good thesis shapes an argument. If you want to understand rhetoric, consider what others say about it, how it's defined in dictionaries, and what people do with it (how it works), then define it for yourself so that it works like a universal key that opens innumerable doors or a seed that, with the right ingredients (water, soil, sunlight) grows into a tree with countless branches. A good definition should help you create or re-create everything you can possibly know about the subject.

Here's the definition I've developed over the years from a variety of sources. This one helps me understand rhetoric as both an art of persuasion (an applied art) and invention (a theoretical art), what historians of rhetoric also call *rhetorica utens* (the *use* of persuasive resources, or *praxis*, πράξης) and *rhetorica docens* (the *study of the use* of persuasive resources, or *theory*, θεωρῆσαι).

> **Rhetoric** is the **art** of **elaborating** or **exploiting ambiguity** to foster **identification** or **division**.

The key words in this definition have been highlighted in bold. Let's begin.

What else can we say about rhetoric as both an applied and theoretical art? Zeno of Citium (c.335–c.263 BCE), provides us with a useful analogy for understanding rhetoric's dual nature. Zeno contrasted rhetoric with dialectic to highlight the creative nature of rhetoric with the logical, argumentative nature of dialectic. In ancient Greece, dialectic named the process of logical deduction, which begins with what people know to be true and systematically derives conclusions from it. Sextus Empiricus, in his treatise *Against the Professors*, explains the difference between rhetoric and dialectic:

> Zeno of Citium, when asked what is the difference between dialectic and rhetoric, clenched his fist and then opened it out and said, "This,"—comparing the compact and short character of dialectic to the clenching, and suggesting the breadth of the rhetorical style by the opening and extension of his fingers. (2.7; 193; also qtd. in Covino, 35)

In 1644, preacher and rhetorician John Bulwer represented these two hands in his book, *Chirologia: or The naturall language of the hand*. He labeled them "eloquentia" (eloquence, which was associated with rhetoric) and "logica" (logic, associated with dialectic). See figure 1.

In *Magic, Rhetoric, and Literacy*, William A. Covino suggests that the open hand and closed fist convey rhetoric's function as the intermediary between the sensible and the conceptual, between what we see and what we know. Working with ideas furnished by the imagination (what the Greeks called "phantasy" or "phantasms"), rhetoric, Covino says, presents external impressions to the mind for assent or agreement. Zeno of Citium used the open hand for rhetoric to suggest that it makes the world of the imagination "graspable," understandable, or believable. Rhetoric is "an agency for speculation" (35). As an art of invention and wonder, rhetoric grasps; it reaches out for the probable, to the uncertain as a method for discovering the available or possible means of persuasion or identification, which can in turn inform the practical application of rhetoric (in argument and other genres) to specific situations. In the image of the open hand, we see the external impressions from divergent sources coalescing in the palm, which is the concept born of experience, the manifestation of the graspable. Rhetoric also works outward, from the conceptual to the impressionable, and through systematic invention, generates multiple perspectives from the common source of experience.

Figure 1. The open hand of eloquence and the closed fist of logic. From *Chirologia: or The naturall language of the hand* (1644) by John Bulwer. https://bit.ly/chirologia

From Invention to Elaboration

Throughout its long history, rhetoric has involved the study of oral and written language of all sorts, including literature, visual symbols, and iconography. Ever since humans discovered that what we say and how we say it makes a difference, we have studied ways to shape our speech and writing to accomplish our goals. Some people seem to be habitually more persuasive than others, so it made sense to early rhetoricians that some system of principles (an art or habit) could explain the why and how of persuasion. That art (what the Greeks called *techne*) could, in turn, be used to teach others the art of speaking (or writing) well. Initially, rhetoric was defined by some as simply "the art of persuasion," a definition that is still with us today. But rhetoric cannot be simply defined by its ends or aims. Rhetoric is also a productive art, supplying conceptual strategies for generating effective discourse. But as rhetoric and other arts became the subject of more intense philosophical scrutiny, philosophers and statesmen in the Western rhetorical tradition like Aristotle (384–322 BCE) and Cicero (106–47 BCE) recognized that rhetoric involved more than performance. It also included the study of the use of language and the ways that rhetoric functioned as a means of uniting and dividing people, of making decisions about morality and justice, and of establishing laws for social and individual conduct—all fundamental aspects of human relations. In this sense, rhetoric is also an analytical art, meaning that it furnishes perspectives for understanding how people use language for partisan interest.

Aristotle, for example, recognized that rhetoric's function was "not to persuade, but to see the available means of persuasion in each case" (Kennedy, *On Rhetoric* I.1.4). Rhetorical inquiry is an activity of mind, a faculty of "supplying arguments" (Kennedy, I.2.7), or of "discovering the possible means of persuasion in reference to any subject whatever" (Freese, *The "Art" of Rhetoric* I.1.2). Even "the most exact knowledge" (Kennedy, I.1.12) alone does not enable one to persuade or communicate effectively due to, as Aristotle often mentions, the corruption or fallibility of the hearer. Rhetoric is the shared act of deliberation, a consideration of the probable, of "things that are for the most part capable of being other than they are" (Kennedy, I.2.11).

The idea that rhetoric considers issues which may be debatable, uncertain, or ambiguous ("other than they are") turns out to be one of modern rhetoric's most distinguishing interests. In the final analysis, our interpretations of experience, which include what we see and read, are open to multiple perspectives, some of which may be more reasonable or profound than others, but all of which may change over time as our circumstances and needs change. It is the inherent probability and social nature of knowledge that leads Aristotle to claim that rhetoric is the art of discovering the *possible* means of persuasion. As our decisions become harder to make or our experience more complex and ambiguous, we find it useful to have a method for discovering what might be spoken, written, or visualized. The better control we have over the means of representing our experience and beliefs, the more likely it will be that we can change our circumstances or foster identification with others. Rhetoric is an art of invention, then, and it plays a central role in the socialized creation of knowledge.

The realm of knowledge is vast, as is our capacity for interpreting it freshly. To say that rhetoric is the art of elaborating ambiguity is to suggest that rhetoric has the capacity to shape experience by generating and utilizing form, and that it is a function of the imagination. As the elaboration of ambiguity, rhetoric helps us discern in the vastness of our experience what is meaningful personally and what may be meaningful to others.

As an art of invention, rhetoric elaborates a subject, situation, or even words that may be unsettled or uncertain, ones that can be developed, extended, and recontextualized. Elaboration in this sense involves tracking down the implications of something, including the terms that name and define it. This elaboration of meaning and significance can happen at the most general of levels (what is justice? what is literature?) or the highly specific (what is justice in this particular case? is this novel literary?). Viewing *elaboration* as an aim of rhetoric recalls classical conceptions of rhetoric as an art of invention, of, as Aristotle put it, "finding the available means of persuasion in any given case." Rhetoric creates knowledge from experience and situations, even as it also functions as an art (or strategy) for manipulating others with words, symbols, or visual representations. What exactly does rhetoric create and elaborate?

Everything! Suppose you want to write an essay or article about the nature and meaning of free speech in public spaces. To elaborate your subject, you can start with your key terms. What do we mean by speech? Do we mean the spoken word? The written? Is a song or a protest sign a kind of speech? What have others said about speech? How does *Merriam-Webster's Unabridged* define it? How does the US Constitution define it? The US Supreme Court? What are speech's aims? How might speech affect others? Then, moving on, what does it mean to be free? What freedoms should be guaranteed? What are the limits of freedom? What restrictions on free speech or freedom generally have governments legalized, enforced, or rationalized? What is "free" speech? What do people think it means? How does the law define it? Does it have any limits? Why or why not? Then we can ambiguate or differentiate these terms even further by placing them in particular contexts. What does free speech mean in a theater? Online? At a protest rally? On a campus or public square? In an essay written for a class? What do these situations have in common? Are *free* and *freedom* substance terms that can mean anything to anyone? Or that mean nothing? Do they even exist in an absolute sense? What happens to our understanding of "free" and "freedom" when illuminated by specific situations? What about free speech necessitated restrictions on hate speech? We could go on and on, tracking down the implications of our key term or terms. Rhetoric becomes the art of elaborating a subject so that we can make informed decisions about what to say or write in any possible situation, while accounting also for purpose (to teach, delight, persuade, or identify, for example), the nature of our audience, the ethical considerations attached to particular contexts (e.g., whether the exercise of freedom carries a responsibility to act in the best interests of a community), and even how people feel about a concept generally as well as its meaning and importance in everyday situations.

Exploitation and the Reduction of Uncertainty

Exploitation is what's called a loaded term: it implies something negative, like taking something that's not your own and putting it to use for your own purposes. *Exploit* (the verb) means "to make use of meanly or unjustly for one's own advantage or profit; take undue advantage of" (*Merriam-Webster's Unabridged*). Exploitation more generally means to convert or transform one thing into another for some gain. It has allegiances to dialectic and logic, both of which begin with certainty (or one specific and unambiguous assertion) and lead through a process of deduction to uncontested truths. The method of development from premise to conclusion mirrors that of rhetorical argument (the closed fist) with one important glitch: rhetorical argument invites an audience to fill in any premises that may be unstated. In the classical form, the dialectical process can be illustrated by this sequence: "All men are mortal. Socrates is a man. Therefore, Socrates is mortal." The rhetorical variation might leave out a premise: "Socrates is a man, so he must be mortal." The audience provides and accepts the missing premise, "all men are mortal." Both the dialectical and rhetorical forms end at the same conclusion. They "exploit" the certainty that all men are mortal or that Socrates is a man to win their argument and end debate.

What exactly does rhetoric exploit? To exploit ambiguity means to take a particular meaning (among many possible) and use it to accomplish some purpose, like winning an argument. Free speech, for example, has a variety of meanings and interpretations depending upon the context, but you may decide to be a purist and argue that speech only refers to spoken or written words, not the more general act of expressing an idea or opinion. Here, you can take one meaning of the more ambiguous "free speech" to claim that throwing cream pies at politicians shouldn't be allowed even when there's no physical harm because pies are not speech The Constitution does not explicitly guarantee the right to throw pies at people.

Elaboration and exploitation act together. Rhetoricians create and express knowledge with the open hand and closed fist. As Deborah Black has argued, the Muslim philosopher and rhetorician Al-Fārābī *(870 CE – 950 CE)* saw the theoretical and creative art of rhetoric operating collaboratively with its practical application (persuasion):

> To be a truly perfect philosopher one has to possess both the theoretical sciences and the faculty for exploiting them for the benefit of all others according to their capacity, which can only be done 'by a faculty that enables him to excel in persuasion.' These persuasive arts are not essential for the philosopher's own knowledge, but they are the very thing that makes that knowledge communicable and relevant to anyone else. (Qtd. in Bizzell et al. 432)

Knowledge is useless if it can't be communicated. Some, including the essayist Michel de Montaigne, believe that ideas depend on words for their very existence ("Of the Education of Children"). Elaboration and exploitation act together.

The Opportunities of *Ambiguity*

The ancient Greek sophist and teacher Gorgias once claimed, according to the Roman historian Sextus Empiricus (160–210 CE), that "nothing exists." How can that be? Let's consider that assertion in a moment. In his speech "On the Nonexistent," Gorgias makes three related claims:

1. Nothing exists.

2. Even if something did exist, it would be incomprehensible to human beings.

3. Even if someone could comprehend what exists, it could not be explained or communicated to anyone else.

These claims seem absurd, the assertions of hopelessness. The world doesn't exist, and even if it did, you couldn't understand it or explain it to anyone? What's the point of anything, then? Don't I exist?

Gorgias is clever. *Nothing* (the word) is what's called a *substance* term—it can refer to *everything* and *nothing* simultaneously. If I say "*nothing* exists," you may counter with "Not!" "I exist." "The world exists." The world is not an empty void where all the things we know (including ourselves) don't exist. In this sense *nothing* refers to "everything that does not exist." However, and here's the key point: *nothing* is also a word comprised of the letters n-o-t-h-i-n-g. The *word* "nothing" clearly exists! I just used the word in a sentence. So there it is, right there. The point is that words can simultaneously refer to things (a word is a sign of a thing) and to other words (as in a dictionary). Words are also things in their own right. *Nothing* is a thing. But it is also *no-thing*.

Words refer to some things that we can't know or comprehend with certainty. This ambiguity is the occasion for and invitation to rhetoric. The word names the condition of language that words have multiple meanings, that the world named or created by words can be understood or imagined in multiple ways. Knowledge, comprised of words, is ambiguous, uncertain, or probable. That doesn't mean that all knowledge is suspect. It just means that people have legitimate and logical reasons to question it. Rhetoric is necessary when knowledge is probable or uncertain, when disagreement or difference is possible.

Ambiguity is also a necessary component in this working definition of rhetoric for a few more reasons: 1) if knowledge is absolute and unequivocal, rhetoric will not be necessary; no one argues about what everyone already believes—when the facts speak for themselves; 2) if the truth or facts are clear and universally accepted, we have no need to debate them with others or to suggest that facts may be other than they are; 3) ambiguity opens the door for rhetoric because it suggests uncertainty, disagreement, or the possibility that there may be more than one way of viewing something. When people disagree about meaning or significance, a course of action, or the value of something, you have the characteristic invitation to rhetoric.

We have already seen that rhetoric can reveal (elaborate) ambiguity. We find so much rhetoric in social life because these days it may be possible to create uncertainty and ambiguity anywhere at any time. People certainly attempt it, and if you give them enough leeway, they may cloud an issue that had once seemed clear and its meaning unambiguous. Good rhetoricians and listening writers can show us why something may be more complicated than it might initially seem. Some might argue that ambiguity is our state of being, and so rhetoric may always be necessary (for its elaboration) or on-call (for its exploitation, the act of taking just one perspective or meaning and running with it).

Ambiguity acts as an invitation to connect or an impulse to separate, to join forces or oppose them. Alertness to ambiguity—seeing the world in all its colors rather than black and white, is the defining characteristic of literacy according to William A. Covino, in *Magic, Rhetoric, and Literacy*. Ambiguity can be upsetting because it makes the world more complex. Sometimes we feel better when there's no doubt about what to do or think. Nevertheless, experience also suggests we should be wary when we feel most certain. The world is almost always more complicated, textured, and nuanced than it initially seems. Rhetoric agitates against complacency. It helps us tolerate and even appreciate uncertainty.

IDENTIFICATION AND DIVISION

From the time of the early teacher-sophists—people who traveled ancient Greece in the fifth century BCE teaching people strategies for effective speaking—definitions of rhetoric have focused on its nature as persuasive discourse. Persuasion involves the use of logical argument and other appeals designed to gain favor, to change minds, to urge action, or even gain sympathy for a cause. It is a kind of pleading that presupposes an antagonistic or at least undecided or uncommitted audience, someone to convert or cajole. Persuasion is only one purpose of rhetoric as a productive art, however. Over time, we have come to recognize that any situation involving the strategic use of symbols to persuade, teach, or delight is analyzable as rhetoric. One common aim in the many uses of language—in literature, politics, law, and even everyday gossip—is identification.

Identification is an important concept in rhetoric because it allows us to see the rhetorical nature of kinds of writing and visual expression that wouldn't usually be thought of as "persuasive" in the traditional sense. There are fairly few occasions when we find ourselves actually changing our minds on the spot in response to what we hear or read and then actually acting on that new way of thinking. However, our attitudes do change gradually, and sometimes not simply in response to direct pleading or urging. Sometimes, for example, we may be moved by a character in a novel or a film to see ourselves or others differently. A biology textbook might teach us to value knowledge when it is acquired by experimentation, even as it may also provide facts about biology. We might empathize with a character depicted in a play, suddenly realizing that we too may have been mistaken by our vanity. Even inanimate objects may function rhetorically when people use them as symbols to induce a reaction of some kind: the atomic bomb, functioned as a symbolic threat for the fifty years of the Cold War. As the aim of rhetoric, identification focuses attention on attitude as a kind of action or readiness to act, a desire to do something, a desire to act or think together. All kinds of symbolic expression may potentially foster identification and change attitudes.

For Kenneth Burke (1897–1993 CE), the primary aim of rhetoric is identification, which he describes as an alignment of interests or motives and that he carefully distinguishes from persuasion. Unlike persuasion, which normally involves explicit appeals, argument, evidence, or coercion, identification allows for an unconscious factor as well. We may identify with someone (or some cause) and thus come to share belief because we imagine or desire to be one with another, or to feel energized or uplifted by our association. In any rhetorical situation there is always a struggle between the forces of identification and division. People can never be identical or divided absolutely. We have bodies and experiences and a common language, each of which can helps us identify with each other. We also have unique experiences that we may interpret differently from others, that keep us divided.

Figure 2. "Hey—are you thinking what I'm thinking?" © John Wilhelm. Used by permission.

Here in Figure 2 we have a nice illustration of how identification works. The image is actually a re-creation of a single-panel cartoon on a "Shoebox Greeting" that shows a similar scene (two doves perched above a child catching snowflakes on their tongue, with the caption, "Hey—are you thinking what I'm thinking?"). Identification acts like an invitation to imagine yourself to be or be like someone (or thing) in some situation that calls out to everyone involved. The situation can be verbal, visual, aural, or all three, but it is always context dependent, as we see here, the signs suggesting a motive or an attitude that precedes action. Clearly, the bird who speaks understands that they both share this situation and, possibly, the motive to act that it encourages. This situation—like so many others in our daily lives—calls forth words (themselves a form of action) and, consequently, the urge to identify with another. Acts of identification like this one may not appear to be rhetorical at first glance. The question "Hey—are you thinking what I'm thinking?" does not make an explicit argument, so the purpose isn't persuasion exactly. Instead, the viewer identifies with either or both birds (the one who asks, the one who hears), and possibly even the child. We may laugh (or groan) because we realize what the birds must be thinking. The rhetorical clincher comes when we put it all together in an "aha!" moment.

Rhetoric enlists readers or viewers in completing an argument in much the same way. Someone presents evidence or makes a claim, jumps to a conclusion, and closes the deal with the audience once they accept that the evidence or claims warrant (lead to) the conclusion. Arguments need not include all the steps of a logical and deductive process, but they can nevertheless be persuasive if the audience fills in the missing steps (often unconsciously), which they will do if they also view the writer as trustworthy and/or feel positively about the conclusion.

For Burke, our passion is the desire for what he calls consubstantiality or "shared substance" and represents an unconscious desire to identify with others. Consubstantiality can be achieved by different means, including the devices of form, which Burke calls a type of rhetorical appeal, the arousal and gratification of desire. We imagine that we share substance even when exactly what we share is ambiguous or the product of some unconscious desire. Here is how Burke puts it:

> A is not identical with his colleague, B. But insofar as their interests are joined, A is *identified* with B. Or he may *identify himself* with B even when their interests are not joined, if he assumes that they are, or is persuaded to believe so.
>
> Here are ambiguities of substance. In being identified with B, A is "substantially one" with a person other than himself. Yet at the same time, he remains unique, an individual locus of motives. Thus he is both joined and separate, at once a distinct substance and consubstantial with another. (20–21)

Consubstantiality may be necessary for any way of life, even if it's purely imaginary. Rhetoric potentially builds community on this fantasy that we share "something." Rhetoric can tear it down as well. In the end, rhetoric relies on an unconscious desire for acting-together, for taking a "substance" together. "In the old philosophies," Burke writes, "substance was an *act;* and a way of life is an *acting-together*; and in acting together, [people] have common sensations, concepts, images, ideas, attitudes that make them *consubstantial"* (21). As mentioned earlier in this essay, the term *substance* itself induces a kind of acting-together. You can see that happen in arguments over quality when people say some "thing" lacks "substance." Such a claim often brings nods of agreement even though, if put to the test, no one would likely agree on just what that "substance" might actually be. Substance becomes purely an acting-together with the term itself referring to nothing in particular. An ambiguous terms serves as an occasion or invitation to agree about "you know not what." It may not matter whether the term has any specific reference because the rhetorical function (inducing agreement or identification, for taking a stance) is to act together, to be social beings.

In naming identification an aim of rhetoric, I don't mean to suggest that identification is the only or ultimate goal of all verbal or symbolic acts. We desire identification precisely because we're also divided. If we were identical with each other (of an identical substance), we wouldn't need to identify at all. (What would be the point?) We are divided, and so we desire consubstantiality. We are identified, and so we desire division. It works both ways.

Rhetorics of Identity

Identification is the alignment of interests or an overlap of experience that may actually exist between people, or it may be asserted or imagined. Both the reality and the fiction suggest that identity itself is not absolute and that it may be a conscious role or the product or unconscious cultural connections. A rhetoric based on the value and necessity of elaborating or exploiting identification should also include the root term *identity*.

Identity is a powerful concept in part because of its ambiguity. We can have one and many, like a parliament of selves, complementary and distinct, each and together naming and defining who we are and how and why we act the ways we do. Drawing from the writing of Kimberlé Crenshaw, Krista Ratcliffe and Kyle Jensen show how language and discourse mediate rhetoric's intersections with knowing (invention) and being (identity). Identity is constructed and negotiated, not essential or unquestionably singular. Good (listening) writers understand that many cultural logics, stories, or myths define us and thus influence motives and actions. They seek this kind of knowledge as a matter of course.

Intersectionality is Kimberlé Crenshaw's term for ways that peoples' lived experience, including discrimination and privilege, shapes identity and can reveal or reify or social hierarchies. Those hierarchies can lead to systemic or ideological bias that govern what Ratcliffe and Jensen call non-conscious identifications. Intersectionality elaborates the ambiguity of identity and the many ways people exploit it to perpetuate inequality and discrimination, especially in the law. In Ratcliffe and Jensen's terms, intersectionality theory

> posits humans' identities and perspectives as compilations of multiple, intersecting cultural categories (gender, race, class, nationality, sexuality, athletic ability, etc.) that inform people's experiences and, thus, identities. That is, a person may identify as a woman but also as a Chicana, a mother, a daughter, a CEO, an American citizen, a homeowner, a political activist, etc. (Ratcliffe and Jensen 6)

As a writer or reader joining a public debate, you can ask this question, says Crenshaw in an interview with *Vox* : "When you're going to sign on to a particular critique by rolling out your identity, exactly how was your identity politics different from what you're trying to critique?" A reflective rhetorician will be aware of the ways her own identities influence her understanding (what can be known) and empathetic to how others might be positioned (identified) as well.

Empathy is the emotional capacity for identification, the desire for what Burke called consubstantiality. Empathy may be necessary for any way of social life, so it plays a central role in rhetoric's function as the strategic use of language and symbols to induce cooperation and build community. Without empathy, we would all be sociopaths, which by definition lack the capacity to identify with another. To the degree that rhetoric acts as the elaboration and exploitation of ambiguity, it brings hope and possibility at times when our differences seem insurmountable. With an aim of identification and an ideal of empathy, your rhetoric, your definitions of rhetoric, as a listening writer helps you understand your many selves and their multiple agencies, an important prelude to persuading, teaching, informing, or portraying others.

Works Cited

Aristotle. *On Rhetoric: A Theory of Civic Discourse*. 2nd ed. Translated by George A. Kennedy, Oxford UP, 2007.

Bizzell, Patricia, Bruce Herzberg, and Robin Reames. *The Rhetorical Tradition: Readings from Classical Times to the Present*. 3rd edition, Bedford/St. Martin's, 2020.

Black, Deborah L. *Logic and Aristotle's Rhetoric and Poetics in Medieval Arabic Philosophy*. Brill 1990.

Bulwer, John. *Chirologia: or The naturall language of the hand*. 1644. https://bit.ly/chirologia.

Burke, Kenneth. *A Rhetoric of Motives*. 1950. U of California P, 1969.

Coaston, Jane. "The Intersectionality Wars." *The Highlight by Vox*, 28 May 2019, https://www.vox.com/the-highlight/2019/5/20/18542843/intersectionality-conservatism-law-race-gender-discrimination. Accessed 3 April 2022.

Covino, William A. *Magic, Rhetoric, and Literacy: An Eccentric History of the Composing Imagination*. SUNY P, 1994

"Exploit." *Merriam-Webster's Unabridged Dictionary*, Merriam-Webster, https://unabridged.merriam-webster.com/unabridged/exploit. Accessed 18 Sept. 2021.

Montaigne, Michel de. "Of the Education of Children." *Essays of Michel de Montaigne*. Translated by Charles Cotton and edited by William Carew Hazlitt, 1877. *Project Gutenberg*, www.gutenberg.org/files/3600/3600-h/3600-h.htm#link2HCH0025.

Ratcliffe, Krista, and Kyle Jensen. *Rhetorical Listening in Action: A Concept-Tactic Approach*. Parlor P, 2022.

Sextus Empiricus. *Against the Professors*. Trans. R. G. Bury. Loeb Classical Library, Harvard UP, 1949.

Teacher Resources for "Elaborate Rhetorics"

Overview and Teaching Strategies

This essay introduces students to rhetoric as both an applied and productive art, then encourages them to reflect on a definition of rhetoric that accounts for both of these functions. The premise is that having a working definition of rhetoric helps students understand that it involves more than just persuasion or, worse, lying, and instead provides the generative principles for elaborating a subject (invention) and contextualizing it in situations that matter. A rich definition is generative; that is, it aids in the invention and discovery of new knowledge. In this case, that knowledge is *about* rhetoric, how and why it works (or not), and what writers should know if they hope to make it work for them.

At least since Plato in *Phaedrus* and *Gorgias*, we've known that writers need more than just the recipe rhetorics provided by handbooks, the prescriptive rules and procedures for producing good writing. Knowledge about rhetoric is often equated with such rules and procedures. This essay suggests, however, that knowledge about rhetoric should include how and why it achieves its effects, how to put it to use to answer questions about what to write and how to write it, as well as what these choices reveal, hide, or ignore. What can our writing do? What difference can it make? Why does answering these questions even matter? In the end, rhetoric is a much more interesting and complex concept than we're led to believe. Because we think *with* concepts, not just *about* them, a healthy appreciation for rhetoric as an art for elaborating or exploiting ambiguity to foster identification helps writers discover what to say and how to say it to achieve their goals.

I encourage students at all levels to develop their own definition of rhetoric, one that includes terms that help them see and explain how writing works across a broad range of media, contexts, and purposes. The rhetorical knowledge they generate can serve them well when faced with unfamiliar situations or genres. They learn to ask smart questions about these situations that can in turn lead to strategies for addressing them without having to rely on what they remember reading in a handbook. A rich definition of rhetoric can act as transferable knowledge and thus transcends the particulars of any given situation.

This sort of rhetorical inquiry can be the cornerstone in courses that value writing about writing (WAW); that teach writers to reflect on and represent identities of privilege, race, gender, class, disability, ethnicity, sexual orientation (the nature and presence/absence of identity, identification, and division); and that encourage students to research and write about applied rhetorics of social justice, activism, and social change.

Sample Assignment

Prompt: You have read about the importance of identification and identity in the productive art of rhetoric. People have long recognized that identity is an important aspect of communication and social life. We have sought new ways to define, reshape, re-imagine, and refashion identity, often focusing on images of the self and the body. As media and medical technologies make it easier to define and reshape images of the self and the body, people have experimented with a variety of techniques that from a rhetorical perspective convey both curiosity and anxiety about what our bodies and our public image convey about identity.

Write an essay that examines a particularly interesting case of what we might call "self-fashioning." You could focus on someone you know or even yourself. Or you could focus on a popular figure. Describe in detail the nature of the image/self that has been fashioned, then consider these questions:

1. What specific techniques do people use to refashion bodies and selves? (Think of changes related to appearance, including what people wear, how they look physically, what they do with their hair, how they decorate the body and the face, whether they literally reshape, re-color, or pierce the body, and so on.)

2. What seems to be the purpose of this self-fashioning?

3. What effects has the self-fashioning had on the individual and their public image?

4. How might social media perpetuate this ethic of performing the self in a public venue? What negative consequences do you see?

5. How might the images of identity people construct reflect or subvert cultural values?

6. What is rhetorical about this self-fashioning?

Discussion Questions and Prompts

1. *Exploring Rhetoric.* Find three uses of the term *rhetoric* in the news, then explain what these uses reveal about the nature and function of rhetoric. What do these uses of rhetoric have in common? How do they differ?

2. *Elaborating Ambiguity.* Find an important ambiguous term in public life, one people refer to often but that may have multiple or uncertain meanings, then elaborate that ambiguity.

3. The word *ambiguous* derives from the Latin prefix *ambi* ("both, around") and the root *agere* ("drive, lead"). *Ambiguous,* according to the *Dictionary of Word Origins* by John Ayto, carries the etymological notion of "wandering around uncertainly" (22; Arcade, 1990). Its relatives include ambivalent, ambidexterous, agent, and act (the latter two from the root *agere*). Ambiguity makes multiple interpretations possible, each of which may be legitimate and thus contestable.

4. *Exploiting Ambiguity.* In some situations, you want to persuade someone to take a specific course of action or to change an attitude. Using the term you chose in #2, choose one of the term's meanings, then write a paragraph that uses that meaning to change someone's attitude about it.

5. Rhetorician Kenneth Burke once wrote in a concrete poem called a "Flowerish" (a pun on "flourish"), "From the very start, our terms jump to conclusions." What do you think he had in mind? In what ways do our terms, our vocabulary, determine what can be known? Spoken? Seen? What might our terms filter from view? Provide one or more examples.

15 What Is Rhetoric? A "Choose Your Own Adventure" Primer

William Duffy

Overview

Providing an introduction to rhetoric is a foundational component of most first-year writing courses.[1] Discussion of rhetorical appeals, for example, is standard fair in these contexts, as are activities that ask students to develop an appreciation for rhetorical situations, audiences, purposes, and even more nuanced concepts such as *kairos* and genre. Unfortunately, it's easy for these concepts—along with the idea of rhetoric itself—to get taken up in these contexts as yet another set of keywords that have static and/or underdeveloped definitions, which in turn limits the ability for students to productively wrestle with the complexities of rhetoric as a resource for their own development as writers. This essay serves as an introduction to rhetoric, but it does so through the medium of a "choose your own adventure" narrative. Divided into ten sections, each of which contains a handful of rhetoric definitions that highlight one of its many qualities, this essay invites students to let their own interests guide how they come to understand rhetoric.

Start Here

"Rhetoric" is a word everyone seems to know but few can define. When I ask my students to define it, almost always one or two will immediately shout out that rhetoric is "logos, ethos, and pathos." I'll point out those are rhetorical *appeals*, shorthand categories for

---

1. This work is licensed under the Creative Commons Attribution-NonCommercial-NoDerivatives 4.0 International License (CC BY-NC-ND 4.0) and is subject to the Writing Spaces Terms of Use. To view a copy of this license, visit http://creativecommons.org/licenses/by-nc-nd/4.0/, email info@creativecommons.org, or send a letter to Creative Commons, PO Box 1866, Mountain View, CA 94042, USA. To view the Writing Spaces Terms of Use, visit http://writingspaces.org/terms-of-use.

classifying the different ways rhetoric can be persuasive to an audience. I'll then ask them to open their phones or laptops and find at least three different definitions to share with the class, which always leads to a discussion about how *what* rhetoric is (how it gets defined) and what rhetoric *means* (what elements of those definitions we find most important) depend on factors like purpose, audience, and occasion, factors that show up as keywords in many of the definitions they locate.

It's easy to identify similarities across definitions of rhetoric, but as a concept it's difficult to pin down. What rhetoric is, not surprisingly, depends on the person doing the looking. And this brings me to you. Yes, *you*. Maybe one of your instructors assigned this essay for homework, or maybe you came across it while doing a web search. Regardless of how you got here, let me offer you an unconventional introduction to rhetoric. While it would be easy for me to describe its history as both a concept and an academic field of study, I just said that what rhetoric is depends on the person doing the looking. For this reason, I'd prefer if you—yes again, I mean *you*—could experience this idea by developing your own understanding of rhetoric. To facilitate this, I've organized this essay as a "choose your own adventure" narrative, which means that as you read, you'll be prompted to make decisions about what to read next. While I haven't calculated how many different readings of this essay are possible, if you are reading this essay for a class, there's a good chance none of your peers will read it exactly like you do, which in turn means your understanding of rhetoric will be different from theirs, even if only slightly.

If you're unfamiliar with the "choose your own adventure" idea, all you need to know is that I've organized this essay into ten numbered sections. I've also included bits of stage direction that ask you questions **in bolded text**. Depending on what you are interested in exploring, the stage directions at the end of each section will point you to which section to read next.

Each section is structured around a handful of definitions of rhetoric that share a similar focus or theme. As you'll see, people have been defining and redefining rhetoric for as long as the word has existed. Once you finish this essay, however much of it you read and in whatever order, you too should be able to develop your own definition. While I don't think you need to read this entire essay, try to cover at least five sections. That should be plenty to help you develop a fuller, more complex understanding of rhetoric.

To begin, let's start with a source that for many of us is the first place we go to when we want to learn about something, Wikipedia. As of the time of this writing, the entry for rhetoric begins this way: "Rhetoric is the art of persuasion, which along with grammar and logic is one of the ancient arts of discourse. Rhetoric aims to study the techniques writers or speakers utilize to inform, persuade, or motivate particular audiences in particular situations" ("Rhetoric"). This is a pretty good definition, but it contains ideas that need unpacking. Rhetoric is not only the "art of persuasion," it's one of the "ancient arts of discourse" we use to study how people "inform, persuade, and motivate" one another.

If you want to learn more about how rhetoric is an art, *continue to Section 1.* **If you want to learn more about how rhetoric is a science,** *skip to Section 2.* **If you want to learn more about the history of rhetoric,** *skip to Section 3.*

1. Rhetoric Is an Art

What does it mean to call something an art? We can answer this question by considering what different arts and artists have in common. Imagine Yo-Yo Ma, Denzel Washington, and Kendrick Lamar sat down to discuss their careers. What would they talk about? Yo-Yo, a famous cellist, might ask Kendrick, a rapper, about his writing process. They might talk with Denzel, an actor, about how he decides which projects to pursue. All three could probably talk about how they respond to criticism, or the qualities necessary to push through creative dry spells. Whatever they end up discussing, the chances are good that what they talk about could be applied to our understanding of rhetoric as an art.

As A.S. Hill explains, "Rhetoric may be defined as the art of efficient communication by language. It is the art to the principles of which, consciously or unconsciously, a good writer or speaker must conform. It is an art, not a science" (1141). Hill was a professor of rhetoric at Harvard and is credited with starting one of the first "freshman writing" programs in the United States, those first-year composition courses that still exist and in which you might currently be enrolled. Notice how Hill is careful to say that rhetoric is not a science, even though he also says rhetoric involves the "principles" that "good" writers and speakers follow. Almost a century later another professor of rhetoric, Karl Wallace, said it "is primarily an art of discourse. It is an art because its principles and teaching are directed to two general ends or functions: the making or producing of utterances and the understanding and appraising of them" (3). This definition is not that different from Hill's, except Wallace identifies the purpose of rhetoric: to produce "utterances," a term that means any written or oral speech, and to evaluate them. In a short essay about effective communication for the

American Water Works Association (yes, apparently even hydraulic engineers care about rhetoric), John Mannion says rhetoric is "the skillful, effective, artistic use of words" (3). Mannion's understanding of rhetoric as an art is simple enough; rhetoric is an art because it requires us to use words skillfully and effectively.

Identifying rhetoric as "the art of efficient communication" or the "artistic use of words" prompts some obvious questions. Is rhetoric still an art if the communication is inefficient or inartistic? And how would we "appraise" these situations? To answer these questions, you will need to read some other sections of this essay. But before you do, I want to point out these definitions from Hill, Wallace, and Mannion were all written for non-academic audiences.

Not surprisingly, academic definitions of rhetoric tend to be more complex. As Charles Bazerman suggests, for example, "Rhetoric is the reflective practical art of strategic utterance in context from the point of view of the participants, both speaker and hearer, writer and reader" (14). Here we see that word "utterance" again, which Bazerman qualifies with the word "strategic," but he also says rhetoric is a "practical art." Sharon Crowley, an historian of rhetoric, argues that "at minimum [we must] conceive of rhetoric as an art of invention, that is, it must give a central place to the systematic discovery and investigation of the available arguments in a given situation" ("Composition is Not Rhetoric"). What do you think of these more academic definitions of rhetoric? Do you see any overlap between these definitions and the ones in the previous paragraph? Have these definitions adequately told us how rhetoric is an art?

You might have some initial thoughts about these questions, but let's push forward. **If you want to consider how rhetoric is a science, *continue to Section 2*. If you want to consider how rhetoric can be understood as effective communication,** *skip to Section 4.*

2. Rhetoric Is a Science

In the opening paragraph of his 1875 textbook, Andrew Dousa Hepburn declared rhetoric "is the Science of the Laws and Forms of Prose. It investigates the method and general principles to which every discourse must conform that is designed to instruct, convince, or persuade" (13). Hepburn's definition is useful for understanding rhetoric as a science because in suggesting that "discourse" (another word for speech or language) "must" adhere to certain laws and principles, he is not only suggesting a natural order to language and how it should be used, he also is suggesting that once we understand how these laws work, we can learn to manipulate them in our efforts "to instruct, convince, or persuade" others.

When rhetoric gets discussed as a science, what we are talking about is our ability to observe and draw conclusions about what makes it work. But as demonstrated in Hepburn's definition, understanding rhetoric as a science can sometimes presuppose a kind of physics determines when our rhetoric will be successful. We can see this mindset at work when Walter Fisher says that "rhetoric refers to the examination of the true nature of speech practices and literary forms of discourse" (170), which of course begs the question, the "true nature of speech practices" *for whom*? The value of these scientific definitions is that they position rhetoric as something that can be investigated and tested, a belief that has sustained rhetoric as an academic enterprise for over two thousand years.

Insofar as you come to understand rhetoric as a science, you come to understand how to dissect it into its various parts and categories, its different effects in different situations, as well as its ability to be understood systematically. "Rhetoric is communication characterized by a high degree of intentionality and high degree of structure," explains Robert L. Scott (440). But we can also think about rhetoric as a science by considering the function of trial and error in our communication with others. According to James McNally, for example, rhetoric can be defined as "sign-behavior exhibiting a pragmatic concentration of meaning (77). The word "sign-behavior" means communication, or the use of things like words, gestures, noises, images, etc. But the key phrase in McNally's definition is this idea of a "pragmatic concentration of meaning," which refers to the success of this sign-behavior—the extent to which it's effective. Like all indeterminate behavior, our communication doesn't always go according to plan; it requires practice and adjustment, just as it requires us to occasionally learn new techniques. **Go back to Section 1 if you want to read about rhetoric as an art. To read about rhetoric's history, *proceed to Section 3*. If you want to consider why the idea of effectiveness is important for the study of rhetoric, *read Section 4*.**

3. Rhetoric Is Old

One of the oldest definitions of rhetoric is also one of its most famous. "Let rhetoric be [defined as] an ability, in each [particular] case, to see the available means of persuasion," says Aristotle in a treatise that dates to the fourth century BCE (Kennedy, *Rhetoric* 36). Many historians credit Aristotle for popularizing the study of rhetoric, at least among ancient Greek elites, but by no means was he the first to recognize rhetoric's importance. Aristotle's teacher, Plato, had a famously critical view of rhetoric. He called it a mere "knack," something akin to a hobby, and said all rhetoric is good for is appealing to people's emotions. Plato's view of rhetoric has remained popular throughout the ages.

In 1690, the philosopher John Locke said that "all the artificial and figurative application of words eloquence [rhetoric] hath invented, are for nothing else but to insinuate wrong ideas, move the passions, and thereby mislead judgment," before calling rhetoric "that powerful instrument of error and deceit" (827). Ezra Pound, the famous poet, echoes Locke: "Rhetoric is the art of dressing up some unimportant matter so as to fool the audience for the time being" (280). Indeed, the first definition for "rhetoric" on Dictionary.com is "the undue use of exaggeration or display; bombast" ("Rhetoric"). Even today when someone denounces an argument as "just rhetoric," they are echoing a long line of critics going back to Plato.

While Plato is credited with coining the word "rhetoric," ancient non-Western cultures had their own famous figures who taught the arts of communication. The Chinese philosopher Confucius, for example, produced works that emphasized, as professor Bo Wang says, "the art of communication in cultivating the moral self and forming reciprocal human relationships" (69), aims that speak to concerns teachers of rhetoric continue to wrestle with when it comes to judging the character of one's words. Interestingly, there is no ancient Chinese equivalent for the word "rhetoric," LuMing Mao reminds us, just as there is no ancient Greek equivalent for the "yin-yang" concept, a symbol that speaks to the idea of reciprocity that Professor Wang mentions as central to Confucius's philosophy of communication.

Another ancient culture that produced fascinating works of rhetoric is that of the Aztecs. When Spain colonized what is now known as Central America, Franciscan monks "recognized as rhetoric what the Aztecs themselves called *huehuetlahtolli*. This Nahuatl word is formed by compounding *huehue*, 'old man,' or 'men of old,' and *tlahtolli*, 'word,' 'oration,' or 'language.' Thus *huehuetlahtolli* is variously translated as 'the ancient word' 'the speeches of the ancients,' or 'the speeches of the elders,'" (Abbott 252), a tradition of Aztec orations that no doubt goes back centuries before the Franciscans translated them for European audiences in the sixteenth century.

The important point is that for as long as humans have existed, there have been teachers passing along orations and other ancient texts to cultivate and enrich the cultures in which they were circulated. **If you want** to learn more about how culture influences rhetoric, *skip to Section 8*. If you want to see how rhetoric gets conflated with persuasion, *read Section 5*.

4. Rhetoric Is Effective Communication

Despite Henry Jones Ripley's assertion that rhetoric "is the science of good writing" (13), rhetoricians typically avoid describing rhetoric as "good" or "bad." Instead, we prefer to think about it in terms of effectiveness. If you've prepared a presentation for your boss about why you deserve a raise, it doesn't matter how many good reasons you offer or how clearly you argue your case. What matters is whether you get a raise, right? If your boss is blown away by the quality of your presentation but then explains why she can't give you a raise, your "good" presentation can also be chalked up as ineffective. My point is simple: rhetoric isn't perfectible.

But successful rhetoric can be approximated by evaluating what makes it *more* or *less* effective in particular situations. In fact, the first definition for rhetoric in the Merriam-Webster dictionary is "the art of speaking or writing effectively" ("Rhetoric"). Defining rhetoric as effective communication is by no means a contemporary practice. After all, consider John of Salisbury's twelfth-century definition that asks, "What is eloquence [rhetoric] but the faculty of appropriate and effective verbal expression?" (McGarry 26).

One way to understand what makes rhetoric effective is whether it is persuasive, but effective rhetoric can mean other things. Edward Channing, who won a Pulitzer Prize in 1926, explains that rhetoric is "a body of rules derived from experience and observation, extending to all communication by language and designed to make it efficient," adding that rhetoric helps us translate thoughts into effective language, "and effective, not in any fashionable or arbitrary way, but in the way that nature universally intends" (31-32). One problem with Channing's definition, and arguably all definitions that suggest prescriptions, is that it draws a line between nature and culture that can't be crossed. But remember, for rhetoric context is everything. As Adetokundo Knowles-Borishade notes, for instance, indigenous African rhetorical traditions didn't rely on theories that just focus on the relations between a speaker, text, and audience; they instead understood rhetoric according to five elements: "(a) Caller-Plus-Chorus, (b) Spiritual Entities, (c) *Nommo* (the Word), (d) Responders, and (e) Spiritual Harmony" (490), elements that, taken together, underscore how indigenous Africans had a more holistic understanding of their place in the natural world than did their Western, colonizing counterparts.

But in its most general sense, effective rhetoric can simply mean rhetoric that works, that achieves its purpose. If I write an assignment prompt for one of my classes, but the students ignore it because I sang the instructions and uploaded them as a song on iTunes, could you blame them for assuming I'd gone crazy? For this reason, I appreciate Paulo Valesio's definition of rhetoric as "the functional organization of discourse"; rhetoric, he adds, "speaks about the ways in which human discourse works and has worked" (7).

Not only can the study of rhetoric help us understand why my students probably wouldn't be persuaded by my assignment prompt song, it also can help us understand how genres like assignment prompts work *as genres*. **To read about why rhetoric goes hand-in-hand with the idea of adaptability,** *skip to Section 7.* **If you want to read about how rhetoric helps us know things,** *read Section 8.*

5. Rhetoric Is Persuasion

One of the most popular ways to define rhetoric is to invoke the idea of persuasion. Aristotle does this in his definition of rhetoric (see Section 3), as do contemporary writers like Sam Leith. Simply put, says Leith, rhetoric is "the art of persuasion: the attempt by one human being to influence another in words. It is no more complicated than that" (1). Depending on how many sections of this essay you've already read, I think we can say in response to Leith that defining rhetoric *is* more complicated.

There is nothing simple when it comes to understanding how human beings attempt to persuade one another, after all. Donald Bryant writes that rhetoric is "the rationale of informative and suasory discourse" and involves "the function of adjusting ideas to people and people to ideas" (404, 413). Bonnie Sunstein and Elizabeth Chiseri-Strater say the same thing, but more clearly. "Rhetoric is commonly defined as the art of persuasion," they say "but it involves far more than the verbal devices that are often connected with propaganda. It is the shaping of discourses (or simply the uses of language) for different purposes and audiences" (Sunstein and Chiseri-Strater 75). And Stephanie Weaver extends rhetoric to "any use of a symbol system (language, written text, images, colors, etc.) to persuade another" ("What is Rhetoric?"). Weaver's definition is helpful because it emphasizes that persuasion can involve more than words. As Wayne Booth, a famous literary critic, once declared, rhetoric is "the art of changing men's [or people's] minds" ("Scope" 95).

As you can imagine, while persuasion has always been one of the goals associated with rhetoric, exploring what persuasion means in various contexts is an ongoing project for rhetoricians. **If you want to learn about what makes rhetoric effective,** *read Section 4.* **If you want to learn about why effective rhetoric must be adaptable,** *read Section 7.*

6. Rhetoric Is Public Action

Some of the most interesting definitions of rhetoric highlight its publicness. Some rhetoricians, such as Kenneth Burke and Robert Hariman, to name just two, would argue all rhetoric is public. There is no such thing as "private" rhetoric, in other words, because even if we are using language privately—perhaps writing in a diary or talking to yourself in the shower—our ability to use language at all is dependent on others for making that language intelligible, even if no one else is present. A prolific theorist of rhetoric, Burke explained in 1950 that "the basic function of rhetoric [is] the use of words by human agents to form attitudes or to induce actions in other human agents" (41). Almost four decades later, Hariman said "[w]e can define rhetoric as a mode of reflection upon the sociality of language" (51). That is, we can understand rhetoric as that which allows us to interact with one another.

Both definitions emphasize how rhetoric is linked to our social life, but they also suggest communication itself is dependent on our ability to use language in ways that are mutually meaningful. Another interesting idea these definitions suggest, one that is abstract but important, is that we need rhetoric to imagine what a public is in the first place. As explained by Thomas Farrell, rhetoric is "the primary practical instrumentality for generating and sustaining critical publicity which keeps the promise of the public sphere alive" (199). Rhetoric is the thing that allows us to create "publics" that in turn allow us to build connections with people outside of our immediate social spheres. Social movements, for example, are dependent on the rhetoric of activists and organizers who must be able to motivate others to join their causes, work that almost always requires supplying the language around which supporters can unify.

While communities are shaped by the languages they share, the study of rhetoric allows us to see how these languages evolve and change over time, and in turn this allows us to see how communities compensate for this change by inventing new ideas, new words, and new forms of interaction to maintain social ties. If you want to see an example of this, open your texting app and look for any of the abbreviations, emojis, or other forms of "text-speak" you use. Gerald Hauser sums up this nicely: "Rhetoric is communication that attempts to coordinate social action" (3). **If you want to further explore the idea of how rhetoric involves more than just words,** *skip to Section 8.* **If you want to continue reading about rhetoric as a kind of social action,** *skip to Section 9.*

7. Rhetoric Is Adaptation

Many definitions focus on rhetoric's purpose, like to persuade or "enlighten the understanding, to please the imagination, move the passions, or to influence the will," as the philosopher and Christian minister George Campbell wrote in 1776 (Golden and Corbett, 145). But there are plenty of definitions that also highlight the skills necessary to use rhetoric effectively. One of the most popular of these skills is the ability to adapt to the rhetorical demands of specific contexts. For John Franklin Genung, a famous teacher of rhetoric in the late nineteenth century, "Rhetoric is the art of adapting discourse, in harmony with its subject and occasion, to the requirements of a reader or hearer" (1). Notice this emphasis on the "subject and occasion" as guideposts for deciding how to adapt one's language according to audience expectations.

Today we use concepts like *genre* and *decorum* to talk about rhetorical situations. For example, some of you might know that career coaches often recommend tailoring your resume for specific job applications. Let's say you are applying for a job at a specialty shoe store for runners, it makes sense that you would include a section on your resume that lists the most recent marathons you've run, but this is something you wouldn't include in the next resume you submit, which happens to be for a job at a local bank. This kind of choice speaks to the importance of adaptation as one of rhetoric's primary mechanisms. "Rhetoric is the art which seeks to capture in opportune moments that which is appropriate and attempts to suggest that which is possible," writes John Poulakos, a definition that captures the idea of adaptability by pointing to the related concept of possibility (36). What Poulakos's definition captures is the importance of reading the room, so to speak, and paying attention to tone of voice, facial expressions, and all the other non-verbal conventions that help us navigate our daily interactions with one another. But the definition also suggests that through this paying attention we can discover opportunities that were previously unavailable.

Like Poulakos, William Covino and David Joliffe's definition suggests the importance of adaptation when they say rhetoric "is primarily a verbal, situationally contingent, epistemic art that is both philosophical and practical and gives rise to potentially active texts" (5). Rhetoric is "situationally contingent," which means its success isn't guaranteed, but it's also an "epistemic art" that produces "potentially active texts." What do you think this means? **To explore the meaning of "epistemic" as it relates to rhetoric, *continue to Section 8*. If you want to consider rhetoric as action, *go back to Section 6*.**

8. Rhetoric Is Epistemic

To call rhetoric epistemic is to invoke what is probably the most technical phrase you'll find in this essay. "Epistemic" is an adjective that comes from the word "epistemology," which means the study of knowledge. When we talk about epistemology, we are talking about how we know things. To call rhetoric epistemic, then, means that rhetoric helps us develop knowledge.

Some epistemologies, or theories of knowledge, stress the importance of symbols, how things like words stand in for things like objects or ideas. Consider George Kennedy's definition, for example, when he says rhetoric is "the energy inherent in emotion and thought, transmitted through a system of signs, including language, to others to influence their decisions or actions" ("A Hoot" 2). Also consider the Islamic philosopher al-Farabi's definition of rhetoric as "a syllogistic art whose purpose is persuasion" (7). While similar to other classical definitions that invoke logic or reasoning (the term "syllogistic" refers to the process of drawing a conclusion based on a set of propositions), Maha Baddar explains that "al-Farabi transforms rhetoric beyond the Aristotelian model into a component of an epistemological structure whose aim is acquiring and communicating knowledge in a manner that accommodates the different capacities of the human intellect" (235). As al-Farabi suggests, rhetoric helps us understand how ideas and beliefs become true for us. Whereas in al-Farabi's definition, we see an emphasis on logic (he calls rhetoric "a syllogistic art"), Kennedy's definition highlights how rhetoric helps us process "emotion and thought." Taken together, they show us how rhetoric can help us appreciate the complexity behind how we learn things.

The definitions in this section so far have been heady, but there are simpler definitions that fit this category. Krista Ratcliffe, for example, says "rhetoric is the study of how we use language and how language uses us" ("The Current"). For Curtis Newbold, "Rhetoric is, essentially, the study of how communication affects our understanding" ("Rhetoric Criticism"). These definitions speak to why one of the first things we do, if we don't understand something, is to ask someone to explain it (or we open Wikipedia or YouTube), and why, if we find that person's explanation insufficient, we ask someone else (or click on a different article or video).

One of the more thorough definitions in this category comes from Richard Cherwitz and James Hikins:

> Rhetoric is the art of describing reality through language. To act rhetorically is to use language in asserting or seeming to assert claims about reality. At the heart of this definition is the assumption that what renders discourse potentially persuasive is that a rhetor (e.g. a speaker or writer) implicitly or explicitly sets forth claims that either differ from or cohere with views of reality held by audiences. (62)

This definition speaks to how things like identity (religion, sexuality, ethnicity, gender, political affiliation, etc.) can constrain not just what arguments will be effective for specific audiences, but whether a specific audience will even listen to you in the first place. *So what?* you might ask. Understanding rhetoric as epistemic helps us see how rhetoric facilitates change, which you can *continue to Section 9* to read about. If you are curious about how such change relies on persuasion, *go back to Section 5.*

9. Rhetoric Changes the World

"Rhetoric is the science which refreshes the hungry, renders the mute articulate, makes the blind see, and teaches one to avoid every lingual ineptitude," writes an unknown definer of rhetoric (Caplan 106), but definitions like this one that list activities for which rhetoric is useful are quite common. For Tania Smith, "Rhetoric is the study and practice of communication that persuades, informs, inspires, or entertains target audiences in order to change or reinforce beliefs, values, habits or actions" ("What is Rhetoric?") Similarly, Abdul-Raof Hussein insists rhetoric "is a linguistic tool which the language user manipulates in order to praise, dispraise, inspire, influence, or entertain the audience" (3).

Rhetoric, quite literally, changes the world. Even if the change is small or marginal or otherwise invisible, change is change. M. Elizabeth Weiser gets it right when she says "rhetoric is the way the world is manipulated around us for the purpose of persuading ourselves and others that something matters and that we should respond to it" (8). **Are you feeling done? If so,** *continue to Section 10.* **If you still have some focus left,** *read one more section and then skip to Section 10.*

10. Everything is Rhetoric

I've subtitled this last section "Everything is Rhetoric" because even if you've just read a few of the preceding sections, it should nevertheless be clear the only thing harder than defining what rhetoric *is* might be deciding what rhetoric *is not*. Whether we understand rhetoric as persuasion, effective communication, or social action, practically every kind of human behavior can be understood as rhetoric.

If everything is rhetoric, then Thomas Rickert's definition does a nice job of summing up the takeaway of this essay: "Rhetoric is revealing and doing—doing as revealing and revealing as doing—and hence integral to our dwelling in the world" (33). Even if all we are doing is thinking, that is still rhetorical labor. And if the activity of thinking can be understood as rhetorical, we must again ask *What is rhetoric not?* Rhetoric is everything and everything is rhetoric.

So how do I define rhetoric? Since I'm a rhetoric professor who also likes thinking about ethics, I like this definition by I.A. Richards with its poetically blunt emphasis on our responsibility to one another to be continuously working out how to maintain relationships: "Rhetoric, I shall urge, should be the study of misunderstanding and its remedies" (3). While this definition might be my favorite, I don't want to shirk the question about *my* definition. For me, rhetoric is the material practice of persuasion and the mechanisms we study to understand such labor. I don't think this definition is any better or worse than others, but it does reflect how I have personally come to understand this thing I write about and teach.

Let me close with an excerpt from Richard Whately's *Elements of Rhetoric* because he talks about the value of defining rhetoric. After sharing various definitions, he suggests that:

> To enter into an examination of all the definitions that have been given, would lead to much uninteresting and uninstructive verbal controversy. It is sufficient to put the reader on his [or their] guard against the common error of supposing that a general term has some real object, properly corresponding to it, independent of our conceptions—that, consequently, some one definition in

every case is to be found which will comprehend everything that is rightly designated by that term. (1-2)

What do you think? Has my examination of rhetoric through these different categories of meaning been "uninteresting and uninstructive"? That depends, doesn't it? Your instructor might ask you to write a response that reflects on your own ideas about some of these definitions, or you might even be asked to critique the effectiveness of my unconventional essay. If this happens, you'll be engaged in the practice of *meta*-rhetoric, or rhetoric *about* rhetoric, which is what I'm doing in this essay. But I'll save that discussion for class.

Works Cited

Abbott, Don P. "The Ancient Word: Rhetoric in Aztec Culture." *Rhetorica*, vol. 5, 1987, pp. 251-64.
Abdul-Raof, Hussein. *Arabic Rhetoric: A Pragmatic Analysis*, Routledge, 2006.
Al-Farabi. *Kitab fi al-Mantiq: Al-Khataba* (A Book on Logic: Rhetoric), edited by Mohamed M. Salim. Cairo: Dar al Kutub, 1976.
Baddar, Maha. "The Arabs Did Not 'Just' Translate Aristotle: Al-Farabi's Logico-Rhetorical Theory." *The Responsibilities of Rhetoric*, edited by Michelle Smith and Barbara Warnick, Waveland Press, 230-242.
Bazerman, Charles. *A Rhetoric of Literate Action, Volume 1.* The WAC Clearinghouse and Parlor Press, 2013.
Blair, Hugh. *Lectures on Rhetoric and Belles Lettres,* edited by Linda Ferreira-Buckley and S. Michael Halloran, Southern Illinois UP, 2005.
Booth, Wayne. "The Scope of Rhetoric Today: A Polemical Excursion." *The Prospect of Rhetoric*, edited by Lloyd Bitzer and Edwin Black, Prentice-Hall, 1971.
Burke, Kenneth. *A Rhetoric of Motives*, U of California P, 1969.
Bryant, Donald. "Rhetoric: Its Function and its Scope." *Quarterly Journal of Speech*, vol. 39, 1953, pp. 401-424.
Caplan, Harry. *Of Eloquence: Studies in Ancient and Medieval Rhetoric*, edited by Anne King and Helen North, Cornell UP, 1970.
Channing, Edward. *Lectures Read to the Seniors at Harvard College*, Boston, Ticknor and Fields, 1856.
Cherwitz, Richard A. and James W. Hikins. *Communication and Knowledge: An Investigation in Rhetorical Epistemology*, U of South Carolina P, 1986.
Crowley, Sharon. "Composition is Not Rhetoric." *Enculturation*, vol. 5, no. 1, 2003. <www.enculturation.net/5_1/crowley.html>. Accessed 1 Aug. 2021.
Covino, William and David Joliffe. *Rhetoric: Concepts, Definitions, Boundaries*, Longman, 1995.
Farrell, Thomas. *Norms of Rhetorical Culture*, Yale University Press, 1993.

Fisher, Walter. "Rhetoric: A Pedagogic Definition." *Western Speech*, vol. 25, 1961, pp. 163-172.
Genung, John Franklin. *The Practical Elements of Rhetoric with Illustrative Examples*, Boston, The Athenaeum Press, 1886.
Golden, James. and Edward P.J. Corbett, editors. *The Rhetoric of Blair, Campbell, and Whatley*, Southern Illinois UP, 1990.
Hauser, Gerald. *Introduction to Rhetorical Theory*, Waveland Press, 2002.
Hepburn, Andrew Dousa. *Manual of English Rhetoric*. Cincinnati, Wilson, Hinkle, & Co., 1875.
Hill, A.S. "From *The Principles of Rhetoric*." *The Rhetorical Tradition: Readings From Classical Times to the Present*, edited by Patricia Bizzell and Bruce Herzberg, Bedford/St. Martin's, 2001, pp. 1149-1151
Kennedy, George, translator. *On Rhetoric: A Theory of Civic Discourse*. By Aristotle, Oxford UP, 1991.
—. "A Hoot in the Dark." *Philosophy & Rhetoric*, vol. 25, no. 1, 1992, pp. 1-21.
Leith, Sam. *Words Like Loaded Pistols: Rhetoric from Aristotle to Obama*, Basic Books, 2012.
Locke, John. "From *Essay Concerning Human Understanding*." *The Rhetorical Tradition: Readings From Classical Times to the Present*, edited by Patricia Bizzell and Bruce Herzberg, Bedford/St. Martin's, 2001, 817-827.
Mannion, John. "Cicero, Where Are You, Cicero?" *Journal (American Water Works Association)*, vol. 83, no. 4, 1991, p. 12.
Mao, LuMing. "Studying the Chinese Rhetorical Tradition in the Present: Re-presenting the Native's Point of View." *College English*, vol. 69, 2007, pp. 216-37.
McGarry, Daniel, translator. *The Metalogicon of John of Salisbury: A Twelfth-Century Defense of the Verbal and Logical Arts of the Trivium*, U of California P, 1955.
McNally, James Richard. "Toward a Definition of Rhetoric." *Philosophy and Rhetoric* vol. 3, no. 2, 1970, pp. 71-81.
Newbold, Curtis. "Rhetorical Criticism." *The Visual Communication Guy*, thevisualcommunicationguy.com/rhetoric-overview/rhetorical-criticism-overview/, Accessed 4 Aug 2021.
Poulakos, John. "Toward a Sophistic Definition of Rhetoric." *Philosophy & Rhetoric*, vol. 16, no. 1, 1983, pp. 35-48.
Pound, Ezra. *Early Writings and Prose Poems*, edited by Ira Nadel, Penguin, 2005.
Ratcliffe, Krista. "The Current State of Composition Scholar/Teachers: Is Rhetoric Gone or Just Hiding Out?" *Enculturation*, vol. 5, no. 1, 2003 http://www.enculturation.net/5_1/ratcliffe.html. Accessed 30 Jul 2021.
"Rhetoric." *Dictionary.com*. www.dictionary.com/browse/rhetoric. Accessed 2 Aug. 2021.
"Rhetoric." *Merriam-Webster.com*. www.merriam-webstr.com/dictionary/rhetoric. Accessed 2 Aug. 2021.
"Rhetoric." *Wikipedia, The Free Encyclopedia*. en.wikipedia.org/wiki/Rhetoric. Accessed 1 Aug. 2021.

Richards, I.A. *The Philosophy of Rhetoric*, Oxford UP, 1965.
Rickert, Thomas. *Ambient Rhetoric: The Attunements of Rhetorical Being*, U of Pittsburgh P, 2013.
Ripley, Henry Jones. *Sacred Rhetoric; or, Composition and Delivery of Sermons*, Boston, Gould, Kendall, and Lincoln, 1849.
Scott, Robert L. "A Synoptic View of Systems of Western Rhetoric." *Quarterly Journal of Speech*, vol. 61, 1975, pp. 439-47.
Smith, Tania. "What is Rhetoric?" *Edu*Rhetor*, 2010, https://edurhetor.wordpress.com/about/rhetoric/. Accessed 4 Aug 2021.
Sunstein, Bonnie Stone and Elizabeth Chiseri-Strater. *Fieldworking: Reading and Writing Research*, Third Edition, Bedford/St. Martin's, 2007.
Valesio, Paolo. *Novantiqua: Rhetorics as Contemporary Theory*. Indiana UP, 1980.
Wallace, Karl. "The Fundamentals of Rhetoric." *The Prospect of Rhetoric*, edited by Lloyd Bitzer and Edwin Black, Prentice-Hall, 1971, pp. 3-20.
Wang, Bo. "*Ren*, Reciprocity, and the Art of Communication: Conversing with Confucius in the Present." *After Plato: Rhetoric, Ethics and the Teaching of Writing*, edited by John Duffy and Lois Agnew, Utah State UP, 2020, pp. 68-85.
Weiser, M. Elizabeth. *Museum Rhetoric: Building Civic Identity in National Spaces*, Pennsylvania State UP, 2017.
Whately, Richard. *Elements of Rhetoric*. London, B. Fellowes, 1841.

Teacher Resources for "What is Rhetoric?: A 'Choose Your Own Adventure Primer"

Overview and Teaching Strategies

In graduate school, I started to collect definitions of rhetoric. I wasn't systematic about it, nor did I have a particular reason for doing so outside of the fact that I had observed *a lot* of definitions for this term. I found around twenty at first, then I had fifty, then a hundred. My list kept growing until one day I realized these definitions had pedagogical value. First-year writing students and others new to the study of rhetoric are often given watered-down definitions that sometimes manage to not only make rhetoric sound vague and uninteresting but also tedious—something for pedants. Indeed, my skin crawls every time I see rhetoric "quizzes" that ask students to identify equally watered-down ideas like *logos*, *ethos*, and *pathos*. So, I decided to introduce students to rhetoric not by simplifying it but by presenting it in all its complexity from the jump.

I didn't want to give students *a* definition of rhetoric, I wanted to give them *all* the definitions. I wanted them to mix up these definitions, get confused, try them out, make their own. Simply dumping pages of definitions into the laps of students isn't helpful, however, which is how the idea for this "choose your own adventure" essay developed. What better way to introduce students to rhetoric than by giving them the opportunity to be persuaded by multiple definitions while also being guided by their own interests? After all, as I say in the chapter, what rhetoric is depends on the person doing the looking.

What makes this essay different from more conventional introductory essays is that it provides information while also inviting readers to participate in the text's own performance as a text. That is, instructors can use this essay to illustrate how rhetoric is an abstract art with material effects. *Or is it a material science with abstract effects?* As one can see, the definitions we choose to explain what rhetoric is and does naturally constrain how we imagine its scope and utility. But that's how rhetoric works.

Discussion Questions

1. How did you end up reading this essay? Go back and retrace your steps: What sections did you read and in what order? Spend a few

minutes reflecting on what this experience says about you. Why did you skip certain sections? What sections were most interesting and why?

2. What is at stake in defining rhetoric as either a science, an art, or both? That is, why does it matter (or not matter) whether we identify rhetoric using these categories?

3. The definitions in each section of this essay are meant to highlight a specific aspect or quality of rhetoric, so the definitions in Section 4 relate to how rhetoric can mean effective communication, the definitions in Section 5 relate to how rhetoric can mean persuasion, etc. But many of these definitions could be classified under more than one section. Pick one definition from this essay that you think could be moved to at least two other sections and explain why.

4. Pick three of the most recent emails you have either received or sent. Thinking about the different approaches to understanding rhetoric outlined in this essay, how would you characterize each of these messages as examples of rhetoric?

5. Invent your own definition of rhetoric. You can make one up from scratch, or you can select ideas or phrases to patch together (this is call "patchwriting") from any of the definitions included in this essay. Once you have a working definition, spend a few minutes freewriting about the choices you considered as you created this definition.

Activities

Persuade the Class

Have students assemble into small groups and instruct each group to select one definition of rhetoric that they believe is the most useful. Then have each group plan an informal presentation in which they must convince the other groups that the definition is the best. After each group presents, the other groups must note what elements of their presentation were persuasive and why. From there, you could conduct a public or private poll, perhaps ranking each presentation, to determine which group came out on top. The discussion could then turn to why students focused on the particular elements of each presentation. Such an activity could easily be stretched over 2-3 class meetings.

Collaborative Writing

Ask each student to develop their own definition of rhetoric (see Discussion Question 5 above) and then instruct students to paste their definition into a shared document, such as a Google Doc, that can be accessed remotely. You could then have small groups of students (perhaps in twos or threes) to start a new shared document where they take each of their classmates' definitions and arrange them into a brief essay like this one. Or you could ask each group to decide on a medium and delivery style of their choosing. Not only would such an activity engage students in critical thinking about rhetoric, but it also encourages them to experiment with collaborative composition. Such an activity could be broken into smaller tasks and extended across multiple class meetings.

16 Thinking across Modes and Media (and Baking Cake): Two Techniques for Writing with Video, Audio, and Images

Crystal VanKooten

Overview

Using the metaphor of baking a cake, this chapter offers students in college writing courses two techniques for writing with video, audio, and images: *integration* and *juxtaposition*.[1] Knowing more about these techniques enables students to approach the analysis and composition of their own and others' multimodal texts with more specificity and control. Drawing on work from writing professors and digital designers, the essay defines and discusses integration and cross-modal reinforcement, as well as sequential and simultaneous juxtaposition, using one student-authored video composition as an example. Overall, students are encouraged to think critically and concretely about *integration* and *juxtaposition* in the multimodal texts they consume and create as they work to become more skilled and rhetorically-sensitive digital writers.

Introduction

When it comes to dessert, who doesn't love cake? It's soft, rich, and sweetly decadent. But if you've ever made a cake from scratch, you know that there are many elements that a baker uses to put together and finish the cake: flour, butter, sugar, eggs, salt,

---

1. This work is licensed under the Creative Commons Attribution-NonCommercial-NoDerivatives 4.0 International License (CC BY-NC-ND 4.0) and is subject to the Writing Spaces Terms of Use. To view a copy of this license, visit http://creativecommons.org/licenses/by-nc-nd/4.0/, email info@creativecommons.org, or send a letter to Creative Commons, PO Box 1866, Mountain View, CA 94042, USA. To view the Writing Spaces Terms of Use, visit http://writingspaces.org/terms-of-use.

filling, and frosting. These elements are combined—or *integrated*—differently depending on how the baker wants the cake to turn out. Put another way, what goes into the mix makes a difference in how the cake tastes in the end. Much like cake, multimodal texts such as videos, websites, posts on social media, and podcasts involve a variety of elements that are combined to make a final product: words, images, sound recordings, music, voices, and video clips, for example. Like master bakers, skilled digital writers know how to combine these elements strategically, sometimes layering several of them together to compose a new whole or sometimes emphasizing one particular mode. This chapter will introduce you to two writing techniques, *integration* and *juxtaposition*, that can help you better understand and describe different combinations of media in a multimodal text, and also help you to compose your own digital product that audiences will really enjoy—to bake your own delicious cake!

But let's be real here: I'm a professor. I'm no master baker, and you probably aren't either. If I'm baking a cake, I'm going to read and follow the directions on the back of the box, and those directions will help me to put the cake ingredients together in a way that—I hope—is really tasty! This chapter is kind of like one set of simple directions on the back of the cake box for your digital writing, a place to start when considering how to describe the modes and media that others put together, *and* how to use those same modes and media to compose your own work. I'll draw from writing professors and digital designers to talk about what *integration* and *juxtaposition* are in relation to writing with video, audio, and images, and I'll show you what these two techniques can look and sound like in one student-authored video made for a writing class. Ultimately, knowing how to recognize, describe, and use these techniques will help you approach the analysis and composition of your own and others' multimodal texts with more specificity, confidence, and control.

What Is a Multimodal Text?

At this point, you may be wondering what exactly a multimodal text is, and why in the world I'm talking about baking in a chapter about digital writing. We'll get there. For now, just stay with me, and think of a multimodal text as a soft and delicious cake that you want to bake for your sister's birthday. You go to the store, choose the "Traditional Chocolate" cake mix, and read that you need to combine cake mix, water, oil, and eggs to make the cake batter. So into the bowl they go, and then, using a spoon—or for those of you who are fancy bakers—a mixer, you stir them together. Next, you bake the cake, let it cool, frost it, and it's ready to eat!

When you and your sister put your forks into a slice, you no longer see the powdery mix, or the water, or the eggs. All of the individual ingredients were *integrated* to create the fluffy, chocolatey dessert you can enjoy. After it's baked, the cake is now what writing professor Bump Halbritter would call "all-there-at-once," meaning it's a whole that comes across as if it isn't comprised of parts and pieces. The baker knows, of course, that many ingredients were combined strategically to make the whole, and those combinations can really affect the taste, texture, and flavor.

This concept of combining elements strategically is useful for cake baking *and* for composing multimodal texts, which of course is why we're spending so much time in this chapter on cake. But what is a multimodal text, anyway? The term *mode* is embedded in the word *multimodal*, and when I talk about a mode, I'm referring to what writing professors Kristin Arola, Jennifer Shepherd, and Cheryl Ball describe as "a way of communicating" (3). When you compose a multimodal text like a video, you blend together images (the visual mode), sounds (the aural mode), and written words (the linguistic mode), much like you mixed together the ingredients for your sister's cake. *Writing Spaces* volume 3 author Melanie Gagich clarifies that *text* is a broad term in writing studies that refers to "a piece of communication that can take many forms" (66). So a multimodal text is a piece of communication that uses multiple ways—or modes—to get its message across.

Arola, Shepherd, and Ball, along with Gagich, also point out that there are many different kinds of multimodal texts that are both digital and non-digital: movies, memes, posters, online articles, slide decks, whole websites, and more. And just as a baker might vary the amount of different cake ingredients to get a different texture or taste, the modes in each different kind of multimodal text can be blended together in various ways. But in baking, you can't experiment with blending if you aren't aware of the ingredients and the effects they can have on cake-eaters, and the same applies for digital media composition. You can't become an advanced digital media author if you don't know how to see and hear past a media product's "all-there-at-onceness." Halbritter advises that we need "an ability to break apart the components" of digital media texts, along with "terminology that identifies and names the relationships within and between the rhetorical elements of a complex piece of audio-visual writing" (108). This is where concepts like *modes, integration,* and *juxtaposition* are helpful. They give us language to talk about how digital texts are composed and how they affect audiences.

INTEGRATION

Integration is defined by professor and political scientist Robert Horn as "the act of forming, coordinating, or blending into a functional or unified whole" (11). In his book about visual language, Horn gets more specific about the integration of words and images, and he talks about nine different kinds of integration of verbal and visual elements: substitution, disambiguation, labeling, example, reinforcement, completion, chunking, clustering, and framing (101-104). I could say a lot about how any of these kinds of integration might apply to our work with digital media, but I'd like to focus us on reinforcement, in part because I've noticed that student writers use this technique a lot—sometimes even a bit too much. According to Horn, visual/verbal reinforcement happens when "the visual elements help present a (generally) more abstract idea. They present the idea a second time, even though it may be clearly interpretable from the words alone" (103). So we could call reinforcement "doubling" or "cross-modal repetition," where an author presents one concept through two (or more) modes of expression: through words *and* images, for example, or through images *and* sound.

Like I said, I've noticed that students tend to use reinforcement a lot when they're new to composing digital compositions. They'll write out a point in a video using words while they simultaneously speak the same exact words in a voiceover. They'll write out facts about a topic on a PowerPoint slide, and then pair the words with a graph that shows the same information. These examples use reinforcement across modes in simple ways, and sometimes, simple is good. A graph might help us see data differently than only reading about it, for example. Many times, though, when authors use cross-modal reinforcement, the visual and the verbal reinforce each other, but for little apparent reason.

Instead, when reinforcement is used to further a specific rhetorical purpose, it can be a useful form of integration. Horn mentions that when using visuals to reinforce words, "visual elements add rhetorical qualities such as mood, style, lightness, and so forth" (103). Applying this idea, an image might be combined with some words not just to use two modes together because we can, but instead to create a specific mood or style like seriousness or whimsy. In addition, disability studies scholar Stephanie Kerschbaum writes about reinforcement using the term *commensurability*, when information is repeated via multiple channels in order to provide greater access for all users and readers. As Kerschbaum makes clear, making digital texts more accessible for audience members with varying abilities is a very good reason to use cross-modal reinforcement.

An Example of Integration: Reinforcement in "A College Collage"

Cross-modal reinforcement has a place, then, when done for a rhetorical purpose and/or for accessibility. Let's talk through an example of what an effective use of reinforcement might actually look and sound like in a multimodal text by looking at a video composed by Evan Kennedy, a student in a writing course that I taught a few years ago. Evan's video is called "A College Collage: Not Going Back," and he made it in response to a video composition assignment in our digital writing class. The assignment was very open, asking students to pick any topic to explore through composing a video that used multiple modes to communicate. Evan chose to make his video about managing mental health during college, and specifically, about his own experiences with mental health through an extended college career at multiple schools. He explores and shares about this topic through combinations of images (many of his own selfies and photos), music (Demi Lovato's popular song "Old Ways"), and sounds (remixed voiceovers from documentary films). I highly encourage you to watch all of Evan's video before you read any further in this chapter (you can access it here: https://youtu.be/RgX4U7Z25c0). Next, I'll talk us through a few sequences where Evan uses different kinds of integration and juxtaposition effectively.

Once you watch the video, you know that "A College Collage" is pretty awesome. For the video's first minute, we hear different voices speaking about mental illness and its effects along with a low driving beat and a crackling, static sound that replays each time a speaker finishes a phrase. We see an empty black screen that switches between various black and white images: notebooks and textbooks falling off of a desk, a person lying on a bed seen through a small window, stacked pill bottles, a man holding the side of his head. In this sequence, Evan has mixed together some cake ingredients—he's integrated various media elements such as spoken words, images, video clips, and sound effects.

Figure 1. "A College Collage" by Evan Kennedy on YouTube, showing an image of stacked pill bottles. Please access Evan's video at https://youtu.be/RgX4U7Z25c0. Screenshot by the author.

Evan effectively uses reinforcement in this opening sequence with the sounds and images. The excerpt from 0:44-0:51 is a good example. A female voice speaks, saying, "Fighting yourself to wake up, get up, take a shower, try and breathe, try and smile, try and act like you believe you have something to live for." Through words, the speaker describes one kind of daily mental health struggle, and reinforcing this spoken message is the image sequence that Evan chose to put with it: a female figure, shadowed, who walks slowly toward us down a hall (see Figure 2). But the image sequence doesn't *exactly* double the content of the spoken words; it adds a feel and tone, along with more information that allows us to interpret the words. The visual is dark, shadowy, somber. We can't see the woman's face. We imagine her struggle to "wake up, get up" as she teeters down the hospital hallway. Together, the words and the image help to communicate the message: that for this woman, it's difficult to wake up and start the day.

The way Evan mixes his ingredients together in this opening sequence to reinforce one another works for me as an audience member. I see it and I hear it; I get it and I feel it—mental illness is a difficult struggle. I wonder what Evan is going to say next about mental health, and I look and listen for more images, words, and sounds to help me better understand the message.

Figure 2. "A College Collage" by Evan Kennedy on YouTube. Evan reinforces the use of spoken words with an image of a woman. Text reads "Woman's voice: Fighting yourself to wake up, get up, take a shower, try and breathe, try and smile." Please access Evan's video at https://youtu.be/RgX4U7Z25c0. Screenshot by the author.

Juxtaposition

Let's go back to your sister's birthday cake. You've already mixed the ingredients and baked the cake. Now, you decide to stack two layers on top of each other and put some filling in the middle, along with frosting around the outside and on top. The filling will add more moisture and a contrasting flavor, but it won't be integrated into the cake in the same way as the other ingredients. It will be positioned next to the other elements for a delicious result. The same is true for the frosting—you smooth it out on the top and sides of the cake, and you taste and enjoy it *along with* bites of cake and filling.

When you use cake filling in the middle of a cake and frosting on the top and outside of a cake, you're baking with the technique of *juxtaposition*, where two or more elements are placed next to one another in a single space or moment "to create meaning and communicate ideas to an audience," as writing professor Sean Morey explains (288). For cake baking, the juxtaposed elements include cake bites and frosting. For digital writing, the juxtaposed elements include images, sounds, and words. In a visual presentation, you can place two or more images side by side and create meanings and patterns that emerge from viewing them together. In a video, you can put sounds and images next to or after one another in time (sequentially) or layered on top of each other at the same moment (simultaneously) to create contrast, to tell a story, to compose a transition, and to do many other things.

Anthropologist and museum researcher Corinne A. Kratz analyzes how juxtaposition works in exhibits, installations, websites, and films. She calls juxtapositions "productive kernals" that can do different kinds of rhetorical work: raise questions, tell stories, imply sequence or narrative, provoke puzzlement or surprise, show contrast or similarity, help to make an argument, or suggest categories (30, 32). Juxtaposition can be seen as a form of integration, but I like to think of it as a related technique where elements are placed in close proximity to one another but still remain somewhat separate. It's layer cake with cake filling; the elements are not fully mixed.

Student writers in my classes use juxtaposition in some of the ways Kratz mentions. For visuals, they often use sequential juxtaposition, where different images are presented in a sequence to tell a story, seen one after the other in progressive time. Students also have used video effects for visuals such as a split screen or a picture-in-picture, which allow for simultaneous juxtaposition as different elements are seen or heard next to or near one another at the same moment in time. The simultaneous juxtaposition of elements can also be composed across modes: images can be placed next to or with sounds or music, for example, or images placed adjacent to written words.

Examples of Juxtaposition: Sequential and Simultaneous Juxtaposition

Let's return to "A College Collage" and look and listen to one portion where Evan utilizes cross-modal sequential and simultaneous juxtaposition to further the message of his video. After the video's introduction at 1:21, Evan uses Demi Lovato's 2015 song "Old Ways" as the soundtrack for the main portion of "A College Collage." Songs are complex, layered pieces of media in and of themselves, and "Old Ways" is no exception. We hear Lovato's voice, the lyrics of the song, various instruments, rhythmic beats, and electronic effects. Writing professor Kyle Stedman claims that "music is a language. It speaks. And as such, it's rhetorically deployed by people who have specific things they want to say with it." As we listen and watch, we notice that Evan is indeed rhetorically deploying "Old Ways" to do a lot more work than a stock background track might do. Many elements of the song—the beat, the lyrics, the changes in pace—are strategically juxtaposed with the images and words we see, and the images themselves are then juxtaposed carefully alongside each other.

From 1:34-1:51, Evan uses Lovato's lyrics to start to tell a story of perseverance amid trial. Lovato sings, "I'm down again / I turn the page / The story's mine / No more watchin' the world from my doorstep / Passin' me by / And I just keep changing these colors…." We hear these lyrics simultaneously juxtaposed with images of a growing stack of books on a shelf and a growing pyramid of empty pill bottles on a table. We see the date "2009" written across the screen. The images are placed in sequential juxtaposition, one after the other, and the changing of the images is coordinated with a hard-hitting percussive beat within each measure of "Old Ways." Hearing this repetitive beat, we anticipate each image change before it appears, and the mix of the images, the date, and the music implies a narrative. We wonder about connections between the modes and media: how are the books and the pill bottles related? Are the pill bottles related to Lovato's lyric about being "down again"?

This fifteen-second sequence ends as the music transitions from verse to chorus. Within the song at 1:41, an ascending electronic scale grows louder, building in volume and pitch to the first line of the chorus. Evan juxtaposes this musical shift with a video clip that zooms in on a lone figure at the end of a hallway (see Figure 3). According to Kratz, one way juxtaposition works is to coordinate elements to heighten the audience's attention (30), and we notice Evan using the music and the clip's zooming movement to do just that—to get us to look and listen closely. As the beat of the chorus drops dramatically, we then see a black and white clip of Evan himself, punching toward the camera on the downbeat, and the visual quickly flips to a red screen with the date "2010."

Thinking Across Modes and Media (and Baking Cake) 275

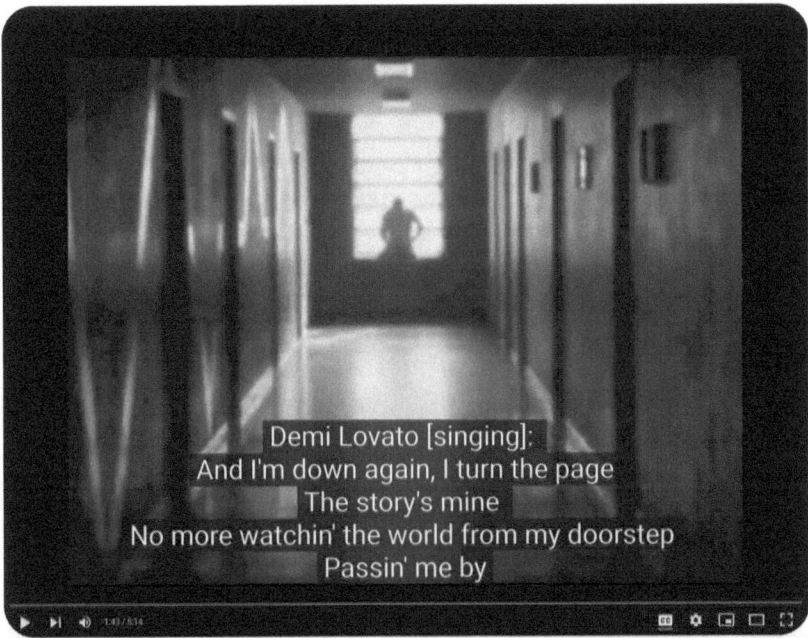

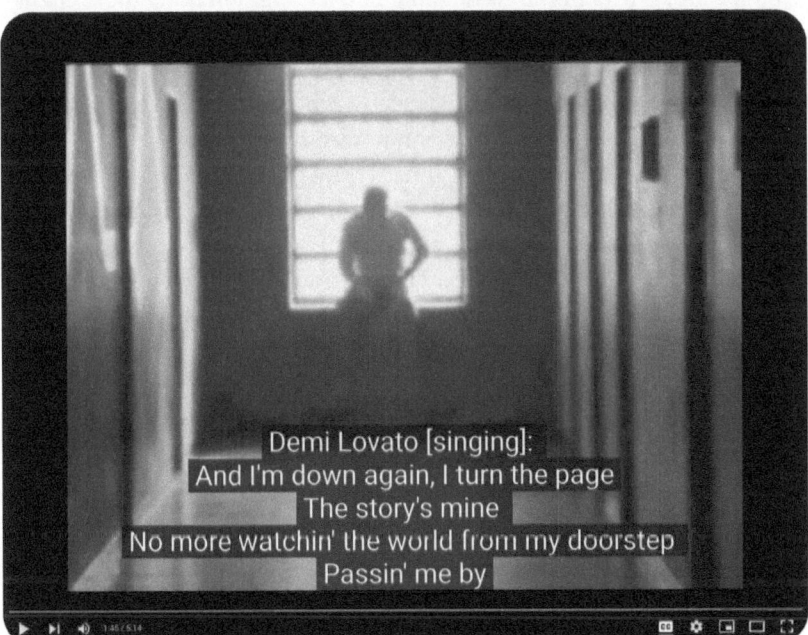

Figure 3. A lone figure illuminated by light from a window at the end of a hallway. Closed captioning shows Demi Lovato lyrics. Please access Evan's video at https://youtu.be/RgX4U7Z25c0. Screenshot by the author.

There's a lot going on here. Evan is both juxtaposing and integrating, using images, clips, music, lyrics, and movement to tell the story of his journey through college with mental health. The juxtapositions are sequential (different images one after another) and simultaneous (music with image); they are within and across visual and aural modes, and they help to make watching this video a captivating and persuasive experience. And the purposes of these juxtapositions are various and align with Kratz's list, working to imply a narrative (of Evan's experiences across time), to heighten attention (to a transition point in the story), or to point out similarities (between Lovato's lyrics and Evan's experiences).

BAKING (AND SHARING) YOUR OWN CAKE

"A College Collage" is chock full of many other moments of integration and juxtaposition that you can watch, listen to, and learn from. It's important to tell you, though, that Evan worked on this video across a span of eight weeks in our writing course. He turned in four different versions of the video, and he was constantly making revisions, listening to feedback from me and others in the class, and going back and making more changes. (If you want to see some earlier versions of "A College Collage," you can view three earlier drafts at this link, https://ccdigitalpress.org/book/transfer-across-media/5-1-evan.html, where I write more about Evan's composition process). The point is that composing these kinds of complex and powerful media sequences takes time, effort, input, and lots of revision. Part of the effort that Evan put in was learning how to see and hear his own work both as "all-there-at-once" and as component pieces that could be tweaked and changed, juxtaposed and integrated in different ways. Then he "taste-tested" his video by giving it to audiences to try, and using their feedback, he went back to the kitchen to mix in different elements that might taste even better.

You can do the same as you read and analyze multimodal texts composed by others or compose your own multimodal texts for class. Think about the whole, and then think about the parts that make up the whole. Taste the cake when it's done (watch the video, read the presentation), and get others to taste it too, during peer review sessions, at the writing center, or anywhere you can get someone to give you feedback on your work. Pay attention to what ingredients you're using and why, listen to feedback on how they come together, and be ready to make changes and taste-test again.

If you're making a PowerPoint presentation, be mindful of how your words and images work together. Is there too much reinforcement between modes? How can you use images to reinforce words or words to reinforce images, but not to simply double the meaning? What images could you use that add value to the words, that might reinforce through an example or through new information? If you're making a video composition, consider and plan how you might juxtapose the modes and media the audience sees and hears. Can you use side-by-side visuals, and if so, what would the effect be on the audience? Can you do more with aligning elements of the musical track with visual and written elements, and how might doing this advance your purpose? Can you tell a story across modes, create a surprising visual moment, or imply a connection between parts?

Thinking critically and concretely about *integration* and *juxtaposition* in the multimodal texts you consume and create is one step toward becoming a more skilled and rhetorically-sensitive digital writer. They're simple concepts with many different applications and outcomes when used across modes and media. And when you can spot them, think about them, and then use them purposefully, you are well on your way to master baker status, digital media style.

Works Cited

Arola, Kristin L., et al. *Writer/Designer: A Guide to Making Multimodal Projects.* 2nd ed., Bedford/St. Martin's, 2018.

Gagich, Melanie. "An Introduction to and Strategies for Multimodal Composing." *Writing Spaces: Readings on Writing*, vol. 3, edited by Dana Driscoll, Mary Stewart, and Matt Vetter, Parlor Press, 2020, pp. 65-85, https://writingspaces.org/?page_id=384.

Halbritter, Bump. *Mics, Cameras, Symbolic Action: Audio-Visual Rhetoric for Writing Teachers.* Parlor Press, 2013.

Horn, Robert E. *Visual Language: Global Communication for the 21st Century.* MacroVU, Inc., 1998, https://openlibrary.org/books/OL400850M/Visual_language.

Kennedy, Evan. "A College Collage: Not Going Back." YouTube, uploaded by Crystal VanKooten, 9 April 2019, https://www.youtube.com/watch?v=RgX4U7Z25c0.

Kerschbaum, Stephanie. "Modality." "Multimodality in Motion: Disability and Kairotic Spaces" by M. Remi Yergeau et al. *Kairos: A Journal of Rhetoric, Technology, and Pedagogy*, 18.1, 2013, https://kairos.technorhetoric.net/18.1/coverweb/yergeau-et-al/pages/mod/index.html.

Kratz, Corinne A. "*Red* Textures and the Work of Juxtaposition." *Kronos*, no. 42, Nov. 2016, pp. 29–47, http://www.jstor.org/stable/44176040.

Morey, Sean. *The Digital Writer*. Fountainhead Press, 2017.
Stedman, Kyle D. "How Music Speaks: In the Background, In the Remix, In the City." *Currents in Electronic Literacy*, 2011, http://currents.cwrl.utexas.edu/2011/howmusicspeaks.

Teacher Resources for "Thinking across Modes and Media (and Baking Cake): Two Techniques for Writing with Video, Audio, and Images"

Overview and Teaching Strategies

This essay introduces students to the concepts of *integration* and *juxtaposition* within digital media composition, framed using theory from Bump Halbritter, Robert E. Horn, and Corrine A. Kratz. In the chapter, I use the metaphor of cake baking to get students to start thinking of texts such as videos, podcasts, or webtexts as composed of various pieces of media that authors can change, combine, and control for rhetorical effect. This essay would be most useful within a unit in a writing course where students have to both analyze and compose digital media texts, as *integration* and *juxtaposition* can be used for analysis and for invention or revision. Students might do a rhetorical analysis activity first, for example, using integration and juxtaposition as a framework. Then, students could compose their own texts that use integration and juxtaposition and reflect on how and why they used the techniques and for what ends.

The chapter offers two examples of effective uses of integration and juxtaposition that come from a student-authored video, "A College Collage" by undergraduate student Evan Kennedy. The examples emphasize using the techniques across various modes that include visuals, sounds, and words. I highly recommend that students view and listen to the example video "A College Collage" in its entirety in order to fully engage with the analysis of the examples in the chapter. "A College Collage" by Evan Kennedy can be found online here: https://youtu.be/RgX4U7Z25c0.

Questions and Activities for Discussion or Reflection

1. Describe a time when you baked something: a cake, a different dessert, or any bread or baked good. What elements and ingredients were included in your baking process, and how were they combined? How does your experience with baking help you to think differently about the digital media texts that you might compose for this class, such as a video or a podcast?

2. After watching and listening to Evan's video "A College Collage," pick a 10-20 second sequence from the video, and write up a rhetorical analysis of the sequence. Focus your analysis on the *integration* and *juxtaposition* you see and hear in the sequence.

3. Look up the different kinds of *integration* that Robert Horn writes about on pp. 101-104 of his book *Visual Language*: substitution, disambiguation, labeling, example, reinforcement, completion, chunking, clustering, and framing. (Horn's book is open access and can be found online here: https://openlibrary.org/books/OL400850M/Visual_language). Using Horn's book as a reference, write up your own definition of one of the types of integration. Where and when might you see, hear, or use this kind of integration?

4. Find a digital media text online that uses integration or juxtaposition effectively. The text you find might be an image, a webpage, an advertisement, a post on social media, or a short video. Write up an analysis of how your chosen text uses integration or juxtaposition to achieve its purposes.

5. Pick a topic, and compose a short audio or video clip that combines at least two media elements strategically for a certain effect. You might combine a song and several images, for example, in a way that aims for surprise, joy, discomfort, or sadness. After composing your clip, write a paragraph that reflects over your authorial choices and their effects on a potential audience.

17 You Are Good for Wikipedia

Matthew A. Vetter and Oksana Moroz

Overview

In a previous *Writing Spaces* essay entitled, "Wikipedia Is Good for You!?," James P. Purdy introduces us to the idea that the online encyclopedia, often devalued in educational spaces, can serve as a starting place for research and a process guide to research-based writing.[1] By observing how Wikipedia editors review each other's work, have conversations about that work, and then revise accordingly, students like you can gain first-hand access and insights into professional writing and research practices that can be applied to research projects. In this chapter, we build on Purdy's essay by acknowledging not only how Wikipedia is good for you but, conversely, how you are good for Wikipedia. This chapter differs from Purdy's contribution in that we discuss how you can become more engaged in the Wikipedia community through various editing and evaluating practices. We want you to consider how you are good for the encyclopedia project in three ways. First, you can diversify the encyclopedia through your participation. Second, you can leverage your access to reputable academic sources of knowledge to improve coverage of certain topics. Third, you can apply critical thinking skills you learn in your writing class to help evaluate information in Wikipedia. Finally, we conclude the essay by providing two examples of our former students who effectively contributed to Wikipedia by connecting their own experiences and identities to their work in the encyclopedia.

---

1. This work is licensed under the Creative Commons Attribution-NonCommercial-NoDerivatives 4.0 International License (CC BY-NC-ND 4.0) and is subject to the Writing Spaces Terms of Use. To view a copy of this license, visit http://creativecommons.org/licenses/by-nc-nd/4.0/, email info@creativecommons.org, or send a letter to Creative Commons, PO Box 1866, Mountain View, CA 94042, USA. To view the Writing Spaces Terms of Use, visit http://writingspaces.org/terms-of-use.

Introduction

Jamie Withorne
@jamiewithorne

My middle school teacher who yelled that "Wikipedia wasn't a reliable source" every day is sharing vaccine conspiracy theories on Facebook.

8:52 PM · Feb 11, 2021 · Twitter for iPhone

41.7K Retweets   **1,317** Quote Tweets   **424.5K** Likes

figure 1. A screenshot of a tweet dated February 2021 from Jamie Withorne (@jamiewithorne) reads, "My middle school teacher who yelled that 'Wikipedia wasn't a reliable source' every day is sharing vaccine conspiracy theories on Facebook."

Check out the tweet above. After you read the actual text, you might notice that, at the time we took the screenshot, this tweet had been liked over 424,500 times and retweeted 41,700 times. Maybe it's gotten even more engagement since.

So, what's remarkable about this tweet? We can't speak for all Twitter users out there, but we can say that this is probably a common enough experience that resonated with people across the Internet, not only in terms of Wikipedia's reliability but also misinformation issues. The tweet mentioned above probably makes people think about some of their own school experiences. Maybe it makes them reflect on issues related to authority and credibility regarding factual information. More than likely, many of the Twitter users that engaged with the tweet did so because they recognized just how much things have changed in the past 10-20 years when it comes to evaluating online sources. But what role does Wikipedia play in all of this?

In Wikipedia, contributors must carefully check their sources to ensure credibility and reliability; otherwise, the information will be removed. As you read this sentence, Wikipedia "develops at a rate of over 1.9 edits per second, performed by editors from all over the world" ("Wikipedia:Statistics"). In fact, the encyclopedia is now both the largest and most widely used in history. In the English language version alone, an average of nearly 600 new articles are created every day. As we write this sentence, the English version includes more than 6,480,638 articles on every topic imaginable ("Wikipedia:Statistics"). That's over 91 times larger than *Encyclopedia Britannica* ("Wikipedia:Size"). Maybe you've heard of it? Significant as the longest-running print encyclopedia in the English language, *Britannica* was continuously printed for 244 years. Yet it doesn't come close to the scope and size of Wikipedia. And while the English language edition of Wikipedia is the most comprehensive and widely accessed, Wikipedia also exists in over 270 other language versions ("Wikipedia:Statistics").

Not only has Wikipedia grown in terms of size over the last two decades since its founding, but the encyclopedia has also matured in terms of accuracy and reliability into what some have called the "Internet's good grown-up" (Harrison), a community that "exists to battle fake news" (Forsyth), and "the last best place on the Internet" (Cooke). Moreover, plenty of scientific studies have shown that Wikipedia is at least as accurate as other encyclopedias and perhaps even more reliable (Brown; Casebourne et al.; Giles; Hwang et al.; Kräenbring et al.; Taraborelli).

Despite all of this, you've likely been told never to use Wikipedia for school projects. Right? It's probably not surprising that Wikipedia was criticized (Gorman) and, in some cases, banned (Cohen) from educational uses. So why the bad rap? Why is Wikipedia still looked down upon, especially by teachers and other academics? James P. Purdy explains the problem that some academics have with Wikipedia in another *Writing Spaces* essay entitled, "Wikipedia Is Good for You!?":

> Usually, teachers do not like two primary aspects of Wikipedia. The first is its open participation: anyone, regardless of background, qualifications, or expertise, can write Wikipedia articles…The second aspect of Wikipedia that many teachers do not like is its changeability: Wikipedia articles do not remain the same over time. (207-208)

What Purdy calls "open participation" is probably the biggest reason it has taken so long for Wikipedia to become more widely recognized as a trustworthy and reliable source. The fact that anyone can make changes to the encyclopedia makes us wonder whether the person writing about a particular topic is knowledgeable about that topic. But the larger purpose of his essay is to explain how Wikipedia can help you, as a writing student, better understand how to use the encyclopedia as 1) a source, and 2) a process guide for researching and writing. It is useful for you to know that Wikipedia can be helpful as a starting place for your research. The processes Wikipedia editors take on when contributing to the encyclopedia are similar to those students should engage in when working on a research assignment.

In this essay, we build on Purdy's work by helping you understand how *your* engagement and contributions to Wikipedia can help the encyclopedia. Not only is *Wikipedia* good for you, as Purdy suggests, but *you* are good for Wikipedia. We believe that Wikipedia's openness, the fact that anyone can contribute, is the encyclopedia's biggest strength. And we want to encourage you to think more deeply about how you can help the Wikipedia project in three specific ways. First, you can improve its diversity. Next, your access to reputable academic knowledge sources enables you to build on its content. Finally, you can apply critical thinking skills that you are learning in your writing or research class to help make the encyclopedia more trustworthy. In the following sections, we discuss how you are good for Wikipedia in these three ways. We ultimately argue that your engagement with the encyclopedia is vital to its continued success. In the conclusion of this essay, we include the voices of other students like you who have learned how to edit Wikipedia and include screenshot images of their contributions.

YOU ARE GOOD FOR WIKIPEDIA'S DIVERSITY PROBLEM

First, while the encyclopedia has come a long way in creating the most comprehensive reference source in history, it still suffers from problems related to what the community calls "systemic biases." More on this later, but the overall problem that causes these biases is that most of Wikipedia's editors are middle-aged, white males whose primary language is English. Because those editors work on topics they are most interested in, other topics or content areas are not represented. If you are reading this as a student, you are probably outside of at least one of those social categories (if not more than one). Your identity (your lived experiences, interests, values, etc.) makes you well-positioned to contribute to Wikipedia, in ways big and small, to develop and focus attention on parts of the encyclopedia that have been overlooked in terms of representing diverse inclusive viewpoints.

So, about those systemic biases. Although Wikipedia calls itself the online encyclopedia "that anyone can edit," it turns out that most people editing (especially the English language version) are male, old(er), and white. You can imagine that these folks probably have a background in technology. Heather Ford and Judy Wajcman, in a research article entitled "'Anyone Can Edit,' Not Everyone Does: Wikipedia's Infrastructure and the Gender Gap," published in the journal *Social Studies of Science*, explore how the overwhelmingly male editorship of the encyclopedia leads to unbalanced coverage and inclusion of people and topics. One powerful example is the lack of coverage of biographical articles about women on Wikipedia. While the statistics are constantly changing, at the time of this writing, it is widely accepted that less than 20% of biographical articles in the encyclopedia cover women (Tripodi). Leigh Gruwell argues in a related article that Wikipedia may discourage women from editing due to its insistence on neutrality or a "Neutral Point of View," which prohibits subjective and/or embodied ways of writing and knowledge-making (for example, personal essays that draw from the author's own experience). Wikipedia's gender gap, as it has come to be known, can be understood as a kind of omission—something missing—in the coverage of topics related to women or women's issues. Remember that the encyclopedia runs on volunteer labor. People edit and improve topics that they are interested in and connect to. And this is a good thing! Wikipedia needs self-motivated people like this that take an interest in a topic to make edits and continually improve the encyclopedia's content. But as long as the group of people reading, engaging, and writing the encyclopedia remains somewhat uniform and stagnant (without a large influx of diversity of identity along the social categories mentioned above), there will always be a problem concerning the issues that are represented well and those that are not represented at all.

Another good example of how the gender gap plays out on Wikipedia is the story of Donna Strickland, a Canadian optical physicist. She was the third woman to be awarded the Nobel Prize in Physics ("Donna Strickland"). Although Strickland had an influential and significant career until being awarded the Nobel Prize, she did not have a Wikipedia article devoted to her until *after* being awarded the Nobel (Bazely). This is a problem for many reasons: gender gap and bias, level of recognizability, the prestige of an award, and marginalization, to name a few. In Wikipedia, male contributors tend to create and edit articles about other dudes. Even more problematic, women are sometimes seen as less notable because of a lack of secondary coverage in sources outside Wikipedia.

This is where you come in. As we mentioned above, if you are reading this as part of a writing course, chances are you are already more diverse than the average Wikipedia editor. You might be younger or have a different gender, sexual, or racial identity. You might come from a challenging socioeconomic background. You might identify as disabled, neurodiverse, or a person with a disability. You might speak multiple languages. You might be diverse in other ways due to your background, past experiences, identity, family, or something else. Diversity is not one thing only, and it is not always visible to others. When engaging Wikipedia, bringing *your identity* to the table can help because the encyclopedia is only as good as the people involved. The community needs multiple volunteers and people with diverse interests, experiences, and identities to contribute to the full breadth of knowledge representation. Our discussion section discusses one specific way you can leverage your identity to improve Wikipedia. Take a look at it and consider engaging.

You Are Good for Wikipedia Because You Have Access to Academic Knowledge

As a student, you have enormous access to knowledge—much more than the average person. Wikipedia articles are most useful (and trustworthy) when they use reliable secondary sources (like academic books or other sources found through a library or library database). For example, you might have run across a "[Citation needed]" tag in a Wikipedia article. This means that another editor has noticed how a statement needs a source to back it up. You can help by adding citations from diverse researchers and other authors while exploring a wide range of reputable, published sources. By tapping into your university's resources, you can evaluate or even improve Wikipedia articles with current and trustworthy information. You can also share the knowledge access you have with the world since Wikipedia is published freely, and anyone with an Internet connection can benefit from its pages.

Think of yourself as the Golden Gate bridge for knowledge equity. You have access to information often unavailable to those outside the college context because of various "paywalls" and restrictions. That way, you are opening a whole new horizon to those not part of academic institutions. We draw from Wikipedia and rhetoric scholar Melanie Kill to support this claim. In a book chapter covering this specific topic, Kill argues that "Wikipedia provides students with a range of opportunities to work as intermediaries between the disciplinary expertise they are studying, a public system of knowledge curation, and a global audience of readers" (389). Not only can you provide access by adding information that would not otherwise be available, but by adhering to the "Neutral Point of View writing style," you can also make that information more accessible (that is, understandable) for global audiences. Furthermore, Wikipedia does not ask you for a subscription or a fee to read its articles. Instead, it encourages you to use, edit, and widely distribute its content.

We suspect that you are probably hesitant (and maybe anxious) to edit a Wikipedia article. And you are not alone. We have heard firsthand from students about the difficulty of accepting Wikipedia as a credible source, as many were told in high school not to use it as a reference (Vetter and Moroz). Or perhaps you are not ready to jump into editing because you are not familiar with the objective, neutral, and factual writing style of Wikipedia (Vetter and Moroz). And that is all OK. We are not asking you to be the next Steven Pruitt (the person with the highest number of Wikipedia edits), but we want you to recognize your resourcefulness and try to add a credible source, edit a small section, or even go big and start an article on an underrepresented topic. Your contributions can be as small as fixing a typo or copy-editing an article or more substantial—integrating new sources, adding images, adding content to underdeveloped articles, or creating new articles altogether. We are confident you can do all that and more!

Now, let's turn to the practical steps you can take to improve the online encyclopedia. If you decide to add a source, you may wonder what a good source in Wikipedia should look like? First, it should be a reliable source. Textbooks, literature reviews, books, or publications written by experts in the field and published by reliable publishers are appropriate. You should not use blog posts, press materials intended to show something in a certain light, or popular press articles, as they tend to be heavily opinionated or biased ("Wikipedia:Reliable"). Remember that Wikipedia wants you to write in an objective and neutral, not subjective style.

When you get to editing, use plain language, be brief, cite sources to back up factual claims, and attribute viewpoints to the people who hold them. You should avoid making conclusions, except when attributed to a specific source. You can paraphrase, use direct quotes, summarize, or transform information from the source, but you still need to make sure you give credit to the author.

While article development in Wikipedia is mainly about generating neutral and fact-based information, many encyclopedia aspects engage you in critical thinking, analysis, and communication, for example, by participating in writing spaces such as talk pages and in-class reflective writing. As you become involved in Wikipedia as a reader, contributor, editor, or writer, you start to understand many processes of creating an article. Wikipedia is unique because it is transparent to anyone in terms of its policies, guidelines, processes, and philosophies, and this transparency can help you better understand how the community works (Vetter and Moroz).

You Are Good for Wikipedia Because You Are a Critical Thinker

Suppose you're learning about and practicing critical thinking skills in your writing class. In that case, you can apply these skills to evaluate both online sources and Wikipedia articles themselves to help improve the encyclopedia's trustworthiness. Unless you have been living under a rock for the past few years, it is painfully clear that most social media platforms are susceptible to issues related to problematic information (things like fake news, propaganda, and misinformation). Need an example? Think about how a former president's claims about bleach as a protectant against COVID-19 spread on Facebook and other social media platforms. Wikipedia is, in some ways, immune to these kinds of things precisely because it has several policies for what makes a reliable source. By helping to evaluate and improve the encyclopedia, you can create a better alternative for reference information.

Your knowledge of digital tools, platforms, and search skills is invaluable when finding and evaluating information. You probably have already used Wikipedia for your queries and could prove to others that Wikipedia can help you answer various questions. Kill acknowledges, "It is often the case that Wikipedia is among the first places students end up when they are looking for information, but seldom do they imagine they might be in a position to curate [or create] knowledge" (404). Can you relate to that? Since Wikipedia has helped you in many ways to get answers to your questions and provided you with information, now it is your turn to pay it forward. Wikipedia needs you to critically assess its contents and improve it, one step at a time.

First, you are capable of spotting if a news piece or an article does not seem to be genuine or valid. You can then use your research skills to find better evidence in the form of secondary sources to back up or disprove that misinformation. Your writing instructor has taught you a thing or two about the credibility of sources and rhetorical situations. This knowledge will help you provide meaningful contributions either in adding a source to Wikipedia or editing the entire article, whatever you choose. When they work to improve a Wikipedia article in a classroom assignment, our students have found that they gain experience in both "looking hard to find research" and "making sure the sources I did find were credible." The way this student describes the process of contributing to Wikipedia, especially the research process, provides an important lesson in critical thinking and source evaluation. Wikipedia articles do not just become "reliable" or "trustworthy" on their own. Their credibility comes from a whole lot of things working together: individual editors like the one we quoted above, who are trying to be careful about the sources they use to contribute; the various references used to build the article; the sources that those references are relying on and their backgrounds, and on and on. This notion of what makes something reliable can be better understood if we move away from traditional strategies for source evaluation that focus on only one source at a time.

One model for evaluating sources that you are probably familiar with is the CRAAP test. It's memorable, right? The acronym stands for certain evaluative categories: Currency, Reliability, Authority, Accuracy, and Purpose/Point of View, which may have been presented to you at a library session or even by your writing instructor. These are wonderful criteria for checking whether a single source is trustworthy and relevant for your research project. However, one thing they do not take into consideration is how the Internet and other new communication technologies have complicated things. It is not enough to evaluate a source by itself. As Dan Melzer discusses in another *Writing Spaces* essay entitled "Understanding Discourse Communities," we also need to consider sources within a broader community. For example, we might ask questions like:

- Is the source itself seen as reliable within a community of experts on the topic?
- What types of evidence (other sources) does the source rely on?
- Additionally, how and why is the source being shared online?

Ellen Carillo and Alice Horning also recommend this approach in their *Writing Spaces* essay from Volume 4: "Effectively and Efficiently Reading the Credibility of Online Sources." In this essay, Carillo and Horning draw from research about "lateral reading" (Wineburg and McGrew) as a better alternative to the CRAAP checklist. More specifically, they provide three steps for reading laterally to assess the credibility of online sources. These steps support the idea that we need to see sources as part of a larger community because all three ask you to "leave the site in question" to 1) determine whether the source "appears on other fact-checking or hoax-busting sites" (such as Snopes.com), 2) find out more about the author, and 3) "explore more about the site [or source] itself" (Carillo and Horning 40-41).

So how do we apply this kind of "lateral reading" for source evaluation to Wikipedia? First, Wikipedia is only as good as the secondary sources it draws from to build each article. When we go back to each source and read laterally across the source and the community or communities it takes part in, we can more effectively evaluate its currency, authority, accuracy, and reliability. As you learn more about this process in your writing and research classes, you build the ability to help ensure Wikipedia's reliability and critically evaluate any information you come across, especially online and on your social media networks.

Hands-On Cases: Abby and Cheyenne

We realize that despite our best arguments, you still might have reservations about engaging with Wikipedia in this way or doubts about your abilities to edit and evaluate the encyclopedia. Therefore, in closing this essay, we want to share how two students, just like you, edited Wikipedia in a course we taught in the spring of 2019. Both students were enrolled in a first-year writing class at the Indiana University of Pennsylvania, where the two authors were co-teaching. Furthermore, despite initial concerns and even some worries, both students used their unique identities and experiences as resources for contributing to the encyclopedia and improving specific articles. In the following sections, we use the pseudonyms Abby and Cheyenne (which these students selected to be used in this essay), describing their work to improve Wikipedia articles and connecting that work to their own experiences and identities with excerpts from their written reflections about the project. And while Abby and Cheyenne might seem like "special cases" or "success stories,"—there are over 100,000 students like them that have worked on a Wikipedia assignment since 2010 ("Changing Classrooms").

Abby's Experience Editing the "Fender Telecaster" Article

As part of their coursework, students in Abby's class wrote a personal essay in which they reflected on their experience editing Wikipedia. Abby begins her essay by recalling previous experiences with Wikipedia in school environments: "Consistently, in both earlier and higher education," Abby writes, "many students, including myself, were told that Wikipedia has no place in the classroom and that it was not allowed to be used as a source because it was unreliable." However, she quickly dismisses these attitudes as "abhorrent and outdated" and proposes that Wikipedia should be "integrated into classrooms at any level of education." What is interesting about Abby's reflection, though, is how her attitude changed. Identifying as a transfer student, Abby confesses that she "had zero clue that [her] English class could be about Wikipedia." However, despite having "doubts about a Wikipedia-centered class," she also recognizes that this approach represents a "great opportunity for students in higher education to learn about many different facets of writing." So, what happened to Abby that might explain this shift in her attitude? To answer this question, we might think further about how Abby was able to use her interests (a hobby, in this example) as a way to connect to the work she was doing in the encyclopedia.

As part of her Wikipedia-based writing project, Abby chose to update the article on "Fender Telecaster." In a class presentation, she explained this choice by discussing how she enjoys playing and learning about the guitar as a hobby. Connecting her experience and interest with the writing assignment further allowed her to make meaningful contributions to the article. Among other edits, Abby worked to create subsections in the article for different Telecaster model "variants," including the "B Bender Telecaster," the "Tele Sub-Sonic," the "Telecaster XII 12-String," and others. While student edits in Wikipedia, like any editor's contributions, are always subject to further revision or even deletion (in some cases), Abby's contributions have remained in the article. Other editors have even built on her contributions ("Fender Telecaster").

Cheyenne's Experience Editing the "Meadville, Pennsylvania" Article

Like Abby, Cheyenne's first reaction to being told that she would edit a Wikipedia article as part of a college writing assignment was disbelief. Her attitude about the online encyclopedia may even line up with what previous teachers have told you in high school or other college classes. "When I first started this class," Cheyenne writes, "I thought this might have been a joke since we were never allowed to use [Wikipedia] to get information or even use the sources that came from it." However, Cheyenne's attitude changed once she realized that the assignment was not, in fact, a joke and that she could leverage her interests to choose an article to work on. Cheyenne describes the experience of selecting an article to work on (her hometown of Meadville, Pennsylvania) and how she figured out what she could add in the following passage:

> When my professor originally introduced to us that we would be picking an article of something that interests ourselves...I thought let's look up Meadville (which is my hometown). When I got to the page, I noticed that most of the information was correct but what could be a section that I could add to make the history of Mead-

ville more interesting. It came across my mind when I thought I should add an attractions portion of it but only of things that Meadville did or has educational purposes. When editing my article, I felt like I was helping students and anyone else who would look up Meadville on Wikipedia to get true and real information while also sourcing my work as I go along.

As a first-year college student, Cheyenne often traveled back and forth between campus and her parents' house to see friends and family on the weekend. Once we realized that she was visiting the town that she was writing about, we suggested to her that she take some photos of the historical features of Meadville and upload them to Wikimedia Commons. Since this is the database used by Wikipedia for images and other media, Cheyenne could also add pictures of the landmarks she was writing about to her article (see Figures 2 and 3).

Figure 2. This image of the Meadville Market House appears in Wikipedia's article "Meadville, Pennsylvania" titled "The Meadville Market House." Via Wikimedia Commons, CC-BY-SA 4.0.

Figure 3. An image of a monument in Meadville, Pennsylvania, with a caption that reads, "A monument in the shape of a scroll dedicated to the founder of Meadville, David Mead." Via Wikimedia Commons, CC-BY-SA 4.0.

What Cheyenne's account tells us is this. First, personal experience (in Cheyenne's case, growing up in Meadville, Pennsylvania) can help students create a unique connection to and improve Wikipedia. Second, adding your photos to a Wikipedia article is a wonderful way to improve the encyclopedia. Finally, while Cheyenne was hesitant about the project at first, she ultimately realized its potential, writing in her reflection, "In my opinion, Wikipedia has a bright future coming if professors keep promoting it out to their students."

Conclusion

Acknowledging the many ways you can benefit from Wikipedia, we want you to consider several key points from the above discussion. First, you are good for Wikipedia because you have multiple aspects of your identity that could help you contribute to the expansion of diversity of the online encyclopedia. Second, your access to academic knowledge makes you a valuable source for those outside academia—everyday readers of Wikipedia. Third, your critical thinking skills are helpful in terms of evaluating the content of Wikipedia, recognizing misinformation, and providing credible sources to verify the facts.

By now, we hope you can understand just how unique you are for Wikipedia's space. Are you inspired to take on an editing task? Or do you feel the urge to email that middle school teacher who warned you not to use Wikipedia? We hope that you are empowered to edit, add, factcheck, copyedit, create, or simply talk to your peers, family, and friends about Wikipedia and what it is all about. Like Abby and Cheyenne, you can explore your interests, identities, and experiences about topics on Wikipedia. Remember: "You Are Good for Wikipedia." This affirmation especially works when you realize that your potential arises from your unique identity. Don't know where to start? Check out the discussion questions and activities we find useful when engaging in Wikipedia writing.

Works Cited

Bazely, Dawn. "Why Nobel Prize Winner Donna Strickland Didn't Have a Wikipedia Page." *The Washington Post*, 8 Oct. 2018, www.washingtonpost.com/outlook/2018/10/08/why-nobel-winner-donna-strickland-didnt-have-wikipedia-page/. Accessed 12 April 2022.

Brown, Adam R. "Wikipedia as a Data Source for Political Scientists: Accuracy and Completeness of Coverage." PS: Political Science and Politics, vol. 44, no. 2, 2011, pp. 339–43, http://www.jstor.org/stable/41319920. Accessed 12 Apr. 2022.

Carillo, Ellen, and Alice Horning. "Effectively and Efficiently Reading the Credibility of Online Sources." *Writing Spaces: Readings on Writing*, vol. 4, edited by Dana Lynn Driscoll, Megan Heise, Mary K. Stewart, and Matthew Vetter. Parlor Press, 2021, pp. 35-50.

Casebourne, Imogen, et al. "Assessing the Accuracy and Quality of Wikipedia Entries Compared to Popular Online Encyclopaedias: A Comparative Preliminary Study across Disciplines in English, Spanish and Arabic." *Epic, Oxford* and *Wikimedia Commons*, 2012. commons.wikimedia.org/wiki/File:EPIC_Oxford_report.pdf. Accessed 13 April 2022.

"Changing Classrooms." *Wiki Education*, wikiedu.org/changing/classrooms/. Accessed 12 April 2022.

Cohen, Noam. "A History Department Bans Citing Wikipedia as a Research Source." *The New York Times*, 21 Feb. 2007, www.nytimes.com/2007/02/21/education/21wikipedia.html. Accessed 12 April 2022.

Cooke, Richard. "Wikipedia Is the Last Best Place on the Internet." *Wired*, 17 Feb. 2020, www.wired.com/story/wikipedia-online-encyclopedia-best-place-internet/. Accessed 12 April 2022.

"Donna Strickland." *Wikipedia, The Free Encyclopedia*, 21 March 2022, en.wikipedia.org/w/index.php?title=Donna_Strickland&oldid=1078488265. Accessed 12 April 2022.

Drury, Alliana. "Wikipedia's Place in Higher Education." *Wiki Education*, 9 July 2019, wikiedu.org/blog/2019/07/09/wikipedias-place-in-higher-education/. Accessed 14 Aug. 2021.

"Fender Telecaster." *Wikipedia, The Free Encyclopedia*, 4 April 2022, en.wikipedia.org/w/index.php?title=Fender_Telecaster&oldid=1080968857. Accessed 12 April 2022.

Ford, Heather, and Judy Wajcman. "'Anyone Can Edit,' Not Everyone Does: Wikipedia's Infrastructure and the Gender Gap." *Social Studies of Science*, vol. 47, no. 4, Aug. 2017, pp. 511–27, doi:10.1177/0306312717692172.

Forsyth, Peter. "How Wikipedia Dodged Public Outcry Plaguing Social Media Platforms." *Wiki Strategies*, 23 Aug. 2018, wikistrategies.net/how-wikipedia-dodged-public-outcry-plaguing-social-media-platforms. Accessed 12 April 2022.

Giles, Jim. "Internet Encyclopaedias Go Head to Head." *Nature*, vol. 438, Dec. 2005, pp. 900–01, doi:10.1038/438900a.

Gorman, Michael. "Jabberwiki: The Educational Response, Part II." *Britannica Blog*, 26 June 2007, Accessed via Wayback Machine, web.archive.org/web/20210224141437/blogs.britannica.com/2007/06/jabberwiki-the-educational-response-part-ii/. Accessed 12 April 2022.

Harrison, Stephen. "Happy 18th Birthday, Wikipedia. Let's Celebrate the Internet's Good Grown-Up." *Washington Post*, 14 Jan. 2019, www.washingtonpost.com/opinions/happy-18th-birthday-wikipedia-lets-celebrate-the-internets-good-grown-up/2019/01/14/e4d854cc-1837-11e9-9ebf-c5fed1b7a081_story.html. Accessed 12 April 2022.

Hwang, Thomas J., et al. "Drug Safety in the Digital Age." *New England Journal of Medicine*, vol. 370, no. 26, June 2014, pp. 2460–2462, doi:10.1056/NEJMp1401767.

@jamiewithorn. "My middle school teacher who yelled that 'Wikipedia wasn't a reliable source' every day is sharing vaccine conspiracy theories on Facebook." *Twitter*, 11 Feb. 2021, 8:52 p.m., twitter.com/jamiewithorne/status/1360044136695554051.

Kill, Melanie. "Teaching Digital Rhetoric: Wikipedia, Collaboration, and the Politics of Free Knowledge." *Digital Humanities Pedagogy: Practices, Principles, and Politics, edited by Brett D. Hirsch, Open Book Publishers, 2012, pp. 389–406. www.jstor.org/stable/j.ctt5vjtt3.21. Accessed 27 July 2021.

Melzer, Dan. "Understanding Discourse Communities." *Writing Spaces: Readings on Writing*, vol. 3, edited by Dana Lynn Driscoll, Mary K. Stewart, and Matthew Vetter. Parlor Press, 2020, pp. 100-115.

Kräenbring, Jona, et al. "Accuracy and Completeness of Drug Information in Wikipedia: A Comparison with Standard Textbooks of Pharmacology." *PLOS ONE*, vol. 9, no. 9, 24 Sept. 2014, doi:10.1371/journal.pone.0106930.

Purdy, James P. "Wikipedia Is Good For You!?" *Writing Spaces: Readings on Writing*, vol. 1, edited by Charles Lowe and Pavel Zemliansky. Parlor Press, 2010, pp. 205-224.

Taraborelli, Dario. "Seven Years after Nature, Pilot Study Compares Wikipedia Favorably to Other Encyclopedias in Three Languages." *Diff*, 2 Aug. 2012, diff.wikimedia.org/2012/08/02/seven-years-after-nature-pilot-study-compares-wikipedia-favorably-to-other-encyclopedias-in-three-languages/. Accessed 13 April 2022.

Tripodi, Francesca. "Ms. Categorized: Gender, Notability, and Inequality on Wikipedia." *New Media & Society*, 27 June 2021, pp. 1-23. https://doi.org/10.1177/14614448211023772.

Vetter, Matthew A., and Oksana Moroz. "English 101: Writing in Wikipedia." *Composition Studies*, vol. 47, no. 2, 2019, pp. 193-202.

"Wikipedia:Reliable Sources." *Wikipedia, The Free Encyclopedia*, 18 Feb. 2022, en.wikipedia.org/w/index.php?title=Wikipedia:Reliable_sources&oldid=1072646679. Accessed 18 Feb. 2022.

"Wikipedia:Size." *Wikipedia, The Free Encyclopedia*. 9 Aug. 2021, en.wikipedia.org/w/index.php?title=Wikipedia:Size_of_Wikipedia&oldid=1037910160. Accessed 10 Aug. 2021.

"Wikipedia:Statistics." *Wikipedia, The Free Encyclopedia*. 5 Aug. 2021, en.wikipedia.org/w/index.php?title=Wikipedia:Statistics&oldid=1037325892. Accessed 5 Aug, 2021.

Wineburg, Sam and Sarah McGrew. "Lateral Reading and the Nature of Expertise: Reading Less and Learning More When Evaluating Digital Information." *Teachers College Record*, vol. 121, no. 11, 2019, pp. 1-40. eric.ed.gov/?id=EJ1262001.

Teacher Resources for "You Are Good for Wikipedia"

Overview and Teaching Strategies

This essay invites students to consider their potential in relation to contributing to and reading Wikipedia through three specific frames of interaction. First, by participating in the Wikipedia community, students bring a more diverse set of identities and positionalities compared to the current editorial demographic. Next, because students have access to academic libraries (and all the resources those institutions provide), they are well-positioned to bridge the uneven divide that currently exists between open access resources and closed or paywalled databases. Finally, because they are actively learning to become critical thinkers and evaluators, students can leverage skills like lateral reading to assess and improve the content, further boosting Wikipedia's credibility. While this essay would pair well with a course that invites students to research and add to an existing Wikipedia article, we also believe that it could serve students and teachers who might be engaging the encyclopedia as a discussion topic or low-stakes activity.

For instance, teachers might ask students to use the citation hunt tool (https://citationhunt.toolforge.org/), which identifies unsourced ("citation needed") statements, to add a reference to a Wikipedia article. In this example, the essay would work well in a larger unit related to online source evaluation, research, misinformation, or digital culture. Teachers interested in replacing a formal writing assignment with a Wikipedia-based project might consider assigning James P. Purdy's previous *Writing Spaces* essay "Wikipedia Is Good for You!?" before asking students to read this piece. Teachers should also be aware of a few organizations to reach out to for help in designing and implementing Wikipedia-based assignments.

Wiki Education (https://wikiedu.org) provides active support for instructors and students trying out Wikipedia-based education, including learning modules, teacher and student training, live advice for pedagogical design, etc. While the Wiki Education Foundation works with college instructors and students in the U.S. and Canada, the Wikipedia Education Program (https://meta.wikimedia.org/wiki/Wikipedia_Education_Program) serves educators at all levels worldwide. So, whether you want to jump into a more robust assignment or just skim the surface, teachers are encouraged to check these resources and get involved in the communities that support them.

Suppose you would like to provide your students with a sample student reflection on their experiences with Wikipedia editing. In that case, you can share Abby's essay entitled "Wikipedia's Place in Higher Education" (https://wikiedu.org/blog/2019/07/09/wikipedias-place-in-higher-education/) published by Wiki Education.

Discussion Questions

1. Let's think back to your middle/high school years. Do you remember that mantra from your teacher: "Do not use Wikipedia for your papers"? What would you reply to that teacher today? How can you prove that Wikipedia is not bad for your writing? What would you say to that teacher after reading this essay?

2. What about Wikipedia's diversity problem? In what areas do you think you can contribute the most? Reflect on your own identities first, and then think about gender identity issues, race, discrimination, diversity, and inclusivity pertaining to Wikipedia's goal of representation. To get started, skim the "Gender Bias on Wikipedia" (https://en.wikipedia.org/wiki/Gender_bias_on_Wikipedia) article to get an idea of what is going on.

3. In groups or with a partner, discuss possible roadblocks or challenges on your way to start editing Wikipedia and ways to overcome those.

4. Look up Wikipedia policies and guidelines related to "Neutral Point of View," "Reliable Sources," and "Verifiability." What do you learn about how the community works together to evaluate information and prevent the spread of misinformation?

5. As a group activity, create a plan for finding an article that needs improvement due to its lack of diverse representation or problematic positioning by adding an additional source, rephrasing some sentences, and/or expanding the topic. Next, look for credible sources in library databases and study them carefully. Finally, contribute to the article by adding an extra source or go big and edit some sentences, adding new relevant information.

18 The Good, the Bad, and the Ugly of Peer Review

Erin E. Kelly

Overview

Academic writing classes regularly require students to engage in peer review: that is, to read and comment on classmates' work in progress in an attempt to make that work better.[1] This chapter shows how such class activities connect to the practices of academic peer review associated with academic publishing. Understanding student peer review as an apprentice version of an academic journal's peer review process (and using the problematic feedback offered by "Reviewer Two" as a negative example) can help students learn to generate constructive criticism; plan and undertake beneficial revisions guided by readers' comments; and, most importantly, see peer review and revision as key elements of writing processes at all levels.

Introduction

"Peer review" is a term students hear in a couple of different contexts in my writing classes. I say we're doing peer review when I require my students to offer feedback on their classmates' (in other words, their peers') work in progress. That feedback can be provided in the classroom after students swap paper copies of drafts, or electronically through a shared repository of documents that allows for commenting, like an online course site or Google Docs. Your instructor might call this same activity – whether it takes place in class or as homework, in person or online – a shared peer response or a draft workshop.

---

1. This work is licensed under the Creative Commons Attribution-NonCommercial-NoDerivatives 4.0 International License (CC BY-NC-ND 4.0) and is subject to the Writing Spaces Terms of Use. To view a copy of this license, visit http://creativecommons.org/licenses/by-nc-nd/4.0/, email info@creativecommons.org, or send a letter to Creative Commons, PO Box 1866, Mountain View, CA 94042, USA. To view the Writing Spaces Terms of Use, visit http://writingspaces.org/terms-of-use.

I also use the term "peer review" when we talk about research. I remind students that if they are seeking high-quality, authoritative academic sources for a research paper or annotated bibliography assignment, they should prioritize peer-reviewed journal articles. Many university libraries allow students to limit their search for articles to "peer-reviewed" materials.

Is there any connection between these two ways that the phrase "peer review" pops up? If so, what's the association? And why should you care? This chapter answers all these questions not just because it's useful to have a broad understanding of peer review (although it is). Crucially, I think learning how to engage in peer review – both as a reviewer offering comments and as a writer responding to reviewers' feedback – is the best way to improve your writing. Peer review develops a piece of writing by connecting its ideas and expressions to a community committed to making it the best it can be, to ensuring it is accurate, ethical, and effective. In other words, peer review is good.

But before we get to what I believe are the benefits of peer review, I need to admit to something kind of ugly: everyone I know has strong feelings about comments they have received on a piece of their writing. Often that's because they've had a painful experience. It's not uncommon for my university faculty colleagues to quote a sentence that a teacher wrote on an essay – possibly in red ink decades in the past – as evidence that they are hopeless at introductions, or unable to summarize clearly, or possibly just not good at writing. And I regularly hear students say they worry about giving honest feedback to a classmate because it will hurt the peer author's feelings.

So, even as I insist that peer review is good, this chapter isn't going to pretend that it always feels good. I'm going to show you a warts-and-all picture of how peer review works for academic writers who publish their research. Done badly, peer review can upset a writer and even damage their writing. But done and used well, it is an effective way to strengthen a piece of writing.

By giving you an honest sense of how academic peer review works, I hope to share some insights about not just why your writing instructor requires peer review but also why even much-published writers make themselves vulnerable by inviting feedback from peers. Along the way, I show how you can make peer review a good experience.

Professional Academic Peer Review

Like your college instructors and university professors, I am an academic writer. All of us have produced complicated undergraduate research essays and most likely completed lengthy master's and doctoral thesis projects. Many of us have also published journal articles or book chapters, and some have even written entire books. These academic publications have gone through the formal process that gets referred to as peer review. (The chapter you're reading right now is one such piece!)

I also have a special perspective on peer review because I serve as an editor for *Early Theatre,* a peer-reviewed academic journal.[2] That means I get to see articles submitted by authors that they want us to consider for publication. I know from the inside the process of picking reviewers for those submissions. I witness how comments from reviewers can lead to great revisions and better publications. And I think a lot about how the peer-review process shapes research.

Even if you don't plan on doing academic writing, much less publishing in peer-reviewed publications, in your own future career, it's useful for you to know about how peer review works beyond the writing classroom. Peer review isn't just a way to make a piece of writing better. It's the foundation for how the research you read about in your textbooks and study in your classes gets tested. It's also the process for authorizing the accuracy, originality, and quality of a piece of writing that shares new and developing knowledge with a larger community. For the rest of your life, medicines you take, technologies installed in the vehicles you drive, and the topics that get taught in your kids' schools will emerge out of research that was peer reviewed.

Briefly, here's how peer review for academic publication generally works.[3] Imagine that Professor Good-Idea comes up with what they think is an exciting new thesis or important discovery. (This key finding would vary based on this person's academic discipline. For a field biologist, it could be the identification of a new species of woodpecker. For a philosopher, it could be an interesting approach to evaluating truth claims.) They want to offer up this idea in a way that will reach others.

---

2. This journal publishes research focused on medieval and renaissance English drama. You can read all the contents for free one year after they are published, if you're interested.

3. I say this is how it "generally works" because journals and publications in varied academic disciplines follow slightly different practices. The system for reviewing scholarly work developed over time and then was adapted. For detailed discussions of this history, read the article by Burnham and then maybe follow up with the book by Shatz.

Professor Good-Idea could share their work by walking down the hall to talk to a group of students. They could post about it on Instagram. They could send a press release to a newspaper or magazine. While those strategies would spread the idea, they wouldn't necessarily reach other experts. What's more, these ways of making an idea public wouldn't help Professor Good-Idea evaluate whether the finding actually is new or important or even accurate. So that's why Professor Good-Idea starts working on a peer-reviewed publication.

Let's say this scholar writes the best version of a journal article they can produce to present their finding. (At different stages of drafting and writing and revising, they likely ask others for advice and feedback. They might even get some help with proofreading and formatting.) When they think the piece is as good as it can be, they submit it to the academic journal in which they hope it will be published. At this point, the journal's editors – people responsible for the publication – make some decisions. If they think the piece is not appropriate for the journal, they will send it back; this is called a desk rejection. More likely, though, if Professor Good-Idea has done quality research and produced a pretty strong piece of writing, the article goes out for peer review.

Peer review in this situation means the editors identify some people who are respected experts in the same field as Professor Good-Idea and who have knowledge of the subject matter. They send Professor Good-Idea's article to those individuals – thought to be the peers of our imaginary professor – and ask them to provide written feedback. Usually that means the editors ask each reviewer for a written response that explains whether the key idea is original, makes a meaningful contribution to the field, and is well-supported. They will also invite comments on how the piece of writing could be improved – what terms to define, what other sources to reference, and what errors to correct. And, they will ask for an overall recommendation: Should this piece be published by the journal or not? Is it possible that it could be published after some changes are made? The editors rely on these recommendations from peer reviewers to determine next steps.

Sometimes, after a round of very positive peer review, a writer gets news from the editors that a piece is being accepted for publication with no or only minor changes. That's great news – and it happens rarely. It's also possible that editors will write to the researcher saying that the piece won't be accepted for publication – and while that sort of rejection can be hard to take, the writer will still receive peer review comments that could help with further revision and rethinking before the author sends it to another journal for consideration. More often, though, an author will receive what's called a "revise-and-resubmit" request – that is, a response from editors saying that they would like to see a revised version of the submission that takes into account the feedback from peer reviewers. A revised submission might go through another round of peer review (or even rejection and then peer review at another journal) before eventually being published.

Let's imagine a happy ending for Professor Good-Idea; after a "revise-and-resubmit" decision from the editors, the writer spends time responding to peer-review feedback and reworks the article. Professor Good-Idea sends the revised piece back to the journal, the editors accept it, and the article gets published.

If it sounds like this peer review-process takes a lot of time and energy, it does. Time between first submission and eventual publication ranges from a few weeks to a few years. And this system is not without flaws. Great articles (and book chapters and even whole books) sometimes go through multiple rounds of rejection and revision and resubmission before they eventually get published.[4] Peer reviewers are people, so they aren't always perfect. Both editors and peer reviewers can be short-sighted, or mistaken, or simply hostile to ideas that challenge their assumptions.

But, at its best, the peer-review system helps to ensure the research that gets published is as good as it can be. A peer-reviewed article is a piece that several independent experts have checked to make sure that its research and the way it's written are accurate, reasonable, and responsible. That's why academic researchers – and your instructors giving you instructions for conducting your own library research – tend to assume peer-reviewed publications are reliable.

BAD REVIEW BY REVIEWER TWO

Even if peer review is generally good for the quality of research published, it can get ugly for individual writers. One way that editors strive to ensure honest, fair feedback is to keep the identities of authors and reviewers anonymous.[5] If you've ever read the comments in an online forum like Reddit or Twitter, you know how rude people can be when they don't have

---

4. See MacDonald for some examples of scientific papers that, after being rejected by one or more journals, went on to win a Nobel Prize. You can find scads of other examples with a simple internet search.

5. Historically, this has been called "blind" review. In an effort to avoid ableist language, the journal I help edit calls it "anonymous" peer review.

to face the person they're attacking – and some reviewers, shielded by anonymity, put vicious comments in their peer review reports.

Note that this sort of viciousness can take different forms. A mean reviewer might reject a submission while failing to give sustained attention to the basic point of the article. An unreasonable reviewer might suggest a piece could be published only after a series of changes that would require lots of impossible, new research. A cruel reviewer might launch personal comments against the author, saying the person who wrote the piece is badly educated, silly, or sloppy.

Editors and academic writers tend to call the person who writes such hurtful reviews "Reviewer Two" because the anonymized peer reviewers' reports sent to an author will often be labeled "One" and "Two." Since most peer-reviewed publications seek two outside reviewers, and since editors tend to present the more positive (and reasonable) review first when sending feedback to an author, the nasty reviewer has the nickname Reviewer Two.

The widespread impact of Reviewer Two types of comments on professional academic writers seems clear based on how many social media accounts there are joking about such feedback. On Twitter alone, you'll find accounts with names like Reviewer2, ShitMyReviewersSay, and WorseReviewer. You can buy coffee mugs that read "Screw You, Reviewer Two" and "I Survived Reviewer Two."

Less amusing are the stories I received when I asked for examples of Reviewer Two types of feedback. A colleague of mine who publishes widely on academic writing revealed that a reviewer said of the manuscript for her (now published) book, "I don't think the author can write." Lots of people shared horror stories when I requested on Twitter that published authors post the Reviewer Two comment that haunts them. But most memorable to me are the people who reached out privately using email or direct messaging because they said the experience of getting a Reviewer Two comment is hard for them to talk about in a public forum.

If scholars who have published multiple peer-reviewed journal articles and received international recognition for their research projects feel shaky after getting harsh, ungenerous, or unfair criticism, then a student starting out as an academic writer is even more likely to be injured when Reviewer Two strikes. At best, tales of the meanest comment you ever got on your writing is fodder for darkly humorous conversations with friends. At worst, attacks on your ideas and expression can give you the sense you don't have anything worth saying or know how to say it. Reviewer Two-style comments – in a classroom setting, from an instructor, or from a publisher –

can wind up silencing the voices of individuals whose ideas have the power to change minds or transform an entire academic field.

The academic peer-review process – peopled with editors and the dreaded Reviewer Two – might seem pretty far away from the peer-review work you do when reading a classmate's draft. Admittedly, the feedback you offer isn't linked to a decision about whether a piece of work will get published or signify that an essay has qualities that mean it shouldn't be taken seriously by experts in a scholarly field. (In fact, you might not know much about the topic on which your classmate is writing!)

But there are some key similarities. When you read your peer's work in progress, you stand in for a larger audience that the author hopes to reach. At best, in an apprentice version of professional academic peer review, you take your classmate's work seriously and think about how it might be improved. And, at worst, if you're not careful, there's the potential for you to offer feedback that isn't helpful – or might even be damaging.

How To Be a Good Peer Reviewer

How can you give honest and even critical feedback – not just empty "I really liked it" kinds of comments – and still avoid being Reviewer Two?

First, be aware that it's easy to edge up to Reviewer Two types of feedback if you're not thoughtful about your response. Problems in a piece of writing can seem obvious after a single, cursory reading, and if that's what we focus on, we can wind up offering nothing but criticism. If you only point out flaws without noting anything that's working, however, you make it difficult for a writer to see what they could develop (instead of just starting over). It's good practice to offer at least one major piece of constructive praise before presenting any criticism. (For advice about writing effective praise with lots of great examples, see DePeter's chapter in *Writing Spaces*, Volume 3.) If you find it challenging to identify and describe the strongest aspect of an essay and explain why it's working, that means you're doing a good job – it takes effort to produce helpful peer reviews, and the more you practice, the better you will get at providing this type of feedback.

Second, remember that when you point out weaknesses that might be addressed or problems that could be fixed in a piece of writing, you are doing so as a peer, not a judge or jury or divine authority. In my experience, the best reviewers of a submitted research article to the journal I help edit see themselves as collaborators in a larger project, one of many voices in an ongoing conversation about a particular topic or question. (For a classic discussion of academic discourse as a conversation, see Booth.) Try to think of yourself as a reader who wants to understand what the writer is trying to communicate to you, and suggest ways they could do it more effectively. Offer specific recommendations of what they might try alongside any criticisms. Cheer on all the ways in which the essay you are reading is working well, and stress how it could be even better.

To help you offer feedback that meets these ideals, I suggest that after reading your classmate's work once, you start by writing answers to the following questions; that is, don't write anything on the draft itself for now:

1. **Originality:** What is the key point that this author is trying to make? What is the central thesis? What is the purpose of this piece? Does this seem like a promising project to you? Why or why not? [Note: If you can't figure out the key point, thesis or purpose, let the author know what you think it is and why you are unsure.]

2. **Argumentation (development):** How does the author develop this argument? Does it seem like there's enough evidence to support the claims being made? Are there points that seem to you to need more support or explanation? [Note: If you are unconvinced by some points that are being presented – or think others will be unconvinced – explain why.]

3. **Argumentation (arrangement):** As you read through this piece from beginning to end, did the order in which points and information appeared seem sensible? Are there places where you felt lost or confused? Can you suggest a way to arrange material that might be more effective? [Note: Imagine an outline for the current version of the essay – does that outline seem logical or effective to you? What changes might you make?]

4. **Readability:** Does the style seem to suit the intended audience of this piece given its key goals? At the sentence level, is it easy to understand? At the word choice level, is the vocabulary appropriate for the subject matter and purpose of the essay? Are there small errors (formatting, etc.) that take attention away from the author's ideas? [Note: This item is not an invitation to proofread or copy-edit. Try to focus only on places where you think a "mistake" has a negative impact on the larger purpose of the essay.]

5. **Overall:** Are there specific examples of strengths or problems you want to call to the attention of the author? Can you offer sugges-

tions for what exactly the author might try to make this piece more effective? [Note: This is a place where you can comment on anything that didn't get covered in the other four items on this list as well as make points that seem related to more than one element.]

These questions are designed to elicit peer review that encounters another writer's work on its own terms and offers constructive feedback; they're not a checklist but rather a guide to engaging with someone else's writing in a holistic way. As you write your answers in a separate document, you should find you tend to stay at a high level of praise and of criticism without getting bogged down in minor details.

And I'm not just saying what you are doing when you comment on a classmate's work is – or should be – a version of professional academic peer review; the list of questions above is a condensed version of the instructions *Early Theatre* sends out to our journal peer reviewers. This set of concerns can apply to almost any piece of academic writing you need to evaluate – including your own. And yet, peer review is especially valuable because even the most skilled writers are challenged by revising their own work. Being a peer reviewer and sharing what you have written as responses to the questions above – by synthesizing your answers in the form of a letter to the author, or even by summarizing orally – helps the author make a plan for how best to revise.

When you serve as a peer reviewer, do unto other writers as you would have them do unto you. You would be hurt by Reviewer Two types of feedback, so don't throw those sorts of comments at your classmate's writing. In a writing class, we want to replicate the good part of peer review – the elements that improve a piece of writing – and avoid the bad part.

Good Uses of Peer Review (and What To Do with Reviewer Two)

All of this might lead you to question: Why do editors send out Reviewer Two peer review reports to authors? If a review is in no way beneficial, we sometimes don't, or we might extract from a set of written comments only the sentences that seem likely to help the author. Sometimes, though, we believe a writer can learn something important from the type of feedback offered by Reviewer Two.

It's perfectly reasonable to be upset or frustrated or sad after getting negative feedback about your work in progress. A mean Reviewer Two-style comment might make you – quite reasonably – angry or hurt. These emotions are real, but you get to choose what to do with them. A critical comment can lead you to walk away from a project (or even jump to the conclusion "I'm a terrible writer"), or it can fuel some great rethinking and revising work. The most skilled writers are often people who have figured out what they can learn from the sort of feedback that initially makes them feel terrible.

There's lots of good advice about how to use the feedback you get. (I particularly recommend Grauman's chapter "What's that Supposed to Mean?" in *Writing Spaces,* Vol. 4.) But general discussions of revision won't necessarily get you past the challenge of what feels like a Reviewer Two-style smackdown. When a comment knocks you back, you need to face it with a growth mindset – to see yourself both as someone who believes you can learn to revise your writing and as someone with the ability to think critically about what has come your way. (See Wells's chapter in this volume for a great introduction to "Dispositions Toward Learning"). And you need a plan.

I recommend you practice responding to Reviewer Two-style comments by first freewriting an unfiltered initial response and then, in a separate step, thinking about how to revise. Just as peer review with your classmates lets you work through an apprentice version of the process used by professional academic writers, it also allows you to experiment with managing feedback that might be incomplete or unclear. Thinking about what you as a writer can take away from comments that are mostly unhelpful or even upsetting can help you revise effectively. I offer you one example here, and you will find more at the end of this essay (see Appendix 1).

Example: I don't understand why anyone would want to write about this boring play.

> My initial response: I hate this reviewer. This is so unfair. Aren't literary scholars supposed to be interested in a wide range of texts? How do I get someone to care about something they think is boring? Maybe I should give up on this topic?

> Planned response: Whether or not this play is "boring" is beside the point – I can make more explicit in my argument that this play hasn't received enough attention from scholars, especially since it connects to a subject that has been discussed a lot lately. Adding a few sentences to my introduction will more clearly establish

the larger implications of this topic and why it's worth reading my argument.

Note that this is an actual example taken from a peer-review report I received – and the "planned response" offers you a sense of how I used this comment to guide revision (and ultimately to get an article published in a highly respected academic journal).

You can also try turning the feedback you get from different readers – say multiple peers in class, a Writing Center tutor, and your instructor – into a formal plan for revision. This is an especially useful process if you have received what seems like contradictory advice – for instance, if your classmate says you are offering too much detail, but a Writing Center tutor suggests your key points need to be supported with more detailed evidence.[6]

In Appendix 2 you'll find a blank chart that offers a system for reflecting on the advice you've received about your work in progress. You can make a version of this chart for yourself to turn feedback from peer reviewers into a to-do (and sometimes also a not-to-do) list. The chart below is a sample version I've filled in with some comments given in response to a research essay that tries to get more people to register to vote.

Features evaluated	Commentary offered	Reflection (Valid or not?)	Planned response
Originality	"I can't tell whether your goal is mostly to motivate people to vote or to vote for a particular candidate. These points seem to get muddled together."	Valid. My goal is to motivate all people who can vote to vote, so I need to look for and rework places that seem to imply I only want people who support the same candidates I do to vote.	Revise my thesis to make my key point more explicit. Highlight sections in my draft that mention a particular candidate currently running, and make sure I'm not implying any favoritism.

---

6. Studies of peer review in academic publishing demonstrate that multiple peer reviewers don't consistently offer the same feedback on a piece of writing; see Fiske. Even if they agree about the general recommendation (say, revise-and-resubmit), they sometimes comment on different elements or offer divergent recommendations. That doesn't mean peer review is a bad process – just that peer reviewers are human.

Features evaluated	Commentary offered	Reflection (Valid or not?)	Planned response
Argumentation (arrangement)	"There are so many examples from past elections, and I'm getting lost. Maybe cut some of these examples?"	Not valid. I think the examples are the strongest part of this essay, so I'm not going to cut any – but maybe I could better explain what each one signifies.	Check and, if it seems necessary, clarify explanations about the significance of every example I include.
Readability	"The writer uses the term 'opponent' all over this essay to refer to the candidate who isn't the incumbent – I think this will offend anyone who doesn't want to vote for the person already in office."	Valid. Interesting comment. I hadn't noticed the implications of this word, and given that I want potential voters to see elections as something other than hostile and angry, I probably need to get rid of this kind of language.	Highlight in yellow any word choices that seem to suggest antagonism or hostility. Then rework that phrasing.

You might also add to your own chart a column that lets you order your planned response tasks. Maybe you want to tackle the easy tasks first (e.g. correcting the spelling of a particular term) and hold off on big jobs (e.g. reordering your examples in the second half of the essay). Maybe you want to manage more global, structural revisions before bothering with small details. In any case, you're likely to find that planning revision as a set of steps makes this stage of the writing process more manageable and effective.

The key way we learn to improve our writing is to think about what we're doing. Getting feedback from readers and then evaluating that feedback offers valuable practice in thinking about thinking. (Giles's essay "Reflective Writing and the Revision Process" offers a helpful overview of "thinking about thinking," also known as metacognition.) By working through a reflective process, we can come to understand that not every nasty comment from a peer reviewer needs to be taken at face value. (For example, we don't necessarily need to change our topic if a reader sniffs, "This is confusing," although we might decide to explain our main point more systematically.) And maybe we can even come to recognize that our own tendency to think harshly about our work in progress could be a step towards identifying a section we might revise later.

Conclusion

The popular fiction author Neil Gaiman offers the following advice about writing: "Remember: When people tell you something's wrong or doesn't work for them, they are almost always right. When they tell you exactly what they think is wrong and how to fix it, they are almost always wrong." It's the job of a peer reviewer to identify what's wrong and to suggest how to fix it, so this quote might not seem to apply to peer-reviewed academic writing. But Gaiman's statement is a helpful reminder that writers need to think critically about suggestions for revision and ponder what changes might improve a project. You can get feedback from a variety of readers, but the choice of what do with their comments and the work you submit is your own.

When you serve as a peer reviewer for another writer's work, you can help them improve it by being honest about exactly what you think is effective. You can even say what you think could be stronger and suggest changes. But if you insist that your perspective is the only one that matters and that a writer who doesn't listen to you is hopeless, you are acting like Reviewer Two. Your own peer review feedback will be good (rather than bad or ugly) if you offer it with the expectation that the writer will make their own decisions regarding how to act on your advice.

You get to do the same with comments you receive – even (maybe especially?) if they come from a Reviewer Two who thinks you should give up. Use criticism to create a plan for revising. Responding to negative feedback is one of the most challenging aspects of the academic writing process even for much-published writers – but thoughtful, effective revision is within your control. Peer review is both something you can get better at and a process that you can rely on to get you to the point where you say with confidence that something you have written is good.

Appendix 1: Sample Reviewer Two Comments for Analysis and Response

1. The first three sentences of this paper are in passive voice, and passive voice isn't good writing. I stopped reading once I realized these sorts of grammar and style problems are all over the essay.
   Initial response:
   Planned response:

2. All the evidence you include in your draft is based on official government data and statistics from medical journal articles about cancer survival rates after surgery. There isn't any sense of what actual people think and feel about having cancer. Why not go out and do interviews with cancer patients?
   Initial response:
   Planned response:

3. I hate math, so no matter how much evidence you offer, I'm never going to think an essay proposing a summer math camp for high school students is a good idea. Why do you want to torture people by making them learn math?
   Initial response:
   Planned response:

4. I find the whole middle section of this draft confusing. You need to cut that section and change your topic.
   Initial response:
   Planned response:

5. [Create your own Reviewer Two style comment here.]

APPENDIX 2: STEPS FOR RESPONDING TO REVIEWERS' FEEDBACK

The blank chart below offers you a system for reflecting on advice you've received about work in progress and can help guide a revision. This system is inspired by a chart presented by Wendy Laura Belcher in her book *Writing Your Journal Article in Twelve Weeks*. Belcher offers advice to academic writers about how to respond to reader reports when they have been told to revise and resubmit their work so that it can be considered for publication. Her guidance is, I think, appropriate for any writer responding to feedback.

As you make your own chart, pay special attention to the "Reflection" column, keeping in mind that you can reasonably decide that a comment is not a valid piece of criticism. It is possible for a peer reviewer to be wrong. But even a bad comment can help you make your writing more effective if it gets you to think about what the reviewer focused on and then consider possible revision options.

REVISION PLAN CHART

Features evaluated	Peer-reviewer comment	Reflection (Valid or not?)	Planned response
Originality			
Argumentation (arrangement)			
Engagement with relevant research (examples)			
Readability			
Other			

Works Cited

Belcher, Wendy. *Writing Your Journal Article in Twelve Weeks,* 2nd ed., Chicago, University of Chicago Press, 2019, https://doi.org/10.7208/chicago/9780226500089.001.0001.

Booth, Wayne. "The Rhetorical Stance." *College Composition and Communication,* vol. 14, no. 3, 1963, pp. 139-145, https://doi.org/10.2307/355048.

Burnham, John C. "The Evolution of Editorial Peer Review." *JAMA,* vol. 263, no. 10, 1990, pp. 1323-1329, https://doi.org/10.1001/jama.1990.03440100023003.

DePeter, Ron. "How to Write Meaningful Peer Review Praise." *Writing Spaces: Readings on Writing,* vol. 3, Parlor Press, 2020, pp. 40-51, https://writingspaces.org/past-volumes/how-to-write-meaningful-peer-response-praise/.

Early Theatre. https://earlytheatre.org/.

Fiske, Donald W. and Louis Fogg. "But the Reviewers Are Making Different Criticisms of My Paper! Diversity and Uniqueness in Reviewer Comments." *American Psychologist,* vol. 45, no. 5, 1990, pp. 591-598., https://doi.org/10.1037/0003-066x.45.5.591.

Gaiman, Neil. "For all the people who ask me for writing advice..." *Neil Gaiman.* 7 May 2012, 12:33 am, https://neil-gaiman.tumblr.com/post/22573969110/for-all-the-people-who-ask-me-for-writing.

Giles, Sandra L. "Reflective Writing and the Revision Process: What Were You Thinking?" *Writing Spaces: Readings on Writing,* vol. 1, Parlor Press, 2010, pp. 191-204, https://writingspaces.org/past-volumes/reflective-writing-and-the-revision-process-what-were-you-thinking/.

Grauman, Jillian. "What's That Supposed to Mean? Using Feedback on Your Writing." *Writing Spaces: Readings on Writing,* vol. 4, Parlor Press, 2022, pp. 145-65, https://writingspaces.org/whats-that-supposed-to-mean-using-feedback-on-your-writing/.

MacDonald, Fiona. "8 Scientific Papers That Were Rejected Before Going on to Win a Nobel Prize." *Science Alert,* 16 Aug. 2016, https://www.sciencealert.com/these-8-papers-were-rejected-before-going-on-to-win-the-nobel-prize.

Reviewer 2. @GrumpyReviewer2. *Twitter.* https://twitter.com/GrumpyReviewer2. Accessed 13 September 2021.

Shatz, David. *Peer Review: A Critical Inquiry.* Lanham, MD, Rowman & Littlefield, 2004.

ShitMyReviewersSay. @YourPaperSucks. *Twitter.* https://twitter.com/YourPaperSucks. Accessed 13 September 2021.

Wells, Jennifer. "Dispositions Towards Learning." *Writing Spaces: Readings on Writing,* vol. 5, Parlor Press, 2023, pp. 17–27.

Worse Reviewer. @Worse_Reviewer. *Twitter.* https://twitter.com/Worse_Reviewer. Accessed 13 September 2021.

Teacher Resources for "The Good, the Bad, and the Ugly of Peer Review"

Overview and Teaching Strategies

Instructors could assign this essay in a first-year or upper-level writing course as students are learning to offer each other peer feedback. Questions, models, and charts in the chapter and appendices can support peer review assignments and revision exercises in or outside of class. However, it might be even more useful to have students work through this material after they have already experienced one round of peer review with classmates and received written feedback from the instructor since it offers strategies for transforming comments on a piece of writing into plans for revision – and provides advice about processing the emotions that come up whenever someone criticizes our writing.

Discussion Questions

1. This chapter offers some examples of Reviewer Two comments, and we can find even nastier ones in the Twitter accounts that are referenced. What is the harshest comment you ever got about your writing? How did you feel about that comment when you first got it, and how do you feel about it now? Do you think the comment presented any valid criticism, or was it just wrong, or mean, or misguided? Imagine exactly how you would respond to that comment if it showed up on something you are currently writing.

2. Writing is an activity that generates a lot of emotions. Why do you think this is? What words come up for you when you describe how you feel when you get a writing assignment or sit down to write? How do you think these emotions affect your writing work? Is there anything about this relationship to your writing that you would like to change? If you would describe yourself as someone who hates writing, what would it take for you to feel good (or even neutral) about your writing?

3. Kelly notes that "even the most skilled writers are challenged by revising their own work." Peer review can help with revision because

it's not just a way of getting someone else's perspective on a piece of your writing; reflecting on peer review comments is a chance to experiment with that different perspective yourself as part of the process of planning a revision. Think about times you have revised your own work and the strategies you used when deciding what changes to make. Whether or not peer review was involved, what ways did you find to get different perspectives on and distance from your work-in-progress while revising?

Activities

Students in higher education classrooms often lack the understanding that the instructors teaching their courses are accomplished researchers – possibly graduate students working on MA or PhD thesis projects; possibly authors of published articles, chapters, or books; and always teachers whose work engages with the scholarship of teaching and learning. While we aren't trying to make all students into academics, much less clones of ourselves, we do them no favors by failing to share our own stories of academic research and writing. By focusing on peer review – and particularly on the label we give to peer-review-gone-wrong, Reviewer Two – this chapter ensures that students see academic writing as produced through collaboration (by writers, reviewers, and editors) and involving revision. Instructors can make clear the importance of drafting, revision, and workshopping by linking such classroom "assignments" or "scaffolding activities" to real experiences of professional academic writing – ideally their own.

- In a class session, walk students through an example of your writing at various stages of development; doing so makes clear not only that you are an academic writer but also that you are not a divine creature who produces brilliant one-and-done drafts. I find it helpful to show my students how an idea developed from a conference paper proposal into a conference paper, then a first draft of a book chapter or article, then a revision of that piece, then another revision, etc. I explain what feedback – from audience members at a conference presentation, colleagues I asked to read work in progress, peer reviewers, editors, etc. – I took into account at each stage of revision. You might share a seminar paper, thesis chapter, or any other piece of writing that has gone through multiple revisions guided by feedback from several readers.

- If you have peer review/reader reports for a piece of writing you published, share these documents, and talk students through how you responded to the feedback you received. Make explicit that by the time a piece of scholarship shows up as a published article or book chapter a student can read and cite, it has been checked, reworked, and revised many times.
- Give students a piece of writing that you consider to be a very rough first draft (maybe two or three typed pages that you pounded out in half an hour without revising, editing, or even proofreading), and ask them to give you feedback on it. If you like, start by asking them to offer mean, nitpicky Reviewer Two types of criticism, and model how you would handle those sorts of comments as well as what ideas for revision you might glean from this feedback.

19 Changing Your Mindset About Revision

L. Lennie Irvin

Overview

Many freshmen enter college with a one-draft writing process where revision means tidying up errors and then submitting the final product.[1] This chapter is about changing your thinking about revision as a foundation for changing your practice of revision. The chapter explores the false concepts about writing and revision and replaces them with new mental models of the revision process. Specifically, it details the big picture concept that writing is an inquiry process where *we discover what we mean as we write it*: through revision, we discover ways to get what we mean closer to what we say and what we say closer to what we mean. Writing is ultimately about thinking and developing our thinking, and one-shot drafts cut short this growth in our thinking and the development of a piece of writing. With this new mindset of writing as an inquiry process in mind, the chapter presents four practices to guide your new approach to the writing process: follow a three-draft sequence to write your papers, always get feedback, reflect between drafts to set revision goals, and save editing for last.

Introduction

What has revision got to do with building a rocket? A lot, it so happens. Perhaps you've seen the video about SpaceX's long drama to develop a rocket that lands successfully. Called "How Not to Land an Orbital Rocket Booster" (https://www.youtube.com/

---

[1]. This work is licensed under the Creative Commons Attribution-NonCommercial-NoDerivatives 4.0 International License (CC BY-NC-ND 4.0) and is subject to the Writing Spaces Terms of Use. To view a copy of this license, visit http://creativecommons.org/licenses/by-nc-nd/4.0/, email info@creativecommons.org, or send a letter to Creative Commons, PO Box 1866, Mountain View, CA 94042, USA. To view the Writing Spaces Terms of Use, visit http://writingspaces.org/terms-of-use.

watch?v=bvim4rsNHkQ) and accompanied by the theme music from Monty Python's Flying Circus, the video shows rocket after rocket crashing and blowing apart: one blows up in mid-air, another lands too hard and explodes, and more land but then tip over into a billowing fireball. Finally, the video shows the first rocket boosters that land successfully. Since that date in 2005, SpaceX has successfully landed its rocket boosters over 200 times (as of 2023). Though writing and revising your college essay, of course, differs from building a rocket (despite sometimes feeling as hard), the process and concepts that drive that process are similar.

Writing is a developmental process in which we discover *what we mean to say* and *how we actually say it* as we work on and rework a piece of writing. We can't expect writing one draft and polishing it up will produce dazzling insights, convincing arguments, and error-free writing just as Elon Musk didn't expect to land his rocket on the first try. Producing a successful piece of writing takes multiple drafts, like SpaceX had to keep building and testing new versions of its rocket after each failure. Revision, it turns out, is about discovery, and growth, and problem-solving.

The prospect of revising your writing may seem about as exciting as going to the dentist, but I invite you to keep an open mind and listen to what I have to share about revision. The heart of your growth as a writer depends upon developing your capacity to revise your writing. But revision is not easy. As a once clueless first-year writer myself, and now as a writing teacher with 30 years of experience, I have seen firsthand how difficult revision is. Much has been written about the terror of the blank page, but little attention has been given to the writer's block of revision. I can't promise that reading this essay will magically transform you into a master of revision, but I invite you to keep reading because what I share will help you become a better reviser and writer.

So what is this secret to revision I have to share? It's simple and it turns out not so secret: for you to become a better reviser of your own writing, you must change your thinking about revision and writing. In fact, research into the difference between "revisers" who made substantial changes to their writing and "non-revisers" who only made surface changes found the most important thing students can learn to improve is to develop new mental models of the revision process (Beach 164). You need new concepts of what revision is and what it entails to be a better reviser.

Before we explore what this new concept of revision is, we need to dispel false concepts about writing and revision that hinder writers before we replace them with a new, more helpful model. Below are some of the flawed attitudes and concepts about revision and writing I suffered from as a first-year writer and see commonly in my students that I believe hinder revision success. Perhaps you will relate?

Flawed Concepts about Writing and Revision

Writing Is about Getting It Down

Sometimes called the transmission or "knowledge telling" model of writing, this belief sees writing in terms of speaking—we say what we have to say, and we are done. Writing is a one-way delivery system of packaging our thoughts and sending them onto the page. With this view, "one shot drafts" are the norm. I've said what I want to say—what else is there? Years of writing essays in one sitting at the last minute or for standardized tests also may have reinforced this view of writing.

Revision Means Tidying up at the End

Following from the "getting it down" model, the next step after you get it down is to clean it up. You've formed the package in your head and painstakingly spit it out on to the page—now that you've got it all down, the most important thing to focus on is correcting errors and wording. Because all the real work getting the writing down is done, revision occurs at the end of the writing process and is reduced to editing and proofreading.

The Most Important Thing about Writing Is Grammar

The "revision means tidying up" model makes sense when we believe grammar is king when it comes to writing. Grammar seems to be the most important thing your teacher wants—right? Years of teachers grading your writing mostly on the basis of grammar may have taught you that. Revision should focus on grammar because grammar is what matters most.

Some of you may be nodding in agreement with these beliefs about writing and revision. They may even seem correct because you've depended upon them to write for years. However, for you to become a better reviser of your own writing, you will need to change your thinking about revision and writing. You need to develop a new mindset about revision.

The Importance of Concepts as Mindsets

Before presenting you with different models of writing and revision, I want to talk about the importance of concepts for your development as a writer (and an individual who is learning and growing). Concepts, you say? That's pretty abstract. Don't I need to know rules and skills? Yes, knowing rules and skills are important, but concepts are the big picture mental frameworks within which we understand and apply rules and skills. Concepts are ideas or mental models we have about the world. These mental models are created and sustained by our beliefs, our theories, our experience, as well as our premises, assumptions, and values. Whether we perceive a concept as truth or opinion, it expresses an idea about something that serves us as knowledge and underpins our thoughts and actions. For example, to say writing is a process may seem like a factual statement, but in reality it is a concept built upon beliefs and theories about how writing happens.

Researchers into concepts have identified two significant aspects about the nature of concepts:

1. Concepts are like portals to new learning (these are called "threshold concepts")

2. Concepts are like ships that enable you to carry learning from one context to another (these are called "transfer concepts")

Jan Meyer and Ray Land describe threshold concepts as representing "a transformed way of understanding, or interpreting, or viewing something without which the learner cannot progress. As a consequence of comprehending a threshold concept there may thus be a transformed internal view of subject matter, subject landscape, or even world view" ("Linkage to Ways of Thinking" 412). Transfer concepts signify knowledge and perspectives that are easy for learners to generalize and apply in a new context, even though it is different. Writing scholars Kathleen Blake Yancey, Liane Robertson, and Kara Taczak have developed a teach for transfer writing curriculum built around "key terms students think with, write with, and reflect with reiteratively during the semester" (5). "Rhetorical situation" is one term they explore as a transfer concept. These key terms represent concepts that enable writers to take what they learn about writing in their first-year writing class and use it in future writing situations.

So what are better concepts about writing and revision than the misconceptions listed above? How will they work as new and improved ways of thinking about writing that will help you revise your papers better and more confidently now and in the future? I'm going to give you one big threshold concept about revision, but like one of those Russian nesting dolls, you'll find other related concepts nested inside this larger one. I think you will find this concept both basic and profound.

Writing Is an Inquiry Process

Writing is not just about getting it down; writing is a process of inquiry. Certainly, we do a lot of writing that resembles speech where we express ourselves and move on. This type of writing might be an email, social media post, or even a journal entry. You may even do this kind of one-shot writing in your college classes with discussion posts, peer response, or essay exams. This kind of "telling" writing is about getting down what you think in the moment. Once you tell what you have to say, you might (or might not) review it for clarity and small errors. Then you're done. That's the "revision is about tidying up at the end" misconception.

But not all writing is simply about knowledge telling, especially in college. Whenever you write something like an essay, a scholarship application, or a report, you are being asked to do something more. Doug Downs and Liane Robertson make this point about writing when they say, "writing is more than transmitting existing information, it is instead a means of *creating new knowledge*" (108). Writing is a "knowledge-making" activity: we discover what we mean as we write it. I want you to sit with that statement for a while and absorb it because as radical as it may seem, I know you have experienced this truth about writing in your past. When we begin to write, we don't have everything figured out, and as we write, what we mean to say grows, changes and becomes clearer. *We discover what we mean as we write it.* And this discovery happens not just while we write, but between drafts when we revise.

Ann Berthoff echoes this belief about writing when she states: "Composing [...] is a means of discovering what we want to say, as well as being the saying of it. [...] It is a process of discovery and interpretation, of naming and stating, of seeing relationships and making meanings" (20). To say writing is a knowledge-making, inquiry process is to say writing is a thinking process founded on revision—as we write we discover, we think and rethink, we write and rewrite. Because language and thought are so connected, as our thinking evolves, so too does our text, and as our text evolves, so too does our thinking. When we engage in this messy inquiry process, we both push our thinking farther and end with a better finished text.

The Problem with "One-Shot" Drafts: Rethink Drafting

You may have mastered one-draft writing because you've been trained to write in this way through years of school and standardized tests. In this model, you figure out what you want to say, write it down, and then review it once for errors. Then you're done. Even if writing the initial draft is a long painful ordeal over many sittings with stops and starts, once the draft is down it's done. I call this the 3-D printing model of writing: the finished text exists in our head like a computer program, and we just hit print and the exact object in our head is reproduced on the page line by line.

The problem with this model for writing is it shortcuts the growth of our thinking. Plus, it ignores this truth about writing—first drafts are always "rough." What we say on the page never matches what we mean in our head, nor does it exactly fit the writing situation. The pressure to write perfectly in a first attempt is simply unreasonable: it's like expecting a batter to hit a home run every time they bat.

Dave Anish and David Russell believe even the term "draft" may be a source of confusion regarding revision for students today. The term "draft" comes from the age of print when we live today in a world of word processing. In their research, they found few students saw draft to mean "iterative," as in multiple versions, but instead saw draft to mean something more fixed and final (Anish and Russell 408). In our age of computers, we are more familiar with the term "version" than "draft." For example, Windows 11 is a version of Windows, and video game companies release beta versions of their game hoping players will find flaws and give feedback before the official release. Although the term "draft" is not going away in common usage, I want you to think "version" when you hear the term "draft." Your drafts are versions of your paper, and the truth is it takes multiple versions to reach a good final copy of your essay. You can't expect to land a rocket on your first try.

Now let me dig in a bit deeper into why your first version should never be your final version, and why a clean-up of your first version is not enough. The difficulty of writing and why we never write perfect first drafts is found in the simple truth that there is a difference between what we mean and what we say in writing. Researchers Carl Bereiter and Marlene Scardamalia described two spaces writers negotiate as they compose: what we mean (the Content Space which represents the thinking and meaning in the writer's head) and what we say (the Rhetorical Space which represents the words on the page) (302-303). The miracle of writing and language is that we are able to transfer what we think and feel inside our consciousness and put it into little black marks on a white page.

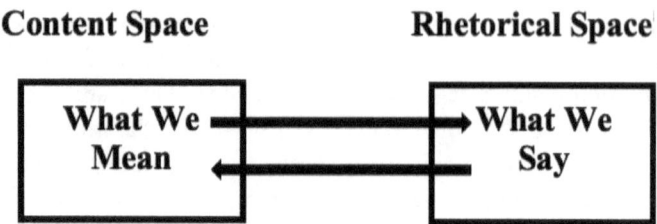

Figure 1. The relationship between Content Space and Rhetorical Space. There are two squares. The one on the left has the words "What We Mean" inside of it and the words "Content Space" above it. The one on the right has the words "What We Say" inside of it and "Rhetorical Space" above it. There are two arrows connecting the squares, each pointing to the other to show that the two ideas inform one another.

When we believe writing is just a matter of getting it down in a one-shot draft, we mistake that we can perfectly (or adequately) get down what we mean on the page in one draft. That's the myth of the 3-D Printing model of writing. But we all know writing does not operate this way. We always experience a gap between what we mean and what we say.

A big step then in appreciating the need for revision is to acknowledge (and respect) this fundamental truth about writing: writing is about getting our thinking and meaning on the page, and there will always be a divergence between what we mean in our head and what we say on the page. To say "writing is an inquiry process" means it is a developmental process in which we discover ways to get what we mean closer to what we say and what we say closer to what we mean.

Peter Elbow compares the writing process to filling a basin of clear water: "Producing writing, then, is not so much like filling a basin or pool once, but rather getting water to keep flowing through till it finally runs clear" (28). Elbow's image of keeping the water flowing through the basin is this work of revision. Each time we work on a piece of writing, we bring what we mean and what we say more into convergence. Each time we review how well our current text is meeting the needs and requirements of the writing task and situation, we find something missing or out of alignment to adjust and fix. Through the work of revision, we get closer to our goal of a successful piece of communication

THE PROBLEM WITH TIDYING UP: INTERNAL REVISION AND EXTERNAL REVISION

Too often revision is believed to involve only the text on the page, but this ignores the importance of our thinking. As an inquiry process, the writing process involving multiple drafts is about the development of our thinking, particularly for college writing. Writing in college is about learning after all.

Donald Murray in his book *The Craft of Revision* talks about this connection of revision to our thinking: "When we revise we do not so much revise the page as revise our thinking, our feeling, our memory, ourselves—who we are" (1). In describing the relationship between what we mean and what we say, Murray develops two categories for revision: "internal revision" and "external revision." Internal revision happens in our head: it is about the change and growth of our thinking about the topic and our understanding of the writing task. External revision happens on the page: it involves the change in our text and how it presents our thinking on the page. ("Internal Revision"). With these ideas about revision, Murry suggests that a dynamic relationship exists between what we mean and what we say. As we internally revise our thinking about the topic and task, it influences our external revision of the text. Changing and developing our thinking should lead to changes and development in our text. Likewise, as we externally revise our text, we trigger internal revision to our thinking. In other words, what we mean always shapes what we say in writing, just as what we write constructs what we mean.

Perhaps you think I am stating the obvious, but recognizing that when you write you are negotiating these two spaces—what's in your head and what's on the page—can help you engage in productive revision. A simple guide for revision is to ask yourself these basic questions:

- Is what I've written really what I mean?
- Is what I mean what I've really written?

Understanding this concept helps you see that issues you identify in your writing may come from problems in your thinking. And as you develop and revise your thinking, you can use this re-thinking as your best guide for re-writing the text on the page.

I'll close this section with a diagram to illustrate how revision is an inquiry process. It emphasizes these two points I've been making:

#1: Revision is about developing both our thinking and writing.

#2: Revision helps us get closer to saying in writing what we mean and appropriately meeting the writing situation.

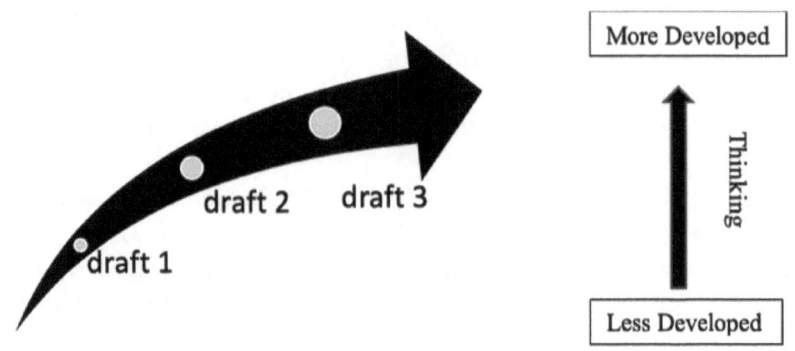

Figure 2. Growth of thinking and writing with revision. There is a large arrow to the left of this image, pointing in an arch towards the right. Along the arrow, there are dots labeled "draft 1," "draft 2", and "draft 3" to demonstrate a progression. The arrow points to an image that has two rectangles, one near the bottom labeled "Less Developed" and one near the top labeled "More Developed." A second arrow, labeled "Thinking," points between these two rectangles, showing that "less developed" leads to "more developed."

Revision as Troublesome Knowledge

Truly acknowledging that writing is an inquiry process with revision hardwired into its DNA may be challenging to you. Meyer and Land talk about how threshold concepts prove to be "troublesome knowledge" for learners at first because once they grasp the concept—once they pass through the portal—there is no going back. Now that you see this connection between writing and thinking and the developmental nature of writing's inquiry process, you can't unsee it. Now that you see revision as the necessary step for growth and improvement in a text, doing a one-shot draft and tidying it up at the end seems insufficient, even absurd.

But accepting the truth of this concept is troublesome—particularly because it means you have to revise. Meyer and Land describe a liminal space as students grapple with a threshold concept where they feel not only unsettling but stuck ("Epistemological Considerations" 377-378). They emphasize the importance of teachers designing their curriculum to help students negotiate these transitions (386). With Meyer and Land's imperative in mind, I am going to make some suggestions about how to approach writing as an inquiry process that I hope will assist developing your ideas and text through revision.

Revising Practices with Inquiry in Mind

Follow a Three-Draft Sequence to Write Your Papers

I want to suggest a sequence for your drafting of a piece of writing. While some writing pieces may take many more drafts, the three-draft sequence below can serve you well for college writing.

Version #1: The Get it Down Draft

Whether you painstakingly write your first draft over many days or dash off a freewriting draft in 30 minutes, consider this first version of your essay to be like a first sketch of your thinking on the topic. As you write and then consider your first draft, don't focus on correctness or perfection. You may not even worry about proper organization or specific support. This draft can be rough and even incomplete. The main goal is to get down your thinking in as complete a draft text as you can. It's too early to worry about the grammar or any other editing concerns!

Version #2: The Development Draft

As you move from first to second draft, your focus will be on developing your thinking and your text. In some classrooms, this development draft may be submitted to peers for feedback and in others to the instructor (or perhaps both). If the first draft is like a sketch, the second development draft is where you fill in the sketch with paint. It's in this second version where you work on a clear expression of your thesis, seek to organize your writing clearly and logically, and try to include full support for your thesis. You also seek to fulfill the requirements of the writing task. But at this point, you are still not worried about correct grammar or documentation. You might call this version your first dress rehearsal of your final draft.

Version #3: The Final Draft

This final draft enables you to troubleshoot and improve your content (your approach to the writing task, thesis, organization, and support), but the focus for the final draft is on readability and careful editing and proofreading. You may do more than two drafts to get to this final draft, but at some point the paper is due and you will have to turn it in to be evaluated for a grade. Now this performance is going live before an audience, and you want to make it as good as you can.

To sum up, as you go from first draft to final draft, your focus for revision gradually shifts from internal revision (what you mean) to external revision (what you say), from a creative and generative phase to a more critical and evaluative phase. Allowing yourself the space and freedom to let your early drafts be rough and provisional without the high bar of being a final draft enables you to see and be open to the changes to content that represent the true growth of your thinking. But you have to let go being perfect in your first or even second draft.

Always Get Feedback

While reviewing your draft on your own is important, getting feedback to assist you with seeing what needs to be improved in your paper is crucial. Research has shown that peer feedback, especially when provided with a sense of the goals and standards of the writing task, is the best source for helping writers make higher order revisions to their writing (Zhang, Schunn, and Baikadi 699). It seems we need this outside perspective to help us see areas for improvement in our writing, especially big picture things about what we are trying to say and how we are saying it. Your class may engage in peer response on drafts, or your instructor may provide feedback for you, but even if you don't get feedback in your class, you can seek out tutors or other readers to read and respond to your draft.

Reflect Between Draft to Set Revision Goals

Between each draft and before starting to revise your essay for the next draft, take a few moments to reflect on your draft. I strongly recommend you do this self-review in writing: get out a pen and piece of paper or open a word processing document and write about where you are with the draft and where you think it needs to go. Review what you've written in terms of the feedback you've received and the goals of the writing task. Ask those key questions I mentioned earlier:

- Is what I've written really what I mean?
- Is what I mean what I've really written?

As you interrogate this relationship between the Rhetorical Space (what you written) and the Content Space (what you mean), keep foremost in your mind what success means for this piece of writing—both in terms of writing a successful essay according to the requirements of the writing task and in terms of saying what you mean and successfully accomplishing your purpose toward your reader (Irvin 18).

This internal understanding of your writing goals and what successfully reaching them looks like will help you identify areas for improvement in your draft. But they won't help unless you have a good understanding of what successfully reaching these goals looks like. For example, you won't be able to diagnose problems in your Introduction without a strong grasp of how to write an Introduction, especially a thesis statement. Likewise, you may not see issues in the formatting of your Works Cited page or know how to fix it unless you know what a successfully formatted Works Cited page looks like. You may need to review the learning materials or specifics of a writing task to be able to see issues in your draft and know how to address them.

The last step in this between-the-draft reflection is to make a plan for what to revise in the next draft. Focus on big picture things first like your thesis, the structure of your essay, the development of your ideas, and how well you are fulfilling the requirements of the writing task. Then use this plan to guide you as you revise your essay for the next draft.

Save Editing for Last (Really)

It takes something akin to an act of faith not to correct the grammar in your first or second drafts. Many of us are so conditioned to think our text must be perfect that we can feel extremely uncomfortable letting something we've written be messy and imperfect. As I mentioned in the three-draft sequence above, I urge you to embrace the messiness and flawed nature of early drafts. Let them be rough. Save the impulse you have for tidying up and perfecting the writing until you truly are at your final draft.

This means making editing a distinct activity in your writing process with the singular goal of readability at the sentence and word level. Print off a fresh copy of your draft, get out a pen, and go through your draft sentence by sentence, word by word. Read passages aloud to hear if they make sense. Look up any grammar rules or usage questions you have.

Only a Beginning

I hope you now have a new mindset when it comes to writing and revision. Re-vision is after all about "seeing again." What I have shared with you is one key concept that will change the way you write and revise. Now that you see writing as an inquiry process, you understand revision is about developing your thinking and text over multiple versions of the essay. Revision is not easy, but it is gratifying work. Heck, it's exciting—like landing a rocket on a drone ship in the middle of the ocean. And as we know by now, we don't land a rocket on our first try.

Works Cited

Anish M., Dave and David R. Russell. "Drafting and Revision Using Word Processing by Undergraduate Student Writers: Changing Conceptions and Practices." *Research in the Teaching of English*, vol. 44, no. 4, May 2010, pp. 406-434.

Beach, Richard. "Self-Evaluation Strategies of Extensive Revisers and Nonrevisers." *College Composition and Communication*, vol. 27, no. 2, 1976, pp. 160- 64.

Bereiter, Carl and Marlene Scardamalia. *The Psychology of Written Composition*. Hillsdale, N. J.: Lawrence Erlbaum Associates, 1987.

Berthoff, Ann E. *The Making of Meaning: Metaphors, Models, and Maxims for Writing Teachers*. Boynton/Cook, 1981.

Downs, Doug and Liane Robertson. "Threshold Concepts in First-Year Composition." *Naming What We Know: Threshold Concepts of Writing Studies*, edited by Linda Adler-Kassner and Elizabeth A. Wardle. Utah State University Press, 2016, pp. 105-121.

Elbow, Peter. *Writing Without Teachers*. Oxford University Press, 2007.

Irvin, L. Lennie. *Reflection between the Drafts*. Peter Lang Publishing Inc., 2020.

Meyer, Jan H., and Ray Land. "Threshold Concepts and Troublesome Knowledge (2): Epistemological Considerations and a Conceptual Framework for Teaching and Learning." *Higher Education*, vol. 49, no. 3, 2005, pp. 373–388, doi: 10.1007/s10734-004-6779-5.

—. "Threshold Concepts and Troublesome Knowledge: Linkages to Ways of Thinking and Practicing." *Improving Student Learning Theory and Practice - 10 Years on: Proceedings of the 2002 10TH International Symposium Improving Student Learning*, edited by Chris Rust. Oxford Centre for Staff & Learning Development, 2003, pp. 412-424.

Murray, Donald M. *The Craft of Revision*, 3rd ed. Harcourt Brace College Publishers, 1998.

—. "Internal Revision: A Process of Discovery." *Research on Composing: Points of Departure*, edited by Charles R Cooper and Lee Odell. NCTE, 1978, pp. 85-104.

Yancey, Kathleen Blake, Liane Robertson, and Kara Taczak. *Writing across Contexts: Transfer, Composition, and Sites of Writing*. Utah State University Press, 2014.

Zhang, Fuhui, Christian D. Schunn, and Alok Baikadi. "Charting the Routes to Revision: An Interplay of Writing Goals, Peer Comments, and Self-Reflections from Peer Reviews." *Instructional Science*, vol. 45, no. 5, 2017, pp. 679–707, doi: 10.1007/s11251-017-9420-6.

Teacher Resources for "Changing Your Mindset About Revision"

Overview and Teaching Strategies

In my syllabus statement of my objectives for Freshman Composition I, I make this statement: "Our most devoted effort will go into supporting substantive revision, for it is during revision that new learning is most likely to occur and your competence to develop." I've found that I have to do a lot of work, though, to get students to engage in "deep revision" of what are commonly called global concerns. In my own study of student revisions and surveying student beliefs about revision, most of my students see revision as a matter of tidying up the one draft they have composed. They mistake editing as revision. I'm not alone in this observation because one of the most frequent findings from research into revision is that new college writers mostly make only surface changes when they revise.

The goal of this essay is to help you teach your students what revision really involves. As Richard Beach found in an early study on revision, the most significant thing we can do as teachers to help our students become better revisers is to work on their mental model—their concept—of what revision is and involves. Luckily, today we have developed the frameworks of "threshold concepts" and "transfer concepts" to help us communicate and teach writing, and this essay is particularly designed to tie into a curriculum designed around these concepts.

I have a few suggestions for how this essay might fit successfully into your course.

- The first one is that you engage your students in a multi-draft writing process which includes peer response (and even reflection) between drafts. Ideally, this includes three drafts to break the pattern of a two-draft sequence which shortcuts the opportunities for writing growth through revision.
- You might also make revision a topic of discussion early in the semester as you review the writing process with your students. Ask them to write their definitions of "revision," "editing," and "proofreading." If your students are like mine, only a few will see any difference between revision and editing. As you review their answers with them, work on establishing clear definitions and distinctions between these activities of the writing process.

- After the final draft of your students' first essay, ask them to do a post-draft reflection where they write a process narrative telling the story of their work on the essay and how the text grew and changed. Students struggle grasping what to do for this kind of meta-cognitive task, so I urge you to take time to explain the task, provide prompts, and even provide models to help them. Then have students share their stories of the writing process where the theme of revision can be highlighted.
- I recommend that you ask students to read this Writing Spaces essay as they begin to revise for the second draft of Essay #1. You might use one or more of the discussion questions included after the chapter (and below) as a homework or in-class journal response to the reading. Then, as your students begin to review their draft and formulate plans for revision, ask them the key questions from the essay: Is what I've written really what I mean? Is what I mean what I've really written?
- Alternatively, you could ask students to read the essay later in the essay as they are asked to revise a previously graded essay or for a final portfolio where revised essays are submitted.

The bulk of the work of fleshing out the model and practices of revision will be up to you. This essay seeks only to re-set students' mental model and mindset regarding revision. Hopefully, it provides a new framework for your students to begin engaging in productive and substantial revision beyond tidying up errors.

Other resources: There are so many good resources about revision and teaching revision, but I want to highlight some other ones I have created for my classes found at "The Write Place: Guides for Writing and Grammar" https://www.lirvin.net/WGuides/default.htm. The guides on the writing process, drafting, and revision may be particularly relevant as complementary resources to this essay.

Discussion Questions

1. Write about some everyday non-school writing that you have done in the last week (like text messages, emails, social media posts or any writing). How much revision do you do on these pieces of writing. Why? Describe the kinds of changes you made?

2. What has been your approach to revising essays in school previous to this class? Describe what you have done in the past to "revise." Talk about one instance of revising following your method.

3. What have been your greatest challenges when you have been asked to revise a draft? Talk about a past experience before this class and a more current experience from revising a draft in this class.

4. Why should your first draft of a college essay never be your last draft (even if you tidy it up)?

5. How is this concept of writing as an inquiry process founded upon revision different and foreign to what you have thought before?

6. How does this essay help you understand what you have been learning about writing and revision so far in this class? How do you think it will affect how you will go about revision in the future?

20 What's the Diff? Version History and Revision Reflections

Benjamin Miller

This essay recommends that writers use digital tools to keep track of what's changing as they write—and to include a quick comment with each notable change, saying what they're trying to achieve.[1] These revisitable histories are helpful in several ways. First, when we notice what we're changing (often unconsciously) on a small scale, like words and phrases, we can think through our reasons for those changes—and then ask if similar reasoning, and similar revision strategies, might also apply at larger scales of paragraphs and beyond. Second, by sharing and discussing these reasons and strategies, we expand our repertoire of revision moves, moving further along the spectrum from novice to expert. Third, if our writing is interrupted—whether by other classes or by world or life events—re-reading the revision notes can help writers recapture momentum and pick up where we left off. And finally, recording what's changing helps us see and celebrate small victories, and realize that there really is progress happening, even when it might not look like it. For example, if each new draft is a scrap-and-start-over of the same three paragraphs until we've clarified our goals for the essay, revision histories can show the progress that word counts alone would leave invisible. Without tracking these mid-draft changes, writers' celebrations can otherwise feel delayed until the project is over, or until a grade comes back—or, worse, never. Noticing and naming progress can generate feelings of interim success to keep ourselves going through difficult stages in the writing process.

---

1. This work is licensed under the Creative Commons Attribution-NonCommercial-NoDerivatives 4.0 International License (CC BY-NC-ND 4.0) and is subject to the Writing Spaces Terms of Use. To view a copy of this license, visit http://creativecommons.org/licenses/by-nc-nd/4.0/, email info@creativecommons.org, or send a letter to Creative Commons, PO Box 1866, Mountain View, CA 94042, USA. To view the Writing Spaces Terms of Use, visit http://writingspaces.org/terms-of-use.

INTRODUCTION

Whether you know it or not, you revise as you write. Even if you produce a first draft and never come back to it, something tells me you at least look back at the sentence you're in the middle of, and sometimes the sentences and paragraphs before that, so you know whether your current thought actually follows on the previous one. Or maybe one of your teachers made a point of telling you to write a rough draft, put the paper away for a while, and come back to it; in that case, you're probably even more aware of revising. But I'll also bet that even within each of those sessions, you were in the middle of saying one thing and thought of a better idea, or a better way of saying it—so you erased, you went back to the middle or beginning of the line, and you restructured it. The writing led to a better understanding, which led you to change what you were writing. And that's revision.

In this essay, I want to help you understand *revision* better. I want to help you think through what you do with words and sentences, because what we do within sentences we can also do with paragraphs, pages, and even larger chunks of writing. Studies have shown that expert writers revise on those large scales more than beginners do, so learning to think big is part of how we grow our expertise as writers.

And the tool I recommend for seeing revision better is *version history*. You may know it better as *track changes*, or (if you're into computer programming) *diffs view*, but the basic idea is this: (1) use digital tools to visibly mark what's changed in your writing from one moment to another; (2) add a note that says what that change is meant to accomplish, or where it gets you; (3) reread the notes later on.

VISIBLY MARKED CHANGES

Before we can talk about what you'll learn in studying your own version histories, I want to make sure we're all on the same page about what I'm describing, and why I find these histories so interesting. Example 1 shows a simple example of a *diff*, a comparison between two adjacent versions of this document. In this case, I generated it with Google Docs, using the File menu to select See Version History. But there are lots of tools you could use; pretty much any word processor these days can compare files, and most can compare versions within the same file. Leaving tool choice aside for now, let's look at the diff together. You should recognize the context: the sentence is taken from the second paragraph above.

Example 1: Substitution at the level of words

> And studies have shown that expert writers revise on those large scales more than beginners do, so learning to think big is part of how ~~you~~ we grow ~~y~~our expertise as ~~a~~ writer_s_.

Not earth-shattering, I know; just a slight shift in wording, from *you* to *we*, from *your* to *our*. But a change doesn't have to be massive to be meaningful. What I meant to accomplish with the change in pronouns was to change my sense of relationship to you as a reader: by including myself in the group that's growing, I signal that I'm still learning, too—including by writing this essay and reflecting on my version history. That's why I'm drawing on examples from this piece, so you can see *how* I'm learning, and what it gets me. True, I'm not exactly a novice, either: I've been publishing and teaching writers for almost two decades; I do think about large-scale changes and restructuring. But as this example shows, thinking about the large scales doesn't mean you stop fiddling with sentences and words as you get more experience.

It might, though, mean you think more about how the small and the large are related, and that's one of the big things studying your version history can help you do. For example, when I think about my reason for that small change above, *you* to *we*, it raises a question that applies to the essay as a whole: what *is* my relationship with readers? And what follows if I'm not separating myself from the lessons I'm trying to impart? For one thing, my examples might shift from things other people have written about to the things I have found concretely helpful, things that don't depend on already having a large revision repertoire. It might mean, in fact, spending more time with the word-level edits we all make, and demonstrating how they can themselves lead to high-level rethinking. And so, here we are: all six paragraphs you just read are entirely new additions. Not a bad outcome for a few small tweaks!

For the change in Example 1, the structure of the sentence stayed the same: the main move was one of *substitution* in place, one pronoun for another. But even within a single paragraph, structural changes are possible. Example 2 shows a diff view from an earlier draft of this essay. I'd written the paragraph in one order, then decided that the last sentence made a better lead sentence—so I switched them around.

Example 2. Reordering at the Level of Sentences

> […] it's an experiment everyone can do: are your changes changing as you study writing and get more focused practice and feedback?
>
> ~~But it's not always easy, in the thick of the writing or after pushing through the thicket, to remember what turns you took, or why; sometimes the new versions just replace what you'd done before, whether figuratively in your memory or literally on your hard drive.~~ In this essay, I want to make the case for using *version control* technology to help track and make visible what's changing in the course of a writing project, so you can then assess how "what changes" has changed in the course of a writing class. <u>Because it's not always easy, in the thick of the writing or after pushing through the thicket, to remember what turns you took, or why; sometimes the new versions just replace what you'd done before, whether figuratively in your memory or literally on your hard drive.</u>

Reordering to highlight main ideas or improve transitions is a strategy worth knowing, if you don't already. But there's also another, related, change in Example 2 that might be obscured by the movement of the full sentence. Do you see it? Between the deleted version (struck through) and the inserted version (underlined), the first word of the sentence changed. In its original position, the idea that "it's not always easy" was a contrast with what came before, a turn, and so I wrote it "but"-first; within the paragraph, though, the two ideas go together, so "but" became "because." Thinking through the reasoning here, we can develop a two-part revision strategy: *First, consider whether a position change makes sense; second, reassess transitions in light of the new position.*

As I said above, the small-scale strategies you can see in these diffs are often worth trying at larger scales. So, knowing that you can reorder sentences within a paragraph, you should start to realize you can reorder whole paragraphs, too. Example 3 shows the whole original paragraph from Example 2 switching places with its neighbor:

Example 3. Reordering at the Level of Paragraphs

> […] to help in future writing projects, I'm more interested in what strategies they used to revise – and in expanding the strategies they have experience with.

~~But it's not always easy, in the thick of the writing or after pushing through the thicket, to remember what turns you took, or why; sometimes the new versions just replace what you'd done before, whether figuratively in your memory or literally on your hard drive. In this essay, I want to make the case for using version control technology to help keep track of what's changing in the course of a writing project, so you can then assess how "what changes" has changed in the course of a writing class.~~

For instance, in one of the classic studies of writing process, Nancy Sommers found that beginning student writers tended to make changes at the level of word, phrase, and sentence, and that most of the word/phrase changes were substitutions that didn't change the overall structure or meaning. Expert writers, on the other hand, tended to make more changes at larger-than-paragraph levels, like theme or section, and they did a lot more cutting and reordering. So it's an experiment everyone can do: are your changes changing as you study writing and get more focused practice and feedback?

<u>But it's not always easy, in the thick of the writing or after pushing through the thicket, to remember what turns you took, or why; sometimes the new versions just replace what you'd done before, whether figuratively in your memory or literally on your hard drive. In this essay, I want to make the case for using version control technology to help keep track of what's changing in the course of a writing project, so you can then assess how "what changes" has changed in the course of a writing class.</u>

According to our two-part strategy from sentence reordering, after we've tried a new position we should reassess transitions in the new position. For sentences, "transitions" meant words or phrases ("but," "because"); scaling up to paragraphs, transitions could be whole sentences. In fact, checking transitions after the paragraph-level reordering helped me realize the "but" was no longer working; the sentence-level reordering in Example 2 was itself a smoothing operation after the paragraph switch. This suggests another strategy: *What you learn at one scale, try applying at another.* Note that I don't mean just small to large; sometimes the learning works in both directions.

Noteworthy Changes Deserve a Worthy Note

Not every diff is so straightforward as the ones shown above: see Example 4, which shows a whole tangle of revisions as I worked through how to talk about the changes in my draft.

Example 4. A more complicated diff to interpret (so maybe not one for the history books)

> That's not to say you'll stop fiddling with sentences and words as you get more experience. I've written plenty over the years, but ~~I~~in those first two paragraphs alone, I ~~count~~can see at least seven ~~edits~~ word-level changes that shifted the emphasis or clarified what I meant~~, edits that feel important enough to me as a writer to name:~~Some wording changes are powerful. For example ~~changed pronouns, including myself by changing you to we in the ; I added new~~ ? The last sentence of paragraph two used to talk about "how you grow your expertise as a writer," until I acknowledged that I'm still growing, so I changed the pronouns to include myself.

I went from planning a list of seven edits to choosing one to focus on; I tried describing some edits as "important" in a single word, then as a whole expanded phrase, then cut both. This moment in the revision process was kind of a mess, really. Why show it to you, then? A few reasons.

First, to make sure I'm not overstating my claim or setting you up for confusion. The truth is, not *every* diff is important or a source of great insight. Sometimes, the best response is to acknowledge that drafting is messy, and move on. Second, following from that truth, the moments that *do* feel like accomplishments are worth marking, so you can find them again later. (See Figure 1, below, where several revisions are marked with notes, and the less interesting moments in the history are marked simply as dates.)

Luckily, many writing tools with version trackers let you add "named versions" within the file's history.[2] You can use these names to say where

---

2. In LibreOffice, you can find the option to name a save under File > Versions… > Save New Version; in Google Docs, timestamps saved automatically under File > Version History can be renamed (though only 40 per document). One version tracker popular among programmers and technical writers, called *git*, tracks only these named versions, which it calls "commits." I kind of love the energy of that: it's like, "Okay, I know you've saved this file, but are you ready to commit to it? Is this an official version you'd want to look at again later?"

you are relative to some point in the process, as in "first draft" or "500 words to go"; or, even better, you can use the notes to briefly describe what's changing, and why. A note like "first draft" doesn't tell you, if you look back at it later, how far you'd gotten by the first draft. By contrast, a note like "reorder Sommers quote from third page to first" or "finished section on barracudas" tells you what you've actually done. A glance back through a series of such notes when the essay is complete can help you call to mind all the highlights of your process and reflect on what you learned—or what you want to ask for feedback on.

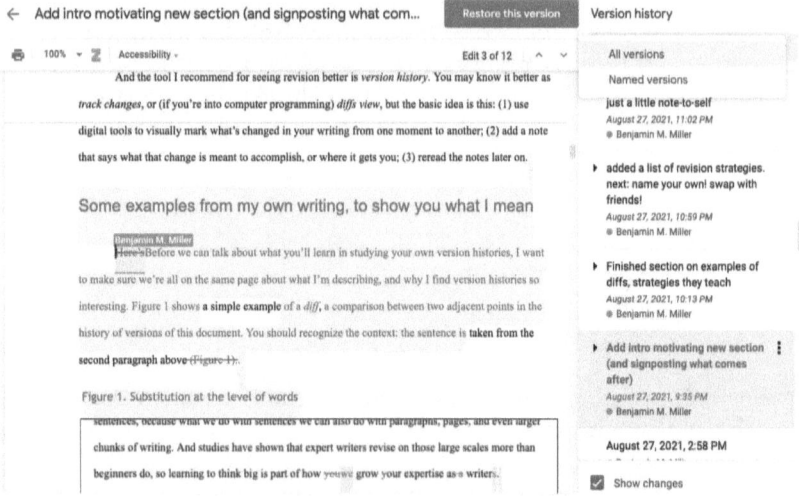

Figure 1. One form of annotated revision history ("named versions"), from a Google Docs version of this chapter. Even the limited space of the annotation allows various kinds of notes: descriptions of what's changed ("Finished section on examples of diffs"), status updates ("Just a little note to self"), plans for future working sessions ("next: name your own! swap with friends!"), etc. Screenshot shows a list of five timestamped versions of a document, with labels including text quoted in the figure caption. An option to show only named versions is unselected. Screenshot by author.

But even before the essay is complete, these notes can be powerful. Pausing to describe what you were just working on—even pausing to decide *whether* to describe what you were working on—opens up a space for reflection. Version notes invite you to think actively about how you're writ-

> NB: Microsoft Word and Apple Pages allow you to compare versions of documents, and Word will even autosave versions to compare, but as of this writing neither Word nor Pages has the built-in capacity to name a save or attach a comment to specific versions.

ing, whether to save a move you just made for future reference or to compare your present writing situation to others you've been in before. And that kind of metacognition, or thinking about your thinking, has been found to be important in developing expertise (*How People Learn* 50, 18).

What's more, if your writing is interrupted (life happens), version notes can be a place to lay down tracks for yourself to return to. Scrolling through just the noteworthy moments when you get back, you might well recover the momentum you had when you left off, allowing you to resume midstream rather than just read the whole draft from the top. Paul Ford, writing in the *New York Times* about open source software, had a memorable take on this kind of process recap. He wrote, "I read the change logs, and I think: humans can do things." If you find yourself in the grip of writer's block, version notes can offer a reminder: you, a writer, can do things.

Looking Back to Look Forward

I'm taking the phrase "revision strategies" from one of the classic studies of writing processes, by Nancy Sommers. By comparing early and late drafts in two groups of writers, she identified four recurring "operations"—addition, subtraction, substitution, and reordering—taking place at four different "levels" of text: word, phrase, sentence, and "theme (the extended statement of one idea)" (Sommers 380). Most interestingly for practical purposes, she found a difference between the two groups based on their experience level. Beginning student writers tended to make changes on the scale of words, phrases, and sentences, and most of the word/phrase changes were substitutions: they didn't change the overall structure or even meaning, since a lot of the substituted words were synonyms. Professional adult writers made small changes, too, but also tended to go beyond—they made more changes at larger-than-paragraph levels, like theme or section, and they did a lot more cutting and reordering.

Their revision *goals* were different, too: the student writers in Sommers's study mostly wanted to "clean up" their early drafts (381), while the experienced writers talked about taking their drafts apart to find the heart of the argument (383-4)—in a sense, using revision to "rough up" the earlier draft and make something better from the pieces. Sommers's experiment was a long time ago, but it's an experiment you can repeat even more easily now, with your own writing: When you have to revisit a first draft, do you look for ways to "clean it up"? Or do you ask yourself what else, what next idea or better explanation, the draft helps you figure out?

What do you think your revision history would have to say about it? It's worth asking, because what we think we're doing and what the evidence shows aren't always the same. In 2018, Heather Lindenman and colleagues published a study comparing students' drafts with reflective memos they'd written about them. They found that many students claimed to have learned new revision skills in their first-year writing courses, but those revision moves weren't actually there when the researchers looked at the diffs. As the authors put it, "students articulated improved writing knowledge in their memos—they talked the talk—but they did not enact it in their revisions—they did not walk the walk" (589). So if you feel like you've realized something new this semester about how to improve your writing, it's worth checking to see if it's actually showing up in your latest drafts. What you expect is changing in your writing, or what you hope is changing, may or may not be visible there.

It's not always easy, in the thick of the writing, to remember what turns you took, or why; sometimes the new versions just replace what you'd done before, whether figuratively in your memory or literally on your hard drive. Using version history can help you keep track of what you've done throughout the course of a writing project, so you can then assess how your strategies have changed—and where they might be useful again in the future.

So before you write a final reflection, on either that piece of writing or a whole course, you'd do well to grab some evidence from your revision history. Or, if you find it's not there yet, you can start making some new history now.

The More Strategies, the Merrier

To find more revision strategies, you may only have to start looking at drafts where something really clicked—where you know your revisions really improved the final product. But to get the most out of it, work with a group. If you share what you find among peers, classmates, or other writing partners, the chances increase that everyone will pick up something new.

In the interest of such sharing, here are a few moves I've noticed recurring in my diffs:

- *Thickening.* Add a new sentence between two existing ones, e.g. to add more detail to an otherwise general statement. Especially useful around quotations that need more context.
- *Prying open.* The scaled-up, paragraph-level version of thickening: add a whole new paragraph between existing paragraphs, e.g. to in-

sert a more concrete example of an abstract idea, or to acknowledge and respond to some possible misreading. Also works with sections (see Example 6).
- *Regrouping.* Sometimes, instead of new material, all you need is a change in punctuation. Adding a period (or a paragraph break) can sometimes let your readers catch their breath and fully understand one thought before you ask them to move on (see Example 5). Section headings can do the same at a larger scale (see Example 6). Conversely, substituting a semicolon for a period can emphasize how closely two ideas are related.
- *Reframing.* Add new material at the beginning of the draft (or paragraph, or section) with the goal of helping readers see how the existing material fits into a larger conversation; see Example 7, below. Note that this could also be considered a scaled-up version of a traditional sentence-level strategy like *adding transitions.*
- *Removing the scaffolding.* Kind of the opposite of reframing: delete preparatory passages that aren't part of the actual building / idea, even though you couldn't have built it without them.
- *Making it explicit.* Add new material at the end of a sentence, paragraph, or section to explain the significance or consequence of what you just said. Say outright what you thought was implied the first time.
- *Fine-tuning.* Substitute individual words to adjust their overtones, so they better match your intended root meaning. (For example, I wanted "overtones" in that sentence rather than "associations," because "overtones" is associated with music and reinforces the musical aspect of "tuning.")

To find these, as I said, I went through my version history and tried to (a) describe the changes I saw, and (b) explain what I hoped each change would accomplish. You can do the same, especially if you already took notes as you went along to mark the revisions of which you're the most proud.

Example 5. Regrouping at the Sentence Level (replacing colon with period)

> In this essay, I want to help you see revision better. I want to help you think through what you do with sentences, because what we

do with sentences we can also do with paragraphs, pages, and even larger chunks of writing.

Example 6. Regrouping to carve out an extra section within an existing one

~~The more strategies, the merrier~~<ins>Where I'm coming from, and where you're going</ins>

I'm taking the phrase "revision strategies" from one of the classic studies of writing process, by Nancy Sommers. By comparing early and late drafts in two groups of writers, she found that beginning student writers tended to make changes at the level of word, phrase, and sentence, and that most of the word/phrase changes were substitutions: they didn't change the overall structure or meaning. Experienced adult writers made those changes, too, but also tended to go beyond—they made more changes at larger-than-paragraph levels, like theme or section, and they did a lot more cutting and reordering.

<ins>The more strategies, the merrier</ins>

Sommers' original article makes from some great reading, despite its kind of boring title [...]

From Discovery to Planning

So far, my advice has mostly been retrospective: I'm asking you to look back at the revisions you've already made, and glean strategies from them. That's not a bad place to start, but the bigger goal is to improve your writing by expanding the ways you know how to improve your writing. This raises an important question: How will you know when to apply one kind of strategy over another—when to add more in the middle or the beginning, when to reorder or regroup?

Example 7. Reframing by adding at the start of a section

Strategy Search Suggestions

<ins>So far, my advice has been mostly retrospective: I'm asking you to look back at the revision you've already made, and glean strategies from them. That's not a bad place to start, but the bigger goal isn't simply to label and catalog all these moves, but rather to use them</ins>

<u>moving forward, to improve your writing by expanding the ways you know how to improve writing. This raises an important question:</u> How will you know when to apply one kind of strategy over another—when to add more in the middle, when to reorder or regroup? Unfortunately, there's no hard and fast rule: it'll usually depend on the particulars of your argument [...]

Unfortunately, there's no hard and fast set of rules: it'll ultimately depend on the particulars of your argument or narrative when you might want to restructure, or thicken, or reframe. Sometimes the best approach is to ask friendly readers where they had questions or had to reread more than once to understand. But since reordering is often both my most challenging and most rewarding revision move, here's what has helped me realize it might be time to try it:

- *Distant callbacks.* If you find yourself saying things like "As I said earlier," it's worth checking how much earlier it was. If readers will have to remember your point from before a whole intervening section, maybe it would make more sense to reposition the new part closer to the first part. On the other hand, maybe all you need is a regrouping: could you add new section titles to help readers anticipate the jump away from the first idea and back to it later? That might make it easier to follow your line of thought.
- *Bringing it down to size,* for example, with a "reverse sentence outline." A reverse outline is one you write after a draft exists, allowing you—like Sommers' experienced adult writers—to search that draft for the shape of an emerging argument, rather than assume the argument is already clear. By outlining in sentences, you essentially scale down the big picture into a paragraph or two: for many writers, a more familiar and manageable space in which to regroup, reorder, and recognize gaps to fill in (or extraneous chunks to cut). Once you've done it with the outline, the corresponding changes you can make in the piece as a whole should be easier to identify.

For regrouping, I think about *needing a break.* Beginnings and endings are positions of power; anything next to a pause gets extra emphasis. Conversely, long stretches without a beginning or ending—whether it's a four-line sentence or a full-page paragraph—seem to suggest there's nothing worth emphasizing. But that's usually not the case! So when I see a long paragraph or sentence, I look more closely for the highlights, and I try to place a period or paragraph break alongside them.

There are troves of authors with additional advice and suggested moves to look into; I've found Wendy Bishop's "Revising Out and Revising In" and E. Shelley Reid's *Solving Writing Problems* to be particularly helpful. Whatever move you choose, if you take a note as you're trying it, you'll be able to come back later and assess how successful it was for your draft. And seeing it in the context of your other named versions will help you consider whether it might work as well, or better, at another point in your process or on another level of scale.

A Parade of Small Rewards

Looking back and looking forward are all well and good, but above all it's the mid-process reflection that keeps me coming back to diffs. Recording what's changing helps us realize that there *is* actual progress happening, even when it might not look like it. As someone who has struggled with writer's block and anxiety for as long as I can remember, many of my first drafts don't look like much of anything, often for a long time. But a look through my diffs shows the progress that word counts alone would leave invisible: the hundreds of words written, then erased; the paragraphs of ideas in a particular order that turned out to be incompatible with another structure, and so had to be cut. In naming each revision, even when the revision move is subtraction, we get to pause and celebrate the writing that was there.

When do you usually celebrate your writing? When the essay is complete? When a grade comes back (depending on the grade)? When you don't have to think about it any more? By acknowledging the hard work and successes of mid-draft changes, version history reminds us that the journey itself is studded with small victories.

Works Cited

Bishop, Wendy. "Revising Out and Revising In." *Acts of Revision: A Guide for Writers*, edited by Wendy Bishop, Boynton/Cook Heinemann, 2004, pp. 13-27.

Ford, Paul. "Letter of Recommendation: Bug Fixes." *The New York Times*, 11 June 2019. *NYTimes.com*, https://www.nytimes.com/2019/06/11/magazine/letter-of-recommendation-bug-fixes-git.html.

How People Learn: Brain, Mind, Experience, and School: Expanded Edition. 2nd ed., National Academy Press, 2000. https://www.nap.edu/catalog/9853/how-people-learn-brain-mind-experience-and-school-expanded-edition.

Lindenman, Heather, Martin Camper, Lindsay Dunne Jacoby, and Jessica Enoch. "Revision and Reflection: A Study of (Dis)Connections between Writing Knowledge and Writing Practice." *College Composition and Communication*, vol. 69, no. 4, June 2018, pp. 581-611.

Sommers, Nancy. "Revision Strategies of Student Writers and Experienced Adult Writers." *College Composition and Communication*, vol. 31, no. 4, Dec. 1980, pp. 378-88.

Teacher Resources for "What's the Diff? Version History and Revision Reflections"

Overview and Teaching Strategies

This essay is intended to support students in making conscious interventions in existing drafts, starting by exposing the specific textual changes from one draft to another: their "diffs." For purposes of reflecting on past and current practices, the chapter may work best if read after students have already begun revising their compositions, as not everyone will have saved work from previous courses. On the other hand, it also encourages students to develop a writerly practice of recording revision intentions alongside each diff they recognize as significant enough to put a label on. Doing so effectively takes, well, practice, and so I would recommend starting relatively early.

I have found that some feedback on version notes—see Supporting Exercise 2, below—can help students learn to write them in a way that still makes sense when read weeks later. Even stating that future-self as an audience, and reminding students of the goal of writing for that audience, seems to help over time. Early on, it can be helpful to model the process in real time (e.g. while revising something together in class), or in a screencast.

Several pieces of comp/rhet scholarship inspired the ideas in this essay and could be similarly inspiring for students to read (or read excerpts from) alongside it. Nancy Sommers' "Revision Strategies of Student Writers and Experienced Adult Writers" would be a natural companion, as I lean on Sommers' analysis, but present only one finding from her complex article. Lindenman et al's "Revision and Reflection: A Study of (Dis)Connections between Writing Knowledge and Writing Practice," which in some ways prompted this piece's deep dive into diffs for a student audience, could also work well for a Writing About Writing course. Finally, the Wendy Bishop chapter I mention, "Revising Out and Revising In," from her collection *Acts of Revision*, is written with an undergraduate audience in mind and offers over 70 suggestions for revision moves, many with fun names. I have often asked my students to pick three of Bishop's exercises, try them in their current drafts, and then discuss in the next class or their final reflections what happened: Would they try it again? At the same or a different point in the process? Why?

DISCUSSION QUESTIONS

1. Which of the revision "moves" described in the essay have you tried in your own writing, and which might you want to try? Are there any you're familiar with, but you think of through different names? How might the names you choose help you think through the move at different scales (word, sentence, paragraph, section, etc.)?

2. This essay sometimes treats revision through a mathematical metaphor: addition, subtraction, substitution, reordering, and regrouping are all things we can do in algebra as well as writing. Are there any other operations or relationships from math that might be relevant to how you think about writing and revision? e.g. What would a distributive property look like in a sentence, or an essay? Are there times you might want to multiply, or to divide?

3. Figure 1 includes a variety of version names, also known as "commit" messages: (a) "just a little note-to-self"; (b) "added a list of revision strategies. next: name your own! swap with friends!"; (c) "finished section on examples of diffs, strategies they teach"; (d) "add intro motivating new section (and signposting what comes next)"; (e) "August 27, 2:58 PM." Which messages tell you the most about the goals or the content of the revision? Which tell you the least?

SUPPORTING ACTIVITIES

1. Look at your own diffs between drafts of a recent project. What revision operations (addition, subtraction, substitution, reordering, regrouping) can you see, at what scales (word/phrase, clause, sentence, paragraph, section)? Try to remember what your goals were in making those changes. Do your revision history and your goals primarily match those of the students or the experienced writers in Sommers' study, at least as Miller has summarized them here?

2. Trade revision histories with a partner and read through the topline version names / "commit" messages. Can you tell what your partner was changing, or why? At what scale (word/phrase, clause, sentence, paragraph, section) would you expect to see those changes? Make a note of particularly clear messages, where you get a

sense not only of what changed, but why: i.e. what the goal of that revision was for your partner. Also make a note of any vague messages, i.e. messages telling you only that *something* changed, but not what. Share these new notes with your partner, and see if you can together rewrite any vague messages to be more like the clear ones.

3. To increase your experience with large-scale structural revision (reordering and regrouping at the paragraph level and above), try a *reverse sentence outline* on index cards. The key difference between this and a more traditional outline is that, rather than listing broad topics (e.g. "senior year of high school") or inert evidence (e.g. "questions on AP exams"), you're listing thoughts, claims, and questions (e.g. "AP exam questions were open-ended, requiring me to decide on my own what information was relevant"). The "reverse" part means that you're outlining a draft that already exists, rather than projecting into the future of a draft you have yet to write.

To make a sentence outline, follow these steps: (1) Number the paragraphs in your draft. (2) Read through your draft, looking for your key points—moments where the thinking moves or the essay turns. Each time you find one, write it onto its own index card as a *single full sentence*. Leave out transitions (e.g. "for example"). If you find you need to compose a new sentence to capture the thought, do so. If a point takes two sentences, use two cards. (Note that instead of using index cards, you could copy all these sentences onto a single sheet of paper. This has the advantage of keeping everything together, making it easier to see the shape of your essay. But it also has the disadvantage of keeping everything together, making it harder to *re*-see the shape of your essay.) (3) As you go, on the *back* of each card, write the number of the paragraph that this idea appeared in. You may have one of these key ideas per paragraph, or two, or three, or none. This in itself is useful information to have; it will help you regroup or consolidate or expand.

Congratulations! With these cards in order, you've produced a basic sentence outline of the thinking moves and turning points in your essay. But noticing the structure as it exists is only one step in re-seeing; to see it as it *might* exist, continue with the next several steps. (4) On the back of each card, write a letter that will help you recover this original order: that is, label the first card A, the second card B, the third C, etc. If you have more than 26 cards, continue with A', B', etc. This is important because of the next step, which is to (5) shuffle the cards, then flip them back to the front (where the sentences are). Rearrange them in such a way as to make a logical paragraph, or short set of paragraphs. If you need to add any new sentences to fill in gaps, do so on new cards, still with one card per sentence and one sentence per card. If some cards don't fit into your new paragraph, or merely duplicate other cards, you can leave them out. (6) When you are done, write down the new sequence of letters in your notebook, so you can recover this revised order. (7) Compare the results of steps 4 and 6. Based on any reorderings, additions, or subtractions you've made to the sentence outline, what reorderings, additions, or subtractions does that suggest for the essay as a whole? Based on your information from step 3, are there any paragraphs you'd like to combine and consolidate? Are there any paragraph breaks you might now add, to highlight your thinking moves?

21 Navigating Your Collaborative Project

Ellen Cecil-Lemkin and Tamara Gluck

Overview

From school to the workplace, managing team projects isn't always easy, but this chapter aims to prepare students for success.[1] In this chapter, we guide students through different tools for working with others, maintaining project goals, and completing projects where technology is at the forefront. We provide information for students on what to expect from their instructors, as well as how to set boundaries with and get to know their team members. This is accomplished through rapport, understanding of access needs, and methods of communicating. We also introduce students to key organizational documents that will allow them to better structure their group work. To this end, we discuss the purpose and creation of a team contract and project schedule. Finally, we introduce various tools which can be used to compose collaboratively across various forms of media. After reading this essay, students will be elevated from novice to navigator of any group project!

The notorious *group project*. As the bane of many college students' experience, working with your peers to successfully complete an assignment or project is rarely an easy feat. It would not surprise us if starting a new collaborative project with team members you've never worked with before caused you to feel a little (or a lot!) anxious about what's to come. Maybe you're worried that you'll have to take on the bulk of the work yourself. Or maybe you're concerned that you won't get along with your team members. These concerns are all perfectly normal, and

---

1. This work is licensed under the Creative Commons Attribution-NonCommercial-NoDerivatives 4.0 International License (CC BY-NC-ND 4.0) and is subject to the Writing Spaces Terms of Use. To view a copy of this license, visit http://creativecommons.org/licenses/by-nc-nd/4.0/, email info@creativecommons.org, or send a letter to Creative Commons, PO Box 1866, Mountain View, CA 94042, USA. To view the Writing Spaces Terms of Use, visit http://writingspaces.org/terms-of-use.

some of your team members may share similar worries. However, collaborating with your peers can be a rewarding experience!

While it may seem like your instructor is assigning a group project just to torture you, there are actually many great reasons for these types of projects. You are probably aware that there's an emphasis on collaboration in the workplace (Bruffee 647; Ede and Lunsford 60; Wolfe 5), and employers are looking for individuals who know how to work in a team. Beyond preparing you for the workforce, these projects have a lot of educational benefits as well. Scholars have found that when you work with a team there are more opportunities to learn and increase your understanding of concepts and materials (Bruffee 644; Wolfe 5), which in turn can promote better writing (Bruffee). Collaborative projects can also lead to developing a community with the people you work with, which can grow into friendships and partnerships for other classes (Brumberger 197; Hunzer 68).

Working with a team, however, doesn't always come naturally. (If you're one of the students who felt anxious at the prospect of working in a team, we're sure you already know this.) Luckily, there are some practical steps that you and your team can take to help ensure that you're all on the same page when it comes to completing your project. There are also some great technologies and tools out there to help you collaborate with your peers. In this essay, we're going to tell you about some strategies and tools you can use to have a positive experience working in a team. We've broken this up into three sections: (1) communication strategies and tools, (2) accountability and organizational strategies, and (3) technologies for collaborating. We will delve into the value of these section topics, discuss what tools are at your disposal, and how to use them to your (and your team's) advantage.

COMMUNICATION STRATEGIES AND TOOLS

It probably comes as no surprise that great collaboration takes strong communication skills. Team members must be willing to communicate with one another to share ideas, acknowledge when they need assistance, and provide support to everyone involved. Reaching a level of comfort when communicating as a team requires rapport—or close, interpersonal bonds that aid in understanding each other's feelings and communicating clearly. Rapport can encourage accountability and provide you with the opportunity to enjoy the collaboration process by creating working relationships with your teammates (Murphy and Valdéz). Rapport doesn't mean that you have to be friends with your team members. While it may seem like a great idea to form groups with your friends, it can complicate the collaborative process and damage friendships if the project doesn't go as planned (Cecil 34-8). Instead, think of rapport as becoming colleagues with your team members—you need to have respect and appreciation for each other in a professional sense. So, remember, even if you are not or do not become great friends with your team members, you can still end up with a successful project as long as you share mutual respect.

Rapport Building

How do you build rapport with your team? The answer is pretty straight forward but often overlooked: spend time getting to know your teammates. Ideally, your instructor will coordinate teams well before you start a major collaborative project. This creates an opportunity for you to test the waters with each other, chat informally, and build rapport before the hard work begins. Even if this isn't the case, there's no time like the present to begin getting acquainted! As a starting point, ask each other basic getting-to-know-you questions to get a feel of your similarities and differences.

Once you know your teammates better, you'll also want to talk about cultural norms and access needs. Ideas of acceptable or unacceptable behaviors differ for people based on parts of the country, different parts of the world, particular gender identities, and involvement in different communities. What you might find rude could be perfectly polite to someone else. For example, you might think that showing up late to a meeting is entirely okay, while someone else could find your tardiness incredibly rude. Understanding these cultural norms ahead of time can help you avoid unnecessary tension. To jump start this discussion, consider:

- What are your assumptions about professional behavior in an educational setting?
- What are your preferences when it comes to communication? For example, do you have particular times that you do or do not want to be reached at, methods of communication (phone call, text, email, etc.), and/or any particular style you prefer (blunt, direct, gentle, diplomatic, etc.)?
- What, to you, does successful collaboration look like? Does it involve everyone getting a chance to share their ideas, having equal input on the project, and/or contributing the same amount of work?
- Why are these values important to you?

After thinking through your team's cultural values, you'll want to consider everyone's access needs. Having a discussion around access needs can open a lot of doors for everyone. Conversations around access will require you to think through what you need from your teammates in order to fully participate. For example, if you have trouble speaking up, you might need your teammates to directly ask you to respond when they introduce a new idea or want solutions. Or, if you're hard of hearing, you may need your teammates to look directly at you or speak loudly when talking. As you continue working on your project, you may find that your access needs change or you find a new way of working which you feel would be more beneficial to yourself and the group. This is to be expected! While you may be uncomfortable speaking up at the beginning of a project, you may later find that you are much more comfortable voicing your opinion. Therefore, we think that it's valuable to speak up about your changing access needs and to check in with your team about theirs. Having this open line of communication will help everyone contribute to the project. To begin a conversation around access needs, you might want to consider:

- Have you ever been a part of a group project that felt particularly inclusive to you as a learner and individual? What specifically about the group made it feel accessible or inclusive to you?
- How do you learn best? Are there ways that your group members can support your learning?
- Do you have any accommodations already in place that might be helpful for your teammates to be aware of?
- What should your team members know about you in order for you to be successful?

Furthermore, as part of your rapport building process, you'll want to challenge any preconceived notions that you have about your teammates based on their gender, race, disability status, sexuality, religion, age, and class. For example, if one of your teammates is considerably older or younger than you, what are your assumptions about them? Then, consider how your assumptions will shape your rapport with this team member and ultimately your collaborative project. Assumptions based on someone's identity markers could hurt your opportunities to learn from one another and work together successfully.

Now that we've addressed the foundations of strong communication skills, we want to turn your attention to some tools to keep you in communication with your team. To help your team determine what tool you might want to use, we've put together a list of some common and easy to use technologies. However, these technologies are just starting points for you to consider, and there may be new and better technology available to you that could work just as well or better. We encourage you to experiment and find out what works best for you and your team.

Asynchronous Chat

When working in a group, everyone likely has their own schedule and time set aside to work on the project; thus, coming up with multiple meeting times to fit everyone's schedule isn't the most realistic approach. Asynchronous chat tools are a great way to overcome this barrier and send information to the group so your teammates can access it on their own time. There are many different services which allow for the "group chat" model, all which have their own characteristics to meet your needs. For example, in an age where Android-users bring green text to group chats, GroupMe is a free texting app for groups regardless of phone operating system. Also, with desktop access for varied communication access points and ease of file sharing, GroupMe comes in handy as both a chat area and sharing of documents. In addition to GroupMe, WhatsApp and Google Hangouts are more common texting tools which may be more accessible to teammates who are international or are better acquainted with such tools, though the mechanics work very similarly, providing more opportunities for video and voice communications.

Discord is one of many resources for asynchronous communication. This is a platform in which you can create a "server" and organize different channels which have their own topics. Though more work goes into setting up a server than simply starting a group chat, it is a valuable tool for more complex projects and larger groups who must collaborate across a greater number of tasks. In addition to providing individual text channels, Discord offers opportunities for more social aspects to further build rapport and to create areas for sending memes, coordinating social meet-ups, and other non-school related functions without clouding up the important task communications. While there are limits to the sizes of files which you can share, Discord in tandem with Google Drive is a powerful and useful combo!

Video Conferencing

There are a variety of different programs out there which enable you to video conference with your team. When meeting in person is difficult, but face-to-face connection is something the group prefers, tools such as

Zoom, Google Meet, and Microsoft Teams present a virtual stand-in for direct contact. Video conferencing can also be used as an informal way to get to know your group members and further build rapport. These tools should be used in place of asynchronous chat when making major decisions and brainstorming. When selecting a video conferencing program, considering what platform your group members are most familiar with and what capabilities the programs have is important to ensure comfort and accessibility. You'll also want to take into account any licensing agreements your school may have with these programs, in case additional features are available to you for free. To find out more, you could ask your teacher or the information technology office at your school.

Project Tracking and Organization

Organizing and tracking the work each member needs to accomplish for the project can get tedious and tiring. Thankfully, there are many online tools that allow for organization of collaborative projects! These resources—such as Trello, Todoist, or Padlet—allow for the creation of different boards and tasks which help track the progress of the project. Trello is built to organize collaborative projects by creating boards to show you what needs to be completed, what's being worked on, who's assigned to each task, and when everything is due. Todoist offers a less complex interface where you can easily input your tasks, assign them to collaborators, and check them off when they're completed. In both programs, multiple users can access and edit the boards to create to-do lists and track the progress of the project. You can input all the tasks created for your project schedule, set reminders for when they are due, and track how much you have left to work on. Padlet functions as a virtual post-it board, building spaces to post content, interact, comment, and create a personalized workspace. While some features for each of these programs are blocked by paywalls, the key features (which can help your team stay organized) are free. Overall, organizing collaborative projects by presenting goals, progress, roles, and due dates provides an effective way to stay accountable, on track, and efficient when working with others.

Accountability and Organizational Strategies

Since you're working with other people, communicating expectations and developing organizational strategies is crucial. These strategies are fundamental to the success of your project; without them, there's a risk of having a turbulent or unsuccessful project. For these reasons, we're introducing you to two important documents: the team contract and project schedule. To develop these documents, we drew heavily from *Team Writing*, a book by Joanna Wolfe—an expert on writing strategies for collaborative projects—with modifications based on our experience. These strategies can also be paired with or augmented by those that Lance Cummings, Rin Jackson, and Moriah Yancey share in "Technologies Of Trust: Creating Networks Of Goodwill For Collaboration."

Team Contract

The team contract is an organizational document designed to establish your group's goals and expectations for the project. This document helps you to communicate with your team about expectations for successfully completing the assignment, brainstorm possible conflicts and how your team will resolve them, and start thinking about the individual strengths each of you bring to the group. While this might seem like unnecessary, additional work, the team contract can help you solve problems before they even start by setting expectations in a neutral environment. The team contract consists of four sections: (1) team goals, (2) division of labor, (3) commitments, and (4) conflict resolution. And, to help you visualize what this document might look like for your team, we've included a sample team contract at the end of this chapter for you to reference, using fictional students and situations (see Appendix 1).

Team Goals

This first section focuses on what you'd like to learn or gain from this project and how your group defines quality work, which can help steer your team towards a rewarding and successful project. When defining what constitutes a successful project, it's really important to move beyond a statement such as "getting an A" and toward breaking down the criteria you will need to accomplish to achieve that A. In the example we've provided, the team has a goal of "Educating ourselves and others about how social media reputation affects school admittance and landing a job by referencing reliable and peer reviewed sources." As you can see, this goal is much more detailed than "getting an A" and can be broken down into concrete steps that the team can implement while completing their project.

To get you started on this section, here are some questions your team can ask yourselves:

- What does quality work look like for this project?
- What do you hope to accomplish as a team?
- What do you hope to learn or gain from this experience?

Division of Labor

For this section, you should determine how you want to structure your team's work. There are lots of different ways to divide the labor amongst team members. For example, each individual member could decide to take on a particular role (e.g., project lead, writer, editor, citation manager, head researcher, or designer), everyone could collectively work on all aspects of the assignment, or some combination of the two. Different methods of labor division may be better suited for different types of assignments, so consider which option might work best for your team and the project at hand. In the example, Juan, Olivia, and Lex assign themselves both individual roles (e.g., Juan is project lead) and overlapping roles (e.g., Juan and Lex are the primary writers).

To get you started on this section, here are some questions your team can ask yourselves:

- What skills and strengths do you have as individuals?
- What are some areas that you'd like to improve upon over the course of this project?
- Based on your previous answers, how would you like to divide the work up?

Commitments

This section will help you and your team be on the same page when it comes to your individual commitment to the project and other important responsibilities that you might have outside of school. You might work at a part-time job (like Olivia), play on one of your school's athletic teams (like Lex), be a part of an on-campus organization (like Juan), have parental responsibilities, or care for a sick family member. All of these responsibilities can impact the amount of time you can devote to your project and when you can meet with your team. When you start assigning tasks for each member and deciding when you'll meet outside of class to work on your project, acknowledging and planning for these commitments can help you all have a smoother collaboration experience.

To get you started on this section, here are some questions your team can ask yourselves:

- How much is everyone willing to contribute to the group? If someone does not want to contribute the same amount, how will that be reflected in the evaluation (if there is one for this project)?
- What are some of the factors that might affect your performance or availability? How can the team assist you with navigating these responsibilities and your commitment to the group project?
- What do you need from your teammates in order to contribute successfully to the project (e.g., due date reminders, clear expectations, and notes)?

Conflict Resolution

This final section might be the most important of the team contract—it will help you decide how possible group conflicts may be resolved in the group, even before they happen. If you have concerns regarding your teammates' contributions, deadline adherence, decision making, or other group issues, then this is the place to address it. Sometimes, when conflict happens, students are nervous or unsure of how to confront their team member about the issue. However, when you plan ahead and anticipate how your team will respond, you can feel more prepared to talk to your team members, since they already know what your team has decided to do. This section might also help prevent conflict, since it brings to attention how everyone's actions can impact the team and what the consequences are.

To get you started on this section, here are two questions your team can ask yourselves:

- What are some conflicts you've encountered in previous groups? How did you resolve them? Did you think this was a fair resolution?
- What are some potential issues (e.g., missed deadline, unacceptable work, and lack of communication) that you are worried might arise during this project? How do you hope that your group will handle them?

Project Schedule

After you've finished creating your team contract and had the opportunity to brainstorm what you want to do for your project, the next step is creating a project schedule (see Appendix 2). The project schedule is a document that lists and assigns tasks necessary for completing the project. In other words, it breaks down all the work that needs to be completed into actionable steps or tasks and evenly distributes this work across team members. By completing this document, you will be able to meet deadlines, complete all the necessary work for your project, and ensure that everyone has a fair and even amount of work.

When deciding how to distribute the work, you don't have to assign everyone to the task in which they are strongest. For example, even if Juan considers himself to be an expert writer, that doesn't mean he should take on the bulk of the writing work. Another team member, like Olivia, might be keen on developing her writing abilities. Allowing her to take on some writing tasks during this assignment can help her develop her writing abilities by learning from her peers—which is one of the goals of collaborative assignments. Therefore, take the time to determine what each of you would like to do by considering everyone's strengths and interests.

To ensure the distribution of work is even across team members, you'll want to assign each task a complexity value. When you assign complexity values to tasks, you are recognizing that each task takes a different amount of time and skill. For example, if you and your team need to create an annotated bibliography (like Juan, Olivia, and Lex), you might determine that finding sources and reading the sources are two different tasks that take varying amounts of time to do well. It's also important to account for recurring work which each team member may do that is not accounted for on a project schedule. For example, Olivia says that she will be a note taker for the group by keeping and distributing notes to the team after each meeting. As such, it may be important to assign Olivia fewer complexity points to account for this additional work that is not tracked on the project schedule.

As you begin working on your project schedule, here are some questions you'll want to consider:

- What are all the steps that your team will need to take in order to complete the assignment? How much work is each of these tasks?
- What part of the assignment are you particularly excited for? How would you like to contribute to that component?
- Are there recurring tasks that are not being accounted for in the project schedule (e.g., scheduling meetings, taking group notes, and reminding the team about deadlines)? How complex are each of these recurring tasks?

With an established team contract and project schedule, you and your team are ready to move onto the real deal: producing your project! In the next section, we've provided some examples of technologies you can use to find the best fit for your team and assignment at hand.

Technology to Support Digital Multimodal Projects

In a world where online work is ever more prevalent and meeting up with team members to work on every detail is unrealistic, options to compose projects long-distance are made easier and more accessible through online means. While multimodal projects are still very relevant, the days of gluing pictures, graphic printouts, and other content to a tri-fold board are becoming less frequent—online and digital productions are vastly more common in academic use. Multimodal refers to multiple modes or methods of communication in a message. This term may be a new addition to your vocabulary, but it is a concept you're already familiar with. Multimodal media ranges from fliers with relevant photos and text to videos or audio components for a project; essentially something that is more than just text-based. (If you're interested in learning more about multimodal composing, we recommend checking out Melanie Gagich's "An Introduction to and Strategies for Multimodal Composing.") This section will discuss tools for creating digital multimodal media, presentation-based, or text-based products.

Multimodal Media Production

For collaboration with a heavy multimodal component, sending the same file back-and-forth isn't the most convenient. To help with this struggle, different multimodal media technologies exist for multiple users to work on one product, from fliers to video production. If you're working on a static design, like a logo, flier, or social media post, Canva has a free platform for multiple users to access in content collaboration and design. With many premade templates to choose from, this technology helps alleviate a lot of pressure that can come from building a project from scratch. Similar to Canva, other tools such as Pixelied and VistaCreate have useful default templates instead of starting with a blank page. These tools allow for more than one person to have access to the project, but typically only one person can actively make edits at a time. Regardless, this is a great way to create crisp and professional materials for classes without needing major graphic design skills. All the tools have countless free-to-use designs and stock images, but there are paywalls for certain upgrades and access to more images and designs. However, a student email address can also unlock one free year of Canva Pro, which grants users access to content behind the paywall. (Many other online resources, such as GitHub, provide access to extended free trials or immense discounts to many multimodal software or programs when you use your student email address.)

If you're looking to create something more interactive, like a website, we recommend trying out Wix or Weebly. Each of these platforms allow you to create free websites with easy-to-use website building templates. Like many of the resources we introduced, they do have additional content hidden behind paywalls, but the vast majority of the resources are free and available to students. With drag and drop editing features, you don't need to have any coding experience to use them, making them fairly intuitive to learn. If you do get stuck, there are loads of free tutorials available online to help you figure out how to put your plan into practice. Additionally, these sites support collaboration. You can easily add collaborators to contribute to the website and determine how much editing access they have. In very little time, your team will have a professional appearing website.

If you're interested in video production, it's worth checking your school's library or computer labs for free access to programs like those available in the Adobe suite. Support for learning these programs may be available through your campus resources or free tutorials online. When creating static projects, you can use programs like Photoshop, Illustrator, and InDesign. Premiere Pro and After Effects are available for video production and motion graphics. If you and your team have access to Apple devices, you can also use iMovie. If this is an option, there is a Cloud sharing method for easier access to projects in-progress; this way, all team members have access to the most updated version. This method might be a little more clunky, since it's not directly tied into the programs like the other options we've suggested, but the video editing programs that do support team collaboration typically require a monthly fee to access.

Finally, if you and your team want to create a podcast, you might want to check out Audition (part of the Adobe suite), Garageband (for Apple users), Anchor, or Podbean. Audition is a more sophisticated and powerful program with more than just podcast options. But don't be intimidated! Adobe provides a simple tutorial for how to create different project types using Audition and includes a pre-set template and default options for easy beginner production. However, you will be limited to working in a space on campus or where you have access to the program, and there are more steps involved if you want your podcast to be published. Both Podbean and Anchor have direct upload for podcast distribution such as Spotify and other popular podcast apps, in addition to their own apps for creating your podcast. Podbean offers basic analytics, up to 5 hours total storage, and a limited monthly upload until you hit paywalls for more advanced features; this includes collaboration, as the free and lower tier packages only allow for one admin per account. On the other hand, Anchor allows multiple people to record and participate simultaneously for each episode, and they have a strong mission statement about keeping the art of podcasting free and without barriers or any paywalls to premium access and storage or upload amounts. Take the time to brainstorm with your team if learning a new medium is right for your project!

Presentation-Based Production

Stitching together everyone's PowerPoint slides before the deadline or figuring out what other visual aides to use when presenting in a group is often stressful and difficult. Google Slides dominates the collaborative presentation space, ensuring each member has equal access to the entire project. This is beneficial in confirming that the design and content are consistent, allowing for more professional outcomes and easier group communication. Another common tool is Keynote; this works similarly to the other presentation tools, as they all allow for simultaneous collaboration and sharing with others. However, Keynote is specific to Apple users only, though there are ways to share the file so it is accessible to PC users, or provide file access through iCloud on Windows. Whatever program you choose to use, verify that your file type is accepted and accessible to your teammates as well as to your instructor.

Text-Based Production

Typing sections of an essay into an email and having one team member piece everything together into an entire essay is not the most efficient or convenient way to write a group essay. You'll have no idea what someone else wrote until (and if) they send it. Instead, consider using a text-based collaborative tool so your team can have equal access to writing and editing your document. The most intuitive example of a collaborative text-based tool is Google Docs. While there are other tools, this remains the most accessible and well-known means for text-based production without any paywall or steep learning curve, especially if you've had experience with Microsoft Word. Available for free and accessible on any computer or mobile device, Google Docs allows multiple people to edit and type into a document simultaneously. You can keep track of what everyone contributes to the document in several different ways, such as through utilizing the "suggesting mode" tool, tracing everyone's contributions by examining the "version history" of the document, or having each team member pick a text color to type their part. This is also helpful when offering edits and suggestions to other users. The comments feature provides a way to add notes and communicate with your group about a specific section or sentence instead of holding an entire meeting to discuss each point.

Conclusion

Collaborative projects offer you the opportunity to expand your skill set, generate and challenge new ideas, build community, and prep for the workforce. Composing as a team does pose some challenges you wouldn't encounter while working on a project individually. However, we've gone over some important considerations, recommendations, and tools to help you navigate this process. If you and your team commit to these practices, then you're setting yourselves up for success. Why should you believe us? We drew on these techniques to work together to write this essay (and had a lot of fun while collaborating), so we really believe that these suggestions will work for you too!

Appendix 1: Team Contract Example

Team Goals

- Educate ourselves and others about how students' social media reputation affects school admittance and landing a job by referencing reliable and peer reviewed sources.
- Learn new skills working in groups, creating a project scope including team contracts, proposals, and schedules.
- Complete all assignments and work by the given deadline.
- Follow all guidelines for each component of the assignment. For example, using correct font, spacing and following the word/page count wanted for each assignment. Also, gathering at least 10 sources for our annotated bibliography and using 8 of those sources in our actual paper.

Division of Labor

- Juan: Juan is going to be the project lead, meaning he is going to be organizing the time schedules and reminding the other groupmates about deadlines. Also, if conflict arises he will take care of the situation by either making a decision himself or talking it out with the rest of the group. Juan will also be co-lead writer because of his interest in developing his writing ability.
- Olivia: Olivia will be in charge of the research and note taking aspect of the project. This means she will make sure that the sources that our group finds are both credible and follow the guidelines that are given in the prompt. Also, she will take notes during our group meetings and distribute these notes to the team members.
- Lex: Lex will be the other co-lead writer to help Juan with the writing portion of the project so that he can handle other responsibilities as well. Lex will also be the lead editor to make sure that the writing portion of the project has little to no mistakes. They will either discuss the writing with the other groupmates or other resources such as the writing center to make the writing quality as good as it can be.

Commitments

- Everyone in the group has their personal commitments and other activities that they are a part of, but Juan, Olivia, and Lex are all willing to put in 100% effort into the project.

- Although Lex is on the tennis team which is a pretty big commitment, they are not worried about managing their time and giving their full effort into the project. They are, however, unable to meet in the mornings because of tennis practice.
- Olivia has a part-time job at the campus bookstore, which will take up some of her time, but she is confident that it will not get in the way of achieving success in this project. She is also worried that her writing skill will affect the group negatively, but plans on stepping her game up and asking for help when needed.
- Juan is worried about other commitments, such as his fraternity, that will affect his participation in the project, but is willing to stay up as late as needed in order to succeed in the project.

Conflict Resolution

- If a problem occurs, the whole group will sit down and discuss the problem until a compromise is reached. However, if the team experiences conflict that is not resolved with 30 minutes of respectful discussion, we will present both sides to their teacher and ask her to decide.
- The team will establish a deadline schedule that each member will need to abide by. If a team member misses a deadline, the project manager will contact the group member through email and text message to see why the deadline was missed. If there is no good reason for why the deadline was missed, the team member will be penalized with a 5 point deduction on their individual grade. If there was a circumstance where there was an emergency, the project manager will discuss with the rest of the group and come to an agreement on whether or not to deduct points.
- If a group member turns in work that does not follow guidelines, assignment criteria, contains many errors, and the quality of the assignment does not meet the expectations of the group, the project manager will contact that group member and give them a one day extension to fix all problems of the assignment. If the team member is having trouble with the assignment they should ask the teacher or the other groupmates to help in completing the assignment with acceptable quality.

Appendix 2: Project Schedule Example

Deadline	Task	Assigned to	Complexity
10/2	First group meeting to discuss everyone's role and Team Contract	Juan, Olivia, Lex	
10/7	Brainstorm ideas for the Team Contract and Project Schedule	Olivia, Juan, Lex	
10/9	Edit Team Contract	Lex	1
10/9	Edit Project Schedule	Juan	1
10/10	Meet at the library at 5:00pm to discuss Proposal	Juan, Olivia, Lex	
10/13	Write initial Proposal	Juan	2
10/13	Make comments on the Proposal	Lex	1
10/13	Edit Proposal	Oliva	1
10/14	Final Team Contract and Project Schedule	Olivia	1
10/14	Final Proposal	Olivia, Juan, Lex	
10/14	Start working on Annotated Bibliography at the library	Olivia, Juan, Lex	
10/21	Each find 4 sources	Olivia, Juan, Lex	
10/21	Work on Annotated Bibliography (in class)	Olivia, Juan, Lex	
10/24	Write first draft of annotations for sources (4 per team member)	Olivia, Juan, Lex	
10/27	Edit citations for Annotated Bibliography	Juan	1
10/27	Edit annotations for Annotated Bibliography	Lex	1
10/28	Final Annotated Bibliography is due	Olivia, Juan, Lex	
10/30	Work on overall rough draft (in class)	Olivia, Juan, Lex	

11/3	Meet at the library to finish rough draft (5:00pm)	Olivia, Juan, Lex	
11/4	Rough draft due	Olivia	1
11/11	Edit the rough draft	Juan	1
11/11	Comment on rough draft	Lex	1
11/11	Take note of their adjustments and make changes	Olivia	1
11/13	Final Paper is Due!	Olivia, Juan, Lex	

Works Cited

Bruffee, Kenneth. "Collaborative Learning and the 'Conversation of Mankind.'" *College English*, vol. 46, no. 7, 1984, pp. 635–52.

Brumberger, Eva R. "Collaborative Projects in a Technical Writing Class: A Cost/Benefit Analysis." *Teaching English in the Two-Year College*, vol. 27, no. 2, 1999, pp. 194–202.

Cecil, Ellen. *Approaches for Collaboration: Student Perceptions on Writing Together*. Miami University, 2015.

Cummings, Lance, et al. "Technologies of Trust: Creating Networks of Goodwill for Collaboration." *Writing Spaces: Readings on Writing*, vol. 4, Parlor Press, 2022, pp. 69–84, https://writingspaces.org/past-volumes/technologies-of-trust-creating-networks-of-goodwill-for-collaboration/.

Gagich, Melanie. "An Introduction to and Strategies for Multimodal Composing." *Writing Spaces: Readings on Writing*, vol. 3, Parlor Press, 2020, pp. 65–85, https://writingspaces.org/past-volumes/an-introduction-to-and-strategies-for-multimodal-composing/.

Hunzer, Kathleen M. "Connecting Writing Process with Personality: Creating Long-Lasting Trust Circles in Writing Classes." *Collaborative Learning and Writing: Essays on Using Small Groups in Teaching English and Composition*, edited by Kathleen M. Hunzer, McFarland & Company, Inc, 2012, pp. 217–24.

Lunsford, Andrea, and Lisa Ede. *Singular Texts/Plural Authors: Perspectives on Collaborative Writing*. Southern Illinois University Press, 1990.

Murphy, Moira, and Cecilia Valdéz. "Ravaging Resistance: A Model for Building Rapport in a Collaborative Learning Classroom." *Radical Pedagogy*, vol. 7, no. 1, 2005, https://radicalpedagogy.icaap.org/content/issue7_1/murphy-valdez.html.

Wolfe, Joanna. *Team Writing*. Bedford / St. Martin's, 2010.

Teacher Resources for Navigating Your Collaborative Project

Overview and Teaching Strategies

This essay is for students working in collaborative project settings for the first time, but it can also provide a refresher for those well versed in teamwork. For this reason, we recommend having students read this chapter as soon as (or, better yet, before) a collaborative project is assigned. However, your work as an instructor should begin even earlier. At the beginning of the semester, you should set the groundwork for your team project by providing students with ample opportunities to get to know one another and having them practice team skills on low stakes assignments, like in-class work or minor homework assignments. This preparation will allow students to begin building rapport with their team and test the collaborative waters well before they're thrown into the deep end with a high stakes assignment. Scaffolded teamwork will help lead your students to a smooth and successful project.

To this end, this chapter introduces fundamental collaboration skills that will prepare students to tackle a variety of team projects (both textual and multimodal) while providing resources on how to build rapport, communicate, set expectations, and create a product. To help students achieve these goals, we've included important discussion questions for students to consider when working in a team. These questions ask students to reflect on their work styles, areas of expertise and growth, expectations for their teammates, and more. Some of these conversations may be more challenging than others, especially the ones in which we invite students to examine their cultural values and access needs. Some students might find these reflective questions to be intimidating or may have difficulty in advocating for their access needs. As such, we think it's important to set aside time for your students to answer these questions with their teams during class time or as a formal homework assignment.

By the end of this chapter, students should feel more comfortable working in a team, acquire organizational strategies for navigating team projects, be able to draw upon different methods for communicating, and have ideas for different technology they can use to complete their projects.

Below, we offer five questions that you can use to help facilitate a discussion around key concepts in the chapter and group work in general.

DISCUSSION QUESTIONS:

1. Have you ever had to work in a team in the past? What do you wish you could have known before you started?

2. What are some of your worries or concerns about working in a team? Did anything in the chapter help you feel more comfortable with the process? What do you still have questions about?

3. What do you believe are some of the most important skills individuals need in order to make a team project successful? What are some expectations you would have of your teammates in a group project?

4. Take some time to think through your strengths as an individual. What abilities do you have which may support your team? Now, consider the skills that you'd really like to develop. What areas would you want to improve on in a collaborative setting?

5. Working with a team requires coordinating tasks on both a team and individual level. This chapter has provided some recommendations on how to coordinate work on a team level. Given these recommendations, how do you plan on managing your own tasks for the project?

22 Writing Science in the First Year of College: Why It Matters to STEM Students and How STEM Students Benefit from It

Chris Thaiss and Stephanie Wade

Overview

This essay aims to help students who have interests in STEM fields make the most of their first year by showing them how to find opportunities to explore STEM topics in typical first-year writing classes, as well as in the STEM courses they will take, and even outside of courses; how strategies such as inquiry-based rhetoric (IRB) apply to science writing in all situations; and how the work of equity, inclusion, and antiracism are foundational to science writing.

Introduction and Background

We are writing specialists who have decades of experience working with scientists and writers. We believe that the communication of science is as important as the research itself; that the ways we approach research and writing can push against systemic inequities; and that all students have the capacity to be successful writers. For these reasons, we aim to illustrate the significance of writing as a vital part of becoming an ethical, successful scientist.

This essay will consider writing both in STEM courses and in first-year writing courses that almost all US college students are required to take. In this article, we will show you:

- the power of scientific literacy and its importance in your education
- ways to get the most out of your required first-year writing course(s)
- how to gain confidence and flexibility via inquiry-based rhetoric (IBR)

- ways to develop antiracist research and writing practices
- how to give and receive useful feedback from teachers and through peer review
- how to deepen learning and improve writing in your STEM classes
- ways to write about STEM outside your courses

The Power of Scientific Literacy and Its Importance in Your Writing Education

The successful transition to college requires adapting to different expectations and practices. In writing, this often includes moving from a rules-based approach to an *inquiry-based rhetorical approach* (IBR), which simply means studying and practicing how writers—including yourself and your classmates—earn readers' trust, make clear claims with good reasons and reliable evidence, and show why their work matters. In other words, pretty much the same goals as good science.

The discipline of writing studies, which most first year writing courses follow, believes in the power of scientific literacy to improve individual lives and communities. The scientific practices of careful study of artifacts, asking good questions, and evaluating data to arrive at evidence creates the backbone of IBR, just as in STEM. These practices help you understand the choices you have as writers. These practices help you make choices that include all community members and achieve goals based on good evidence.

The COVID-19 pandemic has illustrated the dire consequences of scientific *illiteracy*, as misunderstandings and deliberate misinformation have thwarted individual, community, and international responses by undermining respect for science. But the significance of improving public engagement in science dates back at least to the 1600s, when Bernard de Fontenelle wrote an argument for life on other planets, a book that was translated into English and became the most popular nonfiction text in colonial New England. At that time, modern science was a revolutionary discourse, which was just beginning to challenge the authority of organized religion and royalty in Europe.

While this revolution contributed to more freedom for many people, STEM fields have yet to fulfill their liberating potential. Between the 1600s and today, access to—and lack of access to—scientific thinking and its results have affected many issues, such as personal and public health, urban planning, wildlife management, environmental protection, our understanding of race and identity, space exploration—even writing. We invite you to participate in the enactment of STEM communication as an inclusive practice by learning more about writing studies, by reflecting on your past experiences as writers, by listening closely to your peers and to scholars from diverse backgrounds, and by making inclusive choices as researchers and writers.

The field of writing studies, which has roots in classical and modern traditions of rhetoric (Murphy and Thaiss 2020), also includes empirical approaches that follow steps similar to those of scientific research: identifying questions or gaps in knowledge or methods; reviewing literature; collecting data, which often come through observation, surveys, interviews, and careful reading; data analysis; and discussion of the implications of data. For example, research in writing studies (1981) conducted by the team of Linda Flower and John Hayes used think-aloud protocols to document the cognitive processes of writers. This research—which many researchers since have questioned, refined, and built upon—contributed to a cognitive model for understanding writing, which demonstrates that one important difference between successful writers and stymied writers is that successful writers build time to revise into their process.

Ways for STEM Students to Get the Most from Required First-year Writing Course(s)

Even if your past experiences have led you to doubt your strengths as a writer, decades of research in writing studies have shown that all writers can succeed, and your first-year writing class can support your growth in STEM fields in several ways.

First, as you get into the course, look for connections between your interests in STEM and the course. The writing assignments you get in your first-year writing course will be intended to help you develop your general academic writing skills as a college student, but may not initially appear to provide opportunities to write in ways that scientists or engineers write as part of their work. But, as you learn about the assignments and procedures of the course, seek opportunities to connect those assignments with STEM topics you want to write about. For example, most first-year writing courses require some form of **research writing**: most of these assignments will require you to consult sources—and then use those sources to develop your own ideas. (For more on this topic, check out Stephen Lessner and Collin Craig's "Finding Your Way In: Invention as Inquiry Based Learning in First Year Writing," *Writing Spaces*, Vol. 1.)

Second, most of these required first-year courses want students to write about subjects they are interested in—the courses allow choice of topics.

Talk with your instructor regarding topics you might like to pursue. Even if your instructor does not have a formal background in STEM research, the instructor can help you connect your interests in STEM with the classwork and will provide useful feedback on your writing.

For example, one of Stephanie's students who was enrolled in a class on the topic of gardening at Bates College found a way to research her interests in the science of ecology by creating a project on pollinator habitats. A student in a class that she taught about place-based writing at Unity College researched the impact of dams on fish migration. A student in a class about culture she taught at Stony Brook University researched the relationship between culture and nutrition. These examples suggest how you might connect your interests in STEM fields to your writing class.

Third, one common assignment in first year writing classes asks students to reflect on their past experiences with reading and writing. Ask your instructor if you can include your interests in STEM in this assignment. For example, in the classes Chris teaches in Writing in Science, he asks students to write about themselves as scientists and writers. The assignment, "Writing and Science—Your History," asks students to respond to four questions:

1. What are ways that writing has related to your interests as a student and scientist? Describe one or more examples.

2. Have you seen a relationship between your growth as a writer and as a science student? Has one influenced the other? Or have they developed along different, even contrary, paths? Recall specific moments of growth—or frustration.

3. Regarding your future goals, what do you see as challenges for you as a writer and as a scientist?

4. What roles do you see writing playing in your ideal scientific future?

The assignment helps his students set goals for the Writing in Science course—they say that no one has asked them these questions before. Some responses reveal that writing about science has been an important part of their growth. This relationship is true for students whose STEM teachers made writing part of their classes in high school or in college. It's also true for students who decided on their own to write about their scientific interests—in a blog, for example, or on Instagram, or other social media. Or for students who have gone beyond their classes to create presentations for science research competitions—or to write about their STEM work for college applications!

But more of Chris's students say that they have done little writing about their STEM interests—especially in school. Many see school writing as divorced from science, mainly because these students have rarely written in their high school science classes. Their high school writing has been mainly in language arts classes, and in forms, such as essays about literature, that they see unrelated to their interests in STEM. Even more troubling, many of his students have developed fear of writing and look for ways to avoid it.

If you have had experiences like these, it is even more important to look for ways to connect your STEM interests to your first-year writing course, as ways to build your skill and confidence.

How to Gain Confidence and Flexibility via Inquiry-based Rhetoric (IBR)

One way to build confidence in first-year writing is to develop what neuroscientists call *metacognition*, also known as thinking about thinking. For writing, this means assessing your past work and your writing processes. When have you felt good about yourself as a writer, in school or out? What mistakes have you made that you have learned from? How can you take these lessons to new situations?

Metacognition is an essential part of *inquiry-based rhetoric* (IBR), which we introduced earlier. Learning *inquiry-based rhetoric* (IBR) takes time and practice, just as learning lab techniques and applying formulas does. And, just as determining which methods, pipettes, or formulas to use requires experience and the ability to make judgements about the purpose of the experiment and the context, so IBR relies on experience and the ability to make judgements about the purposes, audiences, and situations of the writing.

IBR works against the common misperception of writing as a set of rigid rules. For example, you may have been told never (or always!) to use "I" in your writing, or that every paragraph should have 4-7 sentences, or that all papers have a thesis at the end of the first paragraph. You might also have observed that most published writers, including in STEM, rarely follow these "rules." IBR teaches students how to move beyond so-called 'rules' and instead to understand the choices writers face when composing in various situations (contexts) for diverse readers (audiences) and to make savvy choices.

IBR is part of the broader field of rhetoric, which you will hear about in your first-year writing courses. In brief, rhetoric has two parts. The first part focuses outside the text: on the writer's *purpose, audience,* and *context.* The second part focuses on the text itself: use of *logic*—the ability to make clear claims with related reasons and reliable evidence; *character*—the ability to earn your readers' trust; and *emotions*—the ability to show why the work matters. In many writing classes, you will be taught to read rhetorically: analyzing ways writers use logic, emotions, and character to achieve their purposes for their intended readers.

Strengthening STEM Writing through Cultural Rhetorics and Antiracism

Some writing classes will introduce you to a particular form of rhetoric known as *cultural rhetorics,* and you might have an instructor who practices *antiracist pedagogies.* Cultural rhetorics are "the study and practice of making meaning and knowledge with the belief that all **cultures** are rhetorical and all **rhetorics** are **cultural**" (Bratta and Powell 2016). Cultural rhetoric changes rhetorical analyses and practices in significant ways by illustrating the richness of knowledge available when we pay attention to the work of people who have historically been marginalized in Western, colonial academic institutions in general and in STEM fields in particular. Developing scientific literacy practices that follow principles of cultural rhetorics includes asking questions about audience, purpose, context, logic, emotions, and character. It also requires understanding the impact of racism and other forms of systemic inequality on our personal perspectives and our cultural traditions—including scientific methods and knowledge.

Some scholars and teachers have developed antiracist teaching practices to ensure their classes are inclusive spaces that serve the needs of all students, that value the various forms of knowledge students bring to class, and that use the classroom to address systemic inequities such as racism and sexism. Antiracist teaching practices in STEM and in writing acknowledge that systemic inequity, implicit biases, and micro-aggressions disadvantage Black people, Indigenous people, People of Color, first generation college students, and other people who have been minoritized due to their skin color, ethnicity, gender identity, sexual orientation, and class. Antiracist teaching and writing practices aim to correct these inequities in a number of ways.

For example, Chris's classes of STEM majors from the sciences and engineering are highly diverse ethnically and linguistically. Some writing assignments in these classes are multimodal (using video, photography, and infographic charts, as well as written texts in accessible language). Each student chooses an audience (family members, home communities, special-interest groups, etc.) they would like to reach. Designs of projects use multimodal tools that the students feel can reach the audiences they choose, so that these readers can, the students hope, improve their lives. Sample projects include, among many possibilities, brochures and infographic charts on health topics for medical offices visited by children and parents in communities of color; websites, blogs, and calendars (some multilingual) on nutrition, agricultural practices, and new technologies; oral-visual presentations to high schoolers that encourage them to consider STEM fields.

Nationally, the American Association of Colleges and Universities (AAC&U) through its *Project Kaleidoscope* (PKAL) sponsors annual conferences on Transforming STEM Education. PKAL's central goal is increasing the representation—and success—of BIPOC students and researchers in all STEM fields. Moreover, because many STEM fields have historically failed to recognize and advance the careers of women and of LGBTQ+ scholars, AAC&U has also made gender inclusiveness a continuing goal.

What this means for you as a student and a writer with interests in STEM will depend on your own background; the intersections of race, class, gender identity, sexual orientation, and language in your identity and experience. You will want to reflect on the possibility that you have implicit biases and should work to overcome them. If you come from a privileged background, you will want to be attuned to the possibility that you engage in micro-aggressions and you will need to learn alternatives. If you are a first-generation college student or a BIPOC student, you may want to know about the resources available to help you navigate systems of oppression. Many campuses have programs and offices devoted to supporting students from minoritized backgrounds. #ShutDownSTEM offers many resources organized to address various backgrounds.

You will also want to learn to look for bias in research because much scientific research is inflected by racism and sexism. This bias shows up in the types of questions investigated, the subjects chosen, the types of evidence valued, the methods selected, the language used, and the metaphors employed. "Want to Dismantle Racism in Science? Start in the Classroom," a conversation between science educators, illustrates problems such as the erasure of Black scientists from history, and offers solutions to address racism. For more information in regard to gender, check out Emily

Martin's 1991 article, "The Sperm and the Egg: How Science Has Constructed a Romance based on Stereotypical Male-Female Roles."

In addition to analyzing your behavior and analyzing bias in STEM research, you can actively transfer antiracism to your STEM classes by:

- Working in diverse groups
- Listening across difference
- Creating research questions that serve underrepresented people
- Engaging in inclusive citation practices
- Using inclusive language

The 2020 Conference on College Composition and Communication statement "This Ain't Another Statement! This is a DEMAND for Black Linguistic Justice!" offers important information and resources on antiracism and college writing. You will also find deeper explorations of language justice in two essays in *Writing Spaces*, vol. 4: "Workin' Languages: Who We Are Matters in Our Writing" (by Sara P. Alvarez, Amy J. Wan, and Eunjeong Lee) and "Beyond Language Difference in Writing: Investigating Complex and Equitable Language Practices" (by Christina Sánchez-Martín).

Building Confidence and Rhetorical Awareness through Feedback and Peer Review

Learning *inquiry-based rhetoric* (IBR) develops your metacognitive writing process. To achieve this, you'll closely read your draft to identify which parts you most want your reader to comment on. If your instructor has given you a rubric (list of questions) for the assignment, you can use it to analyze your work, then to frame your request for feedback. If a rubric is not provided, create your own. As an example, here's a rhetorical rubric we provide:

	Questions to Help Writers Set the Agenda for Feedback
Logic	Questions about Critical Thinking and Logic • What is my central claim? • What reasons do I give? • Is my evidence reliable?

Emotions	**Questions about Why the Work Matters** • What gap in research or knowledge of the subject does my work address? • Why does this matter? • What are the implications of my work that I've stated? • What next steps do I see for this research?
Character	**Questions about Genre and Reader Expectations** • What organizational patterns do I follow? • What are the relationships between my points? • Do I provide appropriate detail about my methods and materials? • Who does this research serve? • Are my research methods ethical? • Do my visuals accurately represent my results? • Do I use inclusive language? How understandable would I be to someone reading this draft? • Do I follow ethical and inclusive citation practices (Bali 2020)?
	Questions about Your Goals and Process • How did I generate material, draft, and revise this paper? What worked? What should or might I do differently? • What were my goals as a writer? How did I achieve them? Where would I like to continue to improve?

In addition to feedback from instructors, you will most likely give and receive feedback from classmates via **peer review.** You and the other members of your class will learn how to read your classmates' writing rhetorically, appreciate its strengths, and suggest improvements. Peer review is a vital learning opportunity; it sparks insight into how others conceive writing tasks similar to yours. It gives you permission to ask for their careful response to your work.

Moreover, as a STEM student, you already know that knowledge in any scientific field grows primarily through **peer review,** by which practitioners are called on to review grant applications and articles submitted for publication. If you use the opportunity in your writing class to learn how to perform peer review carefully and respectfully, you will get closer to becoming a STEM student whom future colleagues will value. Successful peer review requires practice in rhetorical reading, which we describe in the next section of this essay. As you perform peer review, you might use a rubric such as that we showed earlier, one designed by your instructor, or one you might create. Find more information about peer review in Ron DePeter's "How to Write Meaningful Peer Response Praise," in *Writing Spaces*, vol 3.

Beyond the First-Year Writing Course: Writing in STEM Classes

In STEM writing, as part of IBR, authors establish their character and earn the trust of readers in several ways that depend on the genre in which the author is writing and the audience the writer aims for. STEM writers situate their work in previous research, summarizing relevant publications; they carefully describe their methods and illustrate their data in clear charts, graphs, and other visuals. STEM writers, like other writers, make clear claims about what their results mean as well as about the limits of their results.

For the genre of formal scientific lab reports for academic audiences, writers carry out IBR through the format of the IMRAD report, which in the 20th century became standard in STEM journals. The IMRAD acronym means Introduction, Materials and Methods, Results, And Discussion. The IMRAD structure includes the following sections:

- An Abstract that summarizes the overall report
- An Introduction that summarizes prior research on this topic, then states the gap in knowledge, the purpose of this research, and perhaps a hypothesis
- A Materials and Methods section that describes the tools used and the steps in the research process
- A Results section that reports the principal findings of the research
- A Discussion section (including a conclusion) that states what the authors consider the significance of the results and necessary further research.

You may be fortunate in your first year to be in a STEM course that actually asks you to read and write in the IMRAD form, perhaps in a lab section that accompanies a large lecture. Writing IMRAD-style reports, as well as reading closely the research articles in journals, will definitely build your powers as a scientific thinker. These articles will often challenge students through difficult, highly technical language, but learning to read and understand these articles is critical for your growth as a scientist.

But other than the practice you'll get in such a course, how do you learn to do these IMRAD exercises well? Fortunately, many guides online as well as STEM writing textbooks focus on the IMRAD report (see our list of resources). Because every journal in science contains articles that use the IMRAD structure, you'll have many opportunities to study articles that will help you learn how to do IMRAD well.

Another helpful practice is to use *rhetorical reading* as a way to apply IBR. Compare articles on the same subject and consider how and why the subject is written about differently. Is there another way that the subject could be written about that seems clearer or truer to you? Put your thoughts into writing. Try out different ways to say things on subjects of interest to you.

You can actively "transfer" the skills of rhetorical reading from your first-year writing class to your work in STEM by analyzing how texts in STEM fields use emotional appeals. (For a fuller discussion of such transfer of ideas, see "The Importance of Transfer in Your First Year Writing Course" by Kara Taczak, *Writing Spaces*, vol. 4.) In STEM writing, authors typically create emotional appeals by demonstrating a gap in the prior research and by explaining the implications of their research to show why their work matters. In the example below, an article titled "A Systematic Review of Empirical Research on Self-Reported Racism and Health" by Yin Paradies (*International Journal of Epidemiology*, 2006), the author briefly summarizes previous studies and then build emotional appeals by noting that his work *updates* and *expands* prior work.

> A handful of previous reviews have attempted to provide an overview of certain aspects of this emerging area of epidemiological research. The first article to consider the health impact of racism (along with sexism and social class) was published by Krieger *et al.* in 1993. This was followed, in 1999, by a review, also by Krieger, of 15 studies examining ethnic and/or racial discrimination and health_and, in 2000, by a review of 13 studies examining racism and mental health for African Americans by Williams *et al.* There were also three reviews published in 2003, with Wyatt *et al._*summarizing 19 studies relating racism to cardiovascular disease for African Americans, Brondolo *et al._*discussing studies relating racism to blood pressure (six studies) and cardiovascular reactivity (11 studies), and Williams *et al._*reviewing 53 population-based

empirical studies of ethnic and/or racial discrimination, which were published from 1998 onwards and related to various health outcomes. Drawing in particular on the most recent review by Williams *et al.*, this paper updates and expands upon these earlier reviews by examining the key characteristics of epidemiological studies of self-reported racism and health—where and when studies have been conducted, the race, age and gender of study populations, study designs, sample sizes, and data sources used. (n.p.)

At the end of the introduction, the author further develops his emotional appeals by signaling that his research has important implications in regard to the health of those who experience racism:

> The nature of associations found between self-reported racism and health is detailed for a range of health outcomes across various study and exposure characteristics along with identified effect modifiers and mediators of these associations. (Paradis n.p.)

Conversely, many first-year STEM courses do NOT give you the opportunity to write reports but are primarily lecture-and-reading courses. These require you to memorize principles, formulae, and substances, on which you will be tested.

Nevertheless, even these courses present opportunities to write to enhance your learning of facts and principles:

- Teachers may include online exercises to help you understand and apply the material. As you engage in these exercises, you solidify knowledge and build powers of expression—even if the process seems difficult at first.
- Because STEM courses often require you to read textbooks in print or online, write notes and explanations for yourself as (1) means to understand all those terms and ideas and (2) make it easier for you to put those terms and ideas into wording that you are comfortable with and likely to remember.
- *Memorizing* means making your perceptions and your connections between ideas part of *your working memory*. Every time you think about a concept and try to express it in related words, you are building your ability to draw on that concept in multiple situations. That is why *writing about ideas and associated concepts* works so well as a memorizing exercise. The same goes for other memorizing methods: drawing, diagramming, and discussing ideas with others. Consider all the ways you have memorized an idea—or perfected a skill—that is important to you. What tools have you

employed to learn that idea or skill so that you can remember and apply it?

Writing about Science Outside Your Courses

Beyond your courses, you may have discovered ways to use writing to deepen your STEM learning and build your powers of expression. Here are some widely-used methods:

1. Start your own blog.

Blogs have proliferated in every STEM discipline (just Google "STEM blogs" and you'll see). Set one up using Blogspot, Wordpress, or another tool. You don't need to publish your blog, but you can if you wish to build a readership. You can start out using your blog as a writing and learning space just for yourself; you can make it public as you gain confidence. Four rewards of blogging:

- Keep a record of your thinking, and return to earlier entries to see how you've grown, which contributes to metacognition
- Read other bloggers, to get ideas for your own blog or perhaps begin to build a blogging community in your area of interest
- Experiment with photos, videos, audio, infographics, and charts
- Practice different writing styles and writing for diverse readers—children, parents, friends, people you admire, people who think differently from you.

2. Write to memorize and reflect on your reading.

Writing about what you read helps you to (1) understand it, (2) remember it, and (3) evaluate it. Too often, students assume that what they read in textbooks or hear in lectures is merely information to be spit back on tests. But *to be a scientist*, you need to become a strong reader: to develop a critical eye and ear not only for *what* other writers write, but also *how* they write. If you learn IBR, you'll have a framework for this analysis. For example, when you read a scientific journal article or a popular article about science, look carefully at how the subject is described. Note differences from one article to another. Ask yourself: "how might I say this differently?"

3. Write about science via social media.

Facebook, Instagram, and TikTok allow for *multi-modal communication*—in words, photos, drawings, video, and sound. They allow researchers to share work in progress. By participating in these conversations, you'll

- learn from ways others use multimodal tools
- learn about emerging research, and
- practice multimodal communication

Moreover, most of these platforms limit the number of words, so you'll practice how to communicate succinctly.

Conclusion

This brief guide introduces you to tools to make the most of opportunities you have in your first year of college to build your skill as a writer and learner in STEM. Equally important, we've explained a conceptual framework, *inquiry-based rhetoric* (IBR), to apply to all the reading and writing you will do in college. This framework includes a related system, *antiracist cultural rhetorics,* that can expand your rhetorical expertise, so that how and why you communicate becomes more inclusive and versatile—while helping in the effort to overcome historical inequities among people, especially in STEM fields.

Works Cited

Alvarez, Sara P., Amy J. Wan, & Eunjeong Lee, "Workin' Languages: Who We Are Matters in Our Writing." *Writing Spaces*, Vol. 4, 2022. 18 March 2022, https://writingspaces.org/?page_id=750

Bala, Maha. "Inclusive Citation: How Diverse are Your References?" *Reflecting Allowed.* May 2020. 8 March 2022, https://blog.mahabali.me/writing/inclusive-citation-how-diverse-are-your-references/

Bratta, Phil, and Malea Powell. "Introduction to the Special Issue: Entering the Cultural Rhetorics Conversations" *enculturation* 21 (2016). 8 March 2022, http://enculturation.net/entering-the-cultural-rhetorics-conversations

De Fontenelle, Bernard. *Entretiens sur la pluralité des mondes* (Paris, 1686); translated as *Conversations on a Plurality of Worlds.* London, 1715. Translator Aphra Behn. 8 March 2022, https://archive.org/details/weeksconversatio00font/page/n3/mode/2up

Flower, Linda, and John R. Hayes. "A Cognitive Process Theory of Writing." *College Composition and Communication*, vol. 32, no. 4, 1981, pp. 365–387. JSTOR, 8 March 2022, www.jstor.org/stable/356600.

Lessner, Steven and Collin Craig. "Finding Your Way In: Invention as Inquiry Based Learning in First Year Writing." *Writing Spaces*. Vol 1, 2010. 8 March 2022, https://wac.colostate.edu/docs/books/writingspaces1/lessner-and-craig-finding-your-way-in.pdf

Martin, Emily. "The Sperm and the Egg: How Science Constructed a Romance Based on Stereotypical Female and Male Roles." *Signs,* vol. 16, no.2, Spring 1999. 8 March 2022, https://doi.org/10.1086/494680

Murphy, James and Christopher Thaiss, eds. *A Short History of Writing Instruction: From Ancient Greece to the Modern United States.* 4th. Ed. London: Routledge, 2020.

Paradies, Yin. "A systematic review of empirical research on self-reported racism and health." *International Journal of Epidemiology* vol. 35.4 (2006): 888-901. 8 March 2022, https://academic.oup.com/ije/article/35/4/888/686369?login=false

Sánchez-Martín, Cristina. "Beyond Language Differences in Writing: Investigating Complex and Equitable Language Practices." *Writing Spaces,* vol. 4, 2022. 25 July 2022, https://writingspaces.org/?page_id=799

ShutDownSTEM. 8 March 2022, https://www.shutdownstem.com/about

Sofia, Maddie. "Want to Dismantle Racism in Science? Start in the Classroom." *NPR.* October 2020. 8 March 2022, https://www.npr.org/transcripts/918864226.

"This Ain't Another Statement! This is a DEMAND for Black Linguistic Justice!" National Council of Teachers of English, 2020. 18 March 2022, https://ncte.org/statement/aint-another-statement-demand-black-linguistic-justice/

Resources

Project Kaleidoscope. American Association of Colleges and Universities. 8 March 2022, https://www.aacu.org/pkal

Transforming STEM Higher Education. American Association of Colleges and Universities. 8 March 2022, https://www.aacu.org/event/2022-stem

Eppendorf Prize Essays by Young Scientists (Winners Video). 4 March 2022, https://www.youtube.com/watch?v=PZOUHREIOb4

Guides to Using IMRAD format

"Scientific Writing: IMRAD Format." Brigham Young University Writing Center, 2020. 18 March 2022, https://rwc.byu.edu.

"Writing an IMRAD Report," George Mason University Writing Center, 2020. 8 March 2022, https://writingcenter.gmu.edu/guides/writing-an-imrad-report

Thaiss, Christopher. "Writing the Research Article" and "Writing the Research Review." *Writing Science in the Twenty-First Century.* Peterborough, Ontario: Broadview Press, 2019. Chapters 5-7.

Teacher Resources for "Writing Science in the First Year of College: Why It Matters to STEM Students and How STEM Students Benefit from It"

Overview and Teaching Strategies

This essay aims to help students who have interests in STEM fields make the most of their first year by showing them how to find opportunities to explore STEM topics in typical first-year writing classes, as well as in the STEM courses they will take, and even outside of courses; how strategies such as inquiry based rhetoric (IRB) apply to science writing in all situations; and how the work of equity, inclusion, and antiracism are foundational to science writing. This essay might be assigned as an option in the beginning of a first-year writing class to reassure STEM students that the FYW course is relevant to their needs. Parts of it might be assigned to prepare students for class work, formal writing activities, and peer review. Also, the essay might be used in first-year STEM classes to explain the importance of writing throughout STEM, or used in other ways depending on the goals and assignments of the specific course.

Throughout the essay, specific uses of writing, sample assignments, and rationales for these are described so that students can employ these tools and teachers can adapt them. Each of the questions below can be turned into a classroom activity by having students work in small groups (in class or in Zoom breakout rooms). Students can share highlights from their small group discussions orally, by writing notes on the classroom chalkboard or white board, by writing notes in collaborative Google Docs, or by writing in class forums set up by their instructors in first-year writing courses or in first-level STEM courses.

Discussion Questions

1. In the section "Ways for STEM Students to Get the Most from Required First-year Writing Course(s)," we discuss ways that students can explore their interests in STEM in their first-year writing classes. Make a list of your interests. Then review your syllabus for your first-year writing class. Note the places in the syllabus where

you think you could explore your interests. If you feel stuck or just have questions, talk with your instructor.

2. We propose IBR (inquiry-based rhetoric) as an alternative to rules-based writing classes. What rules do you remember being taught about writing? How often do you see published writers—including writers in STEM—following these rules? Look for examples of published writers breaking these rules, following other rules, or making their own.

3. In the section on the first-year writing course, we explain how students with STEM interests can expand the typical literacy narrative assignment to include their interests. How did you become interested in STEM? Make a timeline of your life and jot down the moments that have been important to you regarding the development of your interests in STEM. Continue the timeline to project what your future might look like.

4. In the section "Building Confidence and Rhetorical Awareness through Feedback and Peer Review," we offer a rhetorical rubric to help you understand what makes good writing in different genres, for different audiences, and different purposes. Think about your own ideas of good writing. How does the rhetorical rubric match your ideas of good writing? What does it add? What does it leave out?

5. In the section "Strengthening STEM Writing through Cultural Rhetorics and Antiracism," we introduce the connections between antiracism and STEM and call upon readers to reflect on their individual backgrounds to facilitate the process of making STEM more equitable and inclusive. In what ways has your background prepared or failed to prepare you for this work? What resources does your campus offer? What next steps might you take to support yourself and your classmates in the project of improving equity and inclusion in STEM?

6. In the section "Writing about Science Outside of Courses," we suggest that blogs and social media such as Facebook provide important opportunities for you as a science writer. Do you have a favorite blogger or science writer who uses social media? If so, find a few examples of this person's work and write about why you follow them. If not, spend some time exploring your STEM interests on

your favorite social media (for example, using hashtags) and see what you find.

7. In the same section, we write about how social media and much popular science writing "allow for *multi-modal communication*—in words, photos, drawings, video, and sound." If you read such popular science periodicals as National Geographic, or STEM blogs and popular STEM websites, you'll know many examples of multi-modal STEM communication. You may also have heard of STEAM—the joining of STEM research with the arts. Have you engaged in multi-modal STEM? If so, write about what you've tried. If not, write about how you might experiment with communicating your STEM interests through some of these media.

8. In the section "Beyond the First-year Writing Course: Writing in STEM Classes," we note that "*writing about ideas and associated concepts* works so well as a memorizing exercise." To what extent have you used writing as a tool to help you understand and remember ideas, events, or procedures important to you? Reflect on when and how you have used this tool. Can you think of times when you've realized that you should have been more careful to make notes or write about what you had wanted to remember?

Activities for Teaching Rhetorical Reading

In addition to turning the discussion questions above into classroom activities, the following activities related to rhetorical reading can help teachers extend our essay. While we offer the "rhetorical reading rubric" (below) to help guide peer review, this rubric can be used to guide students through the rhetorical reading of the texts the teacher assigns in class:

1. The teacher might assign two or more texts on the same topic in different genres, such as a news article, a blog post, and a research article.

2. The teacher might assign two or more texts from different disciplines on the same topic.

3. The teacher can model rhetorical analysis in class by pointing out features of text as we do using the article by Paradies cited in the essay.

4. Students can continue rhetorical analysis by engaging in informal writing for homework and then share their work in class.

5. The teacher can build these activities into a formal rhetorical analysis assignment that asks students to evaluate the different rhetorical moves writers use in different situations and to consider how they might use these moves in their own writing.

Rhetorical Reading Rubric

Logic and critical thinking:	• The document presents clear claims/points with related reasons supported by reliable evidence.
Emotions (gets the reader to care):	• The document shows how this research addresses a gap in prior research, and (2) shows why this research matters to other researchers or to a broader community.
Character (earns the trust of the reader):	• The document shows understanding of relevant background research. • The document clearly explains methods and relevant materials. • The document uses visual techniques to achieve clarity. • The vocabulary used is accessible to the intended readers. • The document follows the general conventions of writing in the genre and discipline; for example in organization, format, and sentence style.

Activities to Incorporate "Writing to Learn"

Our section "Beyond the First-year Writing Course: Writing in STEM Classes" describes the cognitive and metacognitive benefits of regularly using writing as a tool for memorization and for expanding thinking. It notes that "teachers may include online exercises to help [students] understand and apply the material." Teachers might consider the following:

1. At the beginning of a lecture, pose a question to students related to the theme of the lecture: e.g., "when you hear the term x, what do you think it means? What doesn't it mean?" Ask students to write for just one minute without Googling the term. The question will immediately engage their attention and focus.

2. As the final task toward the end of a lecture, ask students to write for 2-3 minutes to record thoughts/notes about the content of the lecture, perhaps phrased as "information and ideas that you don't want to forget." Such writings might be recorded in an online forum on the teacher's course learning management system.

3. Consider devoting a small part of class time at the beginning of a term, especially in introductory courses for first-year students, to the value of writing as a tool of thinking, remembering, and applying ideas. Consider describing to students your own practices as a researcher who takes careful notes and uses writing informally to expand your thinking.

4. Teachers who set up student writing forums such as that described in a. and b. (above) might consider how frequently they will read or just browse them, and if they will grant them a small amount of course credit. Keep in mind that the writing of exercises like a. and b. is totally informal and spontaneous, and should always be a space for students to write without fear of evaluation. Indeed, teachers might tell students that such spontaneous writings should only be done in personal writing spaces that the teacher will have no access to.

5. Conversely, teachers also may set up such forums more formally, often using them as quasi-public spaces open only to class members and the instructor. These often include regular deadlines, such as weekly, with named topics. In addition to giving students regular incentives to write about their reading and subjects of study, these forums are often used to build a course community, with expectations that students will read one another's entries.

Contributors

David Blakesley is Campbell Chair in Technical Communication at Clemson University, as well as a Fellow of the Rhetoric Society of America. He serves as interim director of Clemson's PhD in Rhetorics, Communication, and Information Design and is president of Clemson's Faculty Senate. He founded Parlor Press in 2002 and serves as its Publisher and CEO. He has authored, co-authored or edited eleven books, including *The Elements of Dramatism* (Longman), *The Terministic Screen: Rhetorical Perspectives on Film* (SIUP), and *Writing: A Manual for the Digital Age* (Cengage). He is currently editor of *KB: The Journal of the Kenneth Burke Society* and co-editor of *The WAC Journal*.

Rachel Hall Buck is Assistant Professor Writing Studies at the American University of Sharjah, where she teaches introductory writing courses, advanced research courses, professional communication for business and engineering courses, and courses in the MA TESOL program. She has previously published on issues related to students' learning in multiple contexts in *Currents in Teaching and Learning*, *Composition Forum*, *Journal of English for Academic Purposes*, *English Language Teaching*, and *International Journal for Educational Integrity*.

Ellen Cecil-Lemkin, PhD, is a teaching faculty member at the University of Wisconsin-Madison, where she helps direct the writing center. Her research focuses on disability, accessibility, and collaboration. Her essays can be found in *College Composition and Communication*, *Teaching English at the Two-Year College*, and *Teaching through the Archives: Text, Collaboration, and Activism*.

Amy Cicchino is Associate Director of the Center for Teaching and Learning Excellence at Embry-Riddle Aeronautical University where she also teaches as adjunct faculty in the humanities/communication department. Her work takes up educator professional development, writing across the curriculum, and digitally enhanced teaching and has appeared in *WPA: Writing Program Administration*, *International Journal of ePortfolio*, and *Writing Center Journal*, among others.

Kristin DeMint Bailey, PhD (she/her), is an independent scholar and former academic who now spends her time writing for clients across the globe. She earned her PhD in English, with a focus on rhetoric and composition, from the University of Wisconsin-Milwaukee, and her co-authors of this article were former students in first-year writing classes she taught as visiting assistant professor at College of DuPage in Glen Ellyn, Illinois. Her dissertation explored the vital roles that university culture centers play in antiracist efforts on college campuses.

Zack K. DePiero is Assistant Professor of English at Northampton Community College in Bethlehem, Pennsylvania. He earned a PhD in Education at the University of California Santa Barbara within its "Language, Literacy, and Composition Studies" program. Through surveys and follow-up interviews, his dissertation explored TAs' perceptions of "good reading" in first-year writing courses, and that research was published in two journals: *Higher Education Research and Development* and the *Journal of College Literacy and Learning*. His research on teacher education and evaluation has been published in two edited collections, *Writing the Classroom* and *Threshold Conscripts*.

Danielle DeRise is a lecturer in the School of Writing, Rhetoric and Technical Communication at James Madison University, where she has taught since 2012 and has served as the Director of First-Year Writing since 2022. Her most recent article, coauthored with a colleague in the Department of Health Sciences and describing a pandemic-era pedagogical collaboration, was published in Currents In Teaching and Learning.

Dr. Kefaya Diab is Assistant Professor in the Writing, Rhetoric, and Digital Studies Department at the University of North Carolina at Charlotte. She identifies as a scholar-teacher-activist who fights the fight to pursue social justice in and outside of academia. Her work has appeared in *Rhetoric Society Quarterly, Composition Studies, Sexual Harassment and Cultural Change in Writing Studies, Community Literacy*, and *Paidea 16*. She received the 2022 Charles Kneupper's Award for her RSQ article "The Rise of the Arab Spring through a Sense of Agency."

Ryan Dippre is Associate Professor of English and Director of College Composition at the University of Maine. He has published on lifespan writing research, writing program administration, and the teaching of writing. Much of his work can be found at the WAC Clearinghouse (wac.colostate.edu).

Contributors

Sydney Doyle is a recent graduate of Park University who earned her bachelor's degree in English writing. She was awarded departmental honors and summa cum laude when she graduated. During her studies at Park, she took a particular interest in nonfiction prose and creative writing. After graduation, she has continued to create various works of writing.

William Duffy teaches in the Writing, Rhetoric, and Technical Communication program at the University of Memphis. He enjoys reading and writing about collaboration, rhetorical ethics, and issues in higher education.

Tamara Gluck is a recent graduate of the University of Chicago Harris school, with a Master of Public Policy. From experience in social work and publishing, Tamara specializes in trauma-informed writing and rhetorical policy analysis. Areas of research include education and social welfare policy, Jewish studies, disability studies, and queer political theory.

An Ha (she/her) is an advanced undergraduate student majoring in psychology and minoring in women's and gender studies at Hope College in Holland, Michigan. She currently serves as the co-president of Women of Color United and is an RA in an all-girls dorm. Her most recent accomplishment was her TedXHope College talk titled "Dear College Student," in which shared a short story she wrote about the transition to college. Another of her short stories was published in an exhibit honoring women of color at the Kruizinga Art Museum in Holland, Michigan.

L. Lennie Irvin is Professor of English at San Antonio College where he serves as a Program Coordinator. He is the author of *Reflection Between the Drafts* (Peter Lang, 2020) and has had essays appear in *Teaching English in the Two-Year College, Composition Forum, The Writing Lab Newsletter*, and *Writing Spaces*.

Erin E. Kelly is Associate Professor in the department of English at the University of Victoria in British Columbia, Canada. She is also the founding director of the UVic's Academic and Technical Writing Program. Her work teaching academic writing to undergraduate and graduate students is informed by her experience (starting in 2011) of serving as an associate editor for the peer-reviewed journal *Early Theatre*.

Angela Laflen is Associate Professor in the English Department at California State University, Sacramento. She teaches in the writing program in the areas of digital writing, online writing pedagogy, and professional writing. Her published work focuses on writing response practices and digital and multimodal literacies, and her work has appeared in *Computers and Writing, Assessing Writing*, and the *Journal of Response to Writing*, among others.

Glenn Lester is Assistant Professor of English at Park University, where he teaches students about writing and reading in first-year writing, literature, and creative writing classes. He holds an MFA in creative writing from the University of North Carolina Greensboro and a BA in English from Hope College. He won the 2021 The Masters Review Novel Excerpt Contest for "Take Warning: The Ballad of Sammy Slug."

Taylor Lucas is a recently graduated student from Park University, where she studied English and communications. In her final semester, she was awarded the 2020–2021 Louisa Davidson Hinde/Carolyn Hinde Zarkaryan Memorial Award for being a student who best represents the spirit of Park University. She now serves as an educator for adult learners looking to strengthen their professional skills.

Jason McIntosh is Assistant Professor of English and Creative Writing and serves as the Writing Program Coordinator at Stephen F. Austin State University. He teaches first-year writing, co-requisite composition, integrated reading and writing, and writing pedagogy courses. His research interests encompass place-based education, the materiality and technologies of writing, and the archiving of composition programs.

Benjamin Miller is Associate Professor of Composition in the English department at the University of Pittsburgh, where he teaches students to write with words, sound, images, and code. He has published poetry (*Without Compass*) as well as digital scholarship (*Distant Readings of Disciplinarity: Knowing and Doing in Composition/Rhetoric Dissertations*), and likes that both kinds of writing reward close attention to punctuation and wording. Ben also enjoys editing collections of others' writing (*Composition and Big Data*; *Journal of Interactive Technology and Pedagogy*).

Oksana Moroz is a Teaching Associate and Mama PhD Candidate at Indiana University of Pennsylvania, where she teaches first-year composition courses and research writing. She serves as a co-chair for AAAL Graduate Student Council. Her research interests revolve around topics of gender and digital identities of English language teachers and multilingual students, writing in Wikipedia, language ideologies, and accents. Oksana's research article, "A Poetic Narrative Autoethnography on Transnational Identity: Tumbleweed," appeared in *Doctoral Students' Identities and Emotional Wellbeing in Applied Linguistics*. She has also published in *Rhetoric Review*, *Explorations in English Language and Linguistics*, *Praxis*, *TESOL Journal*, and *Internationalisation of Higher Education*.

Anthony (AJ) Outlar (he/him) is a full-time police officer with the Chicago Police Department and a criminal justice student at College of DuPage in Glen Ellyn, Illinois, where he also earned an associate's degree in liberal arts. He is also enrolled in the bachelor of arts in criminal justice program at Lewis University in Romeoville, Illinois—a program known for its commitment to social justice and the protection of vulnerable populations.

Alison Overcash graduated from Park University in 2020 with a BA in English. Alison worked as a writing tutor, news reporter, and literary magazine editor in college before joining CBIZ as a content marketing specialist in 2022.

Mattius Rischard is Assistant Professor of English at Montana State University-Northern, where he teaches at teaches at the intersections of African American and Urban Anglophone literatures. Winner of the 2020 New Directions in the Humanities International Award for Excellence, he is a contributor to the redefining volume on intersectional studies of politics in Anglophone literature, *The Routledge Companion to Literature and Class* (2021), and his work also appears in *Texas Studies of Literature and Language* and other journals.

Michelle Sprouse is Assistant Teaching Professor in the Honors College at Bowling Green State University, where she teaches courses in critical thinking. Her research interests include reading in the writing classroom, equitable assessment practices, curriculum design, and the transition to college. She has published in *Pedagogy: Critical Approaches to Teaching Literature, Language, Composition and Culture; Assessing Writing*; and *English Journal*, among others.

Chris Thaiss, Professor Emeritus at UC Davis, served as Clark Kerr Presidential Chair and Director of the University Writing Program. His most recent books are *Writing Science in the Twenty-First Century* (2019), which derives from his teaching of STEM students from many disciplines, and the 4th edition of *A Short History of Writing Instruction: From Ancient Greece to the Modern United States* (2020, co-edited with James J. Murphy). Before coming to UC Davis, he taught at George Mason University, where he co-developed the WAC program and the Writing Center. In 2005, he received Mason's David King Award for career contributions to teaching excellence.

Lisa Tremain is Associate Professor of English and directs the first-year composition program at Cal Poly Humboldt State University. She has published articles and chapters in *Next Steps: New Directions on Writing about Writing, (Re)Considering What We Know*, and *Composition Forum*. Her recent research has turned toward linguistic justice and transfer, equitable frameworks for writing across the curriculum, and pedagogical designs that enact transformation of dominant textual structures, including scholarly genres. She is currently co-editing a scholarly collection in which authors theorize and analyze writing transfer through lenses of radical epistemological justice.

Silvia Vaccino-Salvadore is Assistant Professor at the American University of Sharjah, UAE, where she teaches composition courses. Her research interests include language teacher identities, second language writing, and academic integrity. She has published in the *Journal of Language, Identity & Education* and the *Journal of Second Language Writing*.

Crystal VanKooten is Associate Professor at Michigan State University, where she teaches courses in the Professional and Public Writing major and first-year writing. Dr. VanKooten's work focuses on digital media composition through engagement with how technologies shape composition practices, pedagogy, and research. Her digital book, *Transfer across Media: Using Digital Video in the Teaching of Writing*, is available from Computers and Composition Digital Press.

Matthew A. Vetter is Professor of English at Indiana University of Pennsylvania. His research on Wikipedia has appeared in journals such as *College English, Fast Capitalism, First Monday*, and *Social Media + Society*. He is co-author, with Zach McDowell, of *Wikipedia and the Representation of Reality* (Routledge, 2021).

Stephanie Wade is a lecturer in the Program in Writing and Rhetoric at Stony Brook University. In her prior appointment as assistant director of writing at Bates College, she developed an ecological approach to anti-racist writing instruction that earned the SLAC-WPA Martinson Award for Innovation. Her work has been published in *Community Literacy Journal, WPA: Writing Program Administration*, and the edited collection *Food Justice Activism and Pedagogies*. As part of the Coda Editorial Collective, she publishes creative work related to community engagement in the *Community Literacy Journal*. She serves on the board of directors for the Coalition for Community Writing.

Jennifer Wells is Director of Writing at New College of Florida, where she wears many hats. She has published in *College English, Composition Forum, Praxis,* and *English Journal*, and through Teachers College Press.

www.ingramcontent.com/pod-product-compliance
Lightning Source LLC
Chambersburg PA
CBHW031411230426
43668CB00007B/276